Theology as Hope

Princeton Theological Monograph Series

K. C. Hanson and Charles M. Collier, Series Editors

Recent volumes in the series:

Richard Valantasis et al., editors
The Subjective Eye: Essays in Honor of Margaret Miles

Anette Ejsing
A Theology of Anticipation: A Constructive Study of C. S. Peirce

Caryn Riswold
Coram Deo: Human Life in the Vision of God

Paul O. Ingram, editor
Constructing a Relational Cosmology

Michael G. Cartwright
Practices, Politics, and Performance: Toward a Communal Hermeneutic for Christian Ethics

David A. Ackerman
Lo, I Tell You a Mystery: Cross, Resurrection, and Paraenesis in the Rhetoric of 1 Corinthians

Lloyd Kim
Polemic in the Book of Hebrews: Anti-Judaism, Anti-Semitism, Supersessionism?

Theology as Hope

On the Ground and the Implications of Jürgen Moltmann's Doctrine of Hope

RYAN A. NEAL

☙PICKWICK *Publications* · Eugene, Oregon

THEOLOGY AS HOPE
On the Ground and the Implications of Jürgen Moltmann's Doctrine of Hope

Princeton Theological Monograph Series 99

Copyright © 2008 Ryan A. Neal. All rights reserved. Except for brief quotations in critical publications or reviews, no part of this book may be reproduced in any manner without prior written permission from the publisher. Write: Permissions, Wipf and Stock Publishers, 199 W. 8th Ave., Suite 3, Eugene, OR 97401.

Pickwick Publications
A Division of Wipf and Stock Publishers
199 W. 8th Ave., Suite 3
Eugene, OR 97401

www.wipfandstock.com

ISBN 13: 978-1-55635-463-2

Cataloging-in-Publication data:

Neal, Ryan A.

Theology as hope : on the ground and the implications of Jürgen Moltmann's doctrine of hope / Ryan A. Neal.

xxiv + 254 p. ; cm. Includes bibliographical references.

Princeton Theological Monograph Series 99

ISBN 13: 978-1-55635-463-2

1. Moltmann, Jürgen. 2. Hope—Religious aspects—Christianity. 3. Eschatology. I. Title. II. Series.

BT821.3 N260 2008

Manufactured in the U.S.A.

From first to last, and not merely in epilogue, Christianity is eschatology, is hope.

—Moltmann, *Theology of Hope*, 16

*In equal measure, but for different reasons,
this work is dedicated to*

My Parents

&

My Wife and Kids

Contents

Acknowledgments xi

A Note on Citations and Sources xiii

Abbreviations xv

Introduction xix

PART ONE: The Ground of Hope

1. Resurrection as Hope 3
2. Crucifixion as Hope 41

PART TWO: The Implications: Christian Doctrine as Hope

3. Ecclesiology as Hope 69
4. Trinitarian Doctrine as Hope 95
5. Creation as Hope 130
6. Christology as Hope 153
7. Pneumatology as Hope 174
8. Eschatology as Hope 201

Conclusion 227

Bibliography 233

Acknowledgements

I HAVE INCURRED MANY DEBTS WHILE WRITING THIS BOOK. I MUST FIRST note my indebtedness to a variety of individuals associated with New College, University of Edinburgh, the environment that helped birth this book in its origins as a PhD thesis. Of primary importance is my *Doktorvater*, Dr. John McDowell, who generously offered his time and insight, especially during the formative stages. Additionally, I'd like to thank Professor David Fergusson, my secondary supervisor, who was always available for insight and constructive comments. Dr. Michael Purcell kindly tolerated my wide-ranging questions on christology and eschatology in contemporary theology, typically over pizza on Friday afternoons. Dr. Nicholas Adams patiently taught me the nuances of German language and theology in the weekly "German reading group." Also, my *viva voce* examiners Dr. Adams (University of Edinburgh) and Dr. Stephen Holmes (University of St. Andrews) offered helpful suggestions and questions that have improved this work. All of the above were generous with advice and insight, and each will be able to see (if they so desire) where I have followed their guidance, and alternatively where I have considered their advice, but still gone my own way. I am indebted to each and the errors that remain are mine.

Professor Moltmann was kind enough to meet with me in St. Andrews (30 June–3 July 2003), where he was giving a keynote address. Our encounter evidenced his belief that theology is not a closed system, but rather is a questioning, reforming enterprise that is, in turn, always in need of being questioned and reformed.

Mr. Steven Harring, my *famulus* extraordinaire, helped with numerous editorial and proofing details. A note of thanks is due to the Centre for Jewish-Christian Relations in Cambridge for kindly assisting in finding proper resources related to chapter two. Those whose help was confined to a more specific point are noted in the appropriate footnote.

Thankfully, I was afforded the opportunity to spend some time at Duke University in the summer of 2007, allowing me to complete a preliminary revision of the work due to a Summer Research stipend, granted by Dr. Danny Parker and the Faculty Development Committee of Anderson University, SC.

On numerous occasions I was able to present earlier portions of this book to fellow scholars allowing me to take up their comments and criticisms, and perhaps answer their questions. For this opportunity, thanks are due to the members of the Systematic Theology and Christian Ethics Forum at New College; to the participants of the Scottish Universities' Annual Conference; and to the members of the Society for the Study of Theology.

My parents deserve a special note of thanks for their faithfulness and unwavering support throughout the project.

Finally, my wife and children deserve a special note of thanks. This project is older than our children, and yet through it all, Jennifer offered her interest, understanding and love as she sacrificed her own wishes and revised her own dreams, giving me the opportunity to pursue mine. My own companion in hope, she has not wavered in her love and prayerful support.

A Note on Citations and Sources

To avoid confusion and inserting "[sic]" innumerable times, quotations are verbatim in all instances, including: gender, italicization, and capitalization. Spelling errors are signified with "[sic]".

Inclusive Language

Translating *der Mensch* (the man or human being, m.) and *die Person* (the person, f.) from German is now done predominantly using gender inclusive language; this has not always been the case, and though inclusive language is employed throughout the work, no attempt has been made to alter any quotations at this point.

This study consistently employs male pronouns for God, which follows Moltmann's typical, albeit inconsistent, pattern.

Moltmann's works

Moltmann's name is omitted preceding all citations of his work, abbreviated or not.

Citations refer to the published English translation, when available. At times a German word is enclosed in brackets for greater clarity and precision; in such cases, the relevant German page number is likewise placed in brackets following the English citation. Details of the German texts consulted appear in the bibliography following the relevant English entry. In the event that a work is not available in English, the translations are mine. Throughout, I consulted *The Oxford-Duden German Dictionary*, CD-Rom version (Oxford: Oxford University Press, 1994–97).

Biblical Citations

German biblical citations come from:

Martin Luther, *Die Bibel, mit Apokryphen* (Stuttgart: Deutsche Bibelgesellschaft, 1985).

All references to the Greek New Testament refer to:

Barbara Aland et al., editors, *The Greek New Testament*, 4th edition (Stuttgart: Deutsche Bibelgesellschaft, 2001).

Except when quoting Moltmann's citations:

The Scripture quotations contained herein are from *The New Revised Standard Version Bible*, copyright © 1989, by the Division of Christian Education of the National Council of the Churches of Christ in the U.S.A., and are used by permission. All rights reserved.

Abbreviations

Moltmann's Works
(for full details, see the bibliography)

BP	*A Broad Place*
CG	*The Crucified God*
CJF	*Creating a Just Future*
CoG	*The Coming of God*
CPS	*The Church in the Power of the Spirit*
DGG	Principally refers to Moltmann's two contributions in Michael Welker, ed. *Diskussion über Jürgen Moltmanns Buch "Der Gekreuzigte Gott."*
DTH	Principally refers to Moltmann's 'Antwort' in Wolf-Dieter Marsch, ed. *Diskussion über die "Theologie der Hoffnung" von Jürgen Moltmann*
EB	*In the End—the Beginning*
EG	*Experiences of God*
EH	*The Experiment Hope*
EJM	Principally refers to Moltmann's eight contributions in *God Will Be All in All: The Eschatology of Jürgen Moltmann,* edited by Richard Bauckham
ET	*Experiences in Theology*
FC	*The Future of Creation*
GC	*God in Creation*
GEB	*Im Gespräch mit Ernst Bloch*
GHH	*God: His and Hers,* with Elisabeth Moltmann-Wendel
GL	*The Gospel of Liberation*

GSS	*God for a Secular Society*
HC	Principally refers to Moltmann's three contributions in *Hope for the Church: Moltmann in Dialogue with Practical Theology*, edited by Theodore Runyon
HG	*Humanity in God*, with Elisabeth Moltmann-Wendel
HP	*Hope and Planning*
HTG	*History and the Triune God*
JCTW	*Jesus Christ for Today's World*
JM	*Jewish Monotheism and Christian Trinitarian Doctrine*, with Pinchas Lapide
HD	*On Human Dignity*
M	*Man*
PG	*Passion for God*, with Elisabeth Moltmann-Wendel
PPL	*The Power of the Powerless*
RRF	*Religion, Revolution, and the Future*
SoL	*The Source of Life*
SpL	*The Spirit of Life*
SW	*Science and Wisdom*
TH	*Theology of Hope*
TJ	*Theology and Joy*
ThTo	*Theology Today*
TKG	*The Trinity and the Kingdom*
UZ	*Umkehr zur Zukunft*
WJC	*The Way of Jesus Christ*

Others

ABD	*Anchor Bible Dictionary*, 6 vols.
ANQ	*Andover Newton Quarterly*
ATJ	*The Asbury Theological Journal*
BTB	*Biblical Theology Bulletin*
CUP	Cambridge University Press
EvQ	*Evangelical Quarterly*
EvTh	*Evangelische Theologie*

ExpTim	*Expository Times*
HeyJ	*Heythrop Journal*
HTR	*Harvard Theological Review*
IJST	*International Journal of Systematic Theology*
Int	*Interpretation*
ISBE	*The International Standard Bible Encyclopedia*
ITQ	*Irish Theological Quarterly*
JAAR	*Journal of the American Academy of Religion*
JETS	*Journal of the Evangelical Theological Society*
JPT	*Journal of Pentecostal Theology*
JR	*Journal of Religion*
JTS	*Journal of Theological Studies*
Luth	*Luther's New Testament*
ModTh	*Modern Theology*
MTZ	*Münchener Theologische Zeitschrift*
PRS	*Perspectives in Religious Studies*
RelSRev	*Religious Studies Review*
RRT	*Reviews in Religion and Theology*
SJT	*Scottish Journal of Theology*
SR	*Studies in Religion/Sciences religieuses*
SVTQ	*St. Vladimir's Theological Quarterly*
TDNT	*Theological Dictionary of the New Testament*, 10 vols.
TLZ	*Theologie Literaturzeitung*
TS	*Theological Studies*
TToday	*Theology Today*
TynBul	*Tyndale Bulletin*
UBS[4]	*The Greek New Testament*, 4th edition
USQR	*Union Seminary Quarterly Review*

Introduction

MANY ISSUES AND DOCTRINES VIE FOR PRE-EMINENCE IN MOLTMANN'S theology: eschatology, christology, history, political theology, theodicy, the Kingdom of God, Messianic theology, theology of the cross, and the doctrine of the Trinity.[1] One finds these doctrines and themes in virtually every one of Moltmann's writings, which explains why they have been attached to his theological enterprise as appropriate labels. And while each is important for understanding his theology, none captures the essence of his project from beginning to end.[2] Additionally, as his publications have appeared and interests expanded, identifying one characteristic doctrine as capturing his entire theology has arguably become more difficult.[3] Yet, identifying the core is crucial, and indeed must be found in order to properly understand Moltmann's thought. Hope is the *leitmotiv* of his theology.[4] Not merely one aspect of his proj-

---

1. See, for example, Bauckham, *The Theology of Jürgen Moltmann*, 8–23; Laurence Wood, "Editorial Note," 5; and the numerous doctoral works devoted to Moltmann's work which expound a variety of these elements.

2. Even if one selected eschatological as the proper label, there would still be the need to find the core of his eschatology; a few could be posited as the core: Messiah, promise, history, advent. Christopher Morse claims that promise is the correct entrée to Moltmann's work (Morse, *The Logic of Promise in Moltmann's Theology*). This is arguably a good starting point, but ultimately it confirms the point made here, since Moltmann claims that promise is the "logos of hope" (*ET* 54).

3. The secondary literature is swayed seemingly by the decade it was published; for example, by the 1980s pneumatology and creation emerged as the distinctive doctrines of his program, even though these were latent, at most, prior to 1975 and 1980, respectively.

4. It is unclear whether Moltmann would agree with this assertion. Retrospectively, Moltmann claims that his early work was dominated by historical categories (*SW* 111). In 1973 he subscribes to the label "theology of hope" for his enterprise (*GL* 10), and his essay, "My Theological Career" (*HTG* 165–82) seems to lend weight also, since it is originally entitled "Theologie der Hoffnung. Eine kleine Autobiographie," 235–57. Yet, in 1985, he seems to differentiate between three types of theology: "political theology," "theology of hope," and "trinitarian theology" ("Foreword," in A. J. Conyers, *God, Hope, and History*, ix; see also his prior comments in *DGG* 168).

ect, hope is the whole of it, the supreme doctrine interpenetrating all others.[5] Indeed, hope is his method.[6]

Purpose

The following study is entitled *Theology as Hope*, a play on words intended to convey two meanings, simultaneously.[7] First, the three-word dictum correctly labels Moltmann's entire project. While his theology is correctly regarded as eschatological throughout, there is a specific, identifiable center: from beginning to end, he is developing, exploring, and pronouncing Christian hope.[8] Some find Moltmann's program cacophonous,[9] and admittedly, his wide-ranging interests lead him in a variety of unforeseen directions and discussions of many issues in the field of theology (exhibited rather simplistically by glancing at the main topics of his "contributions"). Yet still, this study insists that his project, once understood, is harmonious: regardless of the various and specific changes in focus and the occasional nature of his key writings, exploring hope is the implicit goal throughout. Retrospectively, Moltmann admits that while writing *TH* his methodology shifted: "I no longer theologized

---

5. Meeks comes the closest to identifying hope as the central doctrine of Moltmann's thought, but because his purpose was to explore the formative influences on Moltmann's thought, he essentially presupposes the notion, instead of examining and/or explicating it. Additionally, his work is much too early to fully consider Moltmann's fuller theology (see Meeks, *Origins of the Theology of Hope*, 8).

6. Of Immanuel Kant's three questions, Moltmann is continually spurred on by answering the third: "What may I hope for?" (see Kant, *Critique of Pure Reason*, A805/B833). Moltmann is interested in the first two questions: "What can I know?" and "What shall I do?" but only the third question receives his full attention (see *TT* 23; see also *TH* 166, 182; *EH* 186; *GL* 30; *JCTW* 79–80; *WJC* 237; *ET* 53). Kant moved the field of eschatology into the practical elements (Kant, "The End of All Things," 217–32; see also *TH* 45–50).

7. The title is a revision of the full title of Moltmann's first programmatic work: *Theology of Hope: On the Ground and the Implications of a Christian Eschatology*.

8. In contrast to the emphasis of love in the Middle Ages and of faith for the Reformers, Moltmann asserts that the modern world "craves the development of a *theology of hope*" (*ET* 53; see also p. 92; *EH* 186). See also Carl Braaten, "Toward A Theology of Hope," 90–111.

9. Some regard Moltmann, typically derisively, as an issue-oriented theologian. Hans Küng summarizes this view best: "I slowly get on with my theological work and don't jump from topic to topic like Jürgen Moltmann" (as quoted in Hartmut Meesmann, "An Account of the Symposium," 130).

about hope, but *from* hope."¹⁰ Indeed, the aim of *TH*, Moltmann insists "is to show how theology can set out from hope and begin to consider its theme in an eschatological light".¹¹ This study advances the thesis that from 1964 forward he never escapes the initial motive of his first programmatic text.¹²

The second meaning of the title, which is clarified and specified by the subtitle, describes the present study. In the pages following, Moltmann's doctrine of hope is investigated as the determining doctrine in his theology, as developed in the principal texts of his *oeuvre*. While this reading insists that hope is the central theme of Moltmann's theology, he is not a practitioner of "monothematic" theology.¹³ Yet, any endeavor to understand his theology must grasp its basic impulse, its driving force. His work, especially as it matures, insists on the coinherence of doctrine, but this study simultaneously presupposes and explicates how he prioritizes hope, as grounded firmly in the dialectic of cross and resurrection, as the determinative doctrine of his claims.¹⁴ Indeed, hope is the essential nature and governing doctrine of Moltmann's thought from beginning to end.

---

10. *HTG* 170, italics original; this may be an unspoken (and altered) reference to Wilhelm Hermann's differentiation of these matters regarding faith.

11. *TH* 13; see also "Resurrection as Hope," 129–47; "Resurrection: The Ground, Power and Goal of Our Hope," 81–9.

12. The scope is 1964–2005, with a chapter devoted to each of his first eight principal texts (*TH*, *CG*, *CPS*, *TKG*, *GC*, *WJC*, *SpL*, and *CoG*). *ET*, his methodology and final "contribution", and *EB*, his "little doctrine of hope", are both used throughout as they shed retrospective light on his doctrine of hope. His autobiography is set for release in the fall of 2007.

The earlier work is largely historical in nature, and has been treated ably elsewhere; see especially Geiko Müller-Fahrenholz, *The Kingdom and the Power*, 15–39; for primary material, see *Christoph Pezel und der Calvinismus in Bremen*; *Herrschaft Christi und Soziale Wirklichkeit Nach Dietrich Bonhoeffer*; "The Lordship of Christ and Human Society," 19–94; *Prädestination and Perseveranz, Geschichte und Bedeutung der reformierten Lehre "de perseverentia sanctorum."*

13. The term is Rowan Williams', who applies it to Karl Barth and Karl Rahner (Williams, *On Christian Theology*, 18–19).

14. To be sure Moltmann emphasizes the incarnational ministry of Jesus (see especially *WJC*), but prioritizes the cross-resurrection event.

Limitations

For precision and concision, limits have been placed on the scope of this project. The present investigation does not proffer an application of Moltmann's hope. Generally most studies of Moltmann's theology focus on its consequential nature, its political and practical direction.[15] While the vast majority of the secondary literature is singularly consumed with the praxis elements of his project, the chief purpose behind his theological program is expressing, defining, and defending hope. Intentionally contrasting these monographs, this study focuses on what is best called, perhaps, his "pure" theology[16] and is written with the goal of filling this gap in the secondary literature. Instead of devoting space to his interest in praxis and ethical considerations, this study spotlights the other side of that dialectical relationship: theory.[17] So, while his understanding of hope is explored with the goal of showing its features, both positive and negative, other aspects of Moltmann's doctrine of hope receive little

---

15. Most monographs detail the political nature of Moltmann's work. While this is not misguided, a greater appreciation of his theological bases is necessary in order to appreciate fully the ethical implications of his work. For helpful studies on the political and/or ethical orientation of Moltmann's theology, see Vincent J. Genovesi, *Expectant Creativity*:; Arne Rasmusson, *Church as Polis*; Nigel Goring Wright, *Disavowing Constantine*. For primary and secondary bibliographic information through 2001, see James L. Wakefield, *Jürgen Moltmann: A Research Bibliography*.

16. The term is Bauckham's; for an exhibition of this method, see Richard Bauckham, "Moltmann's Eschatology of the Cross"; Donald Schweitzer, "The Consistency of Jürgen Moltmann's Theology."

17. Admittedly, the mere suggestion of this division, much less an application of it, may cause some to label this study a fool's errand. There is loud clamor from many corners calling for a closer relation between theory and practice, Moltmann included (see *TKG* 5–9). Admittedly, if pressed too far, such a division would render theology generally, and Moltmann's especially, unintelligible. Setting up this division does not, however, require viewing theory and practice as polar opposites to be applicable or appropriate; it simply provides a necessary and helpful boundary for the present study.

Furthermore, Moltmann understands and operates with such a division, though he seeks to overcome it: "theory and practice, thinking and doing, mutually drive one another" (*HD* 107; see also *HP* vii); "The relation between theory and practice is always circular, and hence must be defined dialectically, not in a linear way" (*ET* 294). The problem is that too few deal with Moltmann's "theory" to set up the dialectic.

attention, namely an existentialist[18] understanding that would lead to a more specific devotion to his vision of an "ethics of hope."[19]

A further limitation of scope provides another unique feature of this study. While other theologians are mentioned, especially as they shed light on his work, the focus is confined to Moltmann's theology. References to the best secondary literature are interspersed throughout, but this study approaches Moltmann's doctrine of hope on his terms, without using someone else's doctrine of hope as either a corrective or criterion.[20]

Method and Outline

The methodological strategy of the present study is both historical and developmental while also being analytical and interrogative. This exploration chronologically shows the developmental nature of Moltmann's doctrine of hope, as it informs and is informed by all other doctrines.

Part I comprises chapters 1–2 and establishes Moltmann's doctrine of hope as grounded in the cross and resurrection. His doctrine of hope is no mere trope or cipher, appearing at first sight substantial but essentially vacuous upon closer inspection.[21] Chapter one focuses on the centrality of the resurrection for his theology, while chapter two evidences his turn to the cross, which formally displaces the resurrection's centrality. This procedure allows a construction and definition of his doctrine of hope as it emerges in the period, without a composition

18. For Moltmann's view of existential hope (typically he juxtaposes hope and fear [*Angst*]), see especially *EG* 39–42 = *JCTW* 50–53.

19. This follows Moltmann who advertises, but never publishes, his "ethics of hope"; see especially *UZ* 13; *DGG* 189; also his "Letter to Karl Barth," 348. For Moltmann's stridently critical view of ethical application which bypasses aesthetics, liberation, freedom and joy, see *TJ*.

20. Critics typically call on Moltmann to embrace a more definable confessional outlook, and use such a standard to judge his work. This method, however, is bound to fail since it seeks to correct his theology by imposing an external standard (with which he disagrees), and this too often entails a misreading of his project. For a helpful discussion of Moltmann's negative (albeit selective) view of creedal and doctrinal formulation, see Richard Clutterbuck, "Jürgen Moltmann as a Doctrinal Theologian," 489–505.

21. Dr. Jeff Keuss (formerly Lecturer of Religious Studies, Glasgow University, Scotland; presently teaching at Seattle Pacific University), in follow-up correspondence (June 10, 2003) to a conference paper I presented at St. Andrews University, asked whether Moltmann's notion of hope was merely a trope or cipher, and ultimately questioned whether it was even possible to determine the contour of Moltmann's hope.

of hope being imposed from the outside. Part II comprises chapters 3–8 and investigates other major doctrines in his program in light of his doctrine of hope. In turn, hope is expounded via ecclesiology, the trinitarian doctrine of God, creation, christology, pneumatology, and eschatology. Those remotely conversant in Moltmann's theology will see immediately that though this study follows the order of publication, it does not follow his pattern of division.[22] Without disrupting the order of publication, the adopted framework argues for a different understanding of his major works in order to more fully comprehend his doctrine of hope, while also attempting to avoid an unnecessary and artificial perspectival distortion.[23] This design seeks to take advantage of the chronological approach, while also integrating the best elements of a topical approach.[24]

---

22. Moltmann's programmatic works are divided into the early trilogy (comprising *TH, CG, CPS*) and the contributions (comprising *TKG, GC, WJC, SpL, CoG, ET*). Between these two groups he switches methodology.

23. Of course, a measure of such distortion threatens all interpretation; the admission here is merely an acknowledgement of the danger of distorting the viewpoint, changing the object or rendering it unrecognizable.

24. Dates of certain assertions are pointed out with the goal of informing rather than overwhelming.

PART ONE

The Ground *of* Hope

THE GROUND[1] OF MOLTMANN'S HOPE IS THE DIALECTIC OF THE CROSS and resurrection.[2] God's promise and subsequent fulfillment in the event[3] of Jesus' death and resurrection show not that God is immutable and impassible, but that he is faithful[4] in keeping his promises (by raising the dead) and participating in suffering.[5] Part I investigates Moltmann's doctrine of hope as he develops it in *TH* and *CG*.

---

1. Ground (instead of basis) is employed throughout to convey the double meaning of *der Grund* as both (1) "foundation" or "basis" and (2) "reason for" or "cause"; many thanks to Dr. Nicholas Adams for delineating this word's dual-role. See Nicholas Adams, "Hope," 309–11.

2. See *TH*; *CG*; *ET* 52. Perhaps one could assert that God is the ground of hope, but this is too broad and though true for Moltmann, the specificity of naming the cross and resurrection is appreciably clearer.

3. While there is some equivocation based on context, from *CG* onward Moltmann typically refers to the dialectical unity of the cross and resurrection of Jesus Christ as one event (see *CG* 204; *WJC* 214; *SpL* 65; *SoL* 15). Earlier, he cited the resurrection alone as an event (*TH* 194, 198).

4. His view on God's essential nature shifts: in 1964 it is future (*TH* 16, 141); in 1995 it is love (*CoG* 329; see also "Liberating and Anticipating the Future," 189–208); in 2000 it is faithfulness (*ET* 36ff., 97; *EB* 163).

5. For explicit comments, see *SW* 58, 198 n. 4. For his most explicit discussion of faithfulness and hope, see *ET* 54–55.

1

Resurrection as Hope

Introduction

"THE CHRISTIAN HOPE FOR THE FUTURE," MOLTMANN WRITES, "COMES of observing a specific, unique event – that of the resurrection, and appearing of Jesus Christ."[1] For Moltmann, the resurrection is "the ground, power and goal of hope."[2] In the late 1950s[3] he determined that theology should begin with eschatology, convinced that although Karl Barth had said quite a lot he had nevertheless "neglected" eschatology.[4] This decision was given further clarity when he encountered the first two volumes of Ernst Bloch's The Principle of Hope,[5] which he read in 1960 (merely two years before he began writing TH).[6] Recalling his initial reaction to the volumes that he read while on vacation, he writes:

---

1. *TH* 194.

2. See "Resurrection as Hope," 129–47; "Resurrection," 81–89; *EH* 56.

3. For biographical details on Moltmann, see especially *UZ* 7–14; "Foreword," in Meeks, *Origins*, ix-xii; *EG* 1–18; *HTG* 165–82; *SoL* 1–9; *GSS* 47–70; *ET* 87–93; "Lived Theology: An Intellectual Biography," *ATJ* 55.1, 9–13; Richard Bauckham, "Jürgen Moltmann," in David F. Ford, 209–10; Bauckham, *Theology of Jürgen Moltmann*, 1–3; Wakefield, *Jürgen Moltmann*, 1–23.

4. *ET* 90; *BP* 109–11. Labeling it "neglect" is slightly unfair, since Barth never finished his eschatology. In 1956–57 Arnold van Ruler helpfully "freed" him from the belief that a new theology could not be done after Barth (see *UZ* 9; *EG* 11; "Politics and the Practice of Hope," 289).

5. 3 vols. Because of its chapter on religion, the third volume was "not allowed to appear" at that time (*ET* 92). The first two volumes "appeared" in 1954–55; the third volume was published in 1959 (Bloch, *Principle of Hope*, 1:xxv–xxvi).

6. He cites 1962–63 (*ET* 92); he met Bloch in 1960 (*GEB* 63).

> I . . . was so fascinated that I did not even notice the beauty of the Swiss mountains. My immediate reaction was, "Why has Christian theology neglected this theme of hope, which is so distinctively its own?" "What is left of the earliest Christian spirit of hope in present-day Christianity?"[7]

While it is perhaps true that without Bloch the school of hope would not exist,[8] it should not be forgotten that Moltmann's decision to begin theology with eschatology was made prior to reading Bloch's *magnum opus*. Only a few years later he began writing his first programmatic book, *TH* (1964; Eng. tr. 1967) which centers on eschatology and hope.[9] The setting for the publication of *TH* was the mood of the 1960s, which Moltmann describes as an era "brimming over with movements of hope and experiences of rebirth and renewal"[10] when "a new utopian rejoicing undoubtedly prevailed among us."[11] Hope was "in the air" and *TH* is marked by its time: the cultural context seemed to summon it.[12] In

---

7. *HTG* 169; see also *UZ* 9–10; *EG* 11; *BP* 79; Moltmann first draws on Bloch's *Principle of Hope* in 1960 (see *HP* 101–29).

8. Capps, "Mapping the Hope Movement," 19.

9. See *UZ* 10; This is not to downplay the formative thinkers that influenced Moltmann from early on, ranging from the biblical scholars Gerhard von Rad and Ernst Käsemann to the philosophies of G. W. F. Hegel and Karl Marx. Karl Barth and Rudolf Bultmann, to whom he reacts throughout his career, should be mentioned along with his Göttingen teachers (Hans Joachim Iwand, Otto Weber, and Ernst Wolf; see *BP* 39–52) as providing a major impetus to his theology. On the principal figures influential to Moltmann, which also expertly situates his early work, see especially Meeks, *Origins*. For an introduction to the formation of his early trilogy, see especially Richard Bauckham, *Moltmann: Messianic Theology in the Making*. Moltmann deems Bauckham's 1987 monograph a "mirror": "in which one recognizes oneself better than one had known oneself before" ("Foreword," in Bauckham, *Moltmann*, vii). For a bibliography of Bauckham's work on Moltmann, see Bauckham, *Theology of Jürgen Moltmann*, 263.

On Moltmann's early view of Bloch, see *GEB*; *EH* 15–29, 30–43; *RRF* 3–18, 148–76; "Hope without Faith," 25–40; *BP* 78–81.

10. *EG* 12, see also "Hope and the Biomedical Future of Man," 89–90; *HTG* 155; *GSS* 48; "The Blessing of Hope," *JPT* 13, 147–48.

Laurence Wood asserts the opposite: "Moltmann wrote *The Theology of Hope* when the 'death of God' theology was prominent. His theological reflections were like a breath of fresh air sweeping away the stench of despair" (Wood, "From Barth's Trinitarian Christology," 65). While this may apply to the 1967 English translation, it applies appreciably less to the German original in 1964; see *WJC* 3.

11. *EJM* 116.

12. *HTG* 170; he points to the Second Vatican Council, the civil rights movement in the USA, and "socialism with a human face" in the USSR; see also *EH* 44; *UZ* 11–12; *SW* 111; *BP* 98–100.

1967, Moltmann asserts that "the unique characteristic of modern times consists in the fact that we are everywhere asking for something that is 'new.' . . . [People] are fascinated by a future which so far nowhere has taken place and hence will be new."[13] It is this type of expectant mentality that accordingly gave rise to a time of hope. Even the title expresses "confidence in the future at a time when there had been a danger of too great a concentration on the past."[14] Indeed, the relatively immediate context was the end of two world wars. Coupled with the fact that two of the central figures in the generation preceding, Barth and Bultmann, had essentially "transposed eschatology into eternity" by insisting on redemption in the category of future beyond history and time,[15] Moltmann's view was distinct from the beginning.[16] As the author of a book so aptly titled, perforce, Moltmann, the "masterful thinker of hope,"[17] became identified as the chief exponent of the hope movement or the "school of hope."[18]

Moltmann's first programmatic text is not strictly devoted to prolegomena, but hope.[19] Yet, due to the interpenetration of all doctrines by eschatology, the text is in many ways the initial steps of, and groundwork for, his theology that continues to this day.[20] As one who shapes theology through eschatology, the text leaves a lasting impression, and

13. RRF 3.

14. Dillistone, "The Theology of Jürgen Moltmann," 145; see also Heinitz, "The Theology of Hope according to Ernst Bloch," 35.

15. CoG 13ff; see also 44–46.

16. To a lesser extent his disagreement with Pannenberg on the role of history is evident in TH as well (see TH 76ff.; WJC 76, 235–36; Meeks, Origins, 59).

17. Johann Baptist Metz, "The Last Universalists," 47.

18. John J. O'Donnell labels this movement the "German eschatological school" (*Trinity and Temporality*, 107). For analysis of Moltmann's role in the "hope movement," see Bauckham, *Moltmann*, 4ff.; Capps, "Mapping," 7ff; Cox, "Gedanken über Jürgen Moltmanns Buch: Der gekreuzigte Gott," 126; Frederick Herzog, "Towards the Waiting God," 53; Morse, *The Logic of Promise*. For general background on the hope movement, see especially Meeks, *Origins*; see also Capps, "Mapping," 1–49; idem, *Time Invades the Cathedral*; idem, *Hope against Hope*, 130–67.

19. Retrospectively, Moltmann labels TH "only prolegomena to eschatology," which rightly corrects the view that TH is intended as eschatology proper (see "Letter to Barth," 348; see also DTH 215).

20. See Volf, "After Moltmann: Reflections on the Future of Eschatology," 234; he likens Moltmann's theology to a "tower" envisioning CoG as the capstone and TH as its foundation. Moltmann describes his theology as "steps" (GC 1).

arguably sets the tone for his career. Indeed, the roots of his entire theological program, determined as it is by eschatology, are buried deeply in *TH*. Yet, upon deeper inspection, a suspicion emerges that this reliance brings to the fore a fundamental problem with his early theology generally, and his eschatology specifically. The core of *TH* is the resurrection, which leads to a central question: to what extent does Moltmann ground hope in the dialectic of cross and resurrection?

In *TH* Moltmann seeks to bring eschatology to the center and invest in it more meaning than its previously allocated status of dealing with "the last things."[21] Eschatology, and with it hope, should not be placed in brackets as an appendix to theology: theology must "make 'eschatology' the very medium of its thought! . . . [and make present] a 'warm stream' of hope in all articles of the Christian faith."[22] Christian hope cannot be confined to the existential present either, for this robs life of its horizon.[23] For, rightly understood, eschatology is "the keynote, the daybreak colours of a new expected day which bathe everything in their light."[24]

The present chapter covers Moltmann's understanding of hope during much of the 1960s. While the focus is squarely on *TH*, other essays are consulted as they shed further light on the importance of the resurrection.[25] The central section of this chapter is devoted to the

---

21. He, of course, belongs to a chorus of recent voices; for appraisals, see Sauter, *What Dare We Hope?* 210ff.; Fergusson, "Eschatology," 226; Gunton, "Dogmatic Theses on Eschatology," 157; Schwöbel, "Last Things First?" 217–41. Daniel Hardy also articulates well this understanding: "Not simply one doctrinal *locus* amongst others, eschatology requires the rethinking of all aspects of theology: what is Christian faith, and what is Christian responsibility, when reshaped by reference to the end of all things in God's purposes?" ("Eschatology as a Challenge for Theology," 151).

22. *EH* 41; see also *EG* 11. Notice the unmistakable allusion to Bloch who labels esoteric Marxism the "'warm stream' in Marxism" ("Hope without Faith," 25–40; *EH* 30ff.).

23. *TH* 265; see also 26–32, 58–69.

24. *EG* 11; see also *TH* 16; *SoL* 40–1; *EB* 87.

25. For overviews and introductions to *TH*, see *EH* 44–59; *HTG* 168–71; *ET* 87–93; Müller-Fahrenholz, *Kingdom and Power*, 40–61; Bauckham, *Moltmann*, 23–52; idem, *Theology of Jürgen Moltmann*, 29–46.

It should be noted that Moltmann's role in the Marxist or revolutionary movements around this time is passed over. For more on Moltmann's view of praxis, revolution, politics, and Marxism (including his participation in the *Paulusgesellschaft*), see especially *RRF* 74–76, 93–97; *HP* 190–93; *UZ* 26ff.; *TJ* 65–75; *M* 47–59; *HD* 43, 98, 168, 174;

nature of the resurrection and its role in grounding hope. Key areas of Ernst Bloch's influence on Moltmann's doctrine of hope will be assessed before concluding the chapter.[26]

Resurrection Hope

The centrality of the resurrection in *TH* is undeniable. Richard Bauckham, Moltmann's foremost commentator, claims that *TH* "might equally well have been called a theology of the resurrection."[27] The physical and theological central chapter of the text, "The Resurrection and Future of Jesus Christ,"[28] lays the foundation for Moltmann's doctrine of hope in the 1960s. In this section Moltmann's view of the resurrection will be appraised because it centrally determines his doctrine of hope. Before embarking on that pursuit, however, his delineation of hopelessness, hope's opposite, needs to be mentioned.

The Sin against Hope: Presumption and Despair

In the "Introduction" to *TH* Moltmann subscribes fully to Josef Pieper's depiction of hopelessness. Following Pieper, he writes:

> hopelessness can assume two forms: it can be presumption, *praesumptio*, and it can be despair, *desperatio*. Both are forms of the sin against hope. Presumption is a premature, selfwilled anticipation of the fulfillment of what we hope for from God.

SpL 329 n. 31; see also Hunsinger, "The Crucified God"; Rasmusson, *The Church as Polis*; Wright, *Disavowing Constantine*, 105–57.

26. Importantly, 1960 and 1961 mark the publication of two essays: (see *HP* 101–29, 130–54) where he mentions the cross of Christ (*HP* 106) and links pain, suffering, love, and hope (*HP* 147–48). These themes are not fully developed and he does not return to them in a full and integrated way until 1967–68. Indeed, the criticism of this time period does not apply to these two early essays, but rather to *TH* and onwards.

27. Bauckham, *Moltmann*, 3; see also Conyers, *God, Hope, and History*, 57; Meeks, "Foreword," in *EH* xi; Wolf-Dieter Marsch, "Zur Einleitung," in *DTH* 11–13; Hendrikus Berkhof, "Über die Methode der Eschatologie," in *DTH* 175.

Moltmann agrees (*TH* 177; *JCTW* 71–87) and in 1989, admits that his focus on the resurrection was "partly due" to its context (*WJC* 3). Indeed, he essentially defines God by the resurrection: "Anyone who says 'resurrection of the dead' says 'God' (Barth). On the other hand, anyone who says 'God' and does not hope for the resurrection of the dead and a new creation from the righteousness of God, has not said 'God'. What other belief in God can be held by those who are 'dead' unless it is 'resurrection faith'?" (*CG* 218).

28. *TH* 139–229.

> Despair is the premature, arbitrary anticipation of the non-fulfillment of what we hope for from God. Both forms of hopelessness, by anticipating the fulfillment or by giving up hope, cancel the wayfaring character of hope. They rebel against the patience in which hope trusts in the God of the promise. They demand impatiently either fulfillment "now already" or "absolutely no" hope.[29]

This summary is instructive, since it provides the reader with Moltmann's understanding of the parameters of hope. Indeed, the lines of demarcation are highlighted, which once crossed, render hope void. This brief description of hopelessness provides a helpful background, allowing one to better appreciate Moltmann's desire to develop a distinctly Christian doctrine of hope, and thereby redress the "neglect" of this key doctrine.[30]

Resurrection and History

For Moltmann, the resurrection of Jesus Christ is present as promise, which validates, but does not fulfill, the promise.[31] On this basis, he avoids using the language of facts taking place in history.[32] At first sight it may seem that he is subscribing to Enlightenment rationalism's suspicion of miracles. He is not avoiding the nature of the resurrection as a miracle by focusing on the subjective level, but rather altering the parameters of the discussion.[33] While a full inspection of this matter is

---

29. *TH* 23; he cites Pieper, *Über die Hoffnung*, 51; the English equivalent is found in *Faith, Hope, Love*, 113. Later Moltmann discusses both presumption and despair by drawing from Pieper, without citing him (*GL* 49–50; *EB* 93–95; see also *HTG* 193 n. 24). See also Elie Wiesel's 1986 Nobel Lecture "Hope, Despair and Memory," 174–79.

30. See *HTG* 169; *UZ* 9–10.

31. *TH* 144–56.

32. *TH* 167ff. Some find Moltmann's pronouncements on this troubling. David Scaer criticizes Moltmann's evasiveness at this point, believing that "The historical question is sidestepped" (Scaer, "Review of *Hope and Planning*," 364). While correctly seeing that "everything depends on the resurrection" for Moltmann, Grace Jantzen is suspicious of his dismissal of the resurrection's importance. Problematically, she only cites *CG* (Jantzen, "Christian Hope and Jesus' Despair," 1–7). If she had looked to Moltmann's prior and more central text on the importance of the resurrection her fears may have been allayed. There, she would have found statements of this type: "because he [God] has raised Christ from the dead, therefore the fulfillment of his promise is certain" (*TH* 145; see also especially 165, 185).

33. See *TH* 177 n. 1; he is critical of D. F. Strauss at precisely this point.

unnecessary, it is important to note that his argument does not deny the historicity of the resurrection *prima facie*, but rather seeks to move its importance away from historical investigation on one side, and existential interpretation on the other. While the verification of the resurrection is moved to the future,[34] the truth of the resurrection is undeniably fundamental to his entire approach: "That the resurrection actually took place is not thereby denied."[35] Moltmann's meaning is clarified by situating his view in relation to two views that he rejects: (1) Pannenberg's enquiry into the resurrection as history,[36] and (2) Bultmann's location of the importance of the resurrection in the subjective decision for faith.[37] Moltmann is convinced that investigating the resurrection via the historical method rests on two erroneous presuppositions: (1) the resurrection is approached as a verifiable event;[38] but more problematic (2) the resurrection is placed on the same plane as other "historical" events. The trouble with this methodology, for Moltmann, is that it devalues the resurrection of its eschatological nature and thus theological importance.[39]

He makes central both the truth of the resurrection and God's promises, while also maintaining that the resurrection is beyond the scope of historical investigation and analogy.[40] If, in so doing, he avoids locating its historical basis,[41] his failure is not to be found in the

34. For a critique, see Placher, "The Present Absence of Christ," 169–79.

35. *TH* 185; see also *EH* 56: "Easter is the historical origin and the continuing basis of the Christian faith, the Christian church, and the Christian hope."

36. While they have numerous similarities, the core difference separating Moltmann from Pannenberg (admittedly bordering on oversimplification), is that while Moltmann's central concern is God's faithfulness as hope, Pannenberg's is God's revelation as history (awaiting the end of history, or history's unification); for explicit comment, see *TH* 112–20; *SW* 111; Pannenberg, *Systematic Theology*, 3:538 n. 53.

37. See especially *TH* 69, 172–90. Of course, others are mentioned in these discussions. The discussion of Pannenberg is unavoidably linked to historical investigation as an analogical discipline, whereby Ernst Troeltsch seeks "the basic similarity of all historic events" (as cited in *TH* 174; see also 177–78). Moltmann is critical, but comparatively less so, of Barth's emphasis on the resurrection as revelation.

38. See also "From the Beginning of Time in God's Presence," 61.

39. "The Blessing of Hope," 152.

40. For an appraisal of recent approaches to the resurrection, see Hunsinger, "The Daybreak of the New Creation," 163–81.

41. Bauckham is not convinced that Moltmann need "renounce any form of historical basis" (*Theology of Jürgen Moltmann*, 42).

accusation that he does not take the event seriously. Indeed, Moltmann asserts that the resurrection's importance is its eschatological significance and so speaks the language of promise, which necessarily points not to the past but to the future and thus requires not historical investigation for verification, but rather the eschaton.[42]

In short, Moltmann is unconvinced that Pannenberg's view of the resurrection has satisfactorily solved the problem of Lessing's "ugly great ditch."[43] Ultimately, Moltmann believes that Pannenberg's appeal to historical investigation, tools, and insight for the relevance of the resurrection necessarily fails. He finds Pannenberg's solution unsatisfactory not because it says too much (some critics believe Pannenberg's appeal to the facts of history is a fools' errand), but rather because it does not say enough. Essentially, Moltmann is making plain that the Christian hope for the general resurrection is rooted in the eschatological significance of the resurrection of Jesus, something which historical investigation can neither research effectively nor report accurately, because it cannot be confirmed. (Moltmann is basically raising the essential point of Kierkegaard's similar questions related to the provisional nature of historical events and the basis of faith.) Historical facts cannot cross Lessing's deep and profound "great ditch." Only an epistemology of eschatological significance can, yet this is only proven in the *eschaton*.[44]

Additionally, later Moltmann makes it clear that it is untenable to "believe in a God, but not in Christ's resurrection . . . 'God yes, but Jesus no' is not a Christian option."[45] While he is quite polemical in his criticisms of historical investigation of the resurrection, those skeptical of Moltmann at this point, perhaps fearing that he is evading altogether the

---

42. Besides *TH*, see *EB* 47.

43. Lessing, "Über den Beweis des Geistes und der Kraft," 4.11ff.

44. Later, Pannenberg defends his earlier view as being misunderstood and in so doing clarifies his views, in seeming reaction to criticisms, including Moltmann's (see especially *Systematic Theology*, vol. 2). He principally attends to the role of anticipation as vital to his views.

45. *JCTW* 72.

meaning of the resurrection,[46] should take note of his decisive polemic against Bultmann, in whom he finds an anti-historical tendency.[47]

Moltmann equally rejects the existentialist approach because it is reductionist in precisely the opposite way. Placing the ultimate meaning of the resurrection in existential terms is faulty because it "has no interest in the historical question."[48] Bultmann epitomizes, for Moltmann, the anti-historical perspective, since he moves the relevance of theology to the preached word and the subjective response of faith, transposing the resurrection from "something that happens to the crucified Jesus to something that happens to the existence of the disciples."[49] This, Moltmann believes, separates theology from any historical grounding, which his entire project seeks to reverse (and his entire project is misunderstood if this is not kept in view).[50]

Each approach is fallacious while making the opposite move: the first procedure seeks to authenticate the resurrection; the second marginalizes this attempt.[51] But centrally for Moltmann, without the resurrection there is no hope. Too easily missed by his critics is the fact that he does not deny the resurrection's facticity, but rather its verifiability according to traditional historical investigation.[52]

More generally, his view of history's importance is partly reactionary. Moltmann is convinced that both Barth and Bultmann, albeit in remarkably different ways, vacate the temporality of the *eschaton*. Indeed, eschatology, according to dialectic theology, threatens to become detemporalized because time and eternity stand in opposition. Moltmann

---

46. After presenting the paper "Jürgen Moltmann's Turn to a Theology of the Cross: Reconsidering the Consensus Judgment" at the 2003 *Society for the Study of Theology* Annual Conference (April 9), a questioner raised precisely this concern.

47. *TH* 58–69, 178ff. For a summary of Bultmann's view of Jesus being raised into the *kerygma*, see Gareth Jones, *Bultmann: Towards a Critical Theology*, 51ff.

48. *TH* 186.

49. Ibid.

50. Indeed, for his decisive criticism of this view, see ibid., 106–12, 230–72; *HP* 56–98.

51. *TH* 187ff.

52. After all Moltmann rightly points out: "If there is a historically strong 'proof' of the resurrection of Jesus, it is not the empty tomb; it is the death-defying return of the disciples" (*CoG* 309). The empty tomb, according to David Fergusson, is "a negative and necessary condition" for the development of resurrection faith (Fergusson, "Interpreting the Resurrection," 300; see also "The Blessing of Hope," 152).

and others of his generation (most notably Pannenberg) have sought to bring the importance of history to bear on theological method, which necessarily impinges on eschatology. Moving beyond the views that he rejects, Moltmann presents his own thesis: the resurrection as promise.

Promise and History[53]

Moltmann looks to the Old Testament[54] to maintain that, rightly understood, history is open to the future based on God's promises.[55] As will be shown, he looks to numerous figures for his understanding of promise. Drawing principally on Gerhard von Rad, he states: "the God who gives his promises in the event of promise is one who makes possible for the very first time the feeling for history in the category of the future, and consequently has a 'historicizing' effect."[56] This statement captures an essential element of Moltmann's argument, which overcomes revelation as epiphany,[57] while also insisting that eschatology be understood historically and *vice versa*: it is "eschatology which first gives history a meaning for theology and does not close it."[58] Following the Old Testament, Moltmann finds this perception of God as promise (to a degree, at least, over against God as presence) in times of fulfillment and judgment; even the latter does not negate a proper understanding of Yahweh's faithfulness to Israel,[59] because now the history of promise is not limited to Israel, but rather is universal.[60] For Moltmann the category of eternity is not the "realm" of God's activity, and immutability is not the supreme designation for God; their replacements are, respectively, history and faithfulness: "God reveals himself as 'God' where he

---

53. This is the title of *TH* chapter 2.

54. For a defense of the locution "Old Testament" instead of "Hebrew Bible," see Seitz, "Old Testament or Hebrew Bible," 61–74; for the salient distinctions between the two, see Collins, *Introduction to the Hebrew Bible*, 1–9.

55. *TH* 97, *passim*; *DTH* 201; *RRF* 201; *ET* 102ff. For Moltmann's differentiation between promise and prophecy, see especially *ET* 93ff.

56. *TH* 100.

57. See ibid., 41, 46.

58. *HP* 81. Morse notes: "when Moltmann discusses the language of promise he does so always in connection with reference to the term 'history'" (*Logic of Promise*, 47).

59. *TH* 100ff.

60. Ibid., 145ff.

shows himself as the same and is thus known as the same. He becomes identifiable where he identifies himself with himself in the historic act of his faithfulness."[61] This quote brings into focus the incontrovertible core of Moltmann's insistence that history, not eternity, is the central category for reality.[62] Thus, "there can be no return to non-historic faith in the ever existing and eternally abiding cosmos. The understanding of history, of its possibilities for good and evil, of its direction and its meaning, lies in the field of hope and can be acquired only there."[63]

Promise, and the hope it helps to produce, is the force of history oriented to the future.[64] "There is therefore only one problem in Christian theology," avers Moltmann, "the problem of the future."[65] In Moltmann's project, the future has priority over the present and the past to such an extent that the future, as it were, draws the present forward in a way that avoids any notion of the future being wholly determined by the present or the past.[66] Indeed, the opposite is the case, as the future determines the present: "Through Christ's resurrection and through hope aroused, the future of God exerts an influence in the present and makes the present historical."[67] Indeed, Moltmann is operating with a vision of the future[68] that is not bound by the past, or else he would be unable to grant the eschaton creative value, indeed *creatio ex nihilo* value,[69] to the future: God promises new life which is "a creative act of

---

61. Ibid., 116. See also *ET* 55: "The essential nature of the God who determines human history through promises such as these is not timeless eternity; it is his identity in time—*his faithfulness*. That is the assurance of the hope awakened by his promise: 'God is faithful, he cannot deny himself' (2 Tim. 2.13)."

62. *TH* 106ff; *HP* 103ff.

63. *TH* 263. Moltmann specifically opposes the Greek cosmology of cyclic recurrence, contrasted with the "Israelite-Christian understanding of reality" (*HP* 104).

64. *TH* 17, 221, 286.

65. Ibid., 16; Compare with Bloch's perspective: "According to Bloch, the initial task of atheism is positing an open space 'above' or 'before' a void where formerly 'God' . . . existed. It nevertheless redefines the God-question as 'the one real thing it can be: the supreme utopian problem, the problem of the end" (Meeks, *Origins*, 82).

66. Besides *TH*, for his later comments, see especially *DTH* 221; *GC* 126–39.

67. *HP* 183; future = *Zukunft* [257]; see also *UZ* 156.

68. Moltmann does not delineate the difference between *Futurum* and *Zukunft* until after *TH* (he first evidences this knowledge in 1966; a full discussion is below).

69. *TH* 209; see also 221; while later he retracts this assertion (*CoG* 75; 350 n. 50), it seems to be aimed directly at Bloch (*GEB* 60).

Yahweh upon his people beyond the bounds of the temporal and the possible."[70]

Important to note is that this view of promise provides Moltmann with the necessary framework to let the future impact present reality and thus, history.[71] Eschatology, while linked to the future, is also tied to history.[72] The category *novum* is integrated into his eschatology,[73] because of the promissory underpinnings of this temporal structure: "The history which is initiated and determined by promise does not consist in cyclic recurrence, but has a definite trend towards the promised and outstanding fulfillment."[74] Indeed, history must be seen as dynamically open: "if there is no future, there is also no real history. If there is no history, our world is not open, but shut in."[75] Moltmann rejects any idea of history's closure, which leads him to emphasize the biblical conception of God as a "God of promise."[76] Imperative in this view is that a promised temporal future (over against timeless eternity) leads not to an abandonment of the present world, but a transformation of it: "In the promises, the hidden future already announces itself and exerts its influence on the present through the hope it awakens."[77] Additionally,

---

70. *TH* 209; the immediate context is the centrality of God's ability to overcome death.

71. For a comprehensive study on the centrality of promise for Moltmann, see Morse, *Logic of Promise*; idem, "God's Promise as Presence," 143–57.

72. Capps, "Mapping," 11.

73. This is based on von Rad and Bloch; see especially *HP* 177; *CoG* 27ff.; Meeks, *Origins*, 87–88.

74. *TH* 103, following Walther Zimmerli. Retrospectively, Moltmann dubs van Ruler the one who "convinced" him of "the Old Testament's surplus of promise towards the New" (*ET* 91; see also *TH* 263; *EH* 44–59).

75. *RRF* 3.

76. *TH* 143; see also 106ff.

77. Ibid., 18, see also 102ff.; 165, 171, 328–31; *GL* 124–26; *ET* 51. Moltmann states that "knowledge of God comes about . . . in view of the historic action of God within the horizon of the promises of God. . . . The name of God is a name of promise" (*TH* 116). This seems to be of a piece with his numerous citations editing Marx's eleventh thesis on Feuerbach. While referencing neither Bloch nor Marx, Moltmann is surely nuancing the latter when he asserts that "The theologian is not concerned merely to supply a different *interpretation* of the world, of history and of human nature, but to *transform* them in expectation of a divine transformation" (*TH* 84); compare, Marx's eleventh thesis: "The philosophers have only *interpreted* the world, in various ways; the point is to *change* it" (Marx, *Early Writings*, 423).

promise is accorded importance because revelation is the form of promise.[78] Thus, for Moltmann, "the *author* and the *content* of the promise are one."[79] More specifically, he follows Iwand for understanding "that the revelation of God in Jesus Christ is grounded alone in God's Word of promise."[80] The promise points beyond the present "into the as yet unrealized future which it announces."[81] In this regard eschatological revelation is not understood as merely divine disclosure, but rather, because it is promise, revelation is a divine separator:

> It is not evolution, progress and advance that separate time into yesterday and tomorrow, but the word of promise cuts into events and divides reality into one reality which is passing and can be left behind, and another which must be expected and sought.[82]

The promise is powerful because it points beyond experienced reality into the *novum*, the unforeseen, albeit promised, future. This, as will be shown, has important ramifications for a proper understanding of the resurrection and hope.

Promissory Perspective

The promise is only verified in the future, and so is a matter of hope: "Promise announces the coming of a not yet existing reality from the future of the truth."[83] Specifically, this means that "the knowledge of the truth presents itself in the form of a question that is open towards the

---

Moltmann also looks to Marx for support when he criticizes Pannenberg's *Revelation as History* (see *TH* 76–86; Pannenberg, "Dogmatic Theses on the Doctrine of Revelation," 123–58). See also Pannenberg's assertion that the future has "ontological priority" (Pannenberg, "The God of Hope," 241). Moltmann typically accords the future transformative import related to history, while it is perhaps truer for Pannenberg that the future serves a more disclosive function for history. This is one of a few central differences between them.

78. Morse, *Logic of Promise*, 44; Herzog, "Towards the Waiting God," 59; *TH* 100ff.

79. *EH* 50.

80. Meeks, *Origins*, 63. Meeks points out that this is a move *contra* Barth who "explained the Word by a concept of revelation grounded in the unity of being and Word in the subjectivity of God" (63); see also *TH* 112–20.

81. *TH* 100.

82. Ibid., 102.

83. Ibid., 83; see also *HP* 20–25.

fulfillment of the promise."[84] Revelation in the appearances of Jesus is "unfinished," and so Moltmann emphasizes the importance of future revelation: "It is still outstanding, has not yet come about, has not yet appeared, but it is promised and guaranteed in his resurrection."[85] Because he is seeking to ensure that both the past and present are not aligned, indeed cannot be aligned, with the promised future, he takes a decidedly negative stance regarding present experience and existence: "If the word is a word of promise, then that means that this word has not yet found a reality congruous to it, but that on the contrary it stands in contradiction to the reality open to experience now heretofore."[86] And similarly: "The future of God among men and the whole creation becomes present in the mode in which the future gains power over the present in promise and experienced hope and decides what will become of the given actuality."[87] And it is here that the power of the resurrection represents and expresses an eschatological promise for the future that has no correspondence with human experience. In *TH* Moltmann finds no hope in the present, which necessitates looking to the future for its ground. In the act of raising Jesus from the dead, God guarantees his promise, while simultaneously contradicting present reality.[88] The concept of promise, therefore, helps to interpret the proper understanding of God's activity. In contradistinction to the God of metaphysics, the God of biblical revelation participates in history in the "event of the cross and resurrection."[89]

---

84. *TH* 86.

85. Ibid., 88; see also 51–53; to be sure, this is situated in terms of critiquing the understanding of revelation as an epiphany of the eternal present.

86. Ibid., 103; see also *HP* 195–97. This changes dramatically as his pneumatology gains influence in his project.

87. Future = *Zukunft* both times (*EH* 40 [62]; see also "Theology as Eschatology," 10). This view caused Rubem Alves (amongst others) to criticize Moltmann's concentration on God's futurity, to the exclusion of the present; see Alves, *A Theology of Human Hope*, 57ff; Grellert, "The Eschatological Theology of Jürgen Moltmann," 269–70; Hefner, "Theological Reflections (4). Questions for Moltmann and Pannenberg," 32–51.

88. *TH* 139, 223.

89. Ibid., 140; Moltmann argues that the resurrection is properly understood with the background of Israel in the Old Testament, indeed in light of the "God of the exodus and the promise" (ibid., 141, see also *TH* 142ff; *ET* 51); Bloch has a similar focus (see Fiorenza, "Dialectical Theology and Hope 2," 388).

This emphasis on promissory presence and revelation has attracted criticism. Langdon Gilkey labels Moltmann's view "incomprehensible": "Not a God who 'will be', but a God who very much already is, is required here."⁹⁰ Gilkey is one in a chorus that deems tenuous and one-sided Moltmann's stress on the future of God's being.⁹¹ While not identical, each complaint is concerned with a stress on the future to the detriment of the present.⁹² Moltmann's eschatology, which Nicholas Adams correctly notes, gives the future "immense weight,"⁹³ while in need of modification and balance, is not necessarily as ill-fated as some maintain. While finding it difficult to articulate the ethical application of this knowledge at this early stage,⁹⁴ Moltmann sees that the promised future correctly shows the present to be provisional and in this way he correctly perceives that this, in turn, enables humanity to set out to change present circumstances in light of the promised future because of the resurrection.⁹⁵ Furthermore, Moltmann's central concern is a criticism of divine eternal presence, and while this provides him reasons to critique present existence, the main point is to ensure that "Promise is itself a mode of presence, but promissory presence must not be confused with eternal presence."⁹⁶

The Resurrection of Jesus Christ

As already mentioned, Moltmann is not exercised by the historical verifiability of the empty tomb, but instead focuses on the resurrection as an eschatological event. This move to characterize the resurrection

---

90. Gilkey, "The Universal and Immediate Presence of God," 86; see also Langdon Gilkey, *Reaping the Whirlwind: A Christian Interpretation of History*, 230.

91. For details and discussion, see Berkhof, "Über die Methode der Eschatologie," 175ff.; Fiorenza, "Dialectical Theology and Hope 1," 148; Frei, "Review of Moltmann's *Theology of Hope*," 268; Macquarrie, "Eschatology and Time," 123.

92. For a summary of Moltmann's position, see *RRF* 177–99.

93. Adams, "Eschatology Sacred and Profane," 283–306. Adams clearly shows problems with Moltmann's incorporation of Bloch's philosophy for Christian eschatology, but it is unclear whether this observation is a criticism.

94. In *TH*, Moltmann's ethical vision is elusive because his theology is not fastened to concrete application (best exhibited, perhaps, in *TH* ch. 5).

95. On this problem of over-emphasis, see Hunsinger, "The Crucified God and the Political Theology of Violence," 266–79, 381.

96. Morse, *Logic of Promise*, 31.

chiefly in eschatological terms is to give it a greater depth of meaning and heightened importance. Thus, the resurrection is

> not a past event, something in history finished and done with; it was an event in the past which still has its future ahead of it. That is to say, it was what theological language describes as an *eschatological* event, in which God's future has acquired potency over the past.[97]

At its strongest his theology of promise expresses mediation: "promise stands between knowing and not knowing, between necessity and possibility, between that which is not yet and that which already is."[98] This extends further: "the Easter appearances of the crucified Christ are a constant incitement to the consciousness that hopes and anticipates, but on the other hand also suffers and is critical of existence."[99] On this basis he concludes: "knowledge of Christ becomes anticipatory, provisional and fragmentary knowledge of his future."[100] This is, indeed, the correct pursuit of ensuring hope's "wayfaring character."[101]

While this is integral to Moltmann's overall argument, the close relation between Good Friday and Easter Sunday is generally assumed while he focuses intently on the resurrection.[102] While he admits later that this one-sidedness was intended,[103] this particular feature is problematic: the basic theme of hope is founded on the resurrection, with no place for the cross to play an essential role in a doctrine of hope.[104]

---

97. *EB* 47; future = *Zukunft* both times [59]. Unfortunately, many critics still seem to lose sight of the freight he places on the resurrection.

98. *TH* 203.

99. *TH* 203.

100. *TH* 203.

101. *TH* 23.

102. For references to the cross, see *TH* 31, 82–85, 163–72, 198, 203, 221, 225–26. Not until 1968, does Moltmann turn toward grounding theology in the cross of Christ. See further: *TH* 177; Bauckham, *Moltmann*, 3; Conyers, *God, Hope, and History*, 57; Wolf-Dieter Marsch, "Zur Einleitung," 11–13; *JCTW* 71–87; indeed, in 1989, Moltmann admits that his focus on the resurrection was "partly due" to its context (*WJC* 3).

103. *CG* 5; *DGG* 166; "Foreword," in Bauckham, *Moltmann*, ix; *HTG* 173–74; *WJC* 3.

104. Moltmann admits in the opening of *CG* that he needed to move past his reliance on Bloch to articulate a theology of the cross (*CG* 5). One explanation of Moltmann's emphasis on God's power is his familiarity with Calvin's thought, which engaged him prior to *TH*; see O'Donnell, *Trinity and Temporality*, 152; Fiorenza, "Dialectical Theology and Hope 1," 145.

Resurrection and Hope

The relationship between resurrection and hope is central. The resurrection alone is given positive value for the importance of hope and it alone is the material ground of hope in *TH*. To be sure, he locates the importance of hope formally in both the cross and resurrection: "The hope that is born of the cross and the resurrection transforms the negative, contradictory and torturing aspects of the world into terms of 'not yet', and does not suffer them to end in 'nothing.'"[105] Yet, this remains only a formal designation, through which he seeks to ensure the continuity of identity: the raised one is the crucified one.[106] Indeed, in Moltmann's early view "The remembrance of the promise . . . bores like a thorn in the flesh of every present" which helps to explain why he deems "all reality inadequate and as such transient and surpassable," indeed "corrupt."[107] As such, reality is the object of Christian hope that is to be transformed.[108] While this is qualified with a notion of promise, the emphasis is derived from Bloch, whose perspective is that "religion is hope, and hope is grounded in the ontic difference between what is and what is not yet, between existence and essence, between present and future."[109] Moltmann adopts this perspective, yet alters it by insisting that the future brings hope via creation *ex nihilo*: "The resurrection of Christ does not mean a possibility within the world and its history, but a new possibility altogether for the world, for existence and for history."[110] When it comes to hope, the present and future are binary opposites: "hope must prove its power. Hence eschatology . . . must formulate its statements of hope in contradiction to our present experience of

---

105. *TH* 197; tellingly, this comment appears just before his section "The Identity of the Lord who Appears as Risen with the Crucified Christ" (*TH* 197–202), which demonstrates that he is not guilty of a deliberate omission, in which he avoids discussing or acknowledging the cross.

106. *TH* 85: "in all the qualitative difference of cross and resurrection Jesus is the same. This identity in infinite contradiction is theologically understood as an event of identification, an act of the faithfulness of God. It is this that forms the ground of the promise of the still outstanding future of Jesus Christ. It is this that is the ground of the hope which carries faith through the trials of the god-forsaken world and of death."

107. *TH* 88, 227, respectively; see also *TH* 21; *HP* 197.

108. *TH* 34.

109. *RRF* 151; see also Marsch, "Zur Einleitung," 8; Bloch, *Principle of Hope*, 2:451.

110. *TH* 179; see also pp. 179–80, 209, 200, 221. While still holding this position, later he qualifies it (*CoG* 75; 350 n. 50).

suffering, evil, and death."[111] Writing in 1965, he states that resurrection hope "allows nothing to remain as it was and is, but rather confronts everything with that transformation which it expects by reproaching it with its unredeemed and unfulfilled condition."[112] In this period, at least, Moltmann avoids linking the cross to hope, as he views resurrection hope in direct opposition to suffering and transience. This oppositional terminology makes plain his desire to emphasize the *novum* and the coming future over against the present. Such a perspective refuses any place for the cross to ground hope.

Is the resurrection of the crucified one solely the ground of a theology of hope? At first glance this seems to be the case. The resurrection exemplifies the power of God, and identifies God as the one who possesses the ability to overcome death. Indeed, it is fundamental to the Christian faith: "if Christ has not been raised, then . . . your faith is in vain."[113] Hope is placed in the God who raises the dead and promises a future. Upon deeper inspection of Moltmann's doctrine at this early stage, problems emerge due to funding a doctrine of hope with the single currency of the resurrection as the power of the promising God, with not enough weight being placed on the crucifixion.[114]

In Moltmann's early work the resurrection alone is the ground of hope causing him to speak in confident, even triumphant terms about the future. It is unfortunate that his understanding of the resurrection is used in this way, rather than in a more expectant manner regarding fulfillment. Throughout *TH* Moltmann insists that the future is open because the resurrection is still to be completed in the eschaton.[115] Yet, he uses this understanding to assert hope as guaranteed, rather than what seems to be called for by his own arguments, which is a more expectant vision.

---

111. *TH* 19.

112. *HP* 173.

113. 1 Cor 15:14.

114. *Contra* Grellert: "Moltmann always speaks of the resurrection in connection with the cross" (Grellert, "The Eschatological Theology of Jürgen Moltmann," 180 n.41).

115. *TH* 92; for Moltmann "historic reality has room for open possibilities ahead." This, in part at least, is due to Bloch's influence; see Moltmann, *Is There Life After Death?*, 7–12.

Moltmann can envision the future as open because the resurrection still must be completed, and vice versa. He avoids keeping this tension, however, by speaking of the future not as fulfillment expected, but fulfillment guaranteed. The grounding of hope is clearly the *novum* of the resurrection. Moltmann develops the openness of the future as an intrinsic basis to his understanding of hope. The open future necessarily gives hope a "wayfaring character."[116] In the end, however, he does not use the open future in this way. He, instead, uses it to give hope a guaranteed character. Yet, to arrive at hope as guaranteed is to disregard the very openness that is the very mark of true hope. Furthermore, it is his understanding of promise, resurrection and future that seem to call this approach into question. Problematically, Moltmann sources his hope with the resurrection, the *novum*, and the future. Though the cross is referenced and discussed in *TH*, other than ensuring that Jesus' identity is the crucified and resurrected one, Moltmann avoids materially grounding his hope in the cross. This lack is the emerging problem with his doctrine of hope in the early period. Before distilling more precisely the impetus of the problems involved with Moltmann's hope in *TH*, a few protests of this critique should be addressed.

Admittedly, a charge leveled against Moltmann for lacking a theology of the cross may sound peculiar, even misguided, at first. Objections may be raised, citing both *CG* and *TKG*, contending that Moltmann centrally identifies the cross as the central doctrine of Christian theology. This point is undeniable, yet unhelpful. Pointing to central themes in *CG* (1972) and *TKG* (1980) has little bearing on his understanding of hope as presented in *TH* (1964). Recalling the methodology employed in the present study, the development of his doctrine of hope is understood best when his writings are appraised chronologically. Limiting the scope to Moltmann's writings of the early- and mid-1960s entails a conscious decision to avoid taking into account the developments that do in fact occur over the ensuing forty years. This procedure advantageously allows one to properly gauge his initial statements of hope and eschatology, thereby distilling more accurately what funds his hope at this early stage. Not allowing consideration of later work and development, this confined outlook produces an interesting view of Moltmann's hope, as advocated in the 1960s. And, more specifically, from this period

116. *TH* 23.

of the 1960s one can see the concentration Moltmann places on the resurrection as the singular ground of hope.

Using the promissory notion of the resurrection as his way of correcting both historical investigation and existential interpretation, Moltmann contends that because it is without analogy, the resurrection is really only known through faith and hope.[117] This line of thinking seems to lead to a doctrine of hope grounded in the promised future, and as such can be expected, because of the God who makes and keeps promises. To the extent that he draws this conclusion, he is on firm ground. He tends to move past this judgment, however, by conflating a promised future with a guaranteed one. Moltmann promotes a promised future, which in his terms is a guaranteed future. He propounds a view of hope as one of guarantee and certainty, because of the resurrecting "God of promise": "the fulfillment of his [God's] promise is certain,"[118] based on the "dependability of God himself," for all the promises of God are "an eschatological certainty in Christ."[119] As such "we enter into the history that is determined by the promised and guaranteed *eschaton*."[120] While there is a future orientation to this fulfillment, it is without reservation.

On one level this view is highly attractive. He clearly looks to the biblical narrative for identifying the ground of hope in the God of promise. And he makes a strong case (implicitly *contra* Bloch) that there will be fulfillment in the future because God is faithful, using the events of Exodus and resurrection as key paradigms.

The problem Moltmann creates in developing hope in a guaranteed, confident tone is that he appears conflicted, working contrary to his own purpose. For, on one level he maintains that promise is the key to history and hope. Yet, promise must always point to the future for verification. Indeed, his entire theological program is unsustainable without this understanding of promise. It is this understanding of history and hope that leads him to argue convincingly that the resurrection of Jesus Christ awaits eschatological confirmation, and so cannot be

---

117. *TH* 172–73; his dialectical epistemology is evidenced in *TH*, yet becomes more pronounced in *CG* and is considered in chapter two.

118. *TH* 145, "is certain" = *ist . . . gewiß* [131]; see the entire section: "The God of Promise" (*TH* 143ff.); see also *TH* 216ff.

119. *TH* 147, certainty = *Zuversicht* [133].

120. *TH* 154, guaranteed = *verbürgten* [139].

merely one event amongst others in history. On another level, however, Moltmann argues for hope as certain. This conclusion seems forbidden by both his specific argument for the promised, awaited future and also the overarching pattern of his theology oriented toward future fulfillment. To conclude that hope is an absolute certainty, however, is to cast aside the promissory understanding and vital key which is essential to true, Christian hope. The problem is that he refuses to maintain hope's proper tension, situated between promise and fulfillment. This tension informs the very identity of hope, as occupying the ground between despair and presumption. He Moltmann does not realize that a fundamental commitment of his project is to avoid presumption. The underlying problem with his hope is its guaranteed, certain fulfillment. This perspective is both a reliance on, and a reaction to, Bloch's alternative vision.

Ernst Bloch's Influence

Bloch pervades Moltmann's understanding regarding hope and also the relationship between the present and future.[121] Moltmann admits that Bloch's "philosophy of the resurrection"[122] provided the "basic categories" for *TH*, which is "a deliberately parallel theological act" to *The Principle of Hope*.[123] In Bloch, labeled by some "a twentieth-century Church Father,"[124] Moltmann finds a properly articulated view of transcendence "conceived with regard to the future before us rather than to an eternity above us or within us. 'The forward-look has replaced the upward-look.'"[125] Moltmann attaches great significance to some of Bloch's distinctive ideas and appropriates them for a doctrine of hope.

121. See Harvey Cox, "Ernst Bloch and 'The Pull of the Future,'" in Marty and Peerman, eds., *New Theology No. 5*, 191–203. For Moltmann's main comments regarding Bloch, see *GEB*; *EH* 15–29, 30–43; *RRF* 177–99; see also *UZ* 10; *EH* 48ff.; *HTG* 169. For secondary analysis of Moltmann's reception of Bloch, see especially Adams, "Eschatology Sacred and Profane," 298–306; Meeks, *Origins*, 16–19, 80–89; Gerald O'Collins, "The Principle and Theology of Hope," 134–44.

122. *FC* 171.

123. *ET* 92; see also 371 n. 75; *UZ* 10; *EG* 11. Glimpses of this mingling occur in 1962, when the Easter event is allied to a Blochian perspective of the future: "There is future in the past (E. Bloch). The proclamation of the resurrection of the crucified Christ means that in this event there is future in the past" (*HP* 86).

124. *GEB* 91.

125. Morse, *Logic of Promise*, 13; see also *RRF* 177–99.

Three areas of influence are key: the future, the nature of God's being, and the question of hope's certainty.

Admittedly, Bloch is rarely referenced explicitly in *TH*.[126] Regarding this point, Geiko Müller-Fahrenholz finds it indicative that Bloch, relatively speaking, is not in fact a major figure.[127] Linking the scarcity of references and citations to Bloch's influence, however, is a *non sequitur*. Müller-Fahrenholz admits as much by remarking: "it is striking that Ernst Bloch is quoted relatively seldom."[128] This, however, inadvertently reveals an unspoken presupposition: the paucity of quotes is "striking" precisely because Bloch's influence extends further than the references acknowledge. While the explicit references do not confirm it, Moltmann purposefully utilizes Bloch without always referring to him.

Bloch's advancement of esoteric Marxism, the "warm stream" of Marxist thought,[129] entailing a refusal to reduce Marxism to economics and materialism (which generated sharp criticism by fellow Marxists), is one of the factors that Moltmann finds appealing.[130] More acutely, however, his importance is his view that hope is a universal characteristic of human existence: humanity "is essentially Utopia-minded, believing in a perfect world and anticipating the future with undying hope."[131] While Moltmann's appropriation of Bloch in *TH* is neither an uncritical "baptism" (as Barth accused)[132] nor an unconditional

---

126. Bloch is not even one of the top ten most frequently cited figures.

127. Müller-Fahrenholz, *Kingdom and Power*, 42.

128. Ibid.

129. *Contra* the systems found in the Leninist or Stalinist conceptions (see Bloch, *Priniciple of Hope*, 1:205–10.). Bloch was criticized by orthodox Marxists since the esoteric movement "posits a future which goes beyond the goal of a classless society" (*EH* 30). On Bloch's advancement of esoteric Marxism, see especially Leszek Kolakowski, "Ernst Bloch: Marxism as a Future Gnosis," 421–49; Fiorenza, "Dialectical Theology and Hope 3," 38; Hudson, *The Marxist Philosophy of Ernst Bloch*, 34ff.; Roberts, *Hope and its Hieroglyph*.

130. *GEB* 11; See Kolakowski, "Ernst Bloch," 422ff.

131. Kolakowski, "Ernst Bloch," 429. For Bloch, "the forward glance becomes all the stronger, the more lucidly it makes itself conscious" (*Priniciple of Hope*, 1:144). And Bloch insightfully observes that "the pull towards what is lacking never ends. . . . The lack of what we dream about hurts not less, but more." (*Priniciple of Hope*, 2:541, as cited in Bauckham and Hart, *Hope Against Hope*, 61–62).

132. *Contra* Barth, who, offering a mixed review of *TH*, asked Moltmann: "To put it pointedly, does your theology of hope really differ at all from the baptized *principle* of hope of Mr. Bloch?" (Barth, *Letters*, 175). After reading *TH*, sent by Moltmann, Barth

adoption of Bloch's philosophy, another image works better: *TH* is arguably "Eine kleine Bloch Musik" (as Wolf-Dieter Marsch asserted).[133] Indeed, Blochian concepts, emphases, and language are coupled with biblical terms to articulate Christian theology.[134] Moltmann asserts: "the future is the real category of historic thinking. . . . Ernst Bloch is right when he insists that 'the nerve of the true historical concept is and remains the new.'"[135] Moltmann relies on Bloch to provide him categories with which to discuss the future and hope. Problems emerge, however, which are consequential to Moltmann's overall purpose. He seems not to realize the problematic way in which he appropriates some of Bloch's understanding and emphases for Christian theology. These elements begin with no less an important understanding than the proper understanding of God's being.

God's Essential Nature

Articulating a proper understanding of God is central to constructing a viable theological program. Moltmann wants to base theology on a scriptural understanding of God, instead of Greek metaphysics.[136] In *TH*, however, Moltmann essentially fuses the New Testament to key

---

admitted to being impressed by the "varied scholarship but also by the spiritual force and systematic power that characterize" the text (see Barth, *Letters*, 175). Critiquing *TH* in a letter to someone else, Barth admits that he "read him [Moltmann] with great openness but [I] hesitate to follow him because this new systematizing . . . is almost too good to be true" (Barth, *Letters*, 174).

Interesting to note, then, is Moltmann's response five months later. On April 4, 1965 Moltmann issued a reply, yet interestingly makes no mention of Barth's probing question referencing Bloch. Instead Moltmann concentrates on another aspect of Barth's letter, the function of the immanent Trinity ("Letter to Barth," 348). Yet it seems that an answer was provided indirectly and in a more public way. Beginning with the 3rd edition of *Theologie der Hoffnung* (1965), an appendix is included that details some differences between Moltmann and Bloch; see also *GC* 335 n. 32; Wolf-Dieter Marsch, "Die Hoffnung des Glaubens," 123). This may be more than coincidental with Barth's probing insight written to Moltmann on November 17, 1964. So, while Moltmann did not provide Barth with a personal response to the question, one indeed was given. And while not mentioning the appendix, Douglas Farrow broadly states that Moltmann "has been replying [to Barth] ever since" (Farrow, "In the End is the Beginning," 425).

133. Marsch, "Zur Einleitung," 10, 14.
134. For some examples, see Bauckham, *Moltmann*, 10.
135. *TH* 263.
136. *TH* 40ff.; *DTH* 215–21.

features of Bloch's understanding, resulting in a view of God that attempts to satisfy the demands of both: "The God spoken of here is no intra-worldly or extra-worldly God, but the 'God of hope' (Rom. 15.13), a God with 'future [*Futurum*] as his essential nature' (as E. Bloch puts it)."[137] What is arguably benign at first becomes problematic, because by the end of the decade Moltmann will have exhibited fully his inconsistent adoption of this view. Moltmann's position on God's nature has confused some commentators. On the one hand, A. J. Conyers (with Randall Otto offering a distinct, yet concurring, opinion[138]) believes that Moltmann "is in substantial agreement with Ernst Bloch's concept of the biblical God."[139] On the other hand, Meeks maintains that "Moltmann does not accept Bloch's ontology as definitive of God's mode of being."[140] So what Conyers sees as "substantial agreement," Meeks sees as clear differentiation. What leads to these opposing views? At different times Moltmann gives credence to both. Upon closer inspection, Moltmann's adoption of Bloch's concept of God is an uneven mixture of agreement and differentiation, and ultimately his formulation betrays incongruence and exhibits problems. Consequently, the matter is more complex than Conyers, Otto, or Meeks envisions and furthermore when

---

137. *TH* 16 [12]; see also *TH* 141 [127]; *RRF* 216; "Der Gott der Hoffnung," 125; *BP* 101; compare, however, the more viable notion: "His essence is . . . the faithfulness with which he reveals and identifies himself in the history of his promise as 'the same'" (*TH* 143); for similar assertions, see also *WJC* 321 and *ET* 55.

138. Otto attributes a biblical understanding to neither, maintaining that "Moltmann's doctrine [of God] is based on Bloch's Ontology of the Not-Yet" (Otto, "The Use and Abuse of Perichoresis," 375). He concludes this quote by baldly asserting: "there can be no God until the end [for Moltmann], which there can finally never be, lest God lose the transcendence of the future as his condition of being." This is the main point of his doctoral dissertation: Randall Otto, *The God of Hope*. Bauckham (one of Otto's dissertation examiners) states that Otto's study exemplifies "polemical determination" (Bauckham, *Theology of Jürgen Moltmann*, 24 n. 6).

139. Conyers, *God, Hope, and History*, 6; Conyers, who is sympathetic to Moltmann's thought, notes how Moltmann agrees with Bloch's formula, but sees no confusion with Moltmann's inconsistent appropriation of it (Conyers, *God, Hope, and History*, 75). This seems to be due to his sources; according to the relevant citations, Conyers relies only on *TH* and *EH*, both of which maintain Moltmann's agreement with Bloch.

140. Meeks, *Origins*, 85; He continues: "Rather he [Moltmann] makes a meticulous distinction between the not-yetness of *futurum* and the not-yetness of *adventus*." Meeks is undoubtedly using "mode of being" for *Seinsbeschaffenheit*, a term linked with *futurum* that Moltmann does adopt; so, Meeks' statement cannot be maintained until 1966 when Moltmann first makes the distinction between the two terms (*FC* 180 n. 53).

attention is paid to the time when Moltmann's assertions are made the problem is even more egregious. To understand fully the problem involved it is important first to grasp Moltmann's differentiation between *Zukunft* and *Futurum* for the meaning of the term future, since it substantially shapes Moltmann's understanding of God and hope.[141]

Two Futures: Futurum *and* Zukunft

Moltmann stresses the qualitative difference between how two words distinctly designate the future.[142] Emil Brunner, Moltmann's source for this distinction,[143] succinctly explains the difference:

> The life of the world to come as distinct from *futurum* is an eschatological concept; it suggests the realization of hope through an event which springs from the beyond, from the transcendent; not like *futurum*, something which grows out of what already exists.[144]

Taking this brief explanation as his starting point, Moltmann elaborates: "*Futurum* means that which will be," that which is extrapolated from

---

141. This problem is not confined to the 1960s; it lingers over the next 35 years as Moltmann later adds to this earlier problem: in 1991 "The essential nature of the triune God *is* this community [of divine persons]" (*SpL* 309); in 1995 God's essential nature is love (*CoG* 239); while in 1999 it is faithfulness (*ET* 55).

142. Moltmann references this important distinction from this point forward; see *DTH* 210–12; "Theology as Eschatology," 11–16; *RRF* 208; *FC* 27–30, 55–56, 180 n. 53; *HP* vii, 181–84; *EH* 52–53; "Verschränkte Zeiten der Geschichte: Notwendige Differenzierungen und Begrenzungen des Geschichtsbegriffs," 221–26; *GC* 132–35; *WJC* 206, 317; *JCTW* 138–40; *CoG* 25; "Kind und Kindheit als Metaphern der Hoffnung," 97; "Foreword," in Althouse, *Spirit of the Last Days*, viii; *SW* 54–55; *EB* 89; "Ernst Blochs Christologie," 13 n. 21; "The Blessing of Hope," 158–59. In practice, Moltmann uses *Zukunft* virtually all the time. While he uses *Zukunft* throughout *TH* to discuss the future, even Christ's future, one could read this as a distinction between *Futur* and *Zukunft* that is not being made, but which the reader might assume incorrectly, based on Moltmann's portrayal of the two terms (see *TH* 202, 224–29 [184, 204–9]). Moltmann makes no such distinction in *TH*, because he was unaware of it (see *DTH* 210).

The distinction emerges in relation to Bloch's usage of *Futur*, and so the terms of the discussion in the 1960s are *Futur* and *Zukunft*. Later, he rightly asserts that the difference informs the concept of time. At the same time, he specifies that the distinction is between *Futur* and *Advent*, not *Futur* and *Zukunft* (see *DTH* 210; *CoG* 25 [42]). This corrects an unspoken assumption in *FC* 29–30.

143. *FC* 180 n. 53; see also van den Brom, "Eschatology and Time," 159ff.

144. Brunner, *Eternal Hope*, 25.

present experience and existence.[145] Similarly: "What 'will be' presupposes here the present tense of the process of becoming and begetting,"[146] because "the *futurum* is *extrapolated* from the factors and processes of the past and present,"[147] and, therefore, simply connotes "that which is going to be."[148] As such *Futurum* can never be totally new.[149]

Moltmann's main point is to distinguish between the future that "will be" from that which is coming:[150] "*Adventus* has its equivalent in the Greek word *parousia*, which also means the arrival of a stranger and another."[151] When *adventus* is used in the New Testament, "it enters the categories of expectation of the prophetic and apostolic hope for the coming of God and the coming of Christ."[152] Both *adventus* and *parousia* are equivalent to the German *Zukunft*: "The future in the sense of *Zukunft* . . . is the 'soul of time'. If we take over this distinction between *Zukunft* and *Future*, then we might say: the present has no future in the sense of *Futur* unless it is the present of the *Zukunft*."[153] While this statement is open to misinterpretation, Moltmann's central point is generally clear:

---

145. *FC* 29; see also *CoG* 25; "God's Kenosis in the Creation and Consummation of the World," 138 = *SW* 54–55. With Bloch, Moltmann asserts that the Latin term *futurum* in a materialistic way is related to the Greek noun *physis*, which "is the producing, the eternally begetting womb of all things. *Physis* is divine. What will be emerges from the eternal process of the becoming and begetting of being" ("Theology as Eschatology," 11–12; see also *GC* 133).

146. *FC* 30. For a comparison between the newness of natality and advent, see Billings, "Natality or Advent," 125–45.

147. "Theology as Eschatology," 14.

148. *FC* 55.

149. "Theology as Eschatology," 15.

150. Moltmann was aware of this distinction at least as early as 1966 (*FC* 180 n. 53) and he utilized it in two articles published that year; see *FC* 29–31; *HP* 178–99.

151. *FC* 29; see also 55; "Theology as Eschatology," 11–14. Adams picks this up as well: "what God will make possible is not constrained by what women and men are able to imagine or plan" (Adams, "Hope," 309). For Moltmann's view of the parousia, see below, pp. 167–72.

152. *FC* 29. While Moltmann seems to imply that *Zukunft* always means "coming" over against *Futur* "what will be," it might be best to state it the other way round: *Futur* always means extrapolation and when Moltmann employs *Zukunft* in comparison then it is distinct from *Futur*. Moltmann does not clarify the matter thusly, however (see *DTH* 211–12). The issue is problematized by the fact that *Zukunft* means future in German indiscriminately.

153. *FC* 30.

Parousia—advent—future—means, as it does in the Old Testament, the unique and then final coming of God and a world which is in total correspondence to him—their coming to the godless and the Godforsaken. Understood in this sense, the future does not simply emerge from the present, either as a postulate or a result; the present springs from a future which one must be expectant of in transience.[154]

This train of thought plainly necessitates Moltmann's critique of Bloch for using *Futurum* to discuss God's essential nature. The reason that commentators disagree on whether Moltmann and Bloch agree is due to the indecisive nature of Moltmann's use of Bloch's understanding of God's essential nature as *Futurum*.

God as Future: Futurum *or* Zukunft?

The question whether Moltmann has adopted Bloch's concept of God as "future" is no small syntactical alteration; it is crucial, especially in Moltmann's project, since he gives it great theological weight and stresses the terminological difference on numerous occasions.

Beginning in the second paragraph of *TH*, Moltmann unreservedly latches onto Bloch's notion of God's essential nature as *Futurum*, quoting him approvingly twice.[155] In his 1966 essay "Trends in Eschatology," however, Moltmann disagrees with Bloch's statement regarding *Futurum* as God's essential nature.[156] This continues in April 1968, when Moltmann stresses the "coming God," and in conjunction to this Old Testament conception of God, he points out that it is the Bible, "the textbook of hope"[157] that is the foundation for regarding "the 'future' [*Zukunft*] as God's mode of being with us."[158] Here he takes Bloch's

---

154. *FC* 29. Moltmann asserts that "the *adventus Dei* takes the place of the *futurum* of being. Exactly this makes for the ontological priority of the *Zukunft* over the other modes of time: that the *Zukunft* is expected from the coming of God" ("Theology as Eschatology," 13).

155. *TH* 16, 141 [12, 127].

156. *FC* 180 n. 53. He also asserts that there is "ambiguity" in the way Bloch uses the term *Zukunft* (*FC* 180 n. 53 [49 n. 53]).

157. *GL* 30; he continues: "every page and every word is concerned with the burning question, 'What may I hope?'" See also *CG* 135; *HC* 131; *EB* x.

158. *RRF* 208 [*UZ* 155]; "Hope and History" (*RRF* 200–220) first appeared in 1968 (*UZ* 167); see also *EH* 39–43 [60–63], which delineates his disagreements with Bloch while using *Zukunft* as a corrective of Bloch.

notion yet turns it on its head by replacing *Futurum* with *Zukunft*. Curiously, and seemingly intentionally, there is no reference to Bloch on this occasion. While Moltmann points only to the Old Testament as his source for this understanding of God, there seems to be an acknowledgement emerging of the problems with Bloch's understanding, or rather with Moltmann's adoption of Bloch's understanding.

That same month (April 1968), Moltmann explicitly denies his previous approval of Bloch's understanding of God: "God's being is coming. He is not a 'God with *futurum* as mode of being' (Bloch), but with the *Zukunft* (future) as his mode to act upon the present and the past."[159] Based on the differences that *Futurum* and *Zukunft* convey regarding the future, neither the vocabulary change nor the critique of Bloch should go unnoticed or be quickly passed over as a minor alteration.[160]

After rejecting Bloch's notion of God's nature as *Futurum* in multiple places, he reverses his previous rejection. Writing in 1970, Moltmann speaks of God's futurity in terms of both *Zukunft* and *Futurum*: "this formula for God can also be translated: 'I will be who I will be.' It contains the future [*Zukunft*] of God. Ernst Bloch is right, therefore, when he speaks of a 'God who has the future [*Futurum*] as the mode of his being.'"[161] The German reveals what the English cannot: these statements are incongruent to the point of unintelligibility.

At the risk of belaboring the point, a few later instances need to be mentioned. In 1989 Moltmann admits that he no longer accepts Bloch's description.[162] In 1995, however, he enigmatically associates Bloch's description of "God 'who has future [*Futurum*] as the essence of his Being'" with God's 'futurity [*Zukünftigkeit*]'.[163] Most flagrant, perhaps,

---

159. "Theology as Eschatology," 13; see also 10. Pannenberg cites the same Blochian concept of God, while not differentiating between the two terms for "future" (Pannenberg, "God of Hope," 240ff.).

160. Meeks contends that Moltmann looks to the biblical perspective to define God's mode of being instead of Bloch's, because in "Bloch's ontology, the future is processed out of the fermenting possibility of matter at the core of nature itself. The future comes from the not-yetness of the present: the *futurum* comes out of the process of the womb *physis* (nature)" (Meeks, *Origins*, 85). Since this is a correct understanding of Bloch, which Moltmann elsewhere clearly opposes, it makes Moltmann's ambivalence regarding vocabulary choice even more problematic.

161. *EH* 48 [68]; see also "Ernst Blochs Christologie," 13.

162. *WJC* 321.

163. *CoG* 23 [41]. Note: although the English translation differs, it is the same German quote as in 1964 (see *TH* 16, 141 [12, 127]).

is the final instance, in the late 1990s. Moltmann attributes the phrase "*Zukunft als Seinsbeschaffenheit*" to Bloch, without providing any indication that he has altered the phrase.[164] He places his own meaning onto Bloch, by inserting *Zukunft* in place of *Futurum*, which alters Bloch's original meaning via misquoting him.[165]

In sum: Moltmann adopts Bloch's original phrase in 1964 and then in a series of assertions exhibits inconsistency by failing to adjudicate the issue decisively. The matter would be simple, and Moltmann would be lauded, if he had simply provided a corrected vision of the future by using *Zukunft* in contradistinction with Bloch's notion of *Futurum*. Plainly, Moltmann finds Bloch helpful for discussing the future and God's being, yet he has difficulty appropriating Bloch's definition.

A critique of the term chosen by Bloch is not issued from the outset in *TH*, instead it is adopted unwaveringly, and only denounced later, albeit inconsistently. The reason Moltmann is able to avail himself initially of the term without qualification seems to be due to the fact that he only started utilizing the distinctive understanding of the two terms in 1966;[166] thus his unconditional acceptance in 1964 is excusable.[167] It is the lack of certainty after 1966 that cannot be dismissed in light of his efforts to show how the two terms are contrasting conceptions of the future. Beyond this problem is another, even more pressing matter.

While Moltmann has apparently wavered in subscribing to Bloch's view of God's "essential nature" (at least regarding vocabulary), the general understanding of God as future remains. Indeed, whether Moltmann consistently accepts Bloch's phrase verbatim matters not.[168] Either way an altered Blochian conception is surrounded by New Testament language, tailored to fit Moltmann's purposes.[169] This inconsistency is

---

164. "Kind und Kindheit," 97. Dated January 1999, but published in 2000. Compare: "Futurum als Seinsbeschaffenheit" (Bloch, *Prinzip der Hoffnung*, 1458; *Theologie der Hoffnung*, 12, 127; see also *UZ* 155).

165. Yet, in 2004 he quotes him correctly: "Ernst Blochs Christologie," 13.

166. *FC* 180 n. 53.

167. He is already using *Zukunft* appropriately in *TH* when discussing Christ's future (*TH* 202, 224–29 [184, 204–9]).

168. Compare especially "Theology as Eschatology," 13, with "Kind und Kindheit," 97.

169. Beyond the example of Moltmann joining Rom 15:13 and Bloch (see above, p. 26), Adams points to a similar instance when Moltmann (*TH* 16–17) ties Col 1:27 "to pure Bloch" (Adams, "Eschatology Sacred and Profane," 301).

deemed problematic. Moltmann can stress that there are two concepts of the future and still invoke Bloch with varying degrees of agreement,[170] because he uses Bloch's terminology while invoking biblical language and citations, while clearly making the resurrection of Christ important for the future, and accordingly label it Christian hope. Beyond the problems involved with Bloch's influence on Moltmann regarding a proper understanding of God's being and the future, there is still another. The final substantive problem with Moltmann's relationship to Bloch in the 1960s is the proper understanding of hope, and serves as the conclusion of the chapter.

Conclusion

Hope: Certain or "Disappointable"?

The chief problem with Moltmann's doctrine of hope in *TH* and the early- and mid-1960s is the confidence with which he speaks of its fulfillment, found supremely in his disagreement with Bloch.[171]

While Moltmann credits Bloch for revealing the Bible's hope orientation, and also the fact that humanity "is essentially Utopia-minded, believing in a perfect world and anticipating the future with undying hope,"[172] it is on a matter of difference between Bloch and Moltmann that shows the true nature of his hope at this early stage and reveals its inadequacies.[173] A central difference between Bloch's conception of

---

170. Or, perhaps, the other way round.

171. See *RRF* 148–76, which is the translation of the appendix to *Theologie der Hoffnung* (added to the 3rd edition); 3rd edition, not the 5th, *contra* Meeks (see *RRF* 148) and Wakefield, *Moltmann*, 93. For full details of the article, see the entry for "Hope and Confidence: A Conversation with Ernst Bloch" in Bibliography I. An important point regarding this article is that its publication precedes *TH*, and most likely would be consistent with Moltmann's view(s) in *TH*. So, while Bloch is rarely referenced in *TH*, it would be erroneous to conclude that he did not influence Moltmann's understanding of hope in *TH*.

172. Kolakowski, "Ernst Bloch," 429. Roberts comments that Bloch had a "single, obsessively-held goal, the as yet undiscovered land of the future." (Roberts, *Hope and its Hieroglyph*, 4).

173. For insightful analysis of Moltmann's reception of Bloch, see Adams, "Eschatology Sacred and Profane," 298–306; Meeks, *Origins*, 16–19, 80–89; O'Collins, "Principle," 134–44.

Regarding *TH*, Balthasar asks: "*For what and for whom does it hope?* Is the object of its hope a risen Christ whose world mission is, however, as yet incomplete? And is its hope

hope and Moltmann's is that while Bloch's hope has a "precarious nature," Moltmann's does not, because the future fulfillment of the victory of the resurrection is a guaranteed certainty.[174]

BLOCH'S HOPE: "THE CATEGORY OF DANGER"

Bloch's three-volume *magnum opus* is a sustained engagement with the importance of hope.[175] Bloch stresses the openness of hope to the extent that it is precarious, and may go unfulfilled because it is open to failure.[176] And although he uses Messianic language,[177] his meaning is finally atheistic: "the future of the risen Christ and the future of God is [for Bloch] . . . 'nothing else but' the future of hidden man and of the hidden world."[178] Moltmann correctly diagnoses the problem: Bloch's hope has no "presupposition of a God of promise marching ahead of us."[179] Indeed, Marxist scholar Leszek Kolakowski asserts that in Bloch's conception "There is no God to guarantee that we shall succeed: God himself is part of the Utopia, a finality that is still unrealized."[180] This, Moltmann rightly sees, will not do: "No enduring hope can be based on 'ontology of not-yet-being.'"[181] To correct this atheistic vision of hope

---

that he may succeed in fulfilling his task?" (Balthasar, "Zu einer christlichen Theologie der Hoffnung," 91). It should be noted that Balthasar discusses Moltmann's theology based on *TH*, *CG*, *CPS*, *TKG*, and also *EH* and *FC*. In totality, he labels Moltmann's theology at its core a theology of the cross (91). Generally, Balthasar's discussion is in more subjective terms (see Balthasar, "Zu einer christlichen Theologie der Hoffnung," 81–102; see also *HTG* 91–109).

174. *RRF* 174–76. Meeks appraises similar issues, but is not critical of Moltmann (see Meeks, *Origins*, 114ff.).

175. Kolakowski, "Ernst Bloch," 427: "most of his imposing volumes consist of variations on the same theme; their repetitiveness is almost without parallel."

176. For Moltmann's analysis of Bloch's hope, see *RRF* 148–76, which is the appendix to the German edition of *TH*.

177. See *GEB* 11–12.

178. *RRF* 152. Indeed, "Bloch's philosophy is atheistic. But it is also thoroughly religious" (*EH* 27).

179. *RRF* 155.

180. Kolakowski, "Ernst Bloch," 424. This is because Bloch "resists all efforts to reinvest the Jesus of the synoptic narratives with triumphalist motifs" (Roberts, *Hope and its Hieroglyph*, 181); *RRF* 155: Bloch's hope has no "presupposition of a God of promise marching ahead of us."

181. "Progress and Abyss: Remembrances of the Future of the Modern World," in Volf and Katerberg, eds., *The Future of Hope*, 18 n. 22; see also *GC* 178–81. For Bloch's earlier treatment of this ontology, see Ernst Bloch, *The Spirit of Utopia*, 191ff.

and articulate a Christian conception of hope Moltmann asserts that a faithful deity is its constitutive ground. Bloch asserts that hope must be "disappointable": hope's openness must allow the possibility of a "heaven without God"[182] and a "hell in which there is no Easter."[183] Moltmann insists the opposite.

Hope as Certain: The Alternative to Hope as "Disappointable"

Moltmann opposes Bloch's understanding of hope on two grounds: it is utopian and atheistic. This necessary rejection, however, is coupled with a desire to view hope as certain. While Moltmann's diagnosis of Bloch's hopeful vision is accurate, his prescription is an over-correction, as he goes too far in drawing out the differences between them.[184] Indeed, while Moltmann rightly opposes Bloch's hope as atheistic, he also goes against the very ground of hope established throughout *TH* by positing the resurrection as promise awaiting fulfillment. While he asserts that "Bloch's hope is 'disappointable,'"[185] Moltmann's vision of hope is endowed with guaranteed confidence because of the resurrection of the crucified Christ.[186]

The cause that leads Moltmann to argue for a guaranteed hope is Bloch. While Bloch, in part, spurred Moltmann to develop theology as hope, it is Bloch's philosophy (which finds utopian daydreaming a proper ground of hope) that causes Moltmann to react so forcefully for guaranteed hope. To correct Bloch, Moltmann posits the faithful God who fulfils his promise(s). This is a move in the right direction, as Moltmann clearly cannot develop Christian eschatology in the same way as the atheistic Jewish philosopher. Yet, surprisingly Moltmann also wishes to take over Bloch's "category of danger" for Christian hope.

While contrasting Bloch's "disappointable" hope with his own certain hope, Moltmann, nonetheless, insists on arguing for a precarious understanding of Christian hope. He simultaneously and critically la-

---

182. *GC* 180.

183. *RRF* 17; see Ernst Bloch, "Kann Hoffnung enttäuscht werden?" I:211ff.; see also Bloch, *Spirit of Utopia*, 200ff; *RRF* 174–76 [*Theologie der Hoffnung*, 333–34].

184. Shakespeare comes to mind here (edited from *Hamlet*): "the Gentleman doth protest too much, methinks."

185. *RRF* 174.

186. Ibid.; see also *JCTW* 57.

bels Bloch's hope precarious, while also taking Bloch's phrase "category of danger" as an appropriate description of Christian hope. The "category of danger," Moltmann avers, "is even more radically characteristic of Christian assurance" than Bloch's understanding of hope.[187] He asserts that "where the ultimate future of God is present in the world, there is crisis—a crisis, moreover, which involves both man's certainties and his wishes."[188] On this basis, he promotes a doctrine of hope informed by the dialectical identity of Christ:

> There is one identity which is maintained through the midst of the infinite qualitative antithesis of death and life. It is that identity in which resurrection is promised. . . . it lies beyond death and life in the event of the promise of God in which man can rely on the faithfulness of God. This identity is promised, and becomes a possible object of hope, in the dialectical point of transformation constituted by the resurrection of the crucified Christ.[189]

In this instance, Moltmann rightly situates hope as pointing beyond death to the promised resurrection. His insistence that the faithfulness of God grounds Christian hope brings out with striking clarity the diametric opposition he has to Bloch's atheistic version. He does not stop the contrast there, however. While wanting to equate Christian hope with danger and openness,[190] ultimately the category of danger is illusory because he refuses to allow a hint of the danger of unfulfilled hopes, as there is in Bloch: "the reality of the not yet (*noch nicht Sein*) . . . is the sphere of the *novum*, . . . the realm of fear as well as hope."[191] Moltmann refuses these categories for the future.[192] Yet for Bloch: "The future can bring everything or nothing, heaven or hell, life or death.

---

187. *RRF* 174; see also *TH* 260.

188. *RRF* 174.

189. Ibid., 169.

190. In *TH* Moltmann grasped the material argument of his doctrine of hope while discussing the cross, but does not maintain it : "The cross is the mark of an eschatological openness which is not yet closed by the resurrection of Christ and the spirit of the Church [*den Geist der Gemeinde*], but remains open beyond both of these until the future of God and the annihilation of death" (*TH* 172 [155]).

191. Ernst Bloch, "Man as Possibility," 63.

192. Indeed, this rejection seems to concretize over the years; this point is returned to in chapters 7 and 8, below.

Thus the future is full of salvation but also full of danger."[193] Since for Bloch the future is undecided, he promotes an uncertain outcome to hope. Moltmann contrasts Christian hope with uncertain hope, seeing them as opposites: "Christian assurance of the future," he writes, avoids "the possibility of its own disappointment."[194] And it is here that Moltmann's call for Christian hope's precarious nature or state of danger is finally undermined, and shown to be only formal, not material. While hope will bring the one who hopes into conflict, objectively there is no danger of failure. This undercuts his claim of hope's precarious nature. While he wishes to avoid Bloch's atheistic version of hope, Moltmann's removal of the possibility of disappointment is wrong, and furthermore his conclusion can only be based on presumption, relegating hope to a non-wayfaring status.[195]

Moltmann wants to have it both ways. His argument favoring the eschatological verification of the resurrection (and thus the verification of God's faithfulness to his promise[s]), calls for a hope that expects fulfillment, yet inherently lacks certainty, because it is still outstanding. This is a central feature of *TH*: God is not the eternal now; he is the God of hope and the future.[196] This emphasis on the eschatological verification of the promising God is correct. Yet, ultimately he has not learned his own lesson, and abandons this line of thought by arguing for a certain, guaranteed hope. Seemingly, because the resurrection awaits eschatological fulfillment it cannot be the basis of an assured hope, but only a "hope against hope." Moltmann does not reach this conclusion. What he offers with the one hand he takes back with the other, as he wants a future eschatological reserve, but also wants guaranteed fulfillment. Not to draw too fine a point on the matter, but it seems that Moltmann has taught an important lesson that he refuses to follow: the constitutive nature of hope necessitates that it is not assured. This is not, ultimately, what Moltmann posits.

While his argument in *TH* calls for the openness of reality, he remains quite certain that it is not open to failure (as in Bloch) but only

193. *RRF* 16.
194. *RRF* 175.
195. See *TH* 22ff.
196. *TH* 26–32; The God of hope is not understood properly in Greek understanding: "'Zeus was, Zeus is, Zeus will be.' ... The future [*Zukunft*] is the Coming of God" (*UZ* 156; see also *CoG* 23).

to fulfillment. Moltmann's vision of certain hope forbids him to argue that hope is actually still in the "category of danger." There seems to be only one plausible way for him to maintain this both/and framework: when contrasting Christian hope with Bloch's version, Moltmann (silently) makes a subject-object switch. This hypothetical solution runs as follows: Moltmann posits objective hope as certain, while also positing subjective hope as dangerous. Indeed, while the doctrine of hope in *TH* is concerned with the provisionality of history in light of the eschaton,[197] he abandons this "open" argument by showing the certainty of Christian hope, compared with Bloch's version.[198] This argument clearly contrasts Bloch's vision, where "salvation and destruction in the world process are not yet settled."[199] There is surely a distinction between Bloch's conception of "brave hope" and Christian hope, for only the former in Moltmann's view is still open to "destruction";[200] indeed, for Bloch "there are only two possibilities, all or nothing, absolute destruction and nothingness or absolute perfection; there is no middle term."[201] Regardless, however, Moltmann asserts that Christian hope is assured because of the faithfulness of the promising God. Beyond the three Blochian influences on Moltmann's understanding of hope detailed so far, there is still another, and it is Moltmann's inability to insist that the cross is constitutive for a doctrine of hope.

Resurrection Hope: Thesis and Synthesis

From *TH* through 1968 Moltmann ostensibly grounds Christian hope in the dialectical identity of the crucified and resurrected one. Yet, this structure is ultimately undermined, because of his conclusion. The argument and the conclusion constitute, respectively, the beginning and end of the dialectic, with the negativity of present reality being the antithesis, instead of the cross.[202] Indeed, the cross is not given its due

197. *TH* 33: "hope that is continually led on further by the promise of God reveals all thinking in history eschatologically oriented and eschatologically stamped as provisional."
198. Seen most clearly in the appendix to *Theologie der Hoffnung*; see also *EH* 27.
199. *RRF* 174–75.
200. Ibid., 174.
201. Kolakowski, "Ernst Bloch," 428.
202. Interestingly, Bowie comments: "Hegel's dialectic is often characterized in terms of the triad of thesis, antithesis, synthesis. This is, however, not the way he pres-

weight in *TH* because the negativity of the present propels Moltmann to concentrate on grounding hope solely on the resurrection as the *novum* over against the present.[203] Because the purpose of *TH*, in part, was to develop a theology of hope rooted in the coming future over against a timeless eternity, he advocates the openness of hope since the promises are yet to be fulfilled within history, typified perhaps in his teaching that the resurrection is still outstanding.[204] *TH* also posits the promised future over against the present. Indeed, the present is the binary opposite of the coming future. This leads Moltmann to argue for the promissory perspective of reality as open to the future. This openness has limitations, however. In contradistinction to Bloch, hope is not open to disappointment. The failure to develop the cross as informing or grounding a doctrine of hope results in a one-sided hopeful vision. There is no antithesis of cross to the thesis of resurrection for hope. While formally the cross plays this role, it is not a constitutive element. In *TH* Moltmann explicitly rejects his later insistence on the cross being integral to God.[205] In this period (1962–68), Moltmann grounds hope in the resurrection: the faithful "God of hope" is most revealed in the newness of the resurrection of Jesus Christ. Indeed, one could read *TH* and conclude that the resurrection alone grounds a doctrine of hope.

Grounding hope in the resurrection alone is one-sided, and ultimately promotes only success and certainty. So, while he speaks of hope being in the "category of danger," this is unfortunately only a rhetorical device, designating an existential perspective; it is not the material point of *TH*, which is the power of the God of the future who guarantees his promise because he is faithful. This perspective is not inherently wrong, but rather extremely one-sided. Moltmann's hope is not sufficiently grounded in the dialectic of cross and resurrection, but instead rooted in the certainty of the future resurrection, where God "will be all in all": as such, the resurrection confirms "the promise which will be fulfilled in all."[206]

---

ents it. The core of the dialectic is rather what Hegel terms the 'negation of the negation'" (Bowie, *Introduction to German Philosophy*, 84).

203. For similar comments, albeit four decades later, see "The Blessing of Hope," 151.

204. See especially *TH* 17ff, 154.

205. See ibid., 171.

206. *TH* 211.

Because he takes such a decidedly negative view of reality in *TH* he is unable to find any resource of hope in the present, but only in the promised future. And this grounding of hope in the resurrection leads him to conclude that hope is assured, and must be pronounced in language exuding confidence and guarantee. Some might defend Moltmann at this very point and argue that he was right to emphasize this aspect of hope in his text. The major reason that this is a deficit is that his theology seems to require a different conclusion. If the dialectical identity of the crucified and resurrected one grounds hope, then the cross must play an integral role. According to Moltmann (following Pieper's categories), hope is neither presumption nor despair.[207] Since he fails to adequately place any limitations on hope, his understanding of hope appears to be presumption, which Moltmann defines thusly: "a premature, selfwilled anticipation of the fulfillment of what we hope for from God."[208] This perspective must be altered if his doctrine of hope is to be properly Christian. Seemingly, the answer lies close to hand: the dialectical relationship of the cross and resurrection that he formally promotes must be forcefully maintained as the material ground of hope. To be sure, the dialectic of cross and resurrection rightly serves as the ground of the identity of Jesus Christ in *TH*, but it fails to be the constitutive ground of Moltmann's doctrine of hope. The dialectic is formally present, yet ultimately resolved in favor of the resurrection. Since there is no other intrinsic limitation to his doctrine at this stage, the tentative conclusion is that the cross has been passed over,[209] the dialectic seemingly synthesized. As such, the thesis (the resurrection) determines the synthesis, because there is no antithesis (the cross) to prevent him from expecting only success.

This changes radically when he turns to the cross. A more nuanced position is forthcoming. In order to overcome such a one-sided articulation of the ground of hope, he turns to the cross in the late 1960s. This turn shows that Moltmann views theology not as a closed system

---

207. See ibid., 22–26; although Moltmann does not refer to him, he still subscribes to Pieper's designation in 2003 (*EB* 93–95).

208. *TH* 23, drawing on Pieper.

209. The phrase "passed over" is odd, perhaps, but others are even less satisfactory. For example, asserting that he does not "integrate" the cross into his doctrine captures the point trying to be made here, but seems even more odd since he insists, in *CG* especially, that the cross cannot be assimilated into Christian theology.

and thus unassailable from without, but rather open to interruption.[210] Chapter two focuses on this turn and its impact on the nature and composition of his doctrine of hope.

---

210. See Metz, "Theological Interruptions," 12–18; similarly, Margaret Miles calls for historical appraisals to be "disrupt[ed]" by elements heretofore "whitewashed" by those seeking to portray history in monolithic terms (see Miles, *The Word Made Flesh*, 5).

2

Crucifixion as Hope

The Context of *Moltmann's Turn to a Theology of the Cross*[1]

THE MAIN CRITICISM LEVELED IN CHAPTER ONE AGAINST MOLTMANN'S doctrine of hope in the early- and mid-1960s is that it is one-sided, and thus incapable of handling, indeed even foreseeing, disappointment. Fulfillment is its only expectation. The adequacy of this complaint can be judged only by appraising his shift in focus from the resurrection to the cross in the late 1960s. Indeed, between *TH* and *CG*, Moltmann turned to the cross. Toward the end of the 1960s, Moltmann exhibits a renewed interest in the cross by spelling out the close interrelation of the resurrection and the cross more explicitly.[2]

The context of the late 1960s is vital to understanding Moltmann's then-developing theology and the moves he makes. Numerous events altered people's conceptions and expectations about societal advancement and improvement. He specifically cites 1968 as representing both the "peak" of the civil rights movement in the United States, and also

---

1. His turn to the cross is mistakenly passed over by most commentators as merely transitional and thus insignificant. Here I can only provide a sketch of the impetus and details of Moltmann's turn; for a full treatment of this important issue and its wider implications for understanding Moltmann's theology, see Neal, "Minority Report: Reconsidering Jürgen Moltmann's Turn to a Theology of the Cross," which questions the validity of the conventional view that Moltmann's turn to the cross is internally necessary, predictable, and simply a slight change in emphasis.

2. The operative word here is "renewed," since prior to *TH* Moltmann is certainly aware of the importance of the cross (see *UZ* 133–47; *HP* 101–29, 130–54; *BP* 43), but for some reason fails to materially integrate it into his discussion.

the "breakdown of hope" generally.[3] Events worldwide caused a shift in thinking "from utopian rejoicing to a bleak apocalypse without hope":[4]

> [T]he Warsaw Pact put a brutal end to "socialism with a human face" [in Czechoslovakia in August 1968], when the papal encyclical *Humanae vitae*[5] blocked the reforming spirit of Vatican II [25 July 1968], when Martin Luther King [Jr.] was murdered [4 April 1968] and Rudi Dutschke[6] shot [11 April 1968], and the carpet bombings of the Vietnam war started. At that time we came to understand the future as by no means open, or an antechamber of unlimited possibilities, but as occupied by counter-forces and counter-utopias.[7]

Of these noteworthy events, the assassination of Martin Luther King, Jr. made an indelible impression on Moltmann, especially since he was in the United States at the time.[8] Recalling the conference that he was attending at Duke, he states: "I left a few days later [after King's assassination] for Tübingen, and I promised my American friends that whenever I returned to their country, I would not speak about the theology of

---

3. *EG* 13; *CJF* 17.

4. *EJM* 118; compare, however, *ET* 305.

5. Pope Paul VI's Encyclical on the regulation of birth; for further comment, see *GSS* 218; *FC* 144–45.

6. Dutschke was a leader of the student revolution in the late 1960s in West Germany. Moltmann rarely mentions the leftist student movement, but it is another hope that came to an end in the late 1960s. The protests were concentrated in West Germany (including Tübingen); it is a bit odd that Moltmann cites Dutschke here, since he is rather critical of the movement (*TJ* 65ff.; *BP* 393 n. 20). Additionally, one scholar describes the student revolution as "a revolution only in name, not in substance, and it soon evaporated. But the students effectively challenged the shallow optimism and the pragmatic mentality of the older generation" (Mommsen, "The Germans and Their Past," 255; see also Peter Pulzer, *German Politics: 1945–1995*, 81–83).

7. *EJM* 118–19; he adds to this discussion elsewhere, see especially *UZ* 11ff.; "Der Gekreuzigte Gott," 407–13; *Gotteserfahrungen: Hoffnung, Angst, Mystik*, 30 (the German discussion is more detailed than the English; compare *EG* 13); *GSS* 52.

For socio-political information on the Federal Republic of Germany in late 1960s, see Jacobsen, "The Role of the Federal German Republic of Germany in the World, 1949–1982," 151.

8. From September 1967 to April 1968, Moltmann was in the U.S. and more specifically on April 4 he was in Durham, North Carolina (*RRF* vii; *FH* ix; *UZ* 167; *EG* 13ff.; *ET* 209; "Lived Theology," 12; Morse, "God's Promise as Presence," 144–151); elsewhere April 6 is incorrectly cited as the date of the assassination (*How I Have Changed*, 17; *PG* 71; *BP* 103). For Moltmann's retrospective discussion on the Civil Rights Movement, see *ET* 201–16; also see Cone, "Martin, Malcolm, and Black Theology," 185–95.

hope any more but of the cross."⁹ It is important to realize the extent to which the failures of these hopes were unforeseen by Moltmann. In 1985 he states: "at the beginning of the 1960s, we were convinced and enthused by hope in action, an active, militant hope, which could ally itself with the friendly tendencies in the world process, in the realm of unlimited possibilities, to lead to success."¹⁰

Besides the cultural changes occurring around the globe that Moltmann mentions, another significant feature of this period is his concerted efforts to mingle the importance of the future and the resurrection with the importance of the cross.¹¹ On 30 October 1967 in his Ingersoll Lecture "Resurrection as Hope" Moltmann states clearly (the title notwithstanding): "Christian hope is not founded on the isolated event of Jesus' resurrection . . . Cross and resurrection therefore inseparably belong together and interpret each other."¹² That same month, tellingly in the context of criticizing Bloch's vision of hope, he writes:

> Where then does Bloch's positive hope preserve the negative element? Where is the cross found in this hope?
>
> Christian theology must go further; it discerns in the crucified Christ the deepest abyss of God-forsakenness and hopelessness on earth. But it also believes in Easter. . . . Out of the humiliated, poor, and abandoned Jesus who was crucified in disgrace, God makes his Messiah of the future, of freedom, and of life.¹³

And in his essay "Theology as Eschatology" (April 1968) along with a future-oriented discussion, he begins to show an interest in questions

---

9. *PG* 71.

10. *HTG* 155. For more on the fulfillment and disappointment of hopes and utopias in the realm of biomedical progress, see *SW* 133–34. Indeed, post-turn, he remarks: hope "can be frustrated but never extinguished" ("Theology in Germany Today," 198).

11. Tellingly, it is not until 1968 (four years after its German publication) that he faults Pannenberg's *Jesus—God and Man*, which he otherwise deems "magnificent," for an insufficient theology of the cross ("Theology as Eschatology," 31 n. 43; for a rebuttal, see Pannenberg, *Systematic Theology*, 2:338).

Related to this is his additional concentration, in 1968 and later, on using anticipation as a further way to demonstrate that the future impacts the present, which in part responds to those critical of his emphasis on the future (*RRF* 212ff.; "Theology as Eschatology," 37–38; *FC* 45–48).

12. *RRF* 52; see also 17–18; *HP* 195ff.

13. *RRF* 17; see also *UZ* 140–42.

related to atheism, which coupled with his self-awareness of his post-Auschwitz situation is the defining context of his proposed theology of the cross.[14] In his inaugural lecture, "God and Resurrection,"[15] given at the University of Tübingen (19 June 1968) Moltmann states: "If the Easter faith makes a puzzle of the cross of the forsaken one, then obviously the cross must first explain this Easter faith."[16] The emphasis is not only on God as future (as in *TH*), now God is supremely identified as the one who experiences history (in *CG* this experience centers on the cross).[17] Whereas in *TH* "divine suffering was firmly outside the walls of Jerusalem in the first century,"[18] Moltmann now makes plain the connection of Easter Sunday to Good Friday.[19] And by implication it is the totality of the cross-resurrection event that is now related to hope: "Resurrection faith is faith in the crucified one; and hope which overcomes the world, which can hope against hope, is born in the community of the crucified one."[20] The relationship between the cross and his doctrine of hope is made explicit, not merely in emphasis, but rather the ground has been arguably reconceived: "Jesus' resurrection is only *indirectly*, but the meaning of his cross is *directly*, the foundation of the Christian hope for justice and life."[21] Indeed, Moltmann is now ensuring that together cross and resurrection ground hope.

In the opening page of *CG*, Moltmann asserts that the cross is, and always has been, the "guiding light" to his theology.[22] The evidence, however, does not support Moltmann's claim. Interestingly, one of the

---

14. In 1968 Moltmann asserts: "If today the theistic representations of the world are outdated, this interrogation of God about evil and pain is not at all outmoded" (*RRF* 100).

15. *HP* 31–55.

16. Ibid., 42–43.

17. Bauckham notes that "the role of criticizing society, which is vital to Moltmann's theology, is largely transferred from hope to the cross" in *CG* ("Moltmann's Eschatology of the Cross," 311).

18. Fiddes, *The Creative Suffering of God*, 13.

19. *HP* 44. Moltmann specifies the frame for a theology of the cross: Jesus' passion begins "in Gethsemane with the experience of God's hiddenness, and ends with the experience of God-forsakenness on the cross" (*SpL* 63–64; see also *TKG* 76; *WJC* 166; "The Passion of Christ and the Suffering of God," 20–23).

20. *HP* 44.

21. *RRF* 53, this essay was first presented in October 1967.

22. *CG* 1.

purposes of *CG* is "to make the theology of hope more concrete," consequently producing "a more profound dimension to the theology of hope."[23] These comments and this motive are admissions of his turn to the cross. It seems the only reason that he would now advocate the need to fully express "solid human hope" is that it has not been enunciated already. Note especially: he does not simply point to the main tenets of *TH* for a proper understanding of how to deal with these disappointments; arguably he cannot because there is so little to support his contention. Apparently, there is a dimension of Christian hope that Moltmann did not make plain in *TH*. Once Moltmann turns to the cross he has a more comprehensive vision, encompassing and drawing on both cross and resurrection. In this way *CG* redresses the central problem of *TH*.

God in the Cross: "A Revolution in the Concept of God"

The specific details of this theology of the cross have a reciprocal relationship with his doctrine of hope, as his emphasis on the cross reshapes the contours of his doctrine of hope. To adequately understand the relationship between God and the cross Moltmann insists: "a revolution [is] needed in the concept of God. Who is God in the cross of the Christ who is abandoned by God?"[24] Indeed, he believes that the doctrine of the Trinity is meaningless[25] unless the cross informs a Christian doctrine of God: "how can the death of Jesus be a *statement about God*? Does that not amount to a revolution in the concept of God?"[26] This question encapsulates well the intent of *CG*. Later he pointedly writes:

> God goes with us, God suffers with us. So where Christ, God's Son, goes, the Father goes too. In the self-giving of the Son we discern the self-giving of God. If this were not so, the Gospel of John could not say "He who sees me sees the Father" (John 14.9). In Christ's God-forsakenness, God goes out of himself, is there, present, dies with a cry for God, by whom he feels forsaken. Where is God in what happens on Golgotha? He is *in* the dying

---

23. *CG* 5.

24. For references to this revolution, see ibid., 4, 142, 152–53, 201, 204, 206–7, 216–17, 246; *GL* 37; *EH* 69; "Foreword," in Ngien, *The Suffering of God*, xi–xii; Kasper, "Revolution im Gottesverständnis?," 144–48.

25. For Moltmann's response to Kant's objection to the doctrine of the Trinity as being vacuous, see *CG* 246.

26. Ibid., 201.

Christ. To the question "why" there are many answers, and none of them adequate. More important is the question "where." And for that Christ himself is the answer.[27]

Following Luther, Moltmann maintains that God is hidden in his revelation,[28] stressing that the cross must take seriously the doctrine of the Trinity, and vice versa.[29]

Moltmann focuses on the crucifixion as the event that is not merely the death of God's son, but rather, when rightly seen, defines the trinitarian being of God.[30] In *CG* he sets out the pillars of his theology of the cross, presenting it as the foundation, the criticism and the criterion of theology.[31] Indeed, "the crucified Christ [is] the foundation and measure of Christian theology as a whole."[32] Reflecting on Luther's understanding,[33] Moltmann, rather one-sidedly in *CG*, maintains that Christian theology must be a thoroughgoing theology of the cross.[34]

---

27. *JCTW* 38; notice the failure to mention the Spirit.

28. On Luther's usage of *Deus absconditus*, see McGrath, *Luther's Theology of the Cross*, 164ff.; on Moltmann and Luther, see Eckardt, "Luther and Moltmann," 19–21; Ngien, *Suffering of God*, 46.

Paul is the major New Testament source (as in *TH*), yet it is Luther's theology of the cross that becomes highly significant and serves as a major tributary of influence (they are the most cited figures in *CG*). Whether Moltmann has followed Luther correctly is disputed. For generally negative appraisals, see Hill, *The Three Personed God*, 169; Eckardt, "Luther and Moltmann," 19–28; Jowers, "The Theology of the Cross as Theology of the Trinity," 245. For generally positive appraisals, see Bauckham, "Moltmann's Eschatology of the Cross," 301–11; Ngien, *Suffering of God*.

29. See *CG* 215–16; *CPS* 61–65; *OC* 93; *ET* 304ff.

30. O'Regan places Moltmann in a group dubbed "post-Hegelians" who, following Hegel, "move from the crucified Christ to the crucified God" (O'Regan, *Heterodox Hegel*, 219). For a critique of this move based on Pauline theology, see Cousar, *A Theology of the Cross*, 50.

31. See *CG*'s subtitle; *CG* 4; *FC* 59–62. Robert W. Jenson intends to "remove the Crucifixion from a kind of centrality it has sometimes occupied in theology," and finds in Moltmann "a similar reorientation" (*Systematic Theology*, 1:179 n. 2).

32. *FC* 59. Here he echoes Martin Kähler's thesis, but elsewhere Moltmann adds the lamenting postscript: "unfortunately [Kähler] did not cling to this principle himself" (*CG* 3).

33. *CG* 207–19; see O'Regan, *Heterodox Hegel*, 209–21.

34. *CG* 211–13. He changes his mind about this: "To know God by suffering God is only one aspect of existential theology. It is one-sided to make it a reason for declaring, as Luther did, that the *theologia crucis*, the theology of the cross, is the only true Christian theology" (*ET* 24).

Seemingly without contradiction, the overriding image of God in *CG*, both implicit and explicit, is that the crucified one is the highest form of iconoclasm, destroying all other images of God.[35] The cross is iconoclastic and scandalous to the degree that it asserts that God experiences the reality of death in the form of divine abandonment:

> The scandal of the cross is marked by the fact that He who proclaimed that the kingdom was near died abandoned by God. He who anticipated the future of God in miracles and in casting out demons died helpless on the cross. He . . . died according to the provision of the law as a blasphemer . . . between two criminals.[36]

For Moltmann the cross mandates divine passibility, as God opens himself to suffering. To achieve this understanding, he rejects the heretofore reliance on both analogical epistemology and two-natures christology, believing that these unnecessarily provide elements of separation between God and suffering.[37] Using analogy to properly understand God is an unnecessary importation of Aristotelian onto-epistemology, which leads to a miscalculation in theology: removing God from being actively involved in history and reality. Analogical thinking, when strictly held, leads to only one conclusion: "God is known only by God."[38] Two-natures christology, in Moltmann's view, establishes a firewall, a static separation of human and divine effectively keeping suffering from the divine and the divine from suffering.[39] This, according to Moltmann, will not do.

---

35. *EH* 118: "Likewise, we contend that the dangerous memory of the cross is our political iconoclasm; the cross is our hope for the politics of liberation." *CG* 108 n. 13: "I am arguing for an iconoclasm of the crucified Christ, because in him, not only the first but also the second commandment seem to be to be fulfilled." See Exod 20:1ff.

36. *CG* 125.

37. For a critique of Moltmann's too-simplistic rejection of two-natures christology, see Webster, "Jürgen Moltmann: Trinity and Suffering," 4–6; Zimany, "Moltmann's Crucified God," 49–57.

38. *CG* 26; see also 210–20.

39. Ibid., 265; "God's Kenosis," 140ff.; he also fears it has a docetic tendency (*CG* 227). See further Jenson's observation: "Regarding Mark 14 (parr.) the reader is faced with a problem, "that either you have God the Son at least momentarily at odds with God the Father, or you have the 'human nature' of Christ somehow abandoned by his 'divine nature' and left on its own over against the Father" (Jenson, "The Bible and the Trinity," 335).

The passion narrative is not play-acting,[40] wherein the divine nature is impassibly unaffected while the human nature suffers. For Moltmann, two-natures christology too easily allows God to be unaffected by history, uninvolved in suffering, and so unable to love, because he remains, even during Golgotha "a self-contained group in heaven."[41] Eschewing two-natures christology, Moltmann asserts that "the cleavage [*der Riss*] of death on the cross goes right through God himself, and not merely through the divine and human [*gottmenschliche*] person of Christ."[42] The cross then has an impact on Jesus Christ, not just his human nature; thus, the cross impacts the Trinity, not only the second member in his human nature. Pain, suffering, and history must affect God, and in this vein he finds the cross as the theological shorthand for a doctrine of the Trinity.[43]

While the text stresses the historical activity of God in the life of Jesus, some deem it mythological due to his placement of the cross in the being of God, prioritizing the immanent over the economic Trinity.[44] While the focus tends toward the Son's experience of abandonment by his Father,[45] other forms of abandonment are stressed as well, each of

40. For a discussion on the church fathers' development of this, see Robert Jenson, *Systematic Theology*, 1:134–37; Jenson, "The Bible and the Trinity," 335–37.

41. *CG* 249; see also *UZ* 10; *HP* 14–15; *DTH* 215, 221; *CPS* 55–56; *ET* 323.

42. *FC* 65 [73]. Here gottmenschliche might be better translated "the divine-human person of Christ." Note: originally this statement is conditional, beginning with "If," but contextually this is a rhetorical device and Moltmann subscribes to the assertion.

43. *CG* 246; see also *HG* 75–82.

44. Rowan Williams compares Moltmann with Hegel, finding in both an attempt to stress the historical, yet ultimately evading the temporal. Williams views Moltmann's theology of the cross as a "transaction in a mythical rather than historical space" (Williams, *On Christian Theology*, 161); John Milbank concurs: Moltmann's "perspective permits him to take in a full, 'mythological' sense, the separation of the Father from Son.... [including] the Hegelian theme of a necessary alienation" (John Milbank, "The Second Difference: For a Trinitarianism without Reserve," 223). Compare, however, Fiddes' insistence that Moltmann's portrayal of divine suffering is more historical in *CG* and *TKG* compared with *TH* (Fiddes, *Creative Suffering of God*, 13).

45. See especially *CG* 145–53, 243, 274–78; *PPL* 117–20. The issue of the Son's abandonment (*Hingabe*) by his Father is crucial to understanding Moltmann's theology of the cross, and its post-Auschwitz claims. Moltmann claims that the Markan record of Jesus' cry does not point to a recitation of Psalm 22 (and is thus triumphant), but rather is a true cry of abandonment. Dennis Jowers vehemently criticizes Moltmann's usage and understanding of this verse (Jowers, "Theology of the Cross," 256–59). For a brief examination of the options in relating Psalm 22 to Jesus' cry, see Donald Juel, *Messianic*

which is historical: as a religious blasphemer, Jesus is abandoned by religious leaders; as a political rebel, he is abandoned by Roman authorities.[46] In addition to these angles, Moltmann presents Jesus' abandonment as virtually comprehensive: even his followers, the females excepted,[47] abandoned him.[48]

Indeed, he places the appropriate emphasis on relating the cross to the resurrection by asserting that one's perspective should not be merely one-sided whereby the resurrection renders the cross intelligible and important, but rather he insists that it is important to emphasize the other direction: the cross also gives the resurrection meaning.[49] Moltmann does not centrally focus on the soteriological implications of the cross, yet many overstate this perceived lack in *CG*.[50] Instead he asserts that Christian theology needs to address first the issue of God and the cross. He seeks not to evaluate the cross in light of who God is, but the other way around: to understand God in light of the cross. To do this competently, Moltmann asserts, requires theology to rightly understand that "at the centre of the Christian faith stands an unsuccessful, suffering Christ."[51]

Exegesis, 114–16; see also Kaiser, *The Messiah in the Old Testament*, 111–18. The sharpest criticism accuses Moltmann of promoting divine child abuse. Dorothee Sölle labels it "theological sadism" (Sölle, *Suffering*, 22–28; idem, "Gott und das Leiden," in *DGG* 112ff.). On the other side, Gunton criticizes Moltmann for stressing the passion of the Son to the point of "rendering the Father passive" (*Act and Being*, 126). For further discussion and Moltmann's response, see *WJC* 172–81; *ET* 375–76 n. 134; *BP* 197–200.

46. See *CG* 128–45.

47. *PG* 59.

48. *CG* 132–33, 166; *WJC* 165–67.

49. Moltmann relates this to the issue of expiation, which when set in an eschatological framework is profitable (*CG* 183).

50. For Moltmann's view of the cross and soteriology, see especially *CG* 162, 182; *PPL* 118–19; *WJC* 181–96; *GSS* 84. He typically places soteriology and atonement in the wider context of God's love. For an example of overstating Moltmann's lack of soteriology, see John Thompson, *Modern Trinitarian Perspectives*, 60. This perceived lack seems attributable to Moltmann's intentional reversal of inquiry: he focuses on the cross and its meaning for God primarily, instead of concentrating on its soteriological importance (*FC* 63–64; *HTG* 172; *ET* 304). For comments on a utilitarian (anthropocentric) approach to the cross which asks: "What importance does it have for me?" see *WJC* 58ff.; *ET* 334–43.

51. *UZ* 14; *PPL* 115; the focus in *CG* is more centrally "dying in forsakenness," and instead of "suffering Christ" it becomes "the crucified God."

This explicit "revolution in the concept of God," whereby the cross determines one's understanding of the Trinity, helps to undergird Moltmann's proposal for a proper doctrine of hope. In *CG* he inveighs against divine impassibility by relying on dialectical epistemology; his pursuit of both these aims is intended to overcome protest atheism.

Overcoming Protest Atheism

Moltmann is convinced that if one follows his theology of the cross, then the arguments in favor of protest atheism are without foundation.[52] To be clear, he respects protest atheism because of its quest for truth:

> Christian faith in God is not a basic naïve trust. It is unfaith that has been overcome: "Lord, I believe, help thou my unbelief." In the fellowship of the assailed and crucified Christ faith grows up in the pains of one's own suffering and the doubts of one's own heart. Here the contradictions and rebellions do not have to be suppressed. They can be admitted. Those who recognize God's presence in the face of the God-forsaken Christ have protest atheism within themselves—but as something they have overcome.[53]

Of course, Moltmann's engagement on this issue is attributable, in part, to the Holocaust: "there would be no theology after Auschwitz . . . had there been no theology in Auschwitz."[54] (It would be difficult to overstate the importance that Moltmann's self-awareness of his "after Auschwitz" context has on his program.) Christian theology must answer specific atheistic protests: "in the face of Auschwitz and Hiroshima . . . how should I believe in the goodness and fatherly rule of a God in heaven?"[55]

---

52. For an excellent examination of the roots of atheism, see Michael Buckley, *At the Origins of Modern Atheism* (New Haven and London: Yale University Press, 1987).

53. *ET* 17. Moltmann edits Bloch's phrase "where there is hope there is religion" into "where there is hope there is atheism" (*HTG* 148; see also *EH* 15ff.). He insists that atheists are "profoundly theological" ("What is a Theologian?," 191). Later Moltmann asserts: "Nonbelief, total atheism, does not exist" (Cabestrero, *Faith*, 129).

54. *CG* 278; see also *GEB* 59; *GSS* 169–90. Related directly to this is Moltmann's use of Elie Wiesel's recollection of the boy on the gallows (see *CG* 273–74; Elie Wiesel, *Night*, 62). For criticism of Moltmann's usage of the story, see Marcel Sarot, "Auschwitz, Morality and the Suffering of God," 135ff. For Wiesel's influence on theology, see Walker, *Elie Wiesel*; Rosenfeld and Greenberg, *Confronting the Holocaust: The Impact of Elie Wiesel*.

55. *UZ* 19.

The answer, according to Moltmann, is to overcome such protests by positing a theology of the cross in trinitarian dimensions:

> Of them [martyrs] and of the dumb sacrifices it is true in a real, transferred sense, that God himself hung on the gallows, as E. Wiesel was able to say. If that is taken seriously, it must also be said that, like the cross of Christ, even Auschwitz is in God himself. Even Auschwitz is taken up into the grief of the Father, the surrender [*Hingabe*] of the Son and the power of the Spirit. That never means that Auschwitz and other grisly places can be justified, for it is the cross that is the beginning of the trinitarian history of God.[56]

Metaphysical atheism views the world as

> a mirror of deity. But in the broken mirror of an unjust and absurd world of triumphant evil and suffering without reason and without end it does not see the countenance of a God, but only the grimace of absurdity and nothingness . . . [Atheism] finds no good and righteous God, but a capricious demon, a blind destiny, a damning law, or an annihilating nothingness.[57]

Moltmann does not dispute this argument: if the world is comprehended as "a mirror of deity," then atheists are right to argue that God is neither righteous nor good.[58] If atheism is correct to view reality analogically, then "belief in the devil is much more plausible than belief in God."[59] Moltmann perceives, however, that protest atheism is ultimately a protest against the God of "theism." As one who regards evil as the "central question"[60] for Christian theology, Moltmann is convinced that theism's doctrine of God does not counter atheism, but rather ineluctably advances its cause: "The unavoidable character of the question of theodicy is found precisely in the fact that neither theism nor atheism solves

---

56. *CG* 278 [266].

57. Ibid., 219–20.

58. See O'Donnell, *Trinity and Temporality*, 112ff.

59. *CG* 220; see Meeks, *Origins*, 57. The result is much the same as the conclusion reached by Job's wife, who believed that the circumstances called for only one response: "Curse God and die" (Job 2:9; see *HP* 33).

60. "Response to the Opening Presentations," 57. Compare *TH* 16: "There is therefore only one problem in Christian theology . . . the problem of the future."

it."⁶¹ For Moltmann, impassibility is a flaw which actually provides the ground of protest atheism. Traditional theism maintains divine impassibility, and this is picked up by protest atheism with the nagging question: if there is a God, why suffering? George Büchner asked, "why do I suffer? That is the rock of atheism."⁶² Yet, Moltmann turns this argument on its head and asserts that suffering does not constitute the absence of God, but rather divine presence. The result of this essential core of *CG* is vital for understanding its impact on hope: God is in suffering and so hope is not rendered unintelligible in the face of suffering, but rather is grounded in the very act of suffering:

> God in Auschwitz and Auschwitz in the crucified God—that is the basis [*Grund*] for a real hope which embraces and overcomes the world, and the ground for a love which is stronger than death and can sustain death. It is the ground for living with the terror of history and the end of history, and nevertheless remaining in love and meeting what comes in openness for God's future.⁶³

Divine passibility, especially the type (voluntary) that Moltmann espouses, ensures hope is found in suffering, because God takes up all suffering, which in *CG* is prototypically found in the cross of Christ.⁶⁴ To respond and move beyond the objections of protest atheism, Moltmann shows that God is active in the suffering of the world through divine love.⁶⁵ Here he consciously rejects the philosophical notion of an apathetic deity.⁶⁶ By concurring with the thrust of protest atheism he sets

---

61. *HP* 33. For a full appraisal of Moltmann's view of theodicy through *GC*, see Patrick S. Maitland-Cullen, "The Theodicy Problem in the Theology of Jürgen Moltmann."

62. As quoted in "Theology as Eschatology," 5 n. 6; see also *HP* 32, 43; *TT* 90.

63. *CG* 278 [267].

64. In *GC* especially he widens this perspective to include the suffering Spirit in creation.

65. *CG* 222, 227–35; *TKG* 33, 57–60; *GC* 85. To help him accomplish this he looks primarily to Abraham J. Heschel. Although he avoids this precise language in *CG*, later Moltmann agrees with Heschel in characterizing the relationship between God and the world as a "relationship of reciprocity." See *TKG* 98: "the relation between God and the world has a *reciprocal* character, because this relationship must be seen as a living one"; see also *TKG* 54ff.; Heschel, *The Prophets*, 5, 9, 224; for criticisms, see Weinandy, *Does God Suffer?* 64–68.

66. *CG* 271; *JM* 47–49; "The 'Crucified God': A Trinitarian Theology of the Cross," 294–95; "The Crucified God," 12; *PG* 73. By rejecting theism outright, instead of a

up a critique of both theism and atheism, and the inferential logic underpinning both.[67]

Dialectical Epistemology

Moltmann's response moves beyond the protests by critiquing the traditional understanding of God as apathetic and presenting a theology of the cross based on a dialectical,[68] instead of an analogical, epistemology.[69] This epistemology links theism to atheism, and so requires substitution. He invokes Aristotle's principles of correspondence: namely,

---

particular view, and by speaking in generalities, Moltmann verges on arguing against a straw man: "The God of theism is poor. He cannot love nor can he suffer" (*CG* 253). Indeed, the God of theism should be replaced if he is poor and unable to love. The framing of the question makes the conclusion all but incontestable. Here Moltmann's framework begs the question: which theologians articulate such a God?

67. *CG* 221; this also previews his attack of monotheism in *TKG*.

68. For detailed explicit comments, see especially *CG* 25ff. Meeks sees the dialectic stemming from both Barth and Bloch (Meeks, *Origins*, 15ff.). Alternatively, Frei states that Moltmann's "methodological principle" or "governing device" is the dialectic, albeit a type related to both Hegel and Marx, instead of Kierkegaard or Barth's early version (Frei, "Review of *Theology of Hope*," 268, 271). Frei does not mention that Moltmann draws on Bloch, who looks to Hegel and Marx's dialectical process as well. Moltmann states that he follows Bloch's interpretation of Marx, and thus gives both Meeks and Frei a measure of validity, while also being more specific (see especially *RRF* 15–18). Fiorenza concurs: Moltmann "borrows the Marxist dialectic as interpreted and understood by Ernst Bloch . . . which he [Moltmann] develops both in dependence on, and in criticism of, Hegel" (Fiorenza, "Dialectical Theology and Hope 1," 146; see also 149). Additionally, Rebecca Chopp, commenting on both *TH* and *CG*, labels Moltmann's formal theological method a "dialectic of contradiction," while assigning the label "dialectic of identification" to his narrative readings; she believes that the latter takes Moltmann past the former to "provoke a witness to the future of hope in the memory of suffering" (Chopp, *The Praxis of Suffering*, 100–101).

On Bloch's reception of Hegel and Marx, see Heinitz, "The Theology of Hope According to Ernst Bloch," 34–41; O'Collins "Principle," 129–44; Fiorenza, "Dialectical Theology and Hope [1–3]."

69. In so doing he seems to be following Iwand (see Meeks, *Origins*, 31). In 1980, however, he maintains that he was following up on a question originally asked by Bloch (*GSS* 272 n. 1).

For Moltmann's discussion of these epistemological issues, see especially *CG* 24–28, 68, 212ff.; *DGG* 150ff.; *GL* 63–70; *FC* 77–79; *WJC* 137–38, 244; *GSS* 135–52; *ET* 169–73. For secondary comments, see Bauckham, "Moltmann's Eschatology of the Cross," 304–8; Bauckham, *Moltmann*, 67–72; Kasper, "Revolution im Gottesverständnis?" 143–44; Lunn, "The Doctrine of Atonement: (3) The Significance of the Cross for Moltmann and Dillistone," 32; O'Donnell, *Trinity and Temporality*, 115; Macquarrie, "Theologies of Hope," 229; Zimany, "Moltmann's Crucified God," 52.

the Platonic formulae "like is only known by like" (epistemological) and "like seeks after like" (sociological) only to dispute their universal validity.[70] His use of dialectical epistemology has attracted criticism.[71] While it can seem both contradictory and counterintuitive, two mundane examples are intrinsically appealing: one knows hot in relation to cold and light in relation to darkness.[72] Framing the discussion in this way enables him to argue that the only way past atheism is to move beyond theism as well.[73]

This dialectical epistemology was operative in *TH*, when he maintained that the revelation of God is dialectical, exemplified with the negation of death in the resurrection: "revelation must be conceived as an event that takes place in promise and fulfillment."[74] While previously revelation focused on promise, life and resurrection, the understanding is paralleled in *CG*, but the point of reference changes to the cross: "in the crucified Christ, abandoned by God and cursed, faith can find no equivalents of this kind which provide it with an indirect, analogical knowledge of God, but encounters the very contrary."[75] In contradistinction to analogical epistemology, Moltmann (following Luther) asserts: "The epistemological principle of the theology of the cross can only be this dialectical principle: the deity of God is revealed in the paradox

---

70. Aristotle, *Metaphysics* II, 4, 1000 b, and *Nichomachean Ethics*, VIII, 4 1155 a, as quoted, respectively, in *CG* 26; see also *GL* 67, 91; *OC* 27–36, 60–63; *GSS* 135–52; *SpL* 257–9; *ET* 151–55.

71. Indeed, in *CG* his polemical move rejecting analogical epistemology is extremely one-sided (see especially *CG* 69). Unfortunately, he does not promote a useful correction to analogy by proffering dialectic as an equal partner or even a handmaiden. Instead, he implies that the entire analogical approach is wrong. Later, he mitigates the one-sidedness dogmatism to a degree in response to Kasper (*DGG* 152–54; see also Kasper, "Revolution im Gottesverständnis?" 144, 147).

72. See *WJC* 244.

73. In part he is following Max Horkheimer (see *CG* 223ff.). Drawing on Horkheimer, Moltmann asks: "Should the murderers triumph over their victims for good? Could their death be their end?" ("Love, Death, Eternal Life: Theology of Hope—the Personal Side," 19, drawing on Horkheimer; see also *CG* 178; *EB* 141). For background on the Frankfurt school, especially Horkheimer and Adorno, see Leszek Kolakowski, "The Frankfurt School and 'critical theory,'" 341–95; Bowie, *Introduction to German Philosophy*, 222–45.

74. *TH* 228.

75. *CG* 68; see also *CG* 69, 80 n. 67.

of the cross."⁷⁶ He answers the atheistic protestors, not by taking the (seemingly) opposite argument and explicating a traditional theistic account, but by rejecting a major premise of the classical understanding of God with its concomitant philosophical restraints because, he believes, they inhibit a proper understanding of God and limit one's description of God to monotheistic, unchangeable, perfect and impassible, which actually prevents moving past protest atheism.⁷⁷ Impassibility, in this view, becomes not a way to preserve divine unity and higher being, but presents the God of theism as open to protest. In this vein he asserts: "'For Christ's sake I am an atheist,' an atheist in respect of the gods of the world and world history, the Caesars and the political demigods who follow them."⁷⁸ While some believe impassibility provides appropriate borders which help to circumscribe a doctrine of God, for Moltmann it is a cage or prison that must be dismantled to fully appreciate the New Testament narrative of divine action in the history of the Son, especially the passion narratives.

Thus, by pursuing a theology of the cross via dialectical epistemology he turns the typical atheistic protest on its head.⁷⁹ So, while Büchner challengingly inquires: "why do I suffer? That is the rock of atheism,"⁸⁰

---

76. Ibid., 27, 31 n. 22, he mentions Schelling, Bloch, Hippocrates; see also *CG* 68–71, 196, 208ff.

77. *CG* 244–45, 252; Moltmann's attack on monotheism blooms fully in *TKG*.

78. *CG* 195; this helps to explain Moltmann's view that "Only a Christian can be a good atheist." He also maintains: "I am a Christian for Christ's sake" (*EG* 17; see also *ET* 46; *BP* 79).

79. While self-consciously countering the atheism of both Dostoevsky and Camus, elsewhere, Moltmann mentions Marx in the context of humanistic atheism (*UZ* 20–23). Camus, according to Moltmann, held that "metaphysical rebellion does not derive from Greek tragedy but from the Bible, with its concept of the personal God" (*CG* 221, see also 251; "What is a Theologian?" 190–91).

Moltmann seems to simplify excessively the issue by exclusively painting the picture in black and white. It is precisely at this point that he encounters a difficulty. Moltmann thinks he "escapes the dispute between the alternative of theism and atheism" (*CG* 252). By his account, then, either theology can continue to assert its theistic basis, and thereby give credence to atheism, or it can abandon both and move to a vision of trinitarian suffering. Regardless of one's (dis)agreement on his vision of divine passibility, the oversimplification involved with Moltmann's account makes it appear that theology is at a crossroads and both options (theism and atheism) lead down the wrong path. Moltmann then pulls the metaphorical rabbit out of the hat and provides the perfect solution.

80. Büchner, as quoted in "Theology as Eschatology," 5 n. 6.

Moltmann retorts: "Why and for whom does God's Christ suffer? ... Büchner is wrong: *this* is the rock of Christian faith."[81] By affirming God's presence and activity in the cross of Christ, Moltmann can avail himself of finding hope in the resurrection and the promised future (*TH*) as well as in the abandonment of the son and suffering (*CG*). Indeed, he unequivocally asserts that it is the very fact that God suffers that hope exists: "At the centre of the Christian faith is the history of Christ's passion. At the centre of this passion is the experience of God endured by the Godforsaken, God-cursed Christ. Is this end of all human and religious hope? Or is it the beginning of the true hope, which has been born again and can no longer be shaken?"[82] Moltmann's path beyond the siblings of atheism and theism is diametrically opposed to the Greek philosophical basis of the traditional understanding of God, which he believes necessitates theism.[83] To fully achieve his aim of reorienting the doctrine of God rooted in the cross, Moltmann emphasizes the suffering love of God, which also reveals a further alteration in his doctrine of hope.

The Suffering Love of God

Led by dialectical epistemology, Moltmann closely links love with suffering.[84] For Moltmann, the Greek apathy axiom can only be understood as a foreign imposition onto the doctrine of God, forcing one to rely on the philosophical restraints of apophatic theology instead of the biblical narrative.[85] When viewed as love, God can be seen as open to suffering. And with this move, Moltmann replaces one axiom with another: a being who loves is open to suffering; (and perhaps more central) a being who cannot suffer, cannot love.[86] Linking divine

---

81. *HP* 43 (italics original); see also 32; *TT* 90. For discussions related to Feuerbach's and Nietzsche's versions of atheism (amongst others) related to protest atheism and the "death of God" movement, see Fiddes, *Creative Suffering of God*, 178–84; O'Donnell, *Trinity and Temporality*, 7–16

82. *PPL* 119.

83. *CG* 221, 251. Typically in *CG*, the term is theism, which becomes monotheism most appreciably in *TKG*.

84. For his view of divine (im)passibility, see below, 119–24.

85. *BP* 393 n. 17.

86. There is no hesitation, and with the inclusion of "almost" John Thompson understates the matter: "Moltmann is critical of the metaphysical view of the *apatheia* of

suffering to divine love necessitates that passibility be viewed not as a defect, but as an attribute of God's very being (though to be sure God freely chooses this): "a God who is incapable of suffering is a being who cannot be involved.... But the one who cannot suffer cannot love either. So he is also a loveless being."[87] Moltmann seeks to avoid presenting God in abstract terms, related to the cosmos only as a distant deity, unable to experience pain, suffering, anguish, and death: "God suffers—suffering is in God."[88] Indeed: "It is on Golgotha that the coming God is present in history."[89]

Christ's death marks the entire theological outlook: "Either Jesus who was abandoned by God is the end of all theology or he is the beginning of a specifically Christian, and therefore critical and liberating, theology and life."[90] Indeed, Moltmann's theology of the cross requires a "revolution in the concept of God" which reaches to his doctrine of hope. Essentially the revolution on the concept of God impresses his view of hope, causing a further revolution.

A Revolution in the Concept of Hope

Moltmann's doctrine of hope changes as he delves into issues related to the absence of God, death in God[91] and "the historical Good Friday of the godforsakenness of Jesus."[92] While the main proposal in *CG* is a

---

God. By contrast, he almost goes to the opposite extreme and makes suffering a central aspect of the nature of God who is love" (Thompson, *Modern Trinitarian Perspectives*, 61).

87. *CG* 222.
88. *DGG* 188; see *CG* 222ff.
89. *GSS* 19.
90. *CG* 4.
91. Bauckham points out that Moltmann silently changes the phrase "death of God" (see *TH* 165–72) to "death in God" (see *CG* 233–4) (Bauckham, "Moltmann's Eschatology of the Cross," 303). According to Moltmann, Hegel's meaning is different than Nietzsche's (*TH* 165ff.).
92. This is not to assert that Moltmann agrees with Hegel's "speculative Good Friday"; see especially *TH* 171; see also *TH* 211: Jesus' resurrection is properly understood as the "conquest of the deadliness of death . . . as a negation of the negative (Hegel), as a negation of the negation of God." Later he asserts that the cross must be more than a negation of the negative (*CoG* 38). The importance of Hegel's influence on Moltmann's view of the cross and Trinity will be assessed in chapter 4. See also O'Regan, *The Heterodox Hegel*, 219–21.

Bauckham asserts that Hegel plays a more prominent role in *TH* than *CG* ("Moltmann's Eschatology of the Cross," 302). In light of *TKG*, Bauckham might wish to

delineation of the proper concept of God in light of the cross, it furthers his doctrine of hope, as it takes into account the importance of the cross. Indeed, his revolution in the concept of God parallels his revolution in the concept of hope.

While in *TH* he sought to ensure that hope is not confined to the present (which led him to stress the future as contradiction), in *CG* he grounds hope in the cross. An example of what would have made his early concentration on hope more complete, thus taking the cross as both informative and integral, comes from his own pen as he develops his theology of the cross. *CG* opens with the programmatic and methodological presupposition: "the crucified Christ [is] the general criterion of theology."[93] This assertion evidences the change that has occurred between *TH* and *CG*. Moltmann stakes out his position most clearly in *CG* "The death of Jesus on the cross is the *centre* of all Christian theology ... All Christian statements about God, about creation, about sin and death have their focal point in the crucified Christ. All Christian statements about history, about the church, about faith and sanctification, about the future and about hope stem from the crucified Christ."[94] In this period, this change reaches his understanding of hope, as he relates the cross to hope directly: "Christian faith therefore has to understand the powerless suffering and the forsaken dying of Jesus, not as refutation of his messianic hope, but rather as its deepest realization under the conditions of a godless and inhuman world which stands under the coming judgment. It has therefore discovered the hope of the suffering ones in the suffering of this 'coming one.'"[95] While Moltmann's early annunciation of hope was rooted primarily in the resurrection, for a proper theology of the cross he asserts that the cross and resurrection mutually inform each other: "Christ's death on the cross is "the significance" of

---

revise his judgment: while Hegel is the most frequently cited figure in *TH*, the underlying argument connecting the cross and its meaning for both the world and the conception of God in *CG* and *TKG* is heavily influenced by Hegel and Moltmann's view of the cross and resurrection as dialectical is arguably more fundamentally central to *CG* than to *TH*. Bauckham is correct to the degree that he is approving Moltmann's move to a stronger historical understanding of the cross in *CG*, over against Hegel's "speculative" account which is the basis of discussion in *TH*. See also Meeks, *Origins*, 34–38; Grellert, "The Eschatological Theology of Jürgen Moltmann," 204ff.

93. *CG* 4.
94. Ibid., 204; italics original.
95. *EH* 64.

his resurrection for us. Conversely, any interpretation of the meaning of his death which does not have as a presupposition his resurrection from the dead is a hopeless matter . . . His resurrection is the content of the significance of his death on the cross 'for us', because the risen Christ is himself the crucified Christ."[96] Thus, Moltmann presupposes the importance of the resurrection throughout *CG*, essentially taking as read his earlier concentration in *TH*. In this way *CG* does indeed deepen *TH* as he takes up the importance of the cross only by ensuring that the proper context is its relationship with the resurrection, thereby providing greater depth to both.[97]

Echoing the imprisoned Dietrich Bonhoeffer, Moltmann maintains: "only the suffering God can help,"[98] making it clear that he is a member of the "new orthodoxy" of a suffering God.[99] While he has a desire to include other themes in his discussion, the central issue, indeed the presupposition of his argument, is in fact the nature of the cross and how it provides a window through which one glimpses the relationship between God the Father and the Son.[100]

Typically, one procures hope from the cross based on one or two (or both) assessments: (1) the cross is a source of hope because Christ died for the sins of the world; (2) the cross is a source of hope because its true meaning is found in the resurrection. In *CG* and later Moltmann argues for number one: "What is the meaning of that terrible happening on Golgotha? . . . that he could be there *for us* in our guilt, freeing us from its burden. That means: God's *atoning intervention* for us."[101] Also in *CG*, he places the cross and resurrection in a mutually informing relationship, whereby each gives the other greater meaning. More centrally, however, Moltmann finds the cross a source of hope because

---

96. *CG* 186.

97. See ibid., chapter 5. And so while *CG* is one-sided, it is less so than *TH* (on the issue of the early trilogy's one-sidedness, see *CG* 5; *DGG* 166; *HTG* 173–74).

98. Bonhoeffer, *Letters and Papers from Prison*, 112; see also *EG* 43; *TT* 17; *HTG* 48; *JCTW* 54; *GSS* 183.

99. See Goetz, "The Suffering God," 385–89.

100. For a brief discussion of *CG* as essentially binitarian and Moltmann's endeavor to overcome it, see below, pp. 178–89. While the Trinity is discussed in *CG* a more substantive pneumatology is not explicated until *CPS* (for an explanation, see *DGG* 184–85).

101. *JCTW* 38; his first reply argues for "*God's solidarity* with us" while the second focuses on atonement.

God is revealed in the event of the Son's abandonment. To some degree Moltmann follows the Israelite concept of judgment being equated with guilt, so that abandonment is equated with God's wrath: "God gave up his own Son, abandoned him, cast him out and delivered him up to an accursed death."[102] Yet, Moltmann's concern for this theological point is not soteriology, but rather divine ontology, specifically the proper relationship between the Father and the Son. He wants to ensure that the cross actually, centrally, and vitally affects God: in the event of the cross God is in suffering and suffering is in God.[103] God is not a distant deity; he is present in the very midst of godforsakenness. As such, God is the God of the godforsaken.[104] Since the suffering and death of Jesus is in God, the Father does not remain unaffected but suffers the death of his Son.[105] This line of thinking leads to a fundamental shift in Moltmann's doctrine of hope, with wide-ranging implications.

Conclusion

In *CG*, the advance in his doctrine of hope centers on the dialectical epistemology that grounds identifying God in the cross. Much has changed between *TH* and *CG*. In *TH*, he insisted that "Christianity stands or falls with the reality of the raising of Jesus from the dead,"[106] while later he maintains that "at the centre of the Christian faith stands an unsuccessful, suffering Christ."[107] Furthermore, recall that in *TH* suffering and present experience are negative and oppositional to hope: "eschatology ... must formulate its statements of hope in contradiction to our present experience of suffering, evil, and death."[108] Compare, however, *CG* where he maintains: "God and suffering are no longer contradictions, as in theism and atheism, but God's being is in suffering and the suffering

---

102. *CG* 242.

103. Ibid., 274–78. Later Moltmann takes issue with Rahner's trinitarian doctrine, but it is perhaps rooted in Rahner's insistence on the two-natures, while Moltmann rejects it (see Rahner, "On the Theology of the Incarnation," 105–20; *HTG* 122–24).

104. *CG*, 242.

105. Ibid., 243.

106. *TH* 165.

107. *UZ* 14; see also *PPL* 115; the focus in *CG* is more centrally "dying in forsakenness," and instead of "suffering Christ" it becomes "the crucified God."

108. *TH* 19.

is in God's being itself."[109] This is extended, without limitation: "There is no suffering which in this history of God is not God's suffering; no death which has not been God's death in the history on Golgotha."[110] A few pages later, this assertion is followed it to its rightful conclusion: "God suffers, God allows himself to be crucified and is crucified, and in this consummates his unconditional love that is so full of hope."[111] As such, CG implicitly constructs an argument that hope, if it is sufficiently Christian, must be grounded in the cross. Christian hope knows that all suffering is in God, and in his faithfulness in suffering he proves that he is no apathetic deity, detached, and unmoved. He is the suffering God, the crucified God. God is not only distantly future; he is present in suffering.

Even in CG, the resurrection is supplemented rather than supplanted as the ground of hope.[112] The cross is a proper ground of hope because it reveals God. Moreover, God is not revealed as merely *capable* of suffering, but God takes suffering into the divine life: he is "the crucified God." And once the intelligibility of the "the crucified God" is established, one sees how Moltmann grounds Christian hope in the cross and resurrection.[113] Indeed: "how can one arouse hope in the name and in the following of a preacher whose hope was cut off by his death?"[114] The answer, Moltmann insists, must be: one cannot unless the crucified one is resurrected. In CG Moltmann concludes that whenever the cross is forgotten the result is that "hope is lost."[115] And while in TH hope generally points forward from the resurrection to the future, in CG this is reversed, as hope sheds light from the resurrection "*backwards*, into

---

109. CG 227; see also "The Crucified God," 18.

110. CG 246.

111. Ibid., 248. The adjective "unconditional" seems theologically unwarranted, yet essential for his soteriology. See also JCTW 46: "But if we discover where God is, and sense his presence in our suffering, then we are at the fountainhead—the source out of which life is born anew."

112. CG 124: "Faith in God is faith in the resurrection ... [God] manifests himself to be the same in the abandonment and in the resurrection of Jesus."

113. It is irrelevant whether one (dis)agrees with Moltmann's doctrine of impassibilty. Of central importance are the far-reaching consequences of it for the remainder of his program, especially his understanding of hope.

114. Ibid., 125.

115. Ibid., 58; contextually he is criticizing the assimilation of Christianity into bourgeois society.

the mystery and suffering of the exalted Lord."[116] While soteriology is not the dominant theme or a major concern of *CG*, it rears its head in relating the cross to hope. Indeed, this procedure of reading the narrative "backwards" engenders viewing the cross as hopeful because it is salvific: "Through his suffering and death, the Christ who was raised from the dead *before us* becomes the Christ *for us*."[117] This both/and approach of understanding the cross and resurrection reads the narrative backward allowing one to find hope in the cross: "Thus the cross of Christ modifies the resurrection of Christ . . . so that it changes from being a purely future event to being an event of liberating love."[118] Indeed, "when it [the cross] is seen in terms of the hope that sheds its light backwards, that means the glory of the coming God has been manifested in the helplessness and shame of the crucified."[119] The result, while not always explicitly drawn out by Moltmann, is clear: neither the cross nor the resurrection alone is sufficient to ground hope. "The multiplicity of the New Testament comes together in the event of the crucifixion and resurrection of Jesus and flows out again from it. It is one event and one person."[120] Since they are best defined as one event, they are inseparable: each requires the other for proper interpretation.

The overall theme for hope in *CG* is precisely this: hope is found in divine suffering, in the event of the Father abandoning the Son on the cross. This move helps to reinforce his prior articulation of hope, by giving it a stronger ground. Yet, this reinforcement is perhaps the most surprising element about *CG* regarding hope. His theology of the cross is relentlessly iconoclastic, and yet fails to supply an adequate antithesis to the thesis proffered in *TH*. In *TH* he argued for the grounding of hope in the resurrection of the crucified one, and in *CG* he argues that hope is grounded in the crucifixion of the resurrected one. Both are necessary and each informs the other. While the failure of his hope in *TH* is its confidence due to its one-sided ground in the resurrection, in *CG* his hope is not so much balanced by the tragedy of the cross but

116. *CG* 180; see also 113, 168, 184; *DTH* 215–29; *HP* 42; for Moltmann's view of Jesus' descent into hell, see "Descent into Hell," 115–19; "The Blessing of Hope," 153.

117. *CG* 184; contextually this is a qualified endorsement of expiation.

118. Ibid., 185.

119. Ibid., 168.

120. Ibid., 204; regarding the event of the cross and resurrection, see *WJC* 213–14, 224.

rather reinforced because God is found not only in the positive activity of new creation, resurrection, and rebirth, but also in abandonment, death, and suffering (both human and divine). His understanding of the assured eschatological resurrection keeps his theology from becoming a negative fatalism, yet enigmatically his theology of the cross supports, equally as strong as *TH*, the confidence of hope. This is a rather odd conclusion. Moltmann insists that the cross must be the center of one's understanding of God and thus the Christian faith; he insists with equal vigor that the cross is pre-eminently iconoclastic for one's understanding of God and the Christian faith. These moves seem to call for an iconoclasm and a questioning of theological assertions, even (or perhaps especially) related to hope. So far it has not. It remains to be seen in Part II whether he finds such a resource. Thus far, the effect his theology of the cross has on his doctrine of hope is rather surprising. Moltmann might have found in his theology of the cross a necessary balance or qualifier that could serve as the antithesis to the resurrection, and thus argue that hope, when effectively grounded in the cross-resurrection event, can only be certain in the eschaton. This move would be an appropriate application of his central arguments in *TH*. He could have used such a presentation to posit the cross as the element that places a question mark on the certainty of eschatological pronouncements.

In *CG*, he fails to find a source for hesitation in articulating his theology of the cross, evidencing his lack of patience with mystery, paradox and the unknown.[121] As such, hope is grounded in the *novum* of the resurrection and also in the suffering and abandonment of the cross. Enigmatically, Moltmann uses the experience of the cross, which in *CG* is offensive, troubling, disconcerting, questioning, and uncomfortable for theology, and uses it to pronounce hope. The cross does not serve to give hope a "glass darkly"[122] aspect, but rather brings hope into clearer focus.

---

121. This may be overstating the matter indefensibly, but his articulation of the cross as the center of theology causes him to say all he is able, indeed arguably more than he should be able. There is little allowance for debating the matter.

122. 1 Cor 13.12: "For now we see through a glass, darkly; but then face to face" (KJV).

Part One

Conclusion:
Hope in the Faithfulness of God

The opening chapters have examined Moltmann's doctrine of hope by discussing first his theology of the resurrection followed by his turn to a theology of the cross, and argued that only together can the cross and resurrection properly articulate and ground Moltmann's doctrine of hope. Without either, hope is invalid. This was a necessary step in showing the development of his doctrine of hope. Read in chronological order one sees the alterations Moltmann makes, and why. In *TH* hope is found in the difference between the future and the present; while this is not abandoned outright, in *CG* hope is found directly in suffering, betrayal and death. While it is true that the resurrection contradicts the cross,[123] it is a contradiction in correspondence to the extent that the two events are best understood as one event, not two.[124] The revolution that requires God to be thought of as intimately involved in the cross, entails a concomitant revolution in the concept of hope: not found in the resurrection only, hope is found in the cross, because God is most present there. That he makes this move relatively early in his career makes what comes after not less important, but more.[125]

While it is clear that he rejects the traditional understanding of God's immutability and impassibility,[126] he does not explicitly state the conclusion of this dual argument for hope. For Moltmann, all theol-

---

123. See especially Bauckham, *Theology of Jürgen Moltmann*, 107.

124. The cross and resurrection is one event (see *CG* 204; *WJC* 214; *SpL* 65; *SoL* 15).

125. Jesus' true identity is based in the cross and resurrection (*WJC* 139).

126. For an opposite conclusion, see Weinandy, *Does God Suffer?* 20 n. 57.

ogy is hope because God is faithful, whether in fulfilling promises and overcoming death, as in the resurrection, or his presence in suffering, typified in the cross. Part I traces the progression: to properly ground hope one cannot look into the future, even God's future, alone, for that would be "flee-the-present" disillusioned escapism; one must integrate the cross into this perspective to properly understand that the dialectical identity of the crucified and resurrected one becomes shorthand for God's faithfulness. Seen together, *TH* and *CG*, both implicitly and explicitly, stress God's faithfulness: God will do what he promises and God is present in suffering.[127] Regardless of the specific issues and problems encountered in *TH* and *CG*, God's faithfulness is a driving force in Moltmann's theology, which grounds his hope. Thus, various statements have been made in Part I regarding the ground of hope: chiefly the "dialectical identity of Jesus Christ as the crucified and resurrected one," and the "dialectical unity of the cross and resurrection" and finally, the "faithfulness of God." Each assertion means the same thing, yet they are used not as reduction of hope, but as amplification of its ground.

In *TH* "the question of God can be answered only in the eschatological horizon opened up by the resurrection,"[128] while in *CG* the question of God can only be answered in the cross. "Hope," Moltmann insists, "recognizes the power and faithfulness of God in this story of the resurrection of the crucified one."[129] What remains to be seen is the nature of hope for Moltmann. Does he seek resolution or does he allow the tension to remain, this side of the eschaton?

The balance of this study continues the chronological approach by ascertaining and perceiving how this early theology casts its shadow on his later principal works, whether positive or negative. His doctrine of hope determines, to a high degree, his theological pronouncements, developments, and direction. The first text to be examined is *CPS*, his messianic ecclesiology.

---

127. Said differently: hope has two elements: "the resolute negation of the negative in the present" coupled with "the anticipation of the positive" (*ET* 56). Contextually, he is summarizing "the reasonableness of hope" (*ET* 51–57).

128. Meeks, *Origins*, 38.

129. *HP* 183.

PART TWO

The Implications:
Christian Doctrine *as* Hope

3

Ecclesiology as Hope

Introduction

FROM THE PERSPECTIVE OF MOLTMANN'S DOCTRINE OF HOPE, *CPS* (the third volume in the early trilogy) is best read as a transitional volume since it takes up the central themes of *TH* and *CG*, while making way for the "contributions."[1] The present chapter plays a similar role regarding this study. Accordingly, it will be shown that the very core of Moltmann's ecclesiology is an outworking of his doctrine of hope: ecclesiology is developed as hopeful, because it is grounded in the paradigm of the crucified and resurrected one.[2] While the church is a community of embodied hope,[3] the present chapter is not concerned with

---

1. Since the volumes were not written according to a pre-set plan, trilogy is the appropriate retrospective label. Interestingly, *CPS* attracted fewer dialogue partners than *TH* and *CG*, which explains why secondary sources are cited less frequently in this chapter and why no *Diskussion* of *CPS* was published (see *HTG* 175–6; Bauckham, *Moltmann*, 114 = Bauckham, *Theology of Jürgen Moltmann*, 119).

CPS largely maintains the dialectic presented in *TH* and *CG*; it is unclear whether Bauckham intends the same when he states that *CPS* "completes this scheme [from *TH* and *CG*]"; Bauckham, *Theology of Jürgen Moltmann*, 5.

2. Miroslav Volf and Maurice Lee lament the fact that "theologians have reflected relatively little on precisely *how* the two [Spirit and Church] are related"; "The Spirit and the Church," 382. Oddly, Moltmann's contribution to this pairing (*CPS*) is not mentioned.

3. As with this study generally, this chapter does not discuss Moltmann's ethics in detail.

ecclesial practice,[4] but rather with the church as a "fellowship of hope,"[5] participating in the trinitarian history of God. This issue is expounded in two ways: (1) the church's mission is situated in the trinitarian history of God; (2) the church should expect suffering by following the crucified one in light of the resurrection.

Insofar as he is able to ground the church in the cross-resurrection "event," he avoids attributing to the church a belief in its ability to bring about its own salvation, optimistically believing it follows in (or perhaps drives) the train of human progress, while also effectively avoiding passive resignation, which can give rise to apocalyptic escapism, as characteristics of the church.[6] For ecclesiology, Moltmann cites the need "to assess the breadth of the horizon of hope opened up through Christ for Christianity as it lives and suffers in history."[7] In this vein, he is wary of "losing" the center or the horizon of the church's activity.[8] The discussion below argues that hope plays this dual function for ecclesiology providing both the center and horizon for the church.

Although he wrote CPS in the 1970s as a European male academic, belonging to an established Protestant church in the Federal German Republic, his "concern was the faith and authenticity of the one church of Christ."[9] The origin of his ecclesiology is his five-year experience

---

4. He rejects infant baptism (CPS 226–42, 314; OC 124–5; HC 47–51) and wishes to unite the Orthodox Eucharist, Catholic Mass, and Protestant communion into a more ecumenical vision, which he labels the Lord's supper (CPS 242–60; HC 52–6; WJC 207).

5. CPS 225.

6. Moltmann is no friend of an anthropocentric ethic that seeks to destroy creation, while the church awaits its rapture (see especially CoG 153).

7. CPS 133.

8. Moltmann does not see the church as a parenthesis (as in dispensational theology) or as a replacement of Israel. For a brief discussion of supersessionism, see Christopher M. Leighton, "Christian Theology After the Shoah," 38–43.

For Moltmann's discussion of the church's relationship with Israel and other world religions, see CPS 133–63; OC 27–30; HC 37–40; HG XII; HD 189–209; JM. He names as "religions of hope" the Abrahamic religions: Islam, Judaism and Christianity (CJF 95; see also CG 135). For Moltmann, Israel must be mentioned separately from "world religions," in contrast to Vatican II language (see CG 134–5). His understanding of New Testament ecclesiology informs his view that the early church was a *"tertium quid"*: "Gentiles did not have to become Jews in order to be Christians, nor did Jews have to become Gentiles" (HC 38; see also CPS 141–4 4).

9. CPS xix; see also OC 95–97.

in the pastorate[10] and his involvement with churches throughout the world.[11] Ecclesiology was on the agenda because of "the contemporary context": the late 1960s brought unrest, resulting in what he deems a "crisis" of relevance for the Protestant church of West Germany, which needed to decide between the conservative or progressive option.[12] Indeed, in 1967 he wrote: "we are everywhere asking for something that is 'new' . . . This is everywhere the case—with the exception perhaps of the church."[13] At the time, he saw the church "at a crossroads": "Either the Protestant church would continue the course that had led to the crisis, from a state church to a people's church, and from a people's church to a church for the people . . . or it would renew itself through forces from below and became [sic] a community church of the people of God in the people."[14] This crisis, then, has a positive effect: "In the crisis of its tradition and in the opportunities afforded by its hope, the church will take its bearings from its foundation [*Grund*], its future [*Zukunft*] and the charge given it. As "the church of Jesus Christ" it is fundamentally dependent on him, and on him alone."[15] The church will "radically

---

10. BP 53–67; "What is a Theologian?" 189–91. He makes it plain that theology is a task of the church (*CPS* 7).

11. *CPS* xix; he names Korea, Kenya, Ghana, Manila, Latin America and also the free church tradition in the U.S. ("Theology in Germany Today," 190). See Bauckham, *Moltmann*, 116 = *Theology of Jürgen Moltmann*, 121; Müller-Fahrenholz, *Kingdom and Power*, 80ff.

12. *HTG* 174; see also *CPS* 16; see Rasmusson, *Church as Polis*, 90ff.

13. *RRF* 3; see also *GSS* 160; *RRF* 14: "No longer is the *incipit vita nova* announced, but instead a *restitutio in integrum*."

14. *HTG* 174–5. While John Zizioulas comments upon numerous contemporaries of Moltmann, it is rather surprising that he avoids discussing Moltmann's theology (including his ecclesiology), especially in relation to Zizioulas' understanding of the local church (see Zizioulas, *Being as Communion*, 247–60).

Moltmann's "from below" ecclesiological methodology is a thread running throughout *CPS*, and is the source of his sometimes vehement attack on the Roman Catholic Church's institutional hierarchy; beyond *CPS*, see especially "Christianity in the Third Millennium," 75–89.

15. *CPS* xviii [11]. The second sentence names Jesus as the ground: "ist sie ihm Grunde auf ihn . . . angewiesen" [11]. To be sure, one of the charges given to the church is theology: "theology is a function of the church" (as quoted in *CPS* 7; he is following Barth and others on this point [see *CPS* 363 n. 3]; see also M. Douglas Meeks, "Moltmann's Contribution to Practical Theology," in *HC* 61–62). Later, Moltmann attributes Johann Baptist Metz with this insight for political theology ("From the Beginning of Time in God's Presence," 54–55).

project itself towards the future it is certain of, because it is the future of Christ, who has called the church to life."¹⁶ The method Moltmann prescribes for the church's hope, then, is to look into the future and then to work in the present in light of this future, regardless of the negative effects or results in the present.

CPS is not Moltmann's first venture into ecclesiology in the trilogy: the final chapter of *TH* is entitled "The Exodus Church,"¹⁷ wherein he describes the church as the "pilgrim people of God," existing "within the horizon of eschatological hope."¹⁸ During this period, he comments: "[The church] has its essence and its goal not in itself and not in its own existence, but lives from something and exists for something which reaches far beyond itself... If we would fathom its *essence*, then we must enquire into that *future* on which it sets its *hopes* and expectations."¹⁹ This prior understanding is not merely amplified in *CPS*, but rather taken up and improved after he turned to his theology of the cross. Indeed, there is a certain degree to which a proper explication of his ecclesiology can be done only in the post-*CG* era for two reasons.²⁰

Suffering

The first advance beyond his ecclesiology of 1964 is the issue of suffering: while the final chapter of *TH* is devoid neither of references to suffering nor the cross,²¹ overall the stress is on the resurrection (as is the entire text), focusing on the role of the risen Christ for the church.²²

---

16. *CPS* xviii; see also *FC* 106ff.

17. *TH* V: 304–38. Furthermore, the origin of *CPS* dates back to a series of lectures given in Bonn 1966), and again in Tübingen (1968 and 1972) (see *CPS* xviii–xix; Tripole, "Ecclesiological Developments," *TS* 34, 20).

18. *TH* 304, 305. Note: the original passage begins: "Christianity is to be understood . . ." For the entire chapter, however, he specifies that "Christianity" refers to "the whole body of believers" (*TH* 304 n. 1). See also *TH* 326.

19. *TH* 325; on the parenthetical inclusion of "the church" for Christianity, see the preceding note.

20. Later, in a memorable aphorism, Moltmann states that such a progression is natural: "A true theology of the cross is Pentecost theology, and Christian Pentecost theology is a theology of the cross" (*SoL* 17).

21. See especially *TH* 333–334; the sole reference to the "crucified Christ" in chapter 5 appears in the final sentence (*TH* 338).

22. See *TH* 325–26, 328–29, 338. Even after turning to the cross his tone can still sound very similar to *TH* (see especially *TJ*).

In the intervening eleven years this changes appreciably. As will be seen, the determining influence and paradigm for the church's ministry and expectation is not the resurrection alone, but rather the cross and resurrection of Jesus Christ. *CPS* is decidedly christological, with Pentecost being virtually presupposed. *CPS* takes up the early motif of the church as an exodus community, but closely related to the pneumatological angle is the role of suffering. While the ministry of Jesus Christ *in toto* is revelatory for the church as the principal foundation for the ministry of the church, the event *par excellence* is his death and resurrection, which is "the centre and quintessence of his history for us."[23] This is a crucial advance over Moltmann's prior understanding.

Spirit

The second advance on his prior understanding of "the exodus church" as expressed in *TH* is the Spirit's role.[24] Inexplicably, there is no explicit reference to the Spirit in *TH*'s final chapter. This marks an advance on *CG* as well, since his theology of the cross is developed initially with a focus on the Father and Son.[25] Later, Moltmann himself concedes the point, admitting that in *CG* he "did not get further than seeing a binity of God the Father and Jesus the Son of God. Where was the Holy Spirit . . . ?"[26] He remedies this lack, which he finds endemic in the west,[27]

---

23. *FC* 81; *contra* Jenson who worries that by looking to the future Moltmann has "relativize[d]" the past as a "norm of development" for the church (Jenson, *Systematic Theology*, 2:239). Seemingly, Jenson's concern is the noticeable lack of sustained comment on the creeds or church fathers in Moltmann's ecclesiology.

24. For comments related to the pneumatological lack in *TH*, see *DGG* 184–87. Secondary scholars' conclusions differ; see Bauckham, *Theology of Jürgen Moltmann*, 151; Donald Claybrook, "The Emerging Doctrine of the Holy Spirit in the Writings of Jürgen Moltmann," 185; Dabney, "Advent of the Spirit," 96–100; Schweitzer, "The Consistency of Jürgen Moltmann's Theology," 203.

25. See especially *DGG* 184–87.

26. *HTG* 174; in places, he lapses into non-trinitarian language (see *CG* 203; *WJC* 137–45). On the relationship between the Spirit and the cross, see below, pp. 182–89. See also Hermannus Heiko Miskotte, "Das Leiden ist in Gott," 79. Compare, however, Moltmann's earlier reference to sinning against the Holy Spirit (*TH* 23). Meeks, commenting on Moltmann's early work, claims to "see clearly its trinitarian nature from the beginning" (Meeks, "Foreword," xi; see also Schweitzer, "The Consistency of Jürgen Moltmann's Theology," 203). Even Moltmann does not go that far (*DGG* 184–87).

27. *DGG* 184–7; later, he attributes this lack to the *Filioque* (*ET* 320; see also *SoL* 15ff.). He devotes *TKG* to resolving the *Filioque* dispute (*TKG* xv).

by beginning to develop pneumatology. Because of the coming of the Spirit at Pentecost, the church exists "in the power of the Spirit."[28]

The Church in the Trinitarian History of God[29]

Recall that in the 1960s Moltmann emphasized present possibilities opened up through the resurrection of Christ. The church is not isolated from the world, but is rather pushed into contradiction with it,[30] which is why one of his early concerns was revolution: "One 'corresponds' to the God of promise by breaking away from the old and setting out into the new . . . Hope, which mobilizes to a new obedience, is therefore always bound up with a criticism of the present."[31] Although revolution is not a watchword in *CPS*, his understanding of the inevitability of facing contradiction with the present because of the promised future still remains strong.[32] Even in *CPS* he insists that "promise, exodus, resurrection and Spirit" (essential components of his ecclesiology) are the "Bible's revolutionary themes."[33] And although he does not include human or divine suffering as a revolutionary theme, he takes up suffering (post-*CG*) as central to Christian existence. Arguably, then, his understanding of revolution contextualized as living in the midst of an unsatisfactory present is stronger post-*CG*, due to his ability to call on the cross's iconoclastic nature. Thus, the originality of Moltmann's ecclesiology, in relation to hope, is that he includes the church in the wider frame of God's trinitarian history; a history which he earlier called a "history of hope."[34] Between remembrance and hope (both of which are grounded in the cross and resurrection), the church is only properly understood in relation to the history of the triune God: "the whole being of the church is marked by participation in the history

---

28. Moltmann qualifies the title by making it clear that the church's fundamental ground is Christ (see especially *CPS* xvii–xix).

29. This is Moltmann's phrase (see *CG* 274–78; *CPS* 50–65); see also Bauckham, *Moltmann*, 111–13; Conyers, *God, Hope, and History*, 125–35.

30. See especially *TH* 196–97.

31. *HP* 18; see also *RRF* 134; "Promissory Perspective" (pp. 15–17, above). For a criticism, see Rasmusson, *Church as Polis*, 90ff.

32. Moltmann rightly refuses to reduce Christian hope to being a private affair (*CPS* 15; *HP* 134–35; 144; 150; 198).

33. *CPS* 17.

34. *CG* 278.

of God's dealings with the world."³⁵ He ties the history of God to the church's activity via the work of the Spirit³⁶ because the Trinity "is the history of love and liberation."³⁷

The church is moving from the past to the future, calling to mind the biblical record of God's people being freed from slavery in Egypt, and the resurrection (which is discussed below).³⁸ In transition to the future, the church moves in hope, involved in the trinitarian history of God.³⁹ This relationship of the church to the trinitarian history is central to Moltmann's ecclesiology.⁴⁰

Trinity in Origin, Trinity in Sending

While his doctrine of the Trinity appears most fully in *TKG*, already in 1975 one of the central elements of Moltmann's doctrine of God is emerging,⁴¹ as he discusses the Trinity "in the sending and origin."⁴² Based on the history of Jesus, one can discern "the order of the history of salvation": "The *missio ad extra* reveals the *missio ad intra*. The *missio ad intra* is the foundation of the *missio ad extra*."⁴³ The Trinity is revealed in the *missio ad extra*, because "As God appears in history as the sending Father and the sent Son, so he must earlier have been in himself."⁴⁴ While this seems to be a silent appeal to Rahner's *Grundaxiom*,⁴⁵ later he explicitly rejects the distinction implied by the very terms economic

---

35. *CPS* 65; see also 75; for the church's role in conversion and soteriology, see ibid., 348ff.

36. For specific comments, see especially *TH* 211; *CPS* 27ff., 50ff.

37. Meeks, *Origins*, 37.

38. "Liberation in the Light of Hope," 423.

39. *CPS* 197: "It is not hope that makes the future into God's future; it is this future that wakens hope."

40. *CPS* 51; without it "ecclesiology remains abstract" (51). See also Bauckham, *Theology of Jürgen Moltmann*, 124ff.

41. Beyond *CPS*, see his 1975 lecture "The Trinitarian History of God" (*FC* 80–96).

42. *FC* 82–86.

43. Ibid., 84; see also *CPS* 54.

44. *CPS* 54. For a criticism of the "speculative" nature of Moltmann's doctrine at this point, see Bauckham, *Theology of Jürgen Moltmann*, 156–57.

45. Rahner's view is discussed more fully in *TKG*, but in *CPS* Moltmann accepts it formally, even while undercutting Rahner's main point. For Rahner's articulation, see *The Trinity*, 22; for two recent criticisms of Rahner's position, see Jowers, *The Trinitarian Axiom of Karl Rahner*; Rauser, "Rahner's Rule."

and immanent: "this terminology is imprecise, for it appears to speak of two trinities. The truth of the matter is that we can speak only of the *one* Trinity and of its economy of salvation."[46]

Rejecting the single *taxis* of Father—Son—Spirit, Moltmann is able to make full use of the historical nature of his doctrine of the Trinity, which he believes is based on two vantage points when perceiving the history of Christ: "from its origin and from its future."[47] The former is the traditional perspective and to it Moltmann adds the latter, by which he means: "If we think forwards, then it [the doctrine of the Trinity] is seen from the point of view of its goal . . . Its future stands in the light of his resurrection from the dead."[48] This places great importance on the eschatological function of his doctrine of God, which is further supported by his plea for an "open Trinity":

> The Trinity in the sending is, from its eternal origin, open to the world and to men . . . The Trinity in glorification is, from its eschatological goal, open for the gathering and uniting of men and the whole creation with God and in God. In it the history of the gathering love of God is completed. Through the sending of the Son and the Spirit the history of the Trinity is opened for the history of gathering, uniting and glorifying of the world in God and of God in the world.[49]

Meaning:

> Formally it [the Trinity in the glorification] corresponds to the Trinity in the sending, but in content it goes beyond it, just as the gathering love corresponds to the seeking love of God yet goes far beyond it through the gathering and uniting of mankind and the world with God.[50]

---

46. "Theological Proposals Towards the Resolution of the Filioque Controversy," 165; this article was written between *CPS* and *TKG*; over time this view concretizes (see *SpL* 290).

47. *CPS* 56; thus, reversing Rahner's assertion. Meeks comments: "This means that the theology of special revelation is theology on the way (*theologia viatorum*) . . . Thus Moltmann shares Iwand's most basic methodological assumption that theological thought at its beginning point has to move from the particular to the universal, from history to eschatology" (Meeks, *Origins*, 32).

48. *CPS* 56.

49. Ibid., 60; see also *TKG* 148–50.

50. *FC* 95.

For Moltmann, one pattern of trinitarian activity cannot adequately convey the activity detailed in the New Testament.[51] (This emerges in *CPS* and is elaborated more fully in *TKG*.) While the pattern of the Trinity "in origin" begins with the Father, relying on any single pattern is insufficient, because "[i]n the framework of the eschatological unity of God we must first talk about the Holy Spirit, then about the Son, and finally about the Father, who is united with the Son through the Spirit."[52] And it is with this reversal, in which the activity moves from the Spirit to the Father through the Son, that the church is involved in the trinitarian history of God as "one element in the movements of the divine sending, gathering together and experience."[53] The relevance of this line of thinking for his doctrine of hope is plain. The path for ecclesiology into this experience of the trinitarian history of God is an approach utilizing the historical (i.e. economic) activity of the three persons, in which he situates the church: "it is the mission of the Son and the Spirit through the Father that includes the church, creating a church as it goes on its way."[54] Thus, the broader context of the church's being and life is the trinitarian history of God, in the openness of the Trinity. Accordingly, *CPS* lays some of the groundwork for his later explicit social doctrine of the Trinity found in *TKG*. For the present chapter, it remains to be seen how his doctrine of hope grounds his ecclesiological insights.

His understanding of trinitarian openness to history is consequential for a proper understanding of his ecclesiology, as well as his doctrine of hope. The sending formula of the Trinity applies to the sending of the church: "If the church sees itself to be sent in the same framework as the Father's sending the Son and the Holy Spirit, then it also sees itself in the framework of God's history with the world and discovers its place and function within this history."[55] It follows from the close relationship between human history and trinitarian history via the work of the Spirit that participation in the trinitarian history of God is a source of hope

---

51. This is perhaps, supreme in the event of the cross, which is discussed in ch. 2, above and ch. 4, below.
52. *FC* 88; see also Conyers, *God, Hope, and History*, 144ff.
53. *CPS* 64.
54. Ibid.
55. Ibid., 11.

for ecclesiology.[56] It is not surprising that Moltmann takes this tack for understanding the church; for, he asserted previously:

> In religious experience hope is turned around. Here we realize that God is not simply the point of our hope in heaven, but that we are his hope on earth. In such experiences man attains the unforgettable impression that he is, together with other people and this whole creation, the utopia of God ... With the experiment "man" and the experiment "world" God has joined a hope.[57]

The reason that this notion of God's trinitarian history is a resource for explicating hope has been detailed in Part I: wherever God is present, there is hope. The Trinity is open to the world seeking unification and glorification, and the church is formed by the promised future (*Zukunft*), regardless of the present failings of the planned future (*Futurum*) that it seeks to help bring about,[58] because at all points the church can affirm that God's ultimate goal is an eschatological glorification, which can be neither prevented nor avoided.[59] The church finds its existence and participation in the trinitarian history of God and is given both the power and paradigm to "go forth outside the camp."

"Let Us Go Forth Outside the Camp"[60]

The church is eschatologically driven by hope as it participates in the history of God: "In the relationship between hope and experience the "nature of the church" is conceived *teleologically* as the inner force that drives it."[61] It should be noted that Moltmann avoids an escapist dualism seeking to retreat from either the present into the future,[62] or from soci-

---

56. Ibid., 198: "we understand this mediation of eschatology and history as the presence of the Holy Spirit."

57. *EH* 27; see also "The Blessing of Hope," 150, 155.

58. This construct is implicit in much of Moltmann's theology; for explicit comments, see especially *HP* 178–99; "Progress and Abyss," 3–26.

59. *CPS* 20, 55–56. What God promises will occur (*ET* 54ff.).

60. Heb 13:13, as quoted in *HP* 146.

61. *CPS* 25.

62. *HC* 130: "Eschatological hope comprises in fact both soul and body, both the individual and society, both heaven and earth."

ety into the convent.⁶³ The church participates in the trinitarian history of God, and is on mission as the exodus community, going forth out of the camp, in at least two ways: one general, one specific. Generally, the church is led in the power of the Spirit through the "wilderness," that is, the present. Specifically, the church must exodus out of captivity to the state. Both of these are handled in turn.⁶⁴

Throughout *CPS*, Moltmann asserts that the church is guided by the event of cross and resurrection and, so, involved in the trinitarian history of God. This involvement prescribes numerous practical corrections, namely an alteration of ecclesial practice and resistance to the state. Yet, what needs to be seen is that these practices are fundamentally determined by his policy of relating the church's existence to the cross and resurrection.⁶⁵ The resurrection alters the church's existence, ensuring that life is "celebrated as the feast of freedom, as joy in existence and as the ecstasy of bliss,"⁶⁶ while the cross serves to sustain the present failures and sufferings, which take place in the present. Indeed, a coherent hope methodology, based in both cross and resurrection, grounds Moltmann's ecclesiology so that the church is the community of hope.

THE CHURCH IN THE POWER OF THE RESURRECTION

In ecclesiological terms, the event of cross and resurrection "evokes conflicts between the powers of the past and the forces of the future, between oppression and liberation."⁶⁷ Moltmann's language reveals the underlying and necessary tension of relating the church to both the cross and resurrection. Thus, the church is variously described as "the exodus church" and "the new *eschatological exodus*," because "Christian faith is alive in the steadfastness of hope."⁶⁸ Indeed, his view of the church "going forth" is properly understood as a "parallel" to the Old Testament exodus,⁶⁹ which, of course, is paradigmatic for God's people by stressing

---

63. *BP* 82–94; *CPS* 93: "This cross-like form of the church cannot be achieved through a mysticism withdrawn from the world."

64. His appeals to wilderness and exodus are reminiscent of *TH*.

65. O'Donnell states that "anticipation and resistance" are the "key words" for understanding the work of the Spirit; *Trinity and Temporality*, 122.

66. *CPS* 109; see also "God's Kingdom," 103.

67. *CPS* 83; see also Tripole, "Ecclesiological Developments," 19ff.

68. *TH* V, *CPS* 83, *HP* 26, respectively.

69. For more on the "exodus church," see especially *CPS* 76–85.

God's faithfulness.[70] Christianity is not a religion of "equilibrium and harmony but ... of conflict and hope."[71] And because he parallels this "going forth" with the resurrection, this understanding is further substantiated[72] by his insistence that this history is lived in and by the power of the Spirit, who is the "Spirit of the resurrection." This understanding of the Spirit's role is not merely added to his prior understanding of the church (from *TH*), but rather transforms it. Indeed, what may have been latent previously is no longer: God's participation "gives man an unambiguous certainty of hope precisely at the place and time when he can see no future ahead."[73] His ecclesiology is heavily informed by his initial impulse of resurrection power, by making it clear that the church is necessarily informed by the resurrecting power of God, which refuses to allow present suffering to lead to a fatalistic outlook, encouraging defeatism. Because the church is involved in the trinitarian history of God, its missionary objective is not the apex of history.[74] This perspective is certainly in part due to his view that the "Spirit of resurrection" is not limited to the church, but is active as the "power of life" for all humanity and creation.[75] This eschewal of ecclesiological triumphalism is advanced by his assertion that the church is not the goal of God's dealings in history, but rather is one element involved in them.[76]

This is not, however, an ecclesiology that consistently prioritizes triumph over perseverance: hope involves the perception and acceptance

---

70. *HP* 146, 148.

71. *CJF* 96; contextually he is discussing the contemporary effect the Exodus has on the "three Abrahamic religions."

72. *HG* 60–1.

73. *EH* 27.

74. Moltmann insists there are other "saving efficacies of the Spirit outside the church" (*CPS* 65). It is difficult to tell whether Moltmann intends this view of the church as reduced or perhaps simply re-focused, compared with more exclusivist ecclesiologies (see *CPS* 348–51).

75. *HP* 22.

76. *CPS* 84: "Its aim is not to spread the Christian religion or to implant the church; it is to liberate the people for the exodus in the name of the coming kingdom"; for a critique of this view, see Bauckham, *Moltmann*, 136–37.
  While this may be a cryptic critique of Catholicism, it does seem to necessarily downgrade the actual role of the church in both society and the kingdom. Regarding the latter half of this statement, see Meeks, *Origins*, 160–61.

of suffering.[77] This is perhaps the most obvious "test" of whether the cross has been adequately integrated into his ecclesiology. The church's existence is marked by suffering and lived in hope: "the confession of hope, the missionary process in which the gospel involves the nations and the obedient acceptance of the cross of the present [is] in the 'power of the resurrection.'"[78] Because the resurrection is "unconcluded *ad opera*" it "exhibits a new reality which does not yet exist."[79]

THE CHURCH UNDER THE CROSS

The fact that Moltmann's theology is heuristic and not static is displayed in his ecclesiology.[80] One can see the effect of his "turn" to the cross has on his understanding of the church, evidenced most clearly by the fact that he takes his initial description from *TH* of the "exodus church" and creatively adds to it, while avoiding supplanting it, in *CPS*: "The true church is 'the church under the cross.'"[81] Indeed, Moltmann specifies that the origin and praxis of the church is the cross.[82]

While there are similarities between *TH* and *CPS* regarding ecclesiology, the distinctive difference in his more mature ecclesiology is his focus on relating the church to the cross. Indeed, while "exodus church" is still applicable, "under the cross" is equally apt for Moltmann's vision of the church, not in formal terms alone, but also in substantive content: "Only by virtue of its remembrance of the one who was crucified can the church live in the presence of the one who is risen—that is to say, can live realistically in hope. The church only follows the promise of Christ and the trend of the Spirit when it accepts its own cross."[83] The church is guided by the messianic future of the risen Christ. An even stronger emphasis can be maintained at this point. In 1978, Moltmann shows how the theses of *TH* and *CG* impact the church: "Diakonia as servanthood under the cross means, therefore, to participate in

77. *HP* 178.

78. Ibid., 20. Moltmann might clarify this by making the connection stronger: the church suffers because it lives in hope.

79. Ibid.

80. See especially *HP* vii-viii.

81. *CPS* 65.

82. Ibid., 89; see especially "The Passion of Christ and the Suffering of God," 26–28.

83. *CPS* 26.

suffering, to accept suffering, and to take on the suffering of others. Such service involves the daily death of the ego and its anxieties. Service under the cross happens in the presence and power of the Resurrected One. For it is only the resurrection hope that makes us ready for selfless love and dying."[84] An important lesson from *CG* is applied to the church. God is on the side of the abandoned, because he has taken up suffering abandonment into the life of the Trinity, and overcome it in the history of the Son.[85] Thus, God's suffering love is an instantiation of hope for the church, because where there is suffering, there is God: "He humbles himself and takes upon himself the eternal death of the godless and the godforsaken, so that all the godless and the godforsaken can experience communion with him."[86] This is why Moltmann maintains: "the anticipation of Christian hope is living and effective only in representing those who have no future."[87] While not negating his understanding from *TH*, in *CG* Moltmann adds a new defining mark of the exodus community, labeling it the "church of the crucified."[88] Indeed it is *CG* that posited the passion of God in the cross as the ground of hope.[89] On this count, Moltmann's ecclesiology seeks to maintain the dialectical unity of the "exodus community" and "the church of the crucified," by insisting that both labels apply. Along with his correct avoidance of prioritizing triumph, Moltmann does not espouse flee-the-present escapism: "Remembrance of the crucified Jesus forbids us to see and use this feast of his resurrection as a flight from earthly conditions of suffering."[90] Yet equally, he does not espouse lethargic resignation when faced with suffering. Because his ecclesiology is informed by his doctrine of hope, when discussing the final mark of the church (suffering), he finds it necessary to mention the resurrection:

84. *HC* 31. The penultimate sentence seems oddly related to Jesus and not the Holy Spirit; see also *CPS* 55.

85. *CG* 277: "Life in communion with Christ is full of life in the trinitarian situation of God. Dead in Christ and raised to new life, as Paul says in Rom. 6:8, the believer really participates in the suffering of the love of God. Conversely, he takes particular suffering of the word, because God has made it his suffering in the cross of his Son."

86. Ibid., 276.

87. *FC* 54.

88. *CG* 52; see also *OC* 82ff.

89. Beyond *CG*, see also *PPL* 113–26.

90. *CPS* 112. See also *HD* 210: "Hope in the kingdom of God makes persons capable of suffering and ready for the future."

> Even though the apostolate is so strongly eschatologically determined by the Easter appearances of the risen Christ, it is equally strongly determined by suffering and sacrifice in discipleship of the Christ who was crucified . . . The fellowship of Christ does not only determine the content of the apostolate; it determines its form in history as well . . . The church is apostolic when it takes up its cross. It then witnesses to the glory of the risen Christ in its fellowship with those who suffer . . .[91]

The christological direction of Moltmann's ecclesiology is most easily found in his emphasis on the suffering of the church. The obvious strength of this proposal is that Moltmann insists that following Christ entails suffering.[92] This, of course, is an application of the main tenets of *CG*, in which he insists that God is active in the present, and open to suffering. Accordingly, there is no incidence of present suffering which is distant from God. Suffering exists in the trinitarian history: "Those who cry out to God in their suffering in essence join in Jesus' dying cry, 'My God, why have you forsaken me?'" When they recognize this, they also recognize that God is not that dark adversary in heaven to whom they cry, but in a very personal sense is the human brother who cries with them and the Spirit which cries in them and will cry for them when they are put to silence."[93] It is because the church exists in the power of the Spirit that the church can go outside of the camp, in hope: "Christianity has continuity in history in so far as it, through hope, reaches out beyond itself. Not in self-preservation but in self-abandonment does Christianity acquire continuance."[94] Indeed, the church gives itself to abandonment, knowing in hope, "that it is 'persecuted, but not forsaken; struck down, but not destroyed; always carrying in the body the death of Jesus, so that the life of Jesus also may be manifested in our bodies' (II Cor. 4.9, 10)."[95] Thus, instances of suffering enigmatically become the place of hope, because suffering ensures God's presence: "If God lives

---

91. *CPS* 361; see also *HP* 145–47. He elaborates on the four-fold description of the church as "the One, Holy, Catholic and Apostolic Church" by developing them into marks of the church. He creatively transposes apostolic succession and identification into the succession of the passion of Christ (*CPS* 360).

92. *GHH* 50ff.

93. *GHH* 75; see also *TKG* 120–21; and for the importance of the cry for Moltmann's own experience as a prisoner of war, see "The Blessing of Hope," 148.

94. *HP* 146–47.

95. Ibid., 147.

among us, he journeys with us too ... If he suffers with us he gives us the assurance of God and ourselves in the great exile of this world."[96]

The Church in Dialectical Tension

Overcoming the one-sidedness of *TH* and *CG*, Moltmann's ecclesiology is determined by both.[97] (As mentioned in Part I, this one-sidedness was purposeful, but *CPS* is less one-sided, arguably because both key insights from *TH* and *CG* are present, and the dialectic maintained.) While colored in a pneumatological light, it is the dialectical unity of the cross and resurrection together that determines the constitutive identity of the church's exodus activity. As such, the church is given the power of exodus by the Spirit of the resurrection. Indeed, the whole point of his (much maligned and misunderstood) rejection of the understanding of the resurrection as "historical" in *TH* applies here: the resurrection "has a confronting impact on the present, opening up the eschatological history of eternal life in the midst of this world of death."[98] This concern is fundamentally determined by the dialectic that was the focus of *TH* and *CG*. Recall that in *TH* he identified the ground of hope accordingly:

> in all the qualitative difference of cross and resurrection Jesus is the same. This identity in infinite contradiction is theologically understood as an event of identification, an act of the faithfulness of God. It is this that forms the ground of the promise of the still outstanding future of Jesus Christ. It is this that is the ground of the hope which carries faith through the trials of the god-forsaken world and of death.[99]

God's faithfulness in the cross and resurrection is the ground of hope. Since the church is grounded in the cross and resurrection, its mission is only intelligible in relation to both. With faith in the resurrection, the

---

96. *GSS* 19.

97. On the issue of one-sidedness, see *HTG* 174–6. Paul, Moltmann's favorite New Testament writer, presents the theme of hope in Romans 8. Yet, Richard Hays points out that Paul places a qualifier on Christian hope, including suffering as a caveat: "the eschatological perspective allows Paul to counsel a high tolerance for ambiguity. Suffering and joy are present together, and the church should expect this paradoxical condition to persist until the parousia" (Hays, *The Moral Vision of the New Testament*, 26). Moltmann is cognizant of this fact (see *CPS* 85–104; *OC* 85–112).

98. "The Blessing of Hope," 152. Interestingly, he labels the resurrection "historical" in this instance (published in 2005).

99. *TH* 85.

church can endure suffering, knowing that in the midst of active suffering God is also present. The dialectical tension of living in hope of the promised resurrection while in the midst of suffering and death is the core of his ecclesiology. His view of the exodus church under the cross is perhaps best exemplified by assessing his adjudication of the proper understanding of Christian religion. While following Christ entails being open to, indeed expecting, suffering, Moltmann invited further opportunity for this result because of his call for the church to maintain distance from the state: "The truth of the gospel is also expressed more in conflict that in general appeasement. At any rate, Jesus did not talk of appeasement."[100]

Religion: Civil or Voluntary?

A more concrete application of the church leaving the camp is his relentless criticism of civil religion.[101] He taught this lesson in both *TH* and in *CG*, and he builds on it in *CPS*. Generally, *TH* propounded the view that existing power structures are not ultimate and will be replaced, while *CG* rather vividly impugns state power by assessing the crucifixion from the angle of the *Imperium Romanum*, where Jesus is put to death as a political rebel.[102] Indeed, the political dimension of Jesus' crucifixion makes clear the lines of demarcation through the incisive question: "Christ—or Caesar?"[103]

Moltmann's criticism of civil religion, which he equates with Constantinian religion, is central to his ecclesiology, which is strongly informed by his hope: "The assimilation of Christianity to bourgeois society always means that the cross is forgotten and hope is lost."[104] The church does not serve the state's interest, but rather needs to maintain critical distance. Superficially, Constantinian religion may be deemed the pinnacle of Christianity's expansion, reach and influence, but

---

100. *GHH* 23; contextually, he is commenting on the need of the church to be opposed to nuclear proliferation.

101. Rasmusson's monograph is an exemplary critical study of Moltmann's rejection of civil religion, but it is telling that he rarely discusses the impact Moltmann's understanding of the cross and resurrection has on his ecclesiology (for an exception, see especially Rasmusson, *Church as Polis*, 109).

102. *CG* 128–45, 325–29.

103. Ibid., 145.

104. Ibid., 58.

Moltmann concludes that ultimately it must be deemed detrimental, because of its effect: the church "had to take on the role of being a unifying state religion for the Roman empire. But as what—the fellowship of Jesus or the religious system that complemented the prevailing social system?"[105] Indeed, the overt expansion of Christianity via supporting the political and civil status quo is deemed entirely contradictory by Moltmann. The point that needs to be made for the present study is that his conclusions are rooted in his prior development of hope, especially related to his turn to the cross, which showed him the nature of political power: "the crucified Christ shows what is really wrong with this world."[106] This is the clearest impression made by his doctrine of hope on ecclesiology.[107]

He rejects infant baptism because it presupposes and supports civil religion, strongly inveighing against any baptismal practice that equates involuntary church association with a state church, because it renders the church an institution that people "belong to" simply as passive registrants based on a past act.[108] Furthermore, his rejection of infant baptism is of one piece with his desire to see the church abandon state ties, in order to avoid becoming an accommodating "tool" for society's benefit.[109] Continuing on from his paradigm of the exodus church, he claims that as long as the church is a state church, it is civil religion, and thus by definition needs liberation from its "Babylonian captivity."[110] In contrast, Moltmann strongly supports the voluntary church, wherein people identify not primarily with a (state) church, but with Christ: "baptism means the public confession of one's new identity in Christ

---

105. *HC* 40. This is similar to his emphasis on praxis over theory (see especially *ET* 294–95). Moltmann has high praise for voluntary congregations, unwedded to the state. It is rather ironic, then, that in the U.S. (a country which typifies this model) some church's (typically conservative ones) are seeking to, in part, reverse this distance so they may have more influence.

106. *FC* 53.

107. See *ET* 366 n. 3; also see Irish, "Moltmann's Theology of Contradiction," 21.

108. *CPS* 226–42, 314; *OC* 124–5; *HC* 47–51.

109. Later he claims (without source attribution): "Even today, over 80% of the German people 'belong' to one or other of the churches, but only 10–15% attend the church to which they 'belong'"; *GSS* 200.

110. See *FC* 106ff.

(Col. 3.3)."¹¹¹ His exposure to "voluntary religion" certified his conviction that civil religion is a deficient form of the church.¹¹² In terms made popular by recent christological debates, he prefers the model of the congregation "from below" compared with understanding it as "a divine institution 'from above.'"¹¹³ Indeed, Moltmann's ecclesiology seeks a "grass-roots level" renewal of the church, where the laity reclaim "the gifts of the Spirit," which will decrease the hierarchical structure.¹¹⁴ For Moltmann, service under the cross does not involve only the clergy.¹¹⁵ While he concurs with Luther's stress on "the priesthood of all believers,"¹¹⁶ Moltmann's ecclesiology draws on "the so-called left-wing" of the Reformation.¹¹⁷ He wants to renew the church by abandoning practices associated with the Constantinian era, which, he asserts, merely serve the state and the institutional ecclesial hierarchal powers that be.¹¹⁸ He laments that such practices "turned a persecuted faith into a 'permitted religion' and ... made it 'the official religion.'"¹¹⁹ The trouble

---

111. *HC* 51; see also *CPS* 225; this sounds like "believer's baptism," but this he rejects, seemingly because it is rooted in the individual's decision of faith, which Moltmann rejects as a basis for salvation (see especially *CoG* 235–55).

112. "Theology in Germany Today," 190–91. See *TH* ch. 5; see also *CPS* 334; "The Challenge of Religion in the '80s: How My Mind has Changed," 466–67. Terminologically, it is important to not that the term used by Moltmann typically is "Evangelical" which virtually always equals "Protestant, not Catholic" in his writings (see *GSS* 191).

113. *GSS* 201; "from above" seems to be code for the Catholic church. He adds a qualifier, pointing to the "irony" that "it should be the Catholic base communities in Latin America which today are" congregational in the Reformation sense (201). On his preference for Protestantism, see *GSS* 191–208.

114. *HC* 21.

115. For Moltmann's relentless rejection of a clergy/laity split, see *CPS* xvi, 2, *OC* 98ff.; *HC* 21, 45, 132; *SoL* 95; "Christianity in the Third Millennium," 80.

116. *GSS* 196; see also *OC* 113–26; *FC* 108–9; "From the Beginning of Time in God's Presence," 56; "What is a Theologian?" 194.

117. Often dubbed the radical reformers: "They were called 'Schwärmer' and 'baptists' and 'sectarians,' but they were rejected" (*OC* 117; *Schwärmer*: enthusiasts, fanatics); see also "Is Protestantism the 'Religion of Freedom'?" 36ff; *PPL* 160–66.

118. This was an emphasis in *CG* as well, where Moltmann used the trial and crucifixion of Jesus to show the necessary reversal of values as they relate to the power structures of the state (*CG* 325–26). Moltmann asserts that "[f]aith in 'the crucified God' robs power and fortune of the careless confidence from which they live and the superstitious fear which is the basis of their rule" (*CG* 154). For a critique of these aspects of Moltmann's theology, see Wright, *Disavowing Constantine*, VI–VII.

119. "The Life Signs of the Spirit," 39–40.

with "civil religion," which its antidote "voluntary religion" avoids, is mingling the interests of the state with the interests of the church: "When religion, church and faith are considered only from the standpoint of their expediency and usefulness for society, they are bound to vanish as soon as the purposes of society can be served by other means."[120] To be sure, the relatively recent historical background of Moltmann's call for critical distance between the state and church is the alternative reactions to the totalitarian state of the Nationalist Socialist dictatorship in Germany (Hitler seized power in 1933), of which two reactions stand out:[121] the Confessing Church's "resistance," explicitly found in the 1934 Barmen Theological Declaration, contrasted with the Lutheran "neutrality" expounded in the Ansbach Decree of 1935.[122] In this instance, "resistance" is rooted in the lordship of Christ in all matters, while "neutrality" is rooted in the "two kingdoms" doctrine.[123] Moltmann believes that the "two kingdoms" doctrine is deceptive, since remaining neutral to the (in)decisions and (in)actions of the state, is, in the final analysis, not indecision, but rather passive acquiescence which while not in intent, but in practice, *ipso facto* always a decision for the state: while formally espousing neutrality, the church is actually aligned with the state, evidenced by a loss in ability to be critical. Espousing neutrality effectively muzzles the church. While viewing state action as hermetically sealed off from church adjudication gives the appearance of separation between church and state, the result is too often a collating of state and church interests: where society is "Christianized," eventually the Church takes "over the functions of the socially essential 'state religion.' The community of Christians and the community of citizens coincided."[124]

His policy of criticizing civil religion is neither accidental nor random; it is integral to his theology. His promotion of a voluntary church, consciously refusing to be wedded to the state is essentially an applica-

---

120. *TJ* 78.

121. There is a third option, which is really none at all: Carl Schmitt's "justification" of Hitler (see *CG* 339 n. 19; *GSS* 25–6, 39–42; *ET* 304, 379 n. 4).

122. See *HD* 81–96 and *HD* 61–77, respectively; see also "Theology in Germany Today," 198–200; *BP* 47.

123. As Moltmann shows, there is not one such doctrine, but many variations of the one, used in various ways (*HD* 63; see also *GSS* 40).

124. *CPS* 224.

tion of this policy and is the logical outworking of the fundamental core of his wider theology.¹²⁵ Moltmann insists that the church can best fulfill the function of embodying the unity of the cross and resurrection by maintaining critical distance from state control or coercion. It was in *CG* that Moltmann most clearly articulated the abuse of state power, evidenced by the crucifixion of Jesus.¹²⁶ In *CPS* this is taken up to call on the church's "liberation from the idols of power,"¹²⁷ insisting that "a missionary church cannot be apolitical."¹²⁸

The church needs critical distance from the state based on one central event, and for two practical reasons.¹²⁹ The central event is the cross of Christ. As shown in *CG*, Golgotha brought into question every aspect of Jesus' ministry, while also questioning the abuse of state power.¹³⁰ The impending result of this, as Moltmann clearly shows, is the nec-

---

125. A closely aligned and equally fruitful example of Moltmann's ecclesiology as rooted in the cross and resurrection is his concern that the church be an open fellowship, which he describes as a church of the people, not for the people (see especially *CPS* 93ff.; *OC* 98–102; *RRF* 141; *HG* 60; *GHH* 19, 50; *HC* 20, 40–42, 45; *WJC* 148; *ET* 147, 262–67). For Moltmann, a church *for* the people is "run" by the ordained, whereas a church *of* the people is a congregation modeled on Jesus' example. In this context, he often refers to the *ochlos*, the common people (UBS⁴); in contrast to the "manifest" church of believers, the poor comprise the "latent" church (*ET* 266; see also "The Passion of Christ and the Suffering of God," 27). For secondary comments, see Bauckham, *Moltmann*, 159–60 nn. 3–4 = *Theology of Jürgen Moltmann*, 130–31 nn. 9–10; J. Stephen Rhodes, "The Church as the Community of Open Friendship," 41–9; Martin Tripole, "A Church for the Poor and the World: At Issue with Moltmann's Ecclesiology," 645–60.

Additionally, Moltmann also has a concern for the handicapped. (On a personal level, his interest is enhanced by the fact that his older brother "was severely disabled" [*SoL* 67; see also *EJM* 44].) For his two essays on the societal problem of the "non-handicapped" relating to the "handicapped" (he disputes the validity of both terms), see *Diakonie im Horizont des Reiches Gottes*, III and IV: "Die Rehabilition Behinderter in einer Segregationsgesellschaft," 42–51; "Befreit Euch—Nehmt einander an," 52–73. He approvingly quotes the World Council of Churches: "Congregations without disabled members are disabled congregations" ("Befreit Euch," 71; see also *PPL* 152–54; *SpL* 192–93).

126. See *CG* IV.

127. *CPS* 89ff.

128. Ibid., 15.

129. See *GSS* 39ff.

130. See also "Civil Religion," 14ff. To be sure, in the case of Jesus' crucifixion, the religious leaders did not merely go along with the state, but rather used the state's means for their own ends.

essary separation of church and state.[131] While Moltmann vehemently advocates such separation, his ecclesiology should not be read as advocating the church's withdrawal from the public square of civil life; he argues precisely the opposite, because of this separation.[132]

Conclusion

Hope in the Church

Typically, Moltmann's theology, and perhaps especially his ecclesiology, is considered from the angle of ethics and praxis.[133] Instead of surveying these issues, this chapter attempted to uncover the determining theological rationale of Moltmann's ecclesiology. This was spotlighted in his call for the church to "go forth out of the camp." All dimensions of his understanding of the church in the trinitarian history of God, to varying degrees, inform his understanding of hope, as they are reciprocally grounded in the cross and resurrection. "The church in the power of the Holy Spirit," writes Moltmann, "is not yet the kingdom of God, but it is its anticipation in history."[134] Ultimately, both *TH* and *CG* positively and profoundly shape the ecclesiological vision Moltmann presents in *CPS*: "The church lives in the history which finds its substantiation in the resurrection of the crucified Christ and whose future is the all-embracing kingdom of freedom. The living remembrance of Christ directs the church's hope towards the kingdom, and living hope in the kingdom leads back to the inexhaustible remembrance of Christ."[135] His call for the church's mission in the history of the triune God in *CPS* calls for elaboration on this history.[136] The church involved in the history of the trinitarian God of the Christian faith is both a hoping church, and the embodiment of hope, grounded in the resurrection of the crucified

---

131. These are not the terms used by Moltmann always, but they are adequate for a 21st century discussion.

132. See *CPS* 342ff.; see also the numerous salient essays in *GSS*.

133. See above, p. xxii n. 15.

134. *CPS* 196.

135. *CPS* 197. Seemingly, one could argue that Part I should have been centered on *TH, CG,* and *CPS,* by arguing that the trilogy is the proper ground of hope. At one point I held this view, but ultimately determined that the ground of hope in the dialectical identity of the crucified and resurrected one is antecedent to all other doctrines.

136. See *FC* 94.

Christ. In this way *CPS* serves as an apt concluding volume to the trilogy as it helps him to transition from the consciously "one-sided" texts to the more "systematic contributions."

In the chapter following, Moltmann's doctrine of God is discussed as presented in *TKG*. Before publishing *TKG*, however, he addresses a variety of issues in the intervening five years (between *CPS* and *TKG*), which help foreground his formal dogmatics.

Transition Period: The Early Trilogy to the Contributions

Between *CPS* and *TKG* Moltmann switched methodologies for his programmatic writings.[137] He moves from the one-sided approach that views all of theology from one angle to what he calls "systematic contributions" (published from 1980–2000), a method not unlike a formal systematic theology, yet begun with an admission of non-comprehensiveness. A few topics are relevant in this period of transition and are discussed briefly.

Hope

In his 1976 "Open Letter" to José Miguez Bonino, Moltmann makes a salient comment about the character of hope.[138] In light of Moltmann's negative assessment of the then-current world political and economic situation,[139] he asserts: "The signs of destruction are increasing. Our hope can no longer afford to be childish and enthusiastic. In common resistance to evil and the flunkies that serve death it must become mature and steady. However we analyze our situation, hope is faithfulness to the resurrection and therefore perseverance in the cross. One learns this

---

137. *BP* 286.

138. He later recants his sharpest criticism of liberation theology as "presentist"; see "Response to the Essays," 134; however, see his rather critical questions from about the same time (*ET* 298–99).

139. This closing sentiment is expressed following his recollection of two events: the first he mentions occurred in December 1974 when "32 leading Protestant church officials greeted the power grab of the military junta in Chile as 'God's answer to the prayers of all believers who see in Marxism a satanic power.'... The God of Jesus Christ does not answer the prayers of those who believe in him through the execution of more than 10,000 poor people." Second, in January 1975 the socialist Yugoslavian government "discontinued the world-renowned journal *Praxis*" and fired eight university teachers associated with the journal ("Open Letter," 62–63).

among the people, in the community of the poor . . ."[140] For Moltmann, following the 1979 General Assembly of the Evangelical churches in Germany, hope is rooted in the "call to hope" or "the command to hope" in the midst of fear and anxiety.[141] The tenor of a self-conscious theology "after Auschwitz" is recognizable: "Christians betrayed their own future and buried their own hopes in Auschwitz . . . The key to the rebirth of our hope is to be found in Auschwitz."[142] While Moltmann's comments are open to misinterpretation if pressed too literally, the overall intent is clear, even if the wording is not: Christian hope's rebirth is to be found only when it adequately addresses Auschwitz. Elie Wiesel's influence is clear as Moltmann states: "Where the Jewish people of hope were annihilated, the Christian hope was annihilated too."[143] (As a precursor, it is instructive to know that Moltmann "actively" entered the Jewish-Christian dialogue in 1976.)[144]

The 1977 Turning Point

In 1976 Moltmann was "eager to experience that which is different and strange," specifically citing African theology, Japanese theology and North American Black theology.[145] There are consequences to such eagerness, he learned. Recalling the lessons learned from the intervening period between 1975 and 1980, he admits that those years allowed him to encounter different theologies, which also brought with it the "painful and then liberating"[146] realization of his inability "to frame a 'theology in context' and a 'theology in movement' (liberation theology, black theology, feminist theology), for I am not living in the Third World, am not oppressed and am not a woman."[147] At a conference he attended in October 1977[148] in Mexico City, Latin American liberation theologians

---

140. "Open Letter," 63; see also Cabestrero, *Faith*, 124.

141. *EG* 19–21; see also *CJF* 16ff., 37ff.

142. *EG* 22.

143. Ibid.; compare, however his late comment: hope "can be frustrated but never extinguished" ("Theology in Germany Today," 198).

144. *HTG* 179.

145. "Open Letter," 57; see also *ET* 183–267.

146. *HTG* 180.

147. *TKG* vii; these comments are from his May 1990 "Preface to the Paperback edition"; see also *WJC* 65; *HTG* 179–80.

148. 1977 is the cited date in at least seven places: *HTG* 180; *How I Have Changed*, 19–20; *ET* 219; "Response to the Essays," 133; Falcke, "Phantasie für das Reich Gottes,"

attempted "to crucify" him, as James Cone described it.¹⁴⁹ Moltmann then made a decision to write the "contributions": "I wanted to overcome my 'one-sidedness' and concentrate on the long-term problems of theology. I no longer wanted to be so controversial."¹⁵⁰ Afterward, Moltmann sees even more clearly the areas of disagreement with the liberation theologians he once thought had a similar orientation and identifies the distance between his own theology and liberation theology.¹⁵¹ At a conference on practical theology in 1978,¹⁵² Moltmann concludes his "Response" with these stinging words: "From the Catholic theologians of liberation we have as yet heard little criticism of the dogma of infallibility. How can a church which does not itself exhibit freedom free peoples?"¹⁵³

RELATING THE EARLY TRILOGY TO THE CONTRIBUTIONS

Moltmann clearly summarizes the relationship between the early trilogy and the contributions: "After a phase of self-critical and positive disengagement in 1977 and 1978 I concentrated on my own "contribution to systematic theology." I am no longer describing the whole of theology at a contemporary focal point, but presenting my part of theology as a contribution to a shared whole."¹⁵⁴ In the late 1970s the task of theology for Moltmann is "[t]o understand God in His trinitarian history"

---

156 (relying on both Moltmann and Müller-Fahrenholz); José Míguez Bonino, "Reading Jürgen Moltmann from Latin America," 106–7; Müller-Fahrenholz, *Kingdom and Power*, 123ff. Alternatively, 1978 is cited in "Adventure of Theological Ideas," 102, and by Chapman, "On Being Human," 69 (following Moltmann's "Adventure" essay). While 1977 has the weight of primary and secondary scholarship, searches to verify the correct year of the conference were fruitless. Decisive, perhaps, is Míguez Bonino's verification, since he participated.

149. See *ET* 219; Müller-Fahrenholz, *Kingdom and Power*, 123.

150. *How I Have Changed*, 20; see *HTG* 180; he labels each text of the trilogy as "one-sided" (*DGG* 166).

151. See "Love, Death, Eternal Life," 4; José Míguez Bonino, "Love and Social Transformation in Liberation Theology," in Burnham, McCoy, and Meeks, *Love: The Foundation of Hope*, 76 n. 18.

152. The 43rd annual Ministers' Week "A Theology of Hope and Parish Practice" at Candler School of Theology, Emory University.

153. *HC* 136; he is also critical of Erik Peterson for criticizing monotheism as a ground of hierarchy (clerical monotheism), yet also converting to Catholicism (*ET* 303–4).

154. *HTG* 168.

explicitly over against the understanding of God as a supreme substance and God as absolute subject.[155] What are the resources for such a task? Moltmann answers with three foci: "Reflection upon the alterability, capacity for suffering, and trinitarian liveliness of God."[156] Here, of course, is a move springing from the strong link he forges between the cross and God, articulated so boldly in *CG*.

Indeed, in 1979, Moltmann is fully cognizant of the direction to which his early trilogy points: "the goal of those three books, whose kind and method should not be continued, is a re-organization of the theological system to a Messianic Dogmatics, in which, under that leading viewpoint of the Trinity and the Kingdom of God, the way is taken from history to freedom. Therein the content of these three books is not abolished [*nicht aufgehoben*] . . ."[157] While he wants to be less controversial, he does not call the "one-sided" trilogy into question.[158] Instead, he sees the texts helpful and fruitful in their own right, "correctly characterized as more pastoral and prophetic than systematic and professorial."[159]

Now begins the investigation of Moltmann's dogmatics, which he labels "systematic contributions." Switching methods he ceases looking at "*the whole of theology in one focal point*" and instead embarks on the long-term issues in theology.[160] Of this project he writes (in 1985): "My systematic contributions set out to discuss in a definite systematic sequence complexes of important concepts and doctrines in Christian theology. In calling them contributions I want to indicate that I do not plan a total system or a dogmatics of pure and universal doctrine."[161] Back in 1975 he asserted the primacy of the Trinity: "Christian theology is hence, inescapably and of inner necessity, trinitarian theology; and only trinitarian theology is Christian theology."[162] And so, it is fitting that the first offering of this agenda is *TKG*, his doctrine of God.

---

155. "Theology in Germany Today," 205; *TKG* 64.
156. "Theology in Germany Today," 205.
157. *DGG* 168; later he labels his contributions "Messianic Theology" (*GC* xvii).
158. *DGG* 166.
159. Ibid., 166–67.
160. *HTG* 180; italics original.
161. Ibid., 180.
162. *FC* 81.

4

Trinitarian Doctrine as Hope

Introduction

In *TKG*, the first volume of his "systematic contributions to theology," Moltmann explores the social trinitarian doctrine of God.[1] While the themes in *TKG* are reminiscent of *CG*, *TKG* is not mere repetition, but rather elaboration of the earlier material.[2] Previously, Moltmann constructed a theology of the cross attacking both atheism and theism, and also the Greek philosophical notions of God as impassible and immutable that underpin them; now, however, he aims centrally at the notion of the absolute subject, with the goal of "surmounting" monotheism.[3]

Additionally, in post-*CG* writings he has been explicating the role of the Spirit through an emerging understanding of the social Trinity

---

1. For an adumbration of these contributions, see *TKG* xi; see also *GC* xvii; *BP* 286ff. For secondary discussion on Moltmann's doctrine of the Trinity, see O'Donnell, *Trinity and Temporality*, 108–58.

2. On the differences between *CG* and *TKG*, see *ET* 306. Generally, *CG* opposes theism, while *TKG* opposes monotheism. Compare, however, Moltmann's criticism of monotheism in *CG* (*CG* 246), and criticism of theism in *TKG* (*TKG* 105ff.). Also, the intent is different: while in *CG* the focus is to refute protest atheism, in *TKG* it is to develop a proper doctrine of God. For more detail on these aspects, see O'Donnell, *Trinity and Temporality*, 23ff., 156ff.; Willis, *Theism, Atheism and the Doctrine of the Trinity*.

3. *TKG* 191; to be sure, hints of this direction appear in the former text, where he disagrees with Schleiermacher and H. Richard Niebuhr: "Christianity cannot therefore any longer be represented as a 'monotheistic form of belief' (Schleiermacher). Christian faith is not "radical monotheism" [Niebuhr]" (*CG* 215; see also 235–37, 243); see also "The Motherly Father," 55; this 1981 essay is reissued in a slightly different form in *HTG* (19–25) and has been retranslated; in the second version "monotheism" is changed to "theism" (*HTG* 24).

involved in history,[4] a further advance on his claim that the cross requires a revolution in the concept of God. While in *CG* the cross is set in terms of God's self-giving, principally in terms of the Father abandoning the Son, he purposely avoided explicating a doctrine of God, proper. Although it occupies relatively little explicit attention, one key piece of evidence manifesting the important emergence of pneumatology is Moltmann's devotion to resolving the *Filioque* dispute in *TKG*,[5] believing that a newly formed doctrine of the Trinity goes "hand in hand" with "overcoming the ecclesiastical dispute."[6]

In the opening of *TKG*, he tellingly asks: "Why are most Christians in the West . . . really only 'monotheists' where the experience and

4. While Moltmann has been accused of depicting the cross in mythical terms (see Williams, *On Christian Theology*, 161; Fiddes, *Creative Suffering of God*, 13), this argument will not hold regarding *TKG*. History is a vital concern for Moltmann, although Müller-Fahrenholz overstates its importance by claiming that it is "*the* theme of [his] theology" (Müller-Fahrenholz, *Kingdom and Power*, 230; see also *SW* 111). For Moltmann's understanding of history for the doctrine of God, see Powell, *The Trinity in German Thought*, 248–53. For Moltmann's adoption and alteration of Joachim of Fiore's scheme, see *TKG* 202–12; see also Bauckham, *Theology of Jürgen Moltmann*, 179–82. For a full consideration of Moltmann's view of history (including references to Joachim), see Conyers, *God, Hope, and History*, III–VI; see also Conyers, "History as Problem and Hope," 29–39.

5. *TKG* xv; see also 178–87; "Theological Proposals Towards the Resolution of the Filioque Controversy," 164–73; "The Unity of the Triune God: Remarks on the Comprehensibility of the Doctrine of the Trinity and its Foundation in the History of Salvation," 169–71; *CPS* 55; *HTG* 58–59; *SpL* 292–5; *ET* 307; *BP* 329; for secondary comments, see especially Bernd Oberdorfer, *Filioque: Geschichte und Theologie eines ökumenischen Problems,* 289–403. Moltmann suggests revising the creed: the Spirit proceeds from "the Father of the Son," because "God the Father is always *the Father of the Son*" (*TKG* 183). Some find Moltmann's formula lacking, believing that it does not emphasize enough the Spirit's role in Christ's coming, life and resurrection (see Dietrich Ritschl, "Historical Developments and Implications of the Filioque Controversy," in *Spirit of God, Spirit of Christ*, 65; Pannenberg, *Systematic Theology*, 1:318–19 n. 181). Later, Moltmann picks up this pneumatic role (*SpL* 292ff.; *ET* 307). For a different criticism, see Bauckham, *Theology of Jürgen Moltmann*, 167–8.

6. *TKG* 179. Inveighing against the West, Moltmann joins a recent trend that finds the addition of the *Filioque* uncanonical. On this development, see Jenson, *Systematic Theology*, 1:149; Pannenberg, *Systematic Theology*, 1:318. Among 20th century theologians, defenders of the *Filioque* are Barth (*Church Dogmatics*, I/1:477ff.); Jenson (*Systematic Theology*, 1:146–61); Kasper is more ambivalent, yet finally opposed to altering the tradition, if it is not deemed heretical (*God*, 214–23). Critics include Congar (*I Believe in the Holy Spirit*, 3:206–14); Pannenberg (*Systematic Theology*, 1:317ff.); Rahner ("*Theos* in the New Testament," 146); T. F. Torrance (*The Christian Doctrine of God*, 187–91).

practice of their faith is concerned?"[7] Lamenting the situation, he sets out to show that social trinitarianism is superior to a monotheistic concept of God, which also overcomes Kant's valid critique[8] that the doctrine of the Trinity is vacuous, indeed impractical and irrelevant.[9] Promoting a doctrine of God that dispenses with the linguistic and conceptual usage of supreme substance or absolute subject, Moltmann insists on speaking of three persons in relationship. Related to this is his view that monotheism is an inappropriate label for the Christian doctrine of God, but rather the simplistic result of misplaced reductionism.[10] Moltmann's trinitarian doctrine is developed as hope, grounded fully in the faithfulness of God, but two other dimensions give Moltmann's trinitarian doctrine its more specific shape: negatively, he is rejecting and reacting to Barth's doctrine, most appreciably, and positively he is relying on Hegel's insistence that God is historically involved and in need of the world. These are addressed in turn in the wider context of showing how Moltmann frames his doctrine of God in direct relation to his doctrine of hope.

The Doctrine of God

Moltmann is unsatisfied with those that subscribe to the young Philip Melanchthon's conclusion: "We adore the mysteries of the Godhead.

---

7. *TKG* 1; see also "Trinitarier und Antitrinitarier," 293–94; *SpL* 290–95. For a lucid study showing how christology can be fitted into Jewish monotheism, see Bauckham, *God Crucified*.

8. At first glance he seems to reject Kant's claim, but a closer reading reveals that Moltmann accepts Kant's criticism of the Trinity being vacuous when understood in theistic terms; yet, Moltmann simultaneously believes his theology of the cross rehabilitates the doctrine of the Trinity, rescuing it from precisely the concerns voiced by Kant (see *CG* 240, 246; *FC* 80–81, 96; *JM* 47; *TKG* 6, 62; *WJC* 58–59). See Immanuel Kant, *The Conflict of the Faculties*, 264: "The doctrine of the Trinity, taken literally, has *no practical relevance at all*, even if we think we understand it; and it is even more clearly irrelevant if we realize that it transcends all our concepts."

9. Additionally, Moltmann concurs with Schleiermacher's assertion that "any new version of the doctrine of the Trinity must be 'a transformation which goes right back to its first beginnings.'" For a critical view of Schleiermacher on this point, see *DGG* 182; for a more sympathetic view, see Powell, *Trinity in German Theology*, 87–103.

10. See *TKG* 172ff.; "Kein Monotheismus gleicht dem anderen: Destruktion eines untauglichen Begriffs," 112–22; "Trinitarier und Antitrinitarier," 293–4. For a helpful summary of the different meanings of monotheism, see Tracy, "God as Trinitarian," 77–79.

That is better than to investigate them."[11] For Moltmann, the Trinity is neither a problem to solve nor a doctrinal embarrassment, but rather the key to understanding the Christian faith. While there is no biblical "proof text" explicitly naming God as Trinity, Moltmann argues that the Trinity is the presupposition of a proper reading of the biblical narrative, since Jesus' life is unintelligible apart from a trinitarian reading.[12] Here the focus is on how his doctrine of God expounds hope, as he extends his argument from *CG* to a doctrine of God, proper.

Throughout *TKG*, he views monotheism as the main enemy: biblically, theologically and politically,[13] which leads many commentators (critical and sympathetic alike) to focus on the political and ecclesial subjugation aspects of his rejection of monotheism.[14] Rather than rehashing these issues and concerns, here the focus centers on God's involvement in the cross and history and the relationship this involvement has with hope.

Monotheism

Moltmann decisively rejects both supreme substance and absolute subject as coherent starting points for a proper doctrine of the Trinity.[15] He first appraises the philosophical view of God as substance, the

---

11. As quoted in *TKG* 1; see *FC* 80; it should be noted that Moltmann's assertions regarding Melanchthon rest on the first edition of *Loci Communes* (1521), but this early perspective was highly contextual and was subsequently altered (Powell, *Trinity in German Thought*, 16–30).

12. *TKG* 62ff; *FC* 80ff.; "God's Kingdom as the Meaning of Life and of the World," 100–103; *HTG* 181. For more on the integral nature of the trinitarian doctrine of God to Christian theology's grammar and structure, see Nicholas Lash, "Considering the Trinity," 183–96.

13. For an attempt to view monarchy as underpinning hope (and thus not as opposites), see Conyers, *God, Hope, and History*, 3–16.

14. Moltmann's critique of monotheism began in *CG* and has continued unabated. Moltmann closely ties *monas* to *monarchia* (*DGG* 170; *TKG* 190–203), following Erik Peterson's article "Monotheism as a Political Problem." For Moltmann's comments on Peterson's thesis, see *CG* 282 n. 43, 325–6, 339 n. 19; "Cross and Civil Religion," 14ff.; *EH* 106; *DGG* 183; *TKG* 130–31, 197; *ET* 303–4, 379 n. 1. See also Bauckham, *Theology of Jürgen Moltmann*, 171–82; Meeks, *Origins*, 151; Neuhaus, "Moltmann vs. Monotheism," 239–43; O'Donnell, "Trinity in Recent German Theology," 166; Otto, "Moltmann and the Anti-Monotheism Movement," 293–308; Sykes, "The Dialectic of Community and Structure," 113–28.

15. See *TKG* 129–50; *GC* 50.

highest object for philosophical enquiry,[16] a view that owes much to Tertullian, who beyond inventing the term *Trinitas*, brought to expression the formula: "*una substantia—tres personae.*"[17] Generally, however, Moltmann is exercised most by the more modern approach, which has held sway since Hegel: God as absolute subject.[18] Setting his sights very high indeed, Moltmann attacks the trinitarian theologies of the two individuals most responsible for the retrieval of trinitarian thought in the twentieth-century: the Roman Catholic Karl Rahner[19] and the Protestant (Reformed) Karl Barth.[20] Of these two, however, it is Barth's view which he raises into representational status to show Christian monotheism's failings and to which he directs his most damning criticisms.[21] Barth proudly championed a doctrine of the Trinity resting in the "soil of Christian monotheism."[22] Indeed, for Barth, the Trinity is

---

16. *TKG* 11; Aquinas' Five Ways is, perhaps, the greatest example (see *TKG* 11–12, 16, 150).

17. Ibid., 16, 177.

18. Ibid., 13–16; since Hegel, the Trinity has been "represented in terms belonging to the general concept of the absolute subject: *one subject—three modes of being*" (ibid., 17; see also pp. 139ff.). Understood in this way, "God . . . with perfect reason and free will, is in actual fact the archetype of the free, reasonable, sovereign person, who has complete disposal over himself" (ibid., 15). Similarly, Moltmann rejects Cartesian [human] "subjectivity" and Aristotelian "metaphysics of substance" in favor of relational metaphysics (*GC* 50); see also *HG* 70–89; *SpL* 19; "Kein Monotheismus," 118; "God is Unselfish Love," 119–20.

He cites Augustine for this view, but even for Moltmann this is not clear (see *TKG* 172); see also Mary T. Clark, "*De Trinitate,*" 91.

19. *TKG* 144–8; For a sympathetic view of Rahner's contribution to recent trinitarian discussion, including crediting *The Trinity* with starting the "first quest for renewal in Trinitarian thought," see McCosker, "Joined-Up Thomism and the Second Quest for Trinitarian Renewal," 332.

Moltmann is troubled by Rahner's insistence that God is "a single divine subject in three 'distinct modes of subsistence'" (*TKG* 148; see also "Kein Monotheismus," 118). Moltmann's judgment is debatable, since in *The Trinity* Rahner speaks of "three subsistences" (pp. 73, 75), specifically denies that God possesses an "absolute subsistence" (60), and denies modalism (pp. 109–10). A note of thanks is due to Dennis Jowers for his comments at this point. Also, compare Rahner's earlier comments, which reveal more complexity than Moltmann allows (Rahner, "*Theos* in the New Testament," 146).

20. *TKG* 139–44.

21. Beyond Barth and Rahner, Moltmann's criticism of Christian monotheism includes Aquinas, Augustine and Tertullian (*TKG* 129ff.; "Unity of the Triune God," 158–60).

22. Barth, *Church Dogmatics*, I/1: 354, as quoted in *TKG* 241 n. 22; see also *ET* 139ff. Earlier, Moltmann criticized Barth for advocating God as eternal presence (*TH* 28, 84;

"one divine subject in three different modes of being,"[23] meaning: "God is 'the one personal God' in the mode of the Father, in the mode of the Son, in the mode of the Spirit."[24] Amongst others,[25] Moltmann fears modalism in Barth,[26] which is rather ironic since this is precisely what he sought to avoid. In Barth's concept of God Moltmann sees a simple unitary aseity,[27] which leads him to find Barth guilty of being "not sufficiently trinitarian."[28] Moltmann's paramount concern with Barth is that he casts trinitarian thinking in a monotheistic mould along the lines of the single solitary subject. On this point, Moltmann finds striking similarities between Barth and the liberal theology which he opposed.[29] Monotheism, Moltmann insists, is not the proper label to affix to the Christian doctrine of God because it is incapable of intelligibly interpreting the narrative of Jesus' life. The doctrine of God requires trinitarian categories, not monotheistic ones.

CG 240; *HP* 20ff). His main criticisms typically rely on *Church Dogmatics* I/1, while Barth increasingly depends on trinitarian language in the later volumes; see further: O'Donnell, "Trinity in Recent German Theology," 165; Powell, *Trinity in German Thought*, 197.

Trevor Hart impartially surveys the doctrine of God in both Barth and Moltmann, and concludes the differences represent an "antinomy"; he advises that trinitarian discourse must constantly attend to both levels when reflecting on the triune God (Hart, "Person and Prerogative in Perichoretic Perspective: The Triunity of God," 100–16).

23. *TKG* 138; see also Susan Brooks Thistlethwaite, "Comments on Moltmann's 'The Unity of the Triune God,'" 181; Bauckham, *Theology of Jürgen Moltmann*, 172ff.

24. *TKG* 141, quoting *Church Dogmatics*, I/1: 359. Moltmann also finds it troubling that Barth prioritizes the lordship of God over his perichoresis (*DGG* 182–84; *TKG* 140–1; *ET* 140).

25. His charge is even more sweeping: "in the Western church trinitarian doctrine has almost without exception a tendency to modalism" (*TKG* 190).

26. *DGG* 183 n. 34; citing Calvin and Barth, Moltmann claims modalism is prevalent in Reformed theology (*DGG* 182). For defenses of Barth against the charge of modalism, see Alan Torrance, "The Trinity," 80–4; Jowers, "The Reproach of Modalism: A Difficulty for Karl Barth's Doctrine of the Trinity," 231–46; Taylor, "In Defence of Karl Barth's Doctrine of the Trinity," 33–46.

27. Discussing *CG*, Miskotte claims that Moltmann is not as trinitarian as Barth (Miskotte, "Das Leiden ist in Gott," 88).

28. *CG* 203.

29. For more on Barth's rejection of liberal theology's concept of God, see Powell, *Trinity in German Thought*, 217–20.

Trinitarianism

To move beyond monotheism, Moltmann articulates a social doctrine of the Trinity.[30] While Pannenberg is correct that Moltmann is guilty of "a wrong terminological decision"[31] in rejecting the term "monotheism," discussions and criticisms of this rejection typically stop short of arriving at the underlying, yet decisive, issue.[32] Moltmann's view is

---

30. *TKG* 19. This leads him to view the *imago dei* differently (see *M* 108ff.; *GC* 233–43). Moltmann sees the image of God in terms of the relationship, sexual differentiation and mutual fellowship of male and female, which is tied to his social trinitarian emphasis, ensuring that the *imago dei* is not understood in the "Western monotheism" sense, which turns it into a further basis of individualism: "Human beings are *imago trinitatis* and only correspond to the triune God when they are united with one another" (*GC* 216; see also *GC* 222–28; *HTG* 137–38, 182; *CJF* 56; *GHH* 40; *JCTW* 86; *CoG* 72–73; *GSS* 78–83, 122; *EB* 113–14). He regards creation of humanity "a condescension, a descent on God's part, since he links his glory with his 'image'" (*EJM* 39; see also *GC* 225–28; *SW* 60–67).

A biographical detail to keep in mind is that while writing *TKG*, Moltmann had before him Andrei Rublev's *Trinity*: "The chalice on the table points to the surrender of the Son on Golgotha. Just as the chalice stands at the centre of the table round which the three Persons are sitting, so the cross of the Son stands from eternity in the centre of the Trinity" (*TKG* xvi; see also *ET* 305–6). The icon captures the essence of social trinitarianism by depicting three persons. Rublev's icon is variously referred to as *Holy Trinity, Angelic Trinity, Old Testament Trinity* (c.1411); to view online, see: http://members.valley.net/~transnat/trinlg.html

31. Pannenberg, *Systematic Theology*, 1:336; see his comments elsewhere: Pannenberg, *Theology and the Kingdom of God*, 71; Pannenberg, "Probleme einer trinitarischen Gotteslehre," 329–34. In a passing reference, Moltmann cites Pannenberg as a subscriber to monotheism (*TKG* 241 n. 22).

32. The problems associated with his rejection of monotheism are multiple; here are two: first, he jettisons the views of innumerable, yet unnamed, theologians (He specifically mentions Schleiermacher [*CG* 214–15]). He provides no real distinction at this point; thus the nagging question: From this tradition, who is included and who is excluded as a (mono)theist? For example, what label do we affix to Aquinas or Augustine; Calvin or Luther; the Cappadocians; Balthasar, Barth, or Rahner? Which of these has understood God (in)correctly? This small sample shows how untenable is Moltmann's tidy assessment. He problematically flattens the differences of emphasis in a host of Christian theological positions, turning a wide spectrum of views into a univocal perspective.

Along with the first, however, is a second problem: if excluded from monotheism, under what label does the Jewish theological tradition find itself? This is both odd and indefensible, especially aggravating in Moltmann's theology. While he is quick to draw from Abraham Heschel, Gershom Sholem, Franz Rosenzweig and Elie Wiesel, (to name only four) they are seemingly excluded from his criticisms of monotheism, yet neither can they support his move to a trinitarian theology. Even Pinchas Lapide, whom agrees

generally decried for its negative aspect (rejecting monotheism), yet its positive contribution (advancing social trinitarianism) is typically left to one side. It is imperative to understand Moltmann's two-fold basis for rejecting monotheism: (1) it cannot contain the narrative of the history of the Son and (2) it cannot be transposed into a doctrine of hope.[33]

The chief problem with the doctrine of the Trinity as Christian monotheism,[34] Moltmann avers, is that it has been restrained by the conceptuality of either substance or one subject. Furthermore, monotheism is deficient because it negatively impacts christology: "Strict monotheism obliges us to think of God without Christ, and consequently to think of Christ without God as well."[35] Moltmann prescribes a social doctrine of the Trinity for Christian theology, which he believes dispenses permanently with the two key heresies that tempt the doctrine of God: (1) Arianism, which denies Christ's unity with God,[36] and (2) Sabellianism, which subsumes Christ into God.[37] His overarching conviction is that social trinitarianism ensures "the deification of Christ . . . [and thus] the Christianization of the concept of God."[38]

The category preferred in Moltmann's doctrine of God is not the unity of three *Hypostases*;[39] the proper vocabulary for the triune God is comprised of terms such as person, perichoresis, relationship, change and event.[40] Moltmann believes that trinitarian theology dictated by monotheism ineluctably emphasizes the one, manifesting an under appreciation of the three. Thus, he maintains: "Only when we are capable of thinking in Persons, relations, and changes in the relations *together*

---

with Moltmann on more than most Jews, is not able to affirm trinitarianism (see *JM*; BP 266–82).

33. Thus Conyers' telling question, which he answers in the negative: "Does Monotheism Cancel Hope?" (*God, Hope, and History*, 3ff.).

34. See *TKG* 129ff.

35. Ibid., 131. For a criticism of this point, see John Cobb, "Reply to Jürgen Moltmann's 'The Unity of the Triune God,'" 174–76.

36. Ibid., 132–35; "Arianism is monotheistic Christianity in its purest form" (ibid., 133; see also 148–50).

37. Ibid., 134–37.

38. Ibid., 132.

39. For his discussion of *persona, prosopon* and *hypostases*, see ibid., 171.

40. See ibid., 171–74. Arguably, Moltmann should not use event to describe the life of trinitarian persons, since it can quite easily entail impersonal activity; yet Moltmann seems to overcome this in *TKG*.

does the idea of the Trinity lose its usual static, rigid quality."[41] While acknowledging the background of Barth's trouble with, and rejection of, the term "person" as a trinitarian category due to its individualistic overtones, Moltmann insists that rejecting the term is a faulty methodological decision, and instead shows how it needs to be understood correctly.[42] To achieve comprehension, one needs to appreciate fully the perichoresis of three persons and the cross for their importance for the doctrine of God.[43] Taking a two-pronged approach he advances social trinitarianism, by insisting, first, on the trinitarian category of perichoresis instead of the single subject of monotheism and, second, on divine passibility over impassibility. These are handled in turn.

Perichoresis Replaces Monotheism

His demand for reversing trinitarian methodology is one side of his anti-monotheism argument (passibility is the other). At its core, *TKG* essentially explicates Moltmann's assertion that "Christian faith [should] no longer be called 'monotheistic' in the sense of the One God."[44] While he can invoke language that borders on being extreme (for example: monotheism is "un-Christian,"[45] "unsuitable" and must be "destroyed"[46]), he is unequivocal in positing perichoretic sociality[47] as the core of his trinitarianism, which will correct Christian monotheism. Traditionally, trinitarian methodology moves from the one (God) to the three (persons),[48] thus monotheism secures the unity of the trini-

---

41. Ibid., 174.
42. Ibid., 139ff.; see also *DGG* 183.
43. *TKG* 171ff.
44. Ibid., 134; see also "Kein Monotheismus," 117–19.
45. *FC* 80: "If Christian theology were to become monotheistic, it would be un-Christian."
46. Notice the subtitle: "Kein Monotheismus gleicht dem anderen: Destruktion eines untauglichen Begriffs," 112–22. Randall Otto often overstates his objection(s) to Moltmann's project, especially related to the doctrine of God (see Otto, "Moltmann and the Anti-Monotheism Movement," 293–308; Otto, "The Use and Abuse of Perichoresis," 366–84).
47. He rejects pantheism later (see *GC* 12, 85ff., 212).
48. At least since Tertullian coined the terms *Trinitas*, *tres personae*, and *una substantia*, theologians have been trying to grapple with how to relate the three persons to their unity (see *TKG* 137–39, 177–78; Kelly, *Early Christian Doctrines*, 109–15).

Arguably, one could assert that the biblical narrative moves in this direction as well. The earliest Christian theologians were, arguably, basing their decisions on the *emerg-*

tarian persons, via either substance or subjectivity. Moltmann argues that moving from one to three to develop the doctrine of the Trinity is doomed to failure, because beginning with monotheism and then trying to integrate three persons into the conceptual structure of one subject can only be done at the expense of each person's individuality.

Moltmann purposely moves from the three to the one, based on trinitarian history: "the starting point for a Christian doctrine of the Trinity must be the biblically attested history of salvation: the story of the Father, the Son, and the Spirit."[49] Rather than presupposing the unity, Moltmann asks "What Divine Unity?"[50] He admits that since he begins with the three persons the problem of maintaining their unity appears: "The unity of the Father, the Son and the Spirit is then the eschatological question about the consummation of the trinitarian history of God."[51] He is convinced that altering the method improves the conclusion.[52] This explains why he reads previous trinitarian theology as essentially an incomplete, and even incoherent, revision of monotheism, which failed to integrate three persons into one absolute subject. As relatively recent examples, he provides Barth and Rahner: both began with the unity and then moved to the tri-unity.[53] Moltmann deems this

---

ing doctrine of God found in the biblical narrative, and thus moving from the one to the three. Most criticisms of Moltmann on this point eventually cite Deut. 6.4: "Hear, O Israel: The Lord is our God, the Lord alone." Yet, in the New Testament one reads of both the Son and the Lord God (Lk. 1.32), and one also finds Jesus Christ being called Lord (John 11:2; 2 Thess 4:15–17).

49. "Unity of the Triune God," 160; see also *TKG* 19. To be sure, the term "revelation" is used here to indicate his reliance on the history of Jesus Christ, and not on the Bible as timeless, propositional revelation: "The foundations of orthodoxy ... are to be found in narrative differentiation. At the centre of Christian theology stands the eternal history [*Geschichte*] which the triune God experiences in himself. Every narrative needs time" (*TKG* 190 [206]). For his most extensive treatment of scripture, see *ET* 134–50.

50. See *TKG* 148–50. His question is a further disputation against the grounds of monotheism, relying on either one divine substance or one divine subject He questions the coherence of both the Nicene Creed and the Athanasian Creed (*TKG* 149).

51. *TKG* 149.

52. Regardless of one's opinion of Moltmann's doctrine of God, it seems unconvincing that moving from three to one is obviously preferable to moving from one to three; the discussion must begin somewhere, and consideration of both the three and the one must be given.

53. While Moltmann is sharply critical, ironically, Rahner also believed trinitarian thinking needed to be revised, because, like Moltmann, he lamented that: "Christians are, in their practical life, almost mere 'monotheists'" (Rahner, *The Trinity*, 10).

approach problematic, by pointing to the methodologically erroneous starting point. Beginning with a single subject is the improper entrée into trinitarian theology. It is better to follow the New Testament narrative of Jesus' history: "Viewed biblically, the main problem is not the Trinity but the unity of God."[54] In the history of the Son one finds not a monotheistic absolute subject, but a tri-unity, that is, three persons perichoretically related.[55] Beginning with one subject for a Christian doctrine of God in the context of the New Testament is absurd on his reading, especially when one is faced with the Gethsemane to Golgotha narrative.[56] The problem is the presupposition: the strictures of monotheism deem the life of Jesus incomprehensible. Framing the discussion in this way allows Moltmann to argue that monotheism is not capacious enough to interpret the struggle of the Father-Son abandonment: "Is it one mode of being of the one God who prays there to the other? How can we assume in the triune God only 'a single will' and 'a single consciousness,' when Jesus' prayer to the Father ends with the words: 'Not my will but thine be done'?"[57] The cross is the event that Moltmann uses to show the deficits of Christian monotheism; that "event" is only intelligible when one acknowledges the activity of more than one subject, thus necessitating a social Trinity. It should be noted that it is unfortunate that his argument is not couched in terms of vociferously defending the notion of the central point of monotheism: the God of the Bible is the one and only "true" God and thus all other claims to deity are improper in comparison.[58] Beginning with such an assertion and only then moving to alter the debate regarding the viability of monotheism as a correct label for the Christian doctrine of God, may have assuaged some rather obvious fears and forestalled attacks on his doctrine of

---

54. "Unity of the Triune God," 160; but compare *TT* 30–34.

55. "Unity of the Triune God," 162; see also *TKG* 171–78.

56. While he typically relies on the Garden to Golgotha narrative to help him argue for three subjects in trinitarian thinking, he also maintains the need to begin with the Old Testament understanding of Yahweh (see *TT* 30–34).

57. *ET* 321–22; see also *CG* 227ff.

58. For his commendation of Rosenzweig's view of the *Shema Israel*, see *CPS* 61; for a critique of his commendation, see Müller-Fahrenholz, *Kingdom and Power*, 138–39.

God. Because he did not take this path, he was led to err in criticizing Christian monotheism, virtually without qualification.[59]

He seeks to overcome the notion of the absolute subject underlying modern monotheism by attacking modalism, which he insists is the tendency of both Barth ("modes of being") and Rahner ("modes of subsistence").[60] These steps lead him to his rather controversial and bold move of positing persons as subjects: beyond using the term person, which both Barth and Rahner generally avoided, Moltmann asserts that the triune God is the unity of three persons, which cannot be rendered as three relations (Barth and Rahner), but rather *as three subjects*.[61] This veritable bombshell was deployed to transform trinitarian thinking. Recall that for Barth the Trinity is "one divine subject in three different modes of being."[62] Moltmann dispenses with not only Barth's preferred term *Seinsweisen* ("modes of being"), but also with the first half of the formula, claiming that the triune God is not one "solitary" subject, but rather three: "the trinitarian history of God [is] the concurrent and joint workings of the three subjects, Father, Son and Spirit."[63] While this

---

59. Bauckham suggests, rightly, that Moltmann would have been better off had he attacked "unitarianism," instead of monotheism (Bauckham, *Theology of Jürgen Moltmann*, 172).

60. *TKG* 18, 139–48; see also *SpL* 290ff.

61. Since Moltmann is following the Eastern tradition at this point, it is surprising he does not endorse the East's aversion to modalism (see *TKG* 190); he notably calls upon Lossky when addressing the *Filioque* dispute (*TKG* 167).

Already in *CG*, Moltmann called for trinitarian discussion along the lines of using the divine names instead of a generic rendering of "God": "The New Testament made a very neat distinction in Christian prayer between the Son and the Father. We ought to take that up, and ought not to speak of 'God' in such an undifferentiated way, thus opening up the way to atheism" (*CG* 247). Moltmann does not consistently adopt this resolution (see *CG* 125, 149–53, 215–16); he repeats the same error in 1989 (*WJC* 85, 165–7) and 1994 (*JCTW* 83). Later, he exhibits the results of such a commitment (see *SpL* 64–5; *ET* 305, 322).

Also, the very title *CG* manifests the problem of using God "generically," since based on the New Testament, "God" almost always refers to the Father alone (Rahner, "*Theos* in the New Testament," 138–48; also see Hengel, "Christological Titles in Early Christianity," 365–9).

62. *TKG* 138; see here Barth, *Church Dogmatics*, I/1: 348–55. Barth's preference of *Seinsweisen* belongs to the realm of relations and revelation, but (in Moltmann's view) not persons, and thus veers too closely to modalism and Sabellianism (*DGG* 182, 183 nn. 34–5; *TKG* 141–3). For more detail on Barth's adoption of *Seinsweisen*, see Hart, "Person and Prerogative in Perichoretic Perspective," 102–9.

63. *TKG* 156; see also 93, 95, 172; *DGG* 175; *GC* 97.

seems to ensure that the Christian doctrine of God avoids modalism,[64] by stressing the "three" so strongly, he has engendered criticisms from Gerald O'Collins and numerous others who fear that Moltmann "verges on tritheism."[65] (Hill and Molnar tantalizingly charge him with both modalism and tritheism,[66] which is ironic, since he sets out to overcome modalism throughout *TKG*.[67]) Moltmann explicitly rejects critics' claims that he is propounding tritheism or modalism: "the trinitarian persons are not to be understood as three different individuals, who only subsequently enter into relationship with one another ... But they are not, either, three modes of being or three repetitions of the One God."[68] Indeed, it may well be that Moltmann evidences tritheistic tendencies because he does not view it as a truly live option in trinitarian discourse. Tellingly, he insists that although modalism has been around for a thousand years, while the opposite "danger" for trinitarian theology, tritheism, is "fictitious," because no one has actually advocated it in the history of Christian theology (a comment that has not insulated him from this very accusation).[69] Even though Moltmann posits three

---

64. See especially *TKG* 174–8; *HTG* 181.

65. O'Collins, *The Tripersonal God*, 158; for further secondary discussion, see Bauckham, *Moltmann*, 106–10; Bauckham, *Theology of Jürgen Moltmann*, 25; Bloesch, *The Holy Spirit*, 238–39; Grenz and Olson, *20th Century Theology: God and the World in a Transitional Age*, 184; Hill, *The Three-Personed God*, 166–75; Hunsinger, "The Crucified God and the Political Theology of Violence," 278; Hunsinger, "Review of Jürgen Moltmann, *The Trinity and the Kingdom*," 131; Milbank, "The Second Difference," 223; Molnar, "The Function of the Trinity in Jürgen Moltmann's Ecological Doctrine of Creation," 210, 227ff.; Neuhaus, "Moltmann vs. Monotheism," 241; O'Donnell, *Trinity and Temporality*, 149–52; Peters, "Trinity Talk: Part 1," 46–47; Peters, *God as Trinity: Relationality and Temporality in the Divine Life*, 103ff.; Thompson, *Modern Trinitarian Perspectives*, 51.

66. Hill, *Three-Personed God*, 172–73; Molnar, "The Function of the Trinity," 222, 228.

67. *TKG* 190.

68. Ibid., 175; of course this assertion is aimed at both Barth and Rahner; for extended discussion, see *DGG* 181–4.

69. *DGG* 182; see also *ET* 382 n. 30; compare however, Moltmann's later assertion that "Sabellian modalism was at times established as church doctrine" (*TKG* 136; see also 144; *DGG* 182). Weber claims: "There really is a kind of permanence in heresy" (as cited in *TKG* 239 n. 1). Moltmann writes: "The standard argument against 'tritheism' practically serves everywhere to disguise the writer's modalism" (*TKG* 243 n. 43).

On Moltmann's claim that there has never been a tritheist, George Hunsinger writes: "If this is true then one can only conclude that Moltmann is vying to be the first. Despite the evident scorn with which he anticipates such a charge, [*TKG*] is about

subjects as the basis for his social trinitarianism, Bauckham correctly asserts that the charge of tritheism fails to stick, upon "careful reading."[70] When properly understood both "perichoresis" and "person" together serve to guard the doctrine of God from either the danger of modalism or tritheism.[71] *Contra* monotheism, Moltmann states: "God's unity . . . must be perceived in the *perichoresis* of the divine Persons. If the unity of God is not perceived in the at-oneness of the triune God, and therefore as a *perichoretic* unity, then Arianism and Sabellianism remain inescapable threats to Christian theology."[72] Seeking to avoid both modalism and tritheism, he explores the perichoretic nature of the trinitarian Persons, by focusing on the unity of the divine persons. As justification for the stress on perichoresis, he cites biblical warrant.[73] Moltmann utilizes not lordship (Barth),[74] or the monarchy of the father (Pannenberg),[75] but rather "the eternal περιχώρησις or *circumincessio*[76] of the trinitarian Persons":

> An eternal life process takes place in the triune God through the exchange of energies. The Father exists in the Son, the Son in the Father, and both of them in the Spirit, just as the Spirit exists in both the Father and the Son. By virtue of their eternal love they live in one another to such an extent, and dwell in one another to such an extent, that they are one . . . Precisely through the personal characteristics that distinguish them from one an-

---

the closest thing to tritheism that any of are ever likely to see" (Hunsinger, "Review of Jürgen Moltmann, *The Trinity and the Kingdom*," 131).

70. Bauckham, *Theology of Jürgen Moltmann*, 25.

71. *DGG* 182

72. *TKG* 150; see also 130.

73. Ibid., xvi; "Unity of the Triune God," 159–60. For a strident critique of social trinitarianism, see Dale Tuggy, "Divine Deception, Identity, and Social Trinitarianism," 269–87. While provocative, his thesis is less useful because he avoids discussing a specific version of social trinitarianism, which results in an attempt to refute a movement, rather than a specific position.

74. *TKG* 63; see Barth, *Church Dogmatics*, I/1:307ff.

75. See especially *TKG* 171ff.; *HTG* xviii-xix; *ET* 317. Moltmann is critical of Pannenberg regarding the monarchy of the Father, but compare Pannenberg's later comments (*Systematic Theology*, 1:300–301 n. 137). Rather surprisingly, Moltmann subscribes to the monarchy of the Father for the "constitution" of the Trinity (*TKG* 177).

76. Later he delineates a distinction between *circumincessio* and *circuminsessio* (*ET* 317–20; *SW* 117–18).

other, the Father, the Son and the Spirit dwell in one another and communicate eternal life to one another.[77]

As such, his doctrine of God "hinge[s] on a concept of dynamic relationality."[78] By this Moltmann ensures that his own doctrine does not prioritize the unity over the three persons.[79]

Through a series of steps he shows how perichoretic unity and self-surrendering passibility serve as the planks of a doctrine of social trinitarianism, over against Christian monotheism.[80] Moltmann (following the sixth century philosopher Boethius) claims that "the trinitarian Persons are not 'modes of being'; they are individual, unique, non-interchangeable subjects of the one, common divine substance, with consciousness and will."[81] He then calls on Richard of St. Victor's view of personhood: "existence means a deepening of the concept of relation: every divine Person exists in the light of the other and in the other. By virtue of the love they have for one another, they ex-ist totally in the other."[82] He does not stop there, however. Moltmann's final step in detailing the contours of social trinitarianism is to call on Hegel's work, which "deepened" the idea of person by insisting on the historical element of personhood. (Hegel is discussed further below; see pp. 115–119) Adding the historical element, Moltmann points out that a proper doctrine of the Trinity must include the element of "self-surrendering love."[83] God is social; he is not one with three "aspects."[84] Indeed,

---

77. *TKG* 174–75; he credits the theology of John of Damascus at this point.

78. Bauckham, *Theology of Jürgen Moltmann*, 15.

79. *HTG* 59: "the unity of the triune God [consists] above all in the unique fellowship, communion, of the three persons." See also *TKG* 148–50.

This move seems to be impelled by another: "The history of salvation is the history of the eternally living, triune God who draws us into and includes us in his eternal life with all the fulness of its relationships" (*TKG* 157). And the pneumatological developments since 1972 are apparent, as the "Spirit draws people into the fellowship of the Son to the Father" (*TKG* 75; notice the anthropological emphasis, instead of a more comprehensive one involving all of creation; compare, however, *TKG* 19–20; *GC*).

80. For his discussion of the unity of the Trinity, see *TKG* 177–8.

81. Ibid., 171. Indeed, "the Father, Son, and Spirit are subjects with will and reason" ("Unity of the Triune God," 165).

82. *TKG* 173; see also *ET* 317–20.

83. *TKG* 174.

84. Ibid., 18ff. Furthermore, understood socially, an appreciation of the relationship of reciprocity between humanity and God is attained.

Moltmann insists that only a social doctrine of God can truly allocate the biblical notion of perichoresis: "only persons can be at one with one another, not modes of being or modes of subjectivity."[85] Preferring "persons" to "relations," Moltmann insists that "the three Persons themselves form their unity, by virtue of their relation to one another and in the eternal perichoresis of their love."[86] This is key, because trinitarian perichoresis is reinforced in Moltmann's reliance on love over against impassibility as being central to both divine ontology and action. "It is the nature of the person to give himself entirely to a counterpart, and to find himself in the other most of all. The person only comes to himself by expressing and expending himself in others."[87]

In his theology of surrender in *CG*, the notion of self-surrendering love and perichoresis is arguably pushed to the point of breaking, as he sees the Father-Son abandonment as differentiation and surrender set (to be sure) in the wider frame of reconciliation. God must overcome godforsakenness and death and he achieves precisely this by taking suffering and death into his very being. Yet, at the precise point of abandonment, Moltmann does not find the dissolution of the perichoresis, but its scandalous expression:

> This deep communion of will between Jesus and his God and Father is now expressed precisely at the point of their deepest separation, in the godforsaken and accursed death of Jesus on the cross. If both historical godforsakenness and eschatological surrender can be seen in Christ's death on the cross, then this event contains community between Jesus and his Father in separation, and separation in community.[88]

Indeed, the separation is a "communion of will": "In the cross, Father and Son are most deeply separated in forsakenness and at the same time

---

85. Ibid., 150.

86. Ibid., 177; see also 148–50; "Unity of the Triune God," 165; He asserts that "[t]he foundations of orthodoxy . . . are to be found in narrative differentiation" (190).

87. Ibid., 174.

88. *CG* 243–44. Arguably, one could subscribe to every tenet of Moltmann's theology, and disagree at this very point, by simply taking Moltmann's theology and pressing it further than he does. He seems to mitigate his strong theology of surrender by asserting that there is a "communion of will"; yet, in *CG*, Moltmann, quite radically at the time, was vehement in articulating the separation of the cross not the communion (see p. 63 n. 121, above). The change may be due to a stronger understanding of the Spirit's role in the cross (see below, 182–89).

are more inwardly one in their surrender."⁸⁹ "The Persons do not merely 'exist' in relations; they also realize themselves in one another by virtue of self-surrendering love."⁹⁰ This necessitates a look at Moltmann's insistence on divine passibility for a doctrine of God.

SUFFERING LOVE REPLACES IMPASSIBILITY

While in *CG* Moltmann's theology of the cross attacked impassibility in relation to the cross, in *TKG* the focus is more on the wider ramifications of passibility for God's involvement in history. A lecture, given twice in 1975, shows the wider frame of his vehement attack on apophaticism for articulating God's being: "we must drop the old philosophical axioms about God's 'nature'. God is not unchangeable, if to be unchangeable means that he could not in the freedom of his love open himself to the changeable history with man and creation. God is not incapable of suffering . . . God is not perfect . . . God is not invulnerable, if this means that he could not open himself to the experience of the cross."⁹¹ The final assertion shows that the cross leads Moltmann to understand God's involvement in history in such intimate terms. This can be asserted more forcefully: the cross becomes the lens through which one properly assesses God's involvement in history. Continuing on from the main arguments in *CG*, Moltmann maintains that cross is of decisive importance for the doctrine of God: "The pain of the cross determines [*bestimmt*] the inner life of the triune God from eternity to eternity."⁹² While in *CG* Moltmann discussed the cross as "death in God" rather than the "death of God" (*TH*), in both *TKG* and *ET* Moltmann retrieves the "death of God" language: "If the Son suffers his death on the cross not just as a human death but also as an eternal death of God-forsakenness, and thus as 'the death of God,' then . . . [the Father] suffers the death of his Son."⁹³ It should not be surprising that one who advo-

---

89. *CG* 244; he goes on to reference the Spirit.

90. *TKG* 174.

91. *FC* 93; see also Moltmann, "The Crucified God," 17; *DGG* 170; *CPS* 62; *GSS* 184; "What is a Theologian?," 196.

92. *TKG* 161 [177].

93. *ET* 304–5; see also *TKG* 80. Notice the similarities to comments in *TH* and his indebtedness to Hegel; see also *JCTW* 37–8. Yet, even in *CG*, he writes: "in the suffering of Jesus, God died on the cross of Christ, says Christian faith, so that we might live and rise again in his future" (*CG* 216). While having a degree of iconoclastic élan, references

cates the position that "In Christianity the cross is the test of everything which deserves to be called Christian"[94] would use this criterion for a proper understanding of God. While also finding Jewish sources helpful for articulating God's *pathos* in history, he materially relates divine suffering to the cross to overcome the Aristotelian epistemological "spell" of impassibility, which is pervasive in the doctrine of God.[95] In replying to the criticism of *CG*, Moltmann explains this further step, in the *Diskussion* volume, which advertises the direction he will go in *TKG*:

> "God is dead and is nevertheless not dead"; this statement, which is fundamental for the Christian faith in the crucified Son of God, becomes paradoxical, if one proceeds from an undifferentiated, monotheistic conception of God. If God is an indivisible, eternal subject, then he can only either be dead or not dead, and because his immortality belongs to his unity and eternity also, he cannot be dead. The Christian statement about the crucified Son of God presupposes a self-differentiation in God: the incarnate Son of God died for us; God, however, the eternal father of Jesus Christ, did not. The unity in this self-differentiation of God, which also contains [*umfaßt*] death, lies in the Holy Spirit, in whom takes place the surrender of the Son to death and through that his resurrection to glory. The one divine life cannot be completed only by one subject or only by one person. Only the doctrine of the tri-unity of God [*Dreieinigkeit Gottes*][96] is in the position to perceive the immense contradiction of the cross and to integrate it into the infinite life of God. Therefore the doctrine of the Trinity constitutes the sublation [*Aufhebung*] of that contradiction—"God is dead" and "God cannot die."[97]

---

to the "death of God" are open to misinterpretation. Whether God refers to the Father or more fully to the triune God, the question remains the same: does God die on the cross? He explicitly denounces this intention: "The Christian statement about the crucified Son of God presupposes a self-differentiation in God: the incarnate Son of God died for us; God, the eternal father of Jesus Christ, however, did not" (*DGG* 175).

94. *CG* 230; see also 7; *EH* 69ff.

95. Namely, Abraham Heschel (*CG* 270–2; *TKG* 25ff.), Gershom Scholem (*TKG* 28), and Franz Rosenzweig (*TKG* 29–30); see also *JM* 56; *EG* 16–17; *ET* 315.

96. *FC* 85: "In German the word 'Trinity' can either be translated by *Dreieinigkeit*—the three in one—or by *Dreifaltigkeit*—the threefold God." He prefers *Dreieinigkeit*, and criticizes Rahner for using *Dreifaltigkeit*, labeling it modalistic (*TKG* 146, 149; see also *FC* 91; *HG* 96; "The Trinitarian Personhood of the Holy Spirit," 311; "Kein Monotheismus," 118).

97. *DGG* 175. Although this essay is not dated, it was published in 1979 and most likely written in 1977–78.

In *TKG* he builds on these themes, and the looming question here is the effect that this view generates regarding God's freedom.

Stated simply, his doctrine of God exemplifies and amplifies his doctrine of hope, because God is identified with both suffering and resurrection. But, to be sure, Moltmann's doctrine of God is strongly informed by his theology of the cross: "The theological concept for the perception of the crucified Christ is the doctrine of the Trinity. The material principle of the doctrine of the Trinity is the cross of Christ. The formal principle of knowledge of the cross is the doctrine of the Trinity."[98] God is not a domineering tyrant, a despot demanding his own way, God is love. This is epitomized, for Moltmann, in the event of the cross. The center of Christian proclamation is Christ's passion. Yet, Christ's passion in the trinitarian presentation of the Gospel necessitates that "God himself is involved in the history of God's passion. If this were not so, no redeeming activity could radiate from Christ's death."[99] For Moltmann, there is no intelligible way to construct a proper doctrine of God or hope loaded with Hellenistic presuppositions of divine negations; one needs to faithfully reflect on the Garden to Golgotha narrative, which consistently supports, indeed requires, a trinitarian conception of God.[100] This explains why he deems "unsatisfactory" any attempt to maintain both divine impassibility and divine suffering, labeling it a "contradiction."[101] Requiring the gospel be read through the lens of *apatheia* serves as a "prison for the statements made by the theology of revelation."[102] This detrimentally influences one's understanding of the doctrine of God: "The concrete 'history of God' in the death of Jesus on the cross on Golgotha therefore contains within itself all the depths and abysses of human history . . . All human history . . . is taken up [*aufgehoben*] into the 'history of God,' i.e. into the Trinity."[103] Indeed,

---

98. *CG* 240–1; see also *JM* 47; *OC* 92; he labels this construct as "scholastic" (*ET* 306).

99. *TKG* 21.

100. For extensive discussion, see *TKG* II; *GHH* 63–76.

101. *GHH* 71.

102. *TKG* 17.

103. *CG* 246 [233]; see also *UZ* 145. Indeed, when framed in monotheistic terms, the phrase the "death of God" is susceptible to the charge of patripassianism, while Moltmann's determination to view the Trinity as three subjects precludes it (*CG* 243; see also "Foreword," in Ngien, *Suffering of God*, xi). The Son dies, while the Father suffers the death of the Son. Although he does not cite him, Moltmann maintains the

God's passibility is not only beneficial to the Christian faith, by providing a basis with which to undercut protest atheism (per *CG*), it is required on the basis of biblical revelation.[104] But, for Moltmann, subscribing to the Greek apathy axiom, "How can Christian faith understand Christ's passion as being the revelation of God?," prevents this.[105] To achieve this he argues for God's passion as being closely related to God's love.[106] Love is constitutive for God's being, pervasive and epitomized in the cross:

> God does not merely love, just as at one point he is angry. He *is* love. His being is love. He constitutes himself as love. That took place on the cross. This definition takes on its full importance only if one constantly keeps in mind the way to it: the dereliction of Jesus on the cross, the giving up of the Son by the Father and the love which does all, gives all, endures all for lost human beings.[107]

This stress on God's love based in divine self-giving in the cross "event" has perplexed some who seek to maintain divine impassibility. They fear that he has gone too far in maintaining that "The pain of the cross determines the inner life of the triune God from eternity to eternity."[108] The crucial matter for most is the viability of God's freedom in such a conception. Yet, it is precisely through this lens that one can better see Moltmann's doctrine of God as a doctrine of hope. This discussion is best contextualized by assessing God's relationship to history.

Hope and History

In positing his social trinitarianism, a vital concern is God's involvement in history. Indeed, history is a central category for trinitarian thinking:

Heideggerian notion that no one suffers their own death, since "suffering presupposes life" (*CG* 243; see also *CG* 76 n. 16; *GL* 134; Kitamori, "Buchbesprechung," 109). Interestingly, Moltmann credits not Heidegger, but rather Wittgenstein for this insight (*CoG* 49).

    104. For Moltmann's view of the Bible, see *ET* 138.

    105. *TKG* 21.

    106. For support, he traces this idea in numerous thinkers, both Christian and Jewish (*TKG* I).

    107. *GHH* 70.

    108. *TKG* 161.

> [History] makes it possible to perceive the living changes in the trinitarian relations and the Persons which come about through the revelation, the self-emptying and the glorification of the triune God . . . [this history] takes place in the Trinity itself, and we have in this sense talked about God's passion for his Other, about God's self-limitation, about God's pain, and also about God's joy and his eternal bliss in the final glorification.[109]

Presupposing central insights from the early trilogy, throughout *TKG* Moltmann articulates God's involvement in history, with the emerging perspective that such involvement is based on need. While he formally agrees with Rahner in identifying the economic Trinity with the immanent Trinity, ultimately he goes further: events in the economy determine God's being.[110] This understanding has been emerging since *TH* at least, but he is more specific from the 1970s forward.[111] He admits, notably after turning to the cross, that in assessing God's relationship to history "there is a tendency for the resurrection to take supremacy over the cross, for the exaltation to acquire ascendancy over the humiliation, and for the joy of God to have more weight than his pain."[112] Since such one-sided articulations are wrong, he declares that both God's passion and joy take place in the history of God, which will be completed in the "eternal felicity of God. That is the final goal of the history of God's passion. But when this goal has been reached, the history of God's passion will not be superseded and a thing of the past. As suffering endured and made fruitful, it remains the ground for eternal joy in the salvation of God and of the new creation."[113] Because of the weight he places on the cross, suffering is constitutive to Moltmann's understanding of God. Yet, because he adds eschatological unification, as a counterweight, his doctrine of God avoids becoming a one-sided unending tragedy. It is best to regard his overall doctrine of God as drawing from the dual insight of his doctrine of hope; so, while he places the cross in a central

---

109. *TKG* 174.

110. See especially ibid., 151; see also *SpL* 290.

111. For example, in 1975, he writes: "God experiences history in order to create history. He goes out of himself in order to gather to himself. He becomes vulnerable, takes suffering and death on himself in order to heal, to liberate and to confer his eternal life" (*FC* 95; see also *CG*).

112. *FC* 95.

113. Ibid.

position, it is always, implicitly at least, with the eschaton in view that he avails himself to claim that God's involvement in history is vital to divine ontology. Yet still, important questions face Moltmann's doctrine of God as it concerns history and hope, especially regarding God being "trapped" in history.

Moltmann's grounding of hope in the cross because God's experience of suffering is exemplified and indeed typified there is reinforced in *TKG* as he calls upon a diverse group of thinkers that insist on theopathy.[114] For Moltmann suffering is constitutive to God's being because he has a high appreciation for the reciprocal relationship God has with the world.[115] In the incarnation, which reaches its apex in the cross and resurrection, God experiences godforsakenness and, perhaps more decisively for Moltmann's doctrine of God, godforsakenness enters into God.[116] The doctrine of the Trinity explicates the history (and glorification) of the Son, and on this basis is a doctrine of hope because the goal of trinitarian glorification and unification is bound up with the future of humanity (a pneumatologically-driven unification that extends to creation most prominently in *GC*). Indeed, trinitarian doctrine is led by doctrine of hope and so further sources hope because it is reliant upon God's faithfulness. Critics typically contest Moltmann's view of impassibility, yet the broader issues cannot be confined to suffering, but must involve the doctrine of the Trinity in relation to the world.[117]

In *CPS* Moltmann asserted that "God is *not perfect* [*vollkommen*] if this means that he did not in the craving of his love want his creation to be necessary to his perfection."[118] In *TKG*, embarking upon a path that rejects "arbitrary" elements of Barth's doctrine,[119] and following the

---

114. See *TKG* 21–60; beyond Jewish sources (especially Heschel), his discussion is wide-ranging, including: nineteenth- and twentieth-century English theology, Miguel de Unamuno, and Nicolas Berdyaev.

115. See especially *DGG* 155, 172–73, 179; *TKG* 98, 161.

116. See especially *TKG* 118ff.; *CG* 276.

117. *TKG* 119: "God does not merely enter into the finitude of men and women; he enters into the situation of their sin and God-forsakenness as well. He does not merely enter into this situation; he also accepts and adopts it himself, making it part of his own eternal life."

118. *CPS* 62 [79].

119. *TKG* 54ff; this, just one in a series of moves showing his disagreement with Barth; see also *DGG* 155.

general tenor of Hegel,[120] he asserted: "God 'needs' the world and man. If God is love, then he neither will nor can be without the one who is his beloved."[121] In silently recanting his previous view,[122] he paves a way between Christian theism and Christian pantheism. This path is forged only when God's liberty is not arbitrary: "If God's nature is goodness, then the freedom of his will lies in his will to goodness."[123] In such a concept, freedom and necessity are not opposites: "If we lift the concept of necessity out of the context of compulsive necessity and determination by something external, then in God *necessity* and *freedom* coincide; they are what is for him axiomatic, self-evident [*selbstverständlich*]. For God it is axiomatic to love, for he cannot deny himself. For God it is axiomatic to love freely, for he is God."[124] Moltmann delineates the proper relationship between God and the world along the lines of necessity. (Here space is devoted to Moltmann's view of God's relationship with history, while God's relationship with creation is delayed until chapter five.) With an emphasis on the economy, Moltmann insists that revelation dictates what may be said about God: "If God is the truth that corresponds entirely to himself, then his revelation can only be true if he entirely corresponds to himself in that revelation. That is to say, not to reveal himself and to be contented with his untouched glory would be a contradiction of himself."[125] Thus, God needs to be involved in history. This is enhanced further because of Moltmann's concomitant assertion that while Jesus is the (revelatory) "Word," his focus typically centers

---

120. O'Regan asserts: "Hegel is very anxious to remove any extrinsic or voluntarist elements.... He is uncomfortable with the notion of a self-sufficient divine outside, or beyond, the context of relation, a divine which may be thought to 'decide' or 'choose' to create a world" (O'Regan, *Heterodox Hegel*, 400 n. 84; see also 144–51). See also Milbank, "The Second Difference," 223.

121. *TKG* 58; also *FC* 119–24; *GC* 86–93; chapter 5 discusses more fully the relationship between creation and God.

122. He does this without pointing out the change in position (*TKG* 106, 236 n. 15).

123. *TKG* 107; he also affirms clearly: "In order to understand the history of mankind as a history *in* God, the distinction between the world process and the inner-trinitarian process must be maintained and emphasized" (*TKG* 107).

124. *TKG* 107 [122]; instead of *axiomatisch*, Moltmann uses *selbstverständlich* which can be translated as axiomatic or as "(perfectly) natural or a matter of course." In this section, Kohl consistently translates *selbstverständlich* as axiomatic; see also *GC* 76.

125. *TKG* 53 [68–9]; see also *DGG* 170.

on the history of Jesus,[126] because God reveals himself in the economy. At this point, however, he makes a decisive and controversial move: the economic Trinity is not the divine exterior (and thus contingent) expression of the immanent Trinity, but the necessary divine self-communication and locale of divine activity,[127] a lesson taught him, in part at least, by Hegel.[128] Compare Moltmann's view: "There is no God other than the incarnate, human God,"[129] with Hegel's: "God does not attain actuality until the Trinity has unfolded in history."[130] (Note Moltmann's stress on the particularity of the second person of the Trinity.) The Trinity is thus involved in history by necessity, a result of Moltmann's view of God, which is best understood as framed by his discussion of God's nature in terms of the dialectic of necessity and freedom.[131] It must be stated that these moves necessitating God's involvement in history are entirely coherent with his desire to formulate hope as certainty. Additionally, Moltmann's argument further underpins his view that there is a dynamic reciprocity between divine and human, which further underlies the stress on God needing the world, *contra* the traditional view of protecting God's freedom.[132] On this point, the Hegelian influence on Moltmann's doctrine of God needs to be examined.[133]

126. In *WJC* Moltmann involves himself more in Jesus' life (and teaching).

127. Molnar laments the "necessary" elements of Moltmann's doctrine of God, fearing that he does not take seriously enough the immanent Trinity (see Molnar, "The Function of the Trinity," 200ff.; *TKG* 167).

128. One might assert that this emphasis derives solely from his reading of the history of the Son in the biblical narrative, but this borders on naïveté. The viability of his move is indebted heavily to Hegel's prior work. Hegel's pronouncements on this issue are pervasive and dense; for expert analysis on this element of his thought, see O'Regan, *The Heterodox Hegel*, 277–83; Powell, *Trinity in German Thought*, 128–34.

129. *TKG* 119.

130. Powell, *Trinity in German Thought*, 128. While there are definite appeals to, and clear parallels with, Hegel for divine self-differentiaion, Moltmann can draw varying levels of support from Richard of St. Victor, Duns Scotus, and Maximus the Confessor for the importance of understanding persons and divine ontology.

131. See especially *TKG* 52–60. O'Donnell, who wrote regarding Moltmann's view of necessity and freedom: "Neither [for Moltmann] does God need the world to fulfill himself" (O'Donnell, *Trinity and Temporality*, 148). Contra O'Donnell, see below: "God in History, pp. 121ff."

132. *TKG* 98: "the relation between God and the world has a *reciprocal* character, because this relationship must be seen as a living one"; see also *TKG* 54ff.

133. For the Hegelian elements related to Moltmann's view of history besides *TKG*, see especially *CG* 244–9, 254; *DGG* 65ff., 175; *FC* 80–96.

God in History

In *TH*, Moltmann denied allegiance to a major premise in Hegel's program: "the godforsakenness of the cross cannot, as in Hegel, be made into an element belonging to the divine process and thus immanent in God."[134] The major thrust of both *CG* and *TKG*, however, exhibits Moltmann's recantation as he makes it clear that god-forsakenness is constitutive to God's being. If God the Father is not intimately involved in the cross event, then the conclusion must be that he "sits enthroned in heaven and allows his Son to come to so miserable an end on earth."[135] This, Moltmann asserts, cannot be the Christian doctrine of God according to the biblical narrative. The emphasis on the Trinity's close relationship with history is without question related to Hegel. While Moltmann forges the main tenets of his social trinitarian doctrine at least partly in reaction and rejection of Barth's doctrine (which is crucial to understanding *TKG*), it is Hegel, whom Moltmann revealingly labels "the philosopher of the Trinity,"[136] who plays a significant role in the development of his understanding.

A central element of *TKG*'s discussion of God's experience of history is the cross. First, Moltmann asserts that pain, death and the cross are central to God, to such a degree that they are a source of the Trinity's being and becoming.[137] Central to this view is his prior insight that "the Trinity is no self-contained group in heaven, but an eschatological process open for men on earth, which stems from the Cross of Christ."[138] In Moltmann's theology, divine openness allows growth in God: "The

---

134. *TH* 171. For a comprehensive study of Moltmann's usage of Hegel, see Spence, "Von Balthasar and Moltmann: Two Responses to Hegel on the Subject of the Incarnation and 'the death of God,'" chapters V–VI; see also McDade, "The Trinity and the Paschal Mystery," 175–91; O'Regan, *The Heterodox Hegel*, 123, 128, 221; Powell, *Trinity in German Thought*, 193–202; Wood, "From Barth's Trinitarian Christology to Moltmann's Trinitarian Pneumatology," 51–69.

135. *GHH* 75.

136. *FC* 82.

137. *DGG* 155, 172–3, 179; *TKG* 161; typically, he is more direct about the world being necessary for the life of God in *DGG* than in *TKG*. Comments favoring God's "becoming" open Moltmann to the charge of being a process theologian; for a good discussion on the salient similarities and differences between Moltmann and process theology, see O'Donnell, *Trinity and Temporality*, 159–203; Cobb, "Jürgen Moltmann's Ecological Theology in Process Perspective," 115–28.

138. *CG* 249; see also *TKG* 148–50.

incarnation of the Son therefore brings about something 'new' even within the Trinity, for God himself."[139] This is based on the history of Jesus. History is constitutive for God's being, and for Moltmann it is God's essential nature, rather than a divine will, that requires God's participation in history.[140]

Similar to rejecting two-natures christology Moltmann insists that it is improper to conceive of God unaffected by the world, when the biblical narrative shows that God himself is involved in history. In the *Diskussion* volume on *CG*, he clarifies his position by asking and answering a central question:

> Does God need the world in order to come to himself? If one understands by "himself" his abstract being for himself and by himself, then one must answer this question in the negative. If one understands by "himself" what the Bible calls his glory, his justice, and his kingdom, then one must answer the question in the affirmative, even if one would not want to put it in the sense of "incompleteness" [*Unvollkommenheit*] of his love and the openness of his hope.[141]

Claiming that God's involvement in the world has no affect on God would be tantamount, in Moltmann's view, to creating a dualism whereby the immanent Trinity remains unaffected by events occurring in the economy. This dualism of the doctrine of God is precisely what Moltmann wishes to dismantle by arguing for the retroactive effect of the economic Trinity on the immanent.[142] The Trinity in sending ultimately shows that the circle in heaven is not closed; it is open: "a trinitarian theology of the cross perceives God in the negative element and therefore the negative element in God, and in this dialectical way is panentheistic . . . all being and all that annihilates has already been taken up [*aufgehoben*] in God and God begins to become 'all in all.'"[143] Moltmann declares that if God is involved in history and time,

---

139. *FC* 93. For more on the openness of God, see *CG* 246ff.; "The Crucified God," 17; *CPS* 54–6; *DGG* 155; *TKG* 94–6, 127; *GSS* 101, 184.

140. Similarly, see *TKG* 167: "The Father begets and bears the Son out of the necessity of his being."

141. *DGG* 155.

142. Notice, however, that he still employs the categories he is trying to overcome.

143. *CG* 277 [266]. Notice the usage of *aufgehoben*, which can be rendered "sublate"; for Hegel "the God of Christianity . . . is a God of narrative elaboration who enters

then these must influence who God actually is, and furthermore, once this ontology is asserted the conclusion is obvious, necessary and a helpful correction of the traditional view: God is neither apathetic nor detached from history, and thus not a closed circle in heaven, and *vice versa*.[144] This construct necessitates his criticism of trinitarian doctrine expounded as one subject. God as absolute subject in three modes of one being does not express clearly enough the experience of God in history from the vantage point of the biblical narrative. And supremely for Moltmann (ever since *CG* at least), unless God is experiencing history, and not above or beyond it, there is no basis for discussing God's involvement in the cross, which, in turn, is the criterion for a Christian doctrine of God and an element grounding his hope. The core of this depiction of God's suffering involvement in history is the cross, which is the point of entry for discussing Moltmann's perspective on God's "free" involvement in history.

GOD IN HISTORY, OR GULLIVER IN LILLIPUT?

Moltmann asks the decisive question for this issue: "Is the suffering God free or is he a prisoner of his own experience of history [*Geschichte*]?"[145] He replies through a series of statements that when brought together amount to a rejection of Barth's view of divine freedom.[146] Moltmann's view might be summarized best by his question: "Does God really not need those whom in the suffering of his love he loves unendingly?"[147] Contextually, he clearly expects the answer to be negative: God needs those he loves. He goes further: "Can God really be content to be sufficient for himself if he *is* love? How is the God who suffers in his love supposed to correspond to a God who exists in untouched glory? How can the God who is glorified in the cross of the Son possess an untouched glory at all?"[148] Moltmann concludes that such an assessment

decisively into finitude if only to sublate it" (O'Regan, *Heterodox Hegel*, 80).

144. *CG* 249; see also *CPS* 55–6; *ET* 323.

145. *TKG* 52 [68]; see also *DGG* 168ff.

146. *TKG* 54ff. The question of God's decision to create is also related to Barth's view (see below "The Necessity of Creation," pp. 132ff.).

147. Ibid., 53.

148. Ibid. Compare O'Regan's assessment of Hegel: "Adequate trinitarian definition, however, ultimately involves all of reality, the 'Immanent Trinity' or 'the holy Trinity' ... not being sufficient and requiring completion in and through its exile in the finite"; *Heterodox Hegel*, 235).

of deity is a *non sequitur* when faced with the narrative of the history of the Son, especially the cross. Statements such as the quote above give weight to critics' charge that Moltmann's doctrine of God is too reliant upon Hegel, in whom they finding disconcerting similarities.[149] Here, this issue is assessed based on its effect on his doctrine of hope: does Moltmann's insistence that God needs the world endanger his doctrine of hope?

Moltmann should be credited for insisting that a doctrine of God must take seriously historical happenings. His insistence on God's involvement in history has caused objections to be raised against his doctrine of the Trinity, supremely revolving around the issue of God "needing" his Other. Moltmann claims that this aspect needs to be understood not as revealing weakness, but as exemplifying strength:

> If he longs for his other, it is not out of *deficiency* of being; it is rather out of the superabundance of his creative fullness. If we talk about the divine longing, then we do not mean any "imperfection of the Absolute" when we transfer the principle of historical movement in this way . . . God longs for his Other, in order that he may put his creative love into action . . . This tension is to be found in God's longing for "his Other," the Other whom he loves and for whose responding love he thirsts.[150]

This section would be enough to raise critics' ire, yet he goes even further. Beyond maintaining God's involvement in history as need or "longing," Moltmann asserts: "The nature of God thus does not stand behind the appearance of history and appearance in history as eternal, ideal being; it is that history itself."[151] Critics generally imply that by interpreting history as the history of the trinitarian God, Moltmann has unfortunately taken these happenings a bit too seriously for divine ontology. Arguments condemning his view of God's activity in history evidence themselves typically in the call for a stronger doctrine of God's freedom.[152] The accusations point to Moltmann envisioning

---

149. See especially *DGG* 169 n. 7; *TKG* 230 nn. 92–93. Most critics find little redeeming in Hegel's legacy at this point; however, see Powell, *Trinity in German Thought*; Spence, "Von Balthasar and Moltmann."

150. *TKG* 45–46. He is qualifying Berdyaev.

151. *FC* 74.

152. For criticisms lamenting Moltmann's lack of protecting God's freedom, see Kasper, "Revolution im Gottesverständnis?" 146; Molnar, "The Function of the Trinity,"

God trapped in history, akin to Gulliver's stop in Lilliput, tied down with hundreds of tethers. This, of course, is partly due to his rejection of distinguishing sharply between the economic and immanent Trinity. Thus, the critics decry, in Moltmann's conception God is not free; he is trapped in history, subjected to suffering and held captive to events outwith his control.[153]

Not only does God experience suffering, suffering is in God.[154] From this, Moltmann asserts that if God is not involved in the cross then the doctrine of God cannot source hope. He makes this move because of his stress on God being on the side of godforsaken humanity. In *TKG* this is expressed most clearly in his usage of love as the central category of understanding God; thus God is open to the "other."[155] God is involved in history not by "deciding," but rather by nature and thus by necessity: "'God is love' means: God is self-communication, and also the desire for self-communication . . . in accordance with the love which is God that he should fashion a creation which he rejoices over, and call to life his Other, man, as his image, who responds to him. Not to do this would contradict the love which God is."[156] Multiple Hegelian parallels are manifest. Hegel involves himself in a "continual invocation throughout the Lectures of the Lutheran theme of 'the death of God.'"[157] He specifically follows the assertion "God himself is dead" (a line contained in a Lutheran hymn), and maintains "that the human, the infinite, the fragile, the weak, the negative are themselves a moment of the divine, that they are within God himself, that finitude, negativity, otherness are not outside of God and do not, as otherness, hinder unity with God.

197–233; Momose, *Kreuzestheologie: Eine Auseinandersetzung mit Jürgen Moltmann*, 86; Thompson, *Modern Trinitarian Perspectives*, 34–35; for a more general appraisal, see Bauckham, *Theology of Jürgen Moltmann*, 24–25.

153. For a critique from the other side, which laments that Moltmann's doctrine of passibility has not gone far enough, see Fiddes, *Creative Suffering of God*, 5–14, 80–86. Williams indicts both Moltmann and Hegel for "evasions of the temporal" (Williams, *On Christian Theology*, 161).

154. *CG* 274–78.

155. See especially *TKG* 57–60.

156. Ibid., 58.

157. O'Regan, *Heterodox Hegel*, 205; see also pp. 212–21. On this, Jüngel asserts: "the pointedly anti-Christian use of the phrase 'God is dead'. . . would scarcely be conceivable without Hegel's mediation between the originally Christian meaning of this phrase and. . . the atheistic feeling of the 'modern age,' as Hegel put it" (Eberhard Jüngel, *God as the Mystery of the World*, 63).

Otherness, the negative, is known to be a moment of the divine nature itself."[158] Although the quote above is from Hegel it could just as easily have come from Moltmann (even though their views are not identical).[159] Paramount for Moltmann, Christ's death informs one's understanding of the term "God." Utilizing Hegel, Moltmann states: "If one describes the life of God within the Trinity as the 'history of God' (Hegel), this history of God contains within itself the whole abyss of godforsakenness, absolute death, and the non-God."[160]

God's "Need" Related to a Doctrine of Hope

Does Moltmann's doctrine of God endanger his doctrine of hope? While arguably critics can point to numerous reasons to answer "yes," if taken on Moltmann's terms, his doctrine of hope is not weakened by his doctrine of God, but rather strengthened. While Moltmann clearly articulates God needing the world, he makes it clear that God is not subject to suffering and history like humanity.[161] At no point does Moltmann posit God as being caught unawares of his own involvement in history, but rather God decides to open himself up to suffering. His doctrine of God's vulnerability stems from the ground of his hope. For Moltmann, God is not Gulliver, but the God of the biblical narratives. And the more one is attuned to the fact that he sees God's interaction in history as hopeful because he sides with fellow victims, one can better see how the life of the Trinity can be seen as further substantiating Moltmann's doctrine of hope precisely because God is involved in history and suffers. For Moltmann, hope is not preserved in focusing on God's freedom, but rather insisting on God's involvement in the world. Thus his doctrine of God does not contradict his doctrine of hope, but

---

158. Hegel, *Lectures on the Philosophy of Religion*, 3:326. Indeed, for Hegel the rendering "'*Gott selbst ist tot*' centers on 'a double divestment or kenosis.'" (O'Regan, *Heterodox Hegel*, 205).

159. For Hegel, the trinitarian persons are "not actual beings"; Powell, *Trinity in German Thought*, 127. For Moltmann's critical comments regarding Hegel, see *CG* 90–92; *TKG* 17–18.

160. *CG* 246; Moltmann follows Hegel's understanding, but seeks to clarify it (*CG* 244): "God died the death of the godless on the cross and yet did not die. God is dead and yet is not dead." See also *CG* 244–49 for Hegelian elements related to Moltmann's view of history.

161. Indeed, Fiddes' critique is aimed at precisely this point; *Creative Suffering of God*, 5–14, 80–86.

rather is fully consistent with it. Indeed, because Moltmann pursues his discussion along the lines of trinitarian activity in the economy, it is possible to read his doctrine of God as merely projection of the human condition onto the divine. Yet, this is a deficient reading of Moltmann's argument, because it places too great a weight on his assertions of God's passibility, and thus misses the core of his social trinitarianism: the cross and the resurrection.

Cross and Resurrection Inform a Doctrine of God

God's involvement in history does not render him passive or inactive, giving in to whatever befalls him, as is often the case with human suffering.[162] Moltmann's doctrine of God remains misunderstood, in part because it is not placed in the wider context of the determining doctrine of his theology: hope.

Because the cross heavily impresses the being of God, Moltmann can be misread as positing trinitarian theology as tragedy. This conclusion, however, is the result of a far-reaching failure to realize that the cross's significance for his doctrine of God is situated in the wider context of his equating God's power with the resurrection (stressed in *TH*) and the kingdom (stressed in *TKG*).

This understanding of God's involvement with the world is driven by his methodology: theology as hope. While some may claim that Moltmann's doctrine of God expounds tragedy, since God is subject to historical events seemingly trapped in history, Moltmann sees it in precisely opposite terms. For Moltmann, the God-world relationship cannot be one-way, where God affects the world, and not vice versa.[163] If this were the case, at least two questions would appear: (1) How does this relationship convey the truth(s) of the cross and resurrection? (2) What hope would there be in such a God? For Moltmann, only because God is intimately involved in the history of the world does hope exist (chapter five, below, discusses how this involvement extends to God's participation in, and need of, creation). Moltmann's trinitarian doctrine of God maintains God's close relationship to the world, because otherwise it too easily posits a God unaffected, unmoved, impassible, "above" creation and outside time. This is similar to his argument for finding

---

162. See especially *TKG* 39–41.
163. See Bauckham, *Theology of Jürgen Moltmann*, 174.

God in the cross so that it becomes a ground of hope for Christian theology, because it is Jesus on the cross suffering and dying in God-forsaken agony, while the Father in heaven suffers the death of his Son. Indeed, for Moltmann to posit a different understanding of God's relationship with history would require a reorientation of his entire theology. Moltmann's doctrine of God expounds hope by centering on the cross as vital to the life of the Trinity, and also by asserting that God needs the world; these two elements are always set in the wider perspective of God's coming kingdom. Of course, one can proof-text Moltmann and find a doctrine of God expounding tragedy, but this is only a partial reading at best, and so it is unfair to Moltmann's doctrine of God specifically, and his overarching program generally. For example, one can quote Moltmann verbatim and misread him: "This world's history of suffering is the history of God's suffering too, the God who does not merely *permit* the evil act because he wishes men and women to be free, but also *endures* the evil act in the victims . . ."[164] Quoting this section alone opens Moltmann to numerous charges. Keep reading, however, and the context provides the necessary qualifier: "If, as Bonhoeffer said, God does not help through his omnipotence but through his powerlessness, not through his untroubled bliss in heaven but through his suffering on this earth, then God is still the determining subject of redemption, both his own redemption from his suffering with us, and the redemption of this unredeemed world too."[165] Of course, this view is underpinned by his doctrine of hope, as he asserts God's faithfulness based on the arguments that guide *TH* and *CG*. This mundane example could be repeated numerous times, but it shows that read closely, from a standpoint of his doctrine of hope, his doctrine of God is reliant on the power of the resurrection, that is, the God of the *Zukunft*, who will make all things new.

The most appreciable comments on this matter address Moltmann's understanding of kingdom and glory.[166] While critics seem to underappreciate the importance it has for his doctrine of God, Moltmann

---

164. *GSS* 184; see also *TKG* 124ff.

165. *GSS* 184; contextually, the final comments represent a rejection of what he deems the "humanist interpretation" of a divine-human collaboration working toward redemption.

166. Of course, this is separate from a "theology of glory," which Moltmann explicitly rejects (*CG* 210, 219–20); on Iwand's influence at this point, see Meeks, *Origins*, 30–41, 56.

has displayed the interrelation between the cross and resurrection typified in suffering and glory,[167] and furthermore because he stresses the future as that which is coming (in contradistinction from a future as disclosure), he places a high premium on the *Zukunft*: "people believe that the omnipotence and omnipresent kingdom in which God 'o'er all things so wondrously reigneth' is already present here and now. That is a fallacy which by-passes the presence of God in history; for in history that presence takes the form of the cross."[168] While the cross determines the being of God for his trinitarian history in the present, it is only coherent when understood in the light of the resurrection: "A theology of the cross without the resurrection is hell itself."[169] As the God of the *Zukunft*, he is fully capable of bringing about his kingdom, defeating the last enemy of death and making all things new, so that he may "be all in all." Although Moltmann more adequately maintains the dialectic in *TKG* compared with *TH*, the ability to call on the resurrection side of the dialectic comes from *TH*: "Christian hope is resurrection hope, and it proves its truth in the contradiction of the future prospects thereby offered and guaranteed for righteousness as opposed to sin, life as opposed to death, glory as opposed to suffering, peace as opposed to dissent."[170]

Moltmann's understanding of God's involvement in history is highly informed by his rejection of impassibility. There is no insulation, no firewall that keeps suffering at bay. While some find this construal of the God/world relationship troubling and deficient, most criticisms are lodged against his formal and material discussion,[171] failing to assess his motive. His understanding of God's involvement in history finds its antecedent in his doctrine of hope. He is not concerned with protecting God's immutability and/or impassibility because he is primarily concerned with God's faithfulness to his promise and in suffering. If one attacks his doctrine of God (besides accusing him of tritheism), one is essentially protesting these points. As such, his doctrine of God is

---

167. *CPS* 59–62; *FC* 90–91; *TKG* 124ff.

168. *GSS* 185.

169. *TKG* 41–42. Contextually, he is lamenting Unamuno's rather one-sided perspective.

170. *TH* 18.

171. For example, see Thompson, *Modern Trinitarian Perspectives*, 33–34.

dictated by the criterion of God's faithfulness (not his freedom) in the cross and resurrection.

The doctrine of God explicates hope because God is involved in history, by necessity. And it is here that Moltmann's doctrine of perichoresis extends beyond the trinitarian persons, and reaches humanity. He roots humanity's freedom in God's: "God demonstrates his eternal freedom through his suffering and his sacrifice, through his self-giving and his patience. Through his freedom he keeps man, his image, and his world, creation, free—keeps them free and pays the price of their freedom."[172] His insistence on the Trinity's openness is not a point of weakening God's freedom,[173] but rather strengthening Moltmann's doctrine of hope, because the openness allows for the future of all creation (which is eschatological glorification) to be tied directly to God's: "It is a *fellowship with God* and, beyond that, a *fellowship in God*. But that presupposes that the triunity is open in such a way that the whole creation can be united with it and can be one within it. The union of the divine Trinity is open for the uniting of the whole creation with itself and in itself. So the unity of the Trinity is not merely a theological term; at heart it is a soteriological one as well."[174] While for some this is absurd at best, and heretical at worst, appeals for Moltmann to take more seriously the immanent Trinity, miss his main point entirely. Moltmann's central goal in articulating a doctrine of God is to source hope in God's faithful activity in the economy.

Conclusion

The present reading of Moltmann's work inspects his doctrines from the perspective of his doctrine of hope. And his doctrine of God, while certainly drawing heavily from the emphases of *CG*, is situated in a wider frame of God's resurrection power. In the perspective of his desire to engender hope, his doctrine of God arguably succeeds at the precise point some find it wanting: God's involvement in history. While his trinitarian doctrine could have been more clear in trying to improve upon (rather than virtual outright rejection and ridicule) previous attempts at constructing a doctrine of God, overall his doctrine of God

172. *TKG* 56.
173. See especially ibid., 55–59, 192.
174. Ibid., 96.

is hopeful because he relentlessly claims that God is in fact involved in history, ensuring the future glorification of God, and also his beloved. In this he follows through with his doctrine of hope.

Moltmann's placement of a qualifier on God's freedom begs a decisive question in relation to hope (which can be asked here, but only answered in the chapter following): what is the effect of qualifying God's freedom on God's faithfulness? An answer emerges in relation with Moltmann's view of the necessity of creation (see below "The Necessity of Creation" in pp. 132ff.).

5

Creation as Hope

Introduction

Following the social trinitarianism of *TKG*, Moltmann offers the second "contribution" of his theological program, *GC*, conceived and presented originally as the 1984–85 Gifford Lectures.[1] He describes it as ecological,[2] messianic, trinitarian, and pneumatological.[3] The title expresses succinctly his application of his previous reflections on the trinitarian orders to his pneumatological focus for his doctrine of creation: "all divine activity is pneumatic in its efficacy . . . Through the energies and potentialities of the Spirit, the Creator himself is present in his creation."[4] Moltmann emphasizes God's present creative activ-

---

1. *GC* 1; *HTG* 127. For overviews of Moltmann's doctrine of creation, see Bauckham, *Theology of Jürgen Moltmann*, 83–90; Müller-Fahrenholz, *Kingdom and Power*, 153–66. Moltmann is the first of his generation to give a set of Gifford Lectures.

2. A doctrine of creation had been on his agenda since 1964, yet he only became aware of the ecological crisis in the 1970s (*GC* 23–29; *CJF* 13–15, 51–55; *WJC* 67–68; *HTG* 170; "Adventure," 104; *ET* 314; *SW* 111). For example, in 1968 he names economic, political and racial (but not ecological) alienation (*UZ* 128ff.), and in 1971, while commenting on creation, he makes no mention of an ecological crisis (*M* 108ff.).

The current chapter does not address the scientific aspects of *GC*. Celia Deane-Drummond, a trained scientist (M.A. in Natural Sciences; Ph.D. in Plant Physiology), deals with these issues in detail in *Ecology in Jürgen Moltmann's Theology*; see also Bauckham, *Theology of Jürgen Moltmann*, 183–98. For Moltmann's explicit comments on spatio-temporal issues post-*GC*, see especially *SW* VI–VII; see also Bauckham, "Time and Eternity," in *EJM* 155–226.

3. See *GC* 4–5, 14, 86, xiv, respectively. He regards a proper doctrine of creation as theocentric (*GC* 197); later, asserting that the biblical notion of "God in creation" relates to the Father (*WJC* 332).

4. *GC* 9; see also xiv; *SoL* 114. He boldly asserts: "God the Spirit is also the Spirit of the universe, its total cohesion, its structure, its information, its energy" (*GC* 16).

ity through the immanent Spirit, ensuring that his doctrine of creation does not promote deism: God is no divine watchmaker, setting the world in motion only to leave it unaffected.[5]

The present chapter shows how Moltmann's doctrine of creation stems from his doctrine of hope as he asserts hope's cosmic scope: hope is not anthropomorphic escapism, but rather encompasses all creation.[6] His emphasis on creation is a switch from his early work, where history was the primary stage of divine action.[7] His doctrine of hope determines to a high degree the shape of his doctrine of creation. His rejection of a doctrine of God as supreme substance or absolute subject in *TKG* continues unabated and influences both his appreciation and critique of Barth's understanding of creation as decree and Tillich's notion of creation as emanation.[8] In the opening of *GC*, he explicitly avoids developing either a monotheistic doctrine of creation which focuses on God as Lord or a "specifically christological doctrine,"[9]

---

5. *GC* 55, 90, 208–10; *FC* 119; *WJC* 286–87; *SW* 122.

6. This move is not new for Moltmann, but has been emerging, and is taken on fully in his program in *TKG* and *GC*.

7. See *GC* 31, 38, 137–38; *SW* 111.

8. *GC* 1, 16–17, 79–86. Although he has been accused of promoting emanation, he explicitly denies it (*GC* 75; *TJ* 40). Compare, however, his equivocal defense of emanation, viewing it as self-determination (*TKG* 54; see also *GC* 82–3). Scholem argues that viewing the first step of creation as contraction (*zimsum*), is opposite of viewing creation as emanation (see Scholem, "Seventh Lecture," 261–62).

Because continuity in Moltmann's *oeuvre* is important for the present study, Christian Link's position should be assessed. Deane-Drummond interprets Link as finding in *GC* "a new departure in Moltmann's thought" (Deane-Drummond, *Ecology in Jürgen Moltmann's Theology*, 52–53). According to Deane-Drummond, Link is asserting that Moltmann is leaving his former considerations behind. But, although Link sees Moltmann developing his doctrine of creation in reference to the ecological crisis, which he "welcomes as a remarkable venture into previously unentered new territory [*unbetretenes Neuland*]," he intends no discontinuity (Christian Link, "Schöpfung im messianischen Licht," 83; see also 83 n. 2). Furthermore, Moltmann is very positive of Link's review ("Zum Gespräch mit Christian Link," 93; see also *TKG* 19–20, 99ff.; *ET* 314).

9. Although Deane-Drummond maintains that Moltmann's doctrine of creation "remains basically Christological and historical in orientation" (Deane-Drummond, *Ecology in Jürgen Moltmann's Theology*, 245), in *GC* Moltmann explicitly avoids developing the christological mediation of creation; see, however, *WJC* 280–8. In *WJC* he affirms that Christ is the ground of creation (287–91); earlier he specifies: "the crucified Christ [is] the ground of his [God's] new creation" (*CG* 217).

instead opting for a focus on "creation in the Spirit."[10] The stress is on the Spirit's immanence, the *Shekinah*, the eschatological sabbath[11] and on God's experience of creation as kenosis (including especially the initial act of creation). There are two issues that are of paramount importance for the present study: (1) the question of the necessity of creation; and (2) understanding creation's eschatological dimensions. The first issue continues and concludes the preceding chapter's questions related to God's freedom, while the second issue shows how the key tenets of his doctrine of hope are paralleled in his doctrine of creation. These are handled in turn.

The Necessity of Creation

The question driving the theological articulation of the necessity of creation is: "Why is there something rather than nothing?"[12] While Moltmann's understanding of creation's relationship to God is not explicated fully until *GC*, he began showing signs of the direction that he would go much earlier.

In 1959 Moltmann asserted the need for theology to begin "identifying God's nature with his faithfulness."[13] At that time, it seems, he had not rejected Barth's position (which stresses God's freedom), because in

---

10. *GC* 9. Following Basil the Great, Moltmann maintains: "The created world is therefore created 'by God', formed 'through God' and exists 'in God'" (*GC* 9; see also *HTG* 73; *SoL* 115; compare, however, *WJC* 287, 281, where the referent is not God, but Christ).

11. These emphases exhibit his penchant for drawing on Jewish sources to fund Christian theology; beyond *TKG* and *GC*, see *SpL* 47–51; "Ernst Blochs Christologie," 9; *ET* 314; see also Lodahl, *Shekinah/Spirit: Divine Presence in Jewish and Christian Religion*, 181–83. The eschatological sabbath is addressed below (see pp. 213–17).

12. *FC* 120 = *SW* 38; see also *GC* 75. Earlier Moltmann asserted that "There is no purposive rationale for the assertion that something exists instead of nothing" (*TJ* 40). For a criticism of Moltmann's solution of the nature-will issue in relation with space-time issues, see Alan J. Torrance, "*Creatio ex Nihilo* and the Spatio-Temporal Dimensions, with special reference to Jürgen Moltmann and D. C. Williams," 96–99.

13. Moltmann and Weissbach, *Two Studies in the Theology of Bonhoeffer*, 49; see also "God's Kenosis," 142 n. 5.

TH (1964) he affirms *creatio ex nihilo*[14] rooted in God's freedom.[15] And in 1971 Moltmann concurs, by asking and answering plainly: "How then can we explain God's freedom relative to his creation? The world as free creation cannot be a necessary unfolding of God nor an emanation of his being from his divine fullness. God is free. But he does not act capriciously."[16] In 1973, however, there is a shift when he maintains that freedom and love can only be related to one another, they cannot be put into any necessary opposition.[17] Replying to Kasper's "fears," Moltmann asserts that "The Trinity is complete in itself" yet quickly adds: the Trinity "is however, open to humans, open to the world and in this respect incomplete [*unvollkommen*] in its being of love, just as the lover does not want to be complete without the beloved."[18] On the same page, he discusses the necessity of the world for God by asking and answering a central question:

> Does God need the world in order to come to himself? If one understands by "himself" his abstract being for himself and by

14. Moltmann affirms *creatio ex nihilo*, *creatio continua*, and evolution (*FC* 119; *GC* 74, 207–8); on his doctrine of creation related to evolution, see Bauckham, *Theology of Jürgen Moltmann*, 190–98. It should be noted that the very notion of creation out of nothing is not derived from the Genesis narratives, principally; Walter Brueggemann cites this revisionist doctrine as "imaginative remembering," rooted in 2 Macc 7:28 (Brueggemann, *Introduction to the Old Testament*, 34). The doctrine of creation *ex nihilo* has been "integral" to a proper understanding of creation since Irenaeus (*GC* 332–33 n. 3). On the theological significance of creation *ex nihilo*, including a discussion of Process thought, which argues against creation out of nothing, based on the existence of evil and more centrally because it is arbitrary, see Fergusson, *The Cosmos and the Creator: An Introduction to the Theology of Creation*, 23–45.

15. *TH* 179; he rejects Bloch's claim that nothing comes from nothing.

16. *TJ* 40. He situates God's freedom to create in a notion of play, which he likens to theatre, dance, music, children playing, beauty, rejoicing and liberty (*GC* 310ff.; see also *TJ* 45–47). Unfortunately, his focus on play is one-sided, since he singularly focuses on the positive connotations. Ultimately, his references need balance: play, at times, has darker elements, and more importantly games have an unknown and uncertain future, which is precisely their appeal; theatre, and even children playing, is rarely one-sidedly devoid of tension and resolution. Yet, Moltmann centers on the positive aesthetically pleasing notions, and as such, his understanding inadequately spotlights only one side of the resources the symbol play could have provided.

17. *DGG* 155.

18. Ibid.; *Unvollkommen* can be translated as incomplete or imperfect. *ET* 323 [282]: "The Trinity is open, not out of deficiency and imperfection [*Unvollkommenheit*], but in the superfluity and overflow of the love which gives created beings the living space for their livingness, and the free scope for their development."

himself, then one must answer this question in the negative. If one understands by "himself" what the Bible calls his glory, his justice, and his kingdom, then one must answer the question in the affirmative, even if one would not want to put it in the sense of "incompletion" [*Unvollkommenheit*] of his love and the openness of his hope.[19]

Yet, to the extent that Moltmann customarily refuses to discuss the Trinity in abstraction (he consistently prefers moving from the particular to the universal), he also rejects the negative answer. In *CPS* (1975) he amplified this understanding by asserting that "God is *not perfect* if this means that he did not in the craving of his love want his creation to be necessary to his perfection."[20] To the decisive question "could God have chosen not to create the world?" he replies in the late 1970s that God has no freedom of choice.[21] And most appreciably in *TKG* (1980) his position is developed explicitly rejecting Barth's "arbitrary" doctrine,[22] by asserting: "God 'needs' the world and man."[23] Seeking to distance himself from creation as decree he speaks highly of Christian panentheism, which bases creation in the divine essence: "Creation is a fruit of God's longing for 'his Other' and for that Other's free response to the divine love. That is why the idea of the world is inherent in the nature of God himself from eternity."[24] Insisting that he is avoiding arbitrary elements of the Nominalist variety,[25] he couples seemingly diametrically opposed notions into a Christian doctrine of

---

19. *DGG* 155.

20. *CPS* 62.

21. *DGG* 170–73; explicitly *contra* Barth, *Church Dogmatics*, IV/1:306ff.

22. *TKG* 54ff; see also *GC* 75; *DGG* 155.

23. *TKG* 58; see also *FC* 119–24; *GC* 86–93. *Contra* O'Donnell: "Neither [for Moltmann] does God need the world to fulfill himself" (O'Donnell, *Trinity and Temporality*, 148).

24. *TKG* 106; this kind of language calls into question the very notion of God "for himself." Positing panentheism as the correct understanding of the God-world relationship helps Moltmann overcome his earlier emphasis of the future as God's essential nature, while also avoiding the pantheism of which he has been accused. While on the surface he can come close to process theology (especially some of his early statements), in *GC* he insists that there is "a fundamental distinction between creation and Creator" (*GC* 79; see also 79–85; *HTG* 18; *SpL* 35).

25. See *DGG* 170; *TKG* 52–56; *GC* 81–83.

creation. The reformulated position is a silent recantation,[26] making creation necessary in the context of the doctrine of God. A *via media* between Christian theism and Christian pantheism is forged only when God's liberty is not arbitrary,[27] as in Christian panentheism: "If we lift the concept of necessity out of the context of compulsive necessity and determination by something external, then in God *necessity* and *freedom* coincide [*Zusammenfallen*]; they are what is for him axiomatic, self-evident."[28] Moving from the economic Trinity to the immanent (although admittedly, these designations are tenuous in his work), Moltmann turns the traditional viewpoint (God creates freely) on its head: "it is impossible to conceive of a God who is not a creative God. A non-creative God would be incomplete [*unvollkommen*] compared with the God who is eternally creative."[29] Viewing God's love as pre-eminent when discussing God's need of creation, he claims that God without creation is contradictory: "It is in accordance with the love which is God that he should fashion a creation which he rejoices over ... Not to do this would contradict the love which God is."[30] In *GC* Moltmann does indeed affirm *creatio e libertate Dei*, but insists that the affirmation must not stop there: "when we say that God created the world 'out of freedom', we must immediately add 'out of love.'"[31] He insists on designating creation as a choice for God, but just below the surface of this admission is a stress on necessity which determines the proper understanding of God's freedom: "In his love God can choose; but he chooses only that which corresponds to his essential goodness ... God does therefore

---

26. He does not point out the change, but following his citations one can trace it (see *TKG* 236 n.15).

27. *SpL* 211–13; *TKG* 107: "If God's nature is goodness, then the freedom of his will lies in his will to goodness"; "In order to understand the history of mankind as a history *in* God, the distinction between the world process and the inner-trinitarian process must be maintained and emphasized."

28. *TKG* 107 [121–22]; see also *GC* 76.

29. *TKG* 106 [121].

30. Ibid., 58 [74]. Indeed, the impetus for God's creativity is love: "*Love is the self-communication of the good. It is the power of good to go out of itself, to enter into other being, to participate in other being*" (*TKG* 57).

On Moltmann's view of the *imago dei*, see principally *M* 108ff.; *GC* 216, 222–23, 233–43; *HTG* 137–38, 182; *CJF* 56; *GHH* 40; *JCTW* 86; *CoG* 72–73; *GSS* 78–83, 122; "Is There Life After Death?" 244–45.

31. *GC* 75.

what for him is axiomatic—what is divine. In doing this he is entirely free, and in this freedom he is entirely himself."[32] This understanding, he believes, enables him to steer clear of two dangers when discussing the relationship of creation to necessity. On one side, his doctrine refuses any tinge of outward duress or pressure on God in the act of creation and, on the other, he seeks to exclude any apparent arbitrariness.[33]

Indeed, for Moltmann, God is neither under outer-compulsion to create, yet, due to God's nature as loving and creative, nor is he free to avoid being creative. This understanding enables Moltmann, seemingly, to subscribe to the best elements of Barth's doctrine (which strongly favors God's freedom), while also refuting the portrayal of God as confronted with a decision to create, that he might have refused.[34] By insisting that one infers the inner-workings of the immanent Trinity based on the activity and revelation in the economy, Moltmann regards any notion of God's "decision" to create inadequate, for two reasons: (1) it is speculative and (2) introduces an arbitrary element in God. These reasons are mutually reinforcing as Moltmann will have nothing to do with God making a decision to do anything. (This latter point is integral to his doctrine, and should not be under-emphasized.) In principle, he opposes God's "free will" based on his rejection of God as absolute subject.[35] It is not the general purpose of stressing God's freedom that Moltmann disallows (indeed he affirms God's freedom), but rather its implication: a doctrine fully concentrated on the free choice of God (à la Barth) regarding the creation of the world necessitates the opportunity that God may have not created in the first place.[36] And for all the relative value that the freedom side of the dialectic contributes to

---

32. *GC* 76.

33. See *GC* 72–79; *GC* 76: "In his free love God confers his goodness: that is the work of his creation." In this section of *GC* Moltmann refers back to *TKG* 52ff., where in the context of discussing God's freedom, he criticizes Barth's "nominalist" arbitrary approach to God's decision to create; see also *TKG* 107.

34. He quotes Barth on this point in order to disagree: "God . . . could have remained satisfied with Himself and with His impassible glory and blessedness of His own inner life. But He did not do so. He elected man . . ." (Barth, *Church Dogmatics*, II/2:166, as quoted in *GC* 82; see also *TKG* 52ff.).

35. *GC* 16–17, 79–86.

36. While earlier his work seemed to align him with Process theology, the more he publishes the more his theology develops a sustained critique of Process thought.

Moltmann's understanding, he substantially qualifies God's freedom to create by supplementing it with the dialectical caveat of necessity.[37]

> What concept of freedom is appropriate for God? If we start from the point of view of the created being, the Creator appears as almighty and gracious. His freedom has no limits, and his commitment to what he has created is without obligation. But if we start from the Creator himself,[38] the self-communication of his goodness in love to his creation is not a matter of his free will. It is the self-evident operation of his eternal nature. The essential activity of God *is* the eternal resolve of his will, and the eternal resolve of his will *is* his essential activity. In other words, God is not entirely free when he can do and leave undone what he likes; he is entirely free when he is entirely himself.[39]

Here Moltmann defines freedom in dialectical relationship with necessity. His understanding of creation is informed by the confluence of necessity, freedom, and love, which condition the divine nature. This understanding moves him to exclude creation as arbitrary for God. As was seen previously, for Moltmann God needs the world, so creation cannot be arbitrary. None of this is too surprising based on his elucidation of God's involvement in the world; its predictability, however, does not determine its coherence.

Creation: Necessity or Faithfulness?

Creation is no mere "stage" arbitrary and incidental to the "drama" of God working in history, but rather necessary and constitutive for God's own being. And upon closer inspection, from the perspective of relating creation to hope, precisely where critics find a flaw, there is a degree of strength, since this scheme ensures creation's eschatological participation. Moltmann removes so-called "arbitrary" decision-making processes from God, because he refuses to discuss the doctrine of God

---

37. See *GC* 74; *TKG* 58–59. The fact that he asserts God's freedom from "preconditions" and "external necessity" is not rejected when qualifying God's freedom to create (*GC* 74).

38. This parallels Moltmann's view in *CG*, when he focuses on the cross and its meaning for God, instead of its meaning for humanity.

39. *GC* 82–83; see also 311; *TJ* 41. He states unequivocally: "the world does not exist of necessity. It exists because God created it out of liberty. He created it freely but not arbitrarily . . . He created what accords with his inmost nature. That is why God's creation is a good creation" (*GC* 82).

without creation. This understanding of freedom could be defended on the grounds that it fortifies divine freedom, removing the perceived error in Barth's view. Framing the issue in this way sets up an either/or decision, exposing a false dichotomy: creation is either arbitrary or necessary. While the intent may have been to reconfigure and strengthen God's freedom from an arbitrary "Nominalist fringe,"[40] ironically by introducing necessity he threatens to undermine the very doctrine he intends to support.

Although critics decry his doctrine of God at this point,[41] the more pressing problem, which goes unnoticed, is the incoherence of this position for Moltmann's own program. Indeed, the most acute problem with his construal of God's freedom is the question it raises in relation to his doctrine of hope. The core of Moltmann's doctrine of hope is God's faithfulness, yet in his doctrine of creation he essentially posits creation as hope because it is "needed" by God, vital to his life. Thus framed, his doctrine of creation has omitted a highly-prized element of his program: God's faithfulness.

While his argument regarding God's freedom focuses on the initial act, it has implications for his eschatology. Stating that creation is necessary for God muddles the picture and calls into question God's faithfulness to his creation. Moltmann has set up the wrong dialectic. It appears that he does not realize fully that the proper dialectic is not freedom and necessity, but rather freedom and faithfulness. When one approaches the topic from faithfulness[42] rather than freedom, his presentation of freedom as qualified by necessity is both unnecessary and unhelpful. Now necessity conditions God's nature, in order to prohibit freedom from being misunderstood. This essentially turns freedom on its head by introducing necessity into God's dealings with the world (whether related to historical involvement or creation). Relating freedom to necessity ensures creation is central to God's being. Yet, Moltmann could

---

40. *GC* 81; see also *DGG* 170; *TKG* 52–56.

41. For salient critiques, see especially Molnar, "The Function of the Trinity," 210ff.; Walsh, "Theology of Hope and the Doctrine of Creation," 53ff. Their criticisms are valid, but like most Moltmann critics, they use an external measure of orthodoxy with which to dismantle his views. In so doing, they miss the more crucial problems facing Moltmann's program at this point.

42. Earlier in a passing comment, he connected "God's nature with his faithfulness" (Moltmann and Weissbach, *Two Studies in the Theology of Bonhoeffer*, 49; compare *TKG* 53; "God's Kenosis," 142 n. 5).

have, and arguably should have, presented his understanding of the necessity of creation along different lines, calling upon faithfulness.

Moltmann's solution is further problematic since it seems that necessity conditions and thus impinges on both freedom and faithfulness. There are resources in his program for a rather simple solution to the problem he seeks to resolve: God's freedom to create is unhindered and unqualified by necessity, and so God is faithful to creation not out of need, but out of faithfulness. This formula would seemingly help him stress God's freedom, while also being coherent with Moltmann's theology, and place creation in a proper relationship with God for initial, continual, and new creation. Even if Moltmann is correct that Barth's doctrine needs to be supplemented (which is debatable), he can avoid any negative implications for continual and eschatological creation, by asserting God's faithfulness to his creation. Unfortunately, he has not learned his own lesson: necessity is not the dialectical balance for freedom; that role is reserved for faithfulness. Though Moltmann's doctrine of creation is determined by his prior assertions related to God needing the world, it would have been more coherent if he had unequivocally invoked God's faithfulness: God's reclamation project of creation will be fulfilled because God has made this promise; God is faithful. This view is merely an extension of his prior theology. Vehemently stressing God's freedom dialectically related to God's faithfulness is the more coherent option for Moltmann to achieve his goal: removing capriciousness and arbitrariness. Instead his position unfortunately places God in need of the world, based on necessity. Regardless whether one finds Moltmann's construal convincing or flawed, God's need for the world places creation in a wider context of "God's eschatological self-deliverance": "the deliverance of or redemption [*Erlösung*] of the world is bound up with the self-deliverance of God [*Selbsterlösung Gottes*] from his sufferings . . . The theology of God's passion leads to the idea of God's self-subjection to suffering. It therefore also has to arrive at the idea of God's eschatological self-deliverance."[43] On this understanding, creation is aligned with redemption because God needs the world and he ensures it will be redeemed and made new, so that God "will be all in all." Creation, then, in the final analysis is not contingent, it is necessary for God's eschatological self-redemption. While he could have detailed his

---

43. *TKG* 60 [75].

doctrine of creation in a simpler and arguably more coherent way, creation as necessity guarantees that creation is not a doctrine limited to the beginning but is central to Moltmann's eschatology, which necessitates understanding creation in eschatological dimensions.

Creation in Eschatological Dimensions

While the previous section showed problems with Moltmann's doctrine of creation related to necessity, this section seeks to show that although necessity appears to be more central than faithfulness to his understanding of God's freedom, ultimately, the core of his doctrine of creation follows the pattern of his doctrine of hope. For Moltmann, a doctrine of creation is more than a description of the events of the Garden of Eden: "God's historical relationship with the world does not merely begin after the Fall;[44] it begins with creation. Creation is aligned towards the future [*Zukunft*]."[45] Throughout *GC* he insists that creation is only understood fully in reference to its eschatological destiny, and in Moltmann's conception this renders creation thoroughly hopeful. The cross-resurrection dialectical pattern sets the frame and fills the content.

Whereas previously he intentionally focused on the cross and its significance for God, writing in the late 1970s he parallels the forsakenness of the cross with the "whole wretched creation," while also paralleling the power of the resurrection with the new creation: "the raising of this one person [Jesus] is hence *nova creatio* for everyone."[46] And in *GC* (while reflecting on Rom 8:19ff.), he links hope to suffering, by advocating a "hope which makes us conscious of 'the sufferings of this present time.' That is the double effect of hope . . . The point where the liberty of the children of God has come so close that we revive in hope is the very point where we become painfully aware of the chains of bondage."[47] Moltmann's doctrine of creation and doctrine of hope are mutually reinforcing. His doctrine of creation complements his doctrine of

---

44. On Moltmann's view of the "fall," see *SpL* 126; *CoG* 90: "It is a negative hubris for human beings to maintain that they are the origin of all unhappiness in the world."

45. *FC* 118 [125–26] = *SW* 36; see also *RRF* 36. He concurs with von Rad: "In Old Testament theology creation is an eschatological concept" (*FC* 118).

46. *FC* 163; see also *TH* 179–80.

47. *GC* 67; see also "Zum Gespräch," 95.

eschatology to such a high degree that they are best understood in reference, one to the other; they are virtually two sides of the same coin.

Creation and Redemption

The doctrine of creation is fundamentally hopeful for Moltmann because it is placed in the wider frame of eschatology, by asserting creation's need of redemption.[48] He sees creation as leading to redemption, rather than to return:

> The goal of this history of creation is not a return to the paradisal primordial condition. Its goal is the revelation of the glory of God. It is true that this end "corresponds" to the beginning in the sense that it represents the fulfillment of the real promise implanted in creation itself; but the new creation of heaven and earth in the kingdom of glory surpasses everything that can be told about creation in the beginning.[49]

Thus, the new creation is not a restorative return to paradisal Eden, but represents God's fulfillment of the promise inherent, indeed "implanted," in creation itself.[50] While resurrection power plays an important role in his understanding of the future of creation, he also relates creation to the cross. By developing the act of creation as divine kenosis and as creation's present situation as threatened by the imposing *nihil*, he ensures that the full weight of his doctrine of hope will impress his

---

48. He believes that viewing creation as merely a stage leading to redemption is incorrect (*GC* 5, 55, 166, 277; *WJC* 286).

Aligning creation with redemption is linked to his goal of surmounting the objectification of nature (*CJF* 60; *SW* 47ff.), which he fears is sustained by a concomitant body-soul dualism. Both of these views cause an incorrect view of the transcendence of God, engendering an anthropocentric world-view. For his various comments on these issues, see *CJF* 75; *HC* 130; *FC* 115–16 = *SW* 33–4; *TKG* 9; *GC* xvi, 6, 18, 36, 197; *WJC* 56ff.; *HTG* 162–4; *CoG* 300; *GSS* 17, 130. He explicitly affirms knowledge of creation "to perceive in order to participate, and to enter into the mutual relationships of the living thing" (*GC* 3). Earlier he was not so negative in characterizing the objectification of nature (*M* 108ff.).

49. *GC* 207.

50. Beyond *GC*, see especially *FC* 116–27 = *SW* 34–47; see also *FC* 170; *CoG* IV. Because Moltmann rightly refuses to limit creation to the origins of the world, he consults both the primary locus of the biblical account of creation (Genesis 1–3) and the New Testament to guide him (*GC* 55ff., 206ff.; *TJ* 45). Sourcing his doctrine of creation in such a way leads him to focus on creation in eschatological terms, finding links between creation, the new creation, the Holy Spirit and hope (see especially *GC* 65).

view of the relationship between God, creation and redemption.[51] The proper context of this relationship is Moltmann's understanding of creation *ex nihilo*.

CREATION OUT OF NOTHING

To comprehend fully Moltmann's understanding of creation out of nothing,[52] one must first understand the Lurian concept of *zimsum* and the impetus behind Moltmann's adoption of it.[53] Giving further insight into the direction he goes in *GC*, already in *TKG* Moltmann followed Isaac Luria[54] in advocating creation as *zimsum*, because with creation "*God's self-humiliation* begins."[55] Asserting that Christian theology, since Augustine, has understood creation one-sidedly and incorrectly as an external act of God,[56] Moltmann calls upon the doctrine of *zimsum* to explain the existence and location of creation.[57] He believes that *zimsum* is the only way to render creation out of nothing comprehensible. Echoing Luria, Moltmann's impetus is a key question: "How can God create out of 'nothing' when there cannot be such a thing as nothing, since his essence is everything and interpenetrates everything?"[58] For his answer, Moltmann adopts *zimsum*, whereby "God withdrew

---

51. Most explicitly, see "God's Kenosis," 137–51 = *SW* 54–67.

52. See "Schöpfung aus nichts," 259–67; this article reappears substantially in *GC*; see *GC* 86–93.

53. Moltmann's usage of *zimsum* has exercised commentators and drawn criticism; see Walsh, "Theology of Hope," 72; see also Breshears, "Creation Imaginatively Reconsidered: Review of *God in Creation*," 337–51; Deane-Drummond, *Ecology in Jürgen Moltmann's Theology*, 202–5; Fiddes, "Review of *God in Creation*," 263–65; Fiddes, *The Promised End*, 262; Jim McPherson, "Life, the Universe and Everything: Jürgen Moltmann's *God in Creation*," 39–42; Alan J. Torrance, "*Creatio ex Nihilo*," 90.

54. He accesses Luria's thought through Gershom Scholem's descriptions (*TKG* 237 n. 22); see Scholem, "Isaac Luria and His School," 260–64. *Contra* Phillips, who gives Moltmann too much credit by asserting that Moltmann "develops" *zimsum* (Benjamin Blair Phillips, "The Crisis of Creation," 9).

55. *TKG* 59.

56. Indeed, he questions the very notion of an outward aspect of God at all (*GC* 86), and is highly critical of the "patriarchal" view of creation as something God makes (*GC* 312ff.).

57. Moltmann calls upon *zimsum* from 1980 forward (see *FC* 120; *TKG* 108ff.; *GC* 86ff.; *WJC* 328–9; *SpL* 47ff.; *CoG* 297–308; *SW* 60–64, 119ff.).

58. *TKG* 108–11; *GC* 98; *CoG* 297; see also Scholem, "Isaac Luria and His School," 260–62.

his omnipresence in order to concede space for the limited presence of the creation. In this way creation comes into being in the space of God's *kenosis*."⁵⁹ "The first act of all is not an act of revelation but one of limitation."⁶⁰

While valid objections can be raised against Moltmann's speculation,⁶¹ there are at least two important elements of this adoption for his project. The first is that *zimsum* renders creation as kenosis for God.⁶² *Zimsum* serves to ground creation in a "humble" act, more in line with "motherly categories" of "letting-be, by making room" over against masculine metaphors of "making."⁶³ The second reason that *zimsum* appeals to Moltmann is less obvious, perhaps, but more crucial: it puts creation

---

59. *SW* 62 = "God's Kenosis," 146; see also *GC* 87; Moltmann believes that *zimsum* solves the problem of absolute space (*GC* 152–57; see also *SW* 62ff., 119ff.).

60. Scholem, "Isaac Luria and His School," 261. While the precise terminology differs at points, this is the concept of *zimsum* that Moltmann adopts fully.

61. The problems vary in significance: (1) he seeks to show creation's motherly side, but still discusses *zimsum* in terms of power (*TKG* 109; *GC* 87); (2) how does *zimsum* relate to trinitarian perichoresis? (see especially *CoG* 296ff.); (3) he seems to imply that the *nihil* is in God from the beginning. See especially Walsh, "Theology of Hope," 72–74; Deane-Drummond, *Ecology in Jürgen Moltmann's Theology*, 201–6.

62. *TKG* 59; *GC* 86–90; "God's Kenosis," 146–47 = *SW* 62–64. The adoption of *zimsum* seems to require a notion of zero-sum space, or absolute space which is a container that God indwells fully and so must vacate a portion in order to create. This emphasis ensures that creation exists in God (*CoG* 296ff.; see also *SW* 119–24). This is especially the case for Moltmann since he forbids the notion that God could have created a space in which to create the world outside himself (see *GC* chapter 6; *CoG* 296–308). For a more conflicted view, see *SW* 119.

63. *GC* 88; see also *TKG* 109, 162–66; *HTG* xiii–xvi, 1–25. Moltmann is inconsistent in what *zimsum* actually means regarding power. Calling to mind the Christ-hymn of Philippians 2, Moltmann interprets the act of creation as a divine kenosis: "Even in order to create heaven and earth, God emptied himself of his all-plenishing omnipotence, and as creator took upon himself the form of a servant" (*GC* 88; see also "God's Kenosis," 146–47 = *SW* 62–64). He views the creation of the world as an expression of God's love, "not a demonstration of his boundless power" (*GC* 75–76); yet compare his insistence, only a few pages later, that *zimsum* "is the affirmative force of God's self-negation which becomes the creative force in creation and salvation" (*GC* 87). And later he comments: "When God restricts himself so as to make room for his creation, this is an expression not of powerlessness but of almighty power" (*SW* 120). Moltmann seems conflicted. The solution is found, perhaps, in his initial comments, where Moltmann views creation as having two sides: an inward, feminine, restriction of space, and an outward, masculine, creation in space; indeed "Act I" veils and "Act II" reveals (*TKG* 110). The important point of this scheme is his insistence that creation is an act of kenosis: Act I always precedes and to some degree conditions Act II (see *TKG* 108–11).

in an eschatological light. Placing creation in need of redemption from the *nihil* renders *zimsum* integral to his divine eschatology: God's initial self-limitation [*Selbstverschränkung*] is matched by the eschatological de-restriction [*Selbstentschränkung*] at the new creation.[64] Although his stated goal is to better appreciate the truth of creation *ex nihilo*, it benefits his eschatology by conceptualizing the eschatological reversal of *zimsum*, when God "will be all in all."[65] While it may appear that his attempt to Christianize *zimsum* is principally related to God,[66] this is only part of the rationale. It contextualizes for Moltmann creation's relationship to the cross and resurrection, because it posits the impending *nihil* which must be overcome.

Overcoming the Nihil

Recall that Moltmann's doctrine of creation does not deal only with how things were in the beginning, but instead on how they are, and indeed how they will be. In this vein, Paul's comments in Romans 8:19–23[67] strongly impress Moltmann's understanding of both the futility and future of creation:

> Enslavement through the bondage of transience, and a yearning openness for the future . . . determine[s] the present condition of the world. And this is not only true of the world of men and women; it applies to the whole creation . . . It is a destiny to which creation is subjected: a continual process of annihilation, an all-embracing fellowship of suffering, and a tense and anxious openness for a different future.[68]

---

64. *GC* 86ff. Note: Kohl translates *(Selbst)entschränkung* as either delimitation or derestriction, but these are antonyms in English. The latter is correct and will be used to describe Moltmann's view; see, for example, *GC* 89 [101].

65. See *CoG* 294.

66. Phillips, "The Crisis of Creation," 105ff.

67. Rom 8:19–23: "19For the creation waits with eager longing for the revealing of the children of God; 20for the creation was subjected to futility, not of its own will but by the will of the one who subjected it, in hope 21that the creation itself will be set free from its bondage to decay and will obtain the freedom of the glory of the children of God. 22We know that the whole creation has been groaning in labor pains until now; 23and not only the creation, but we ourselves, who have the first fruits of the Spirit, groan inwardly while we wait for adoption, the redemption of our bodies."

68. *GC* 39; see also 6, 67–68; *FC* 12, 29; *WJC* 253, 280, 304; *CoG* 91–92. While his mature view is relatively clear (creation is redeemed and nature is fallen), commentators are conflicted about Moltmann's early view of nature (*FC* 163; *GL* 33; "Hope and

The context for understanding "the present condition of the world" is to be found in Moltmann's view that, historically speaking, God's self-humiliation occurs first in creation, then in the cross.[69] Whereas in *CG* and *TKG* Moltmann centrally locates God's capacity for suffering in the abandonment of the Son, in reference to creation he not only points to God's suffering on Golgotha, but also to the Old Testament understanding that God "opens himself in his Shekinah for the sufferings of his people."[70] He relates this understanding to creation by explaining the relationship between creation and the *nihil*:[71] "The space which comes into being and is set free by God's self-limitation is a literally God-forsaken space. The *nihil* in which God creates his creation is God-forsakenness, hell, absolute death."[72] This, then, is creation's predicament.[73] What is the creator's response? Here Moltmann relies on the dialectic that grounds his doctrine of hope. To convey his meaning, he emphasizes the cross's role for creation:

> If he [God] desires its [creation's] salvation, then in the sending and surrender of his own Son he exposes himself to the annihilating Nothingness, so that he may overcome it in himself and through himself, and in that way give his creation existence, salvation and liberty ... He pervades the space of God-forsakenness with his presence. It is the presence of his self-humiliating, suffering love for his creation, in which he experiences death itself.

---

the Biomedical Future of Man," 93-97). For the key discussion, see John O'Donnell, "Exploring the Human: Theology in Dialogue," 128-9; Schubert Ogden, "Response to Jürgen Moltmann," in Cousins, *Hope and the Future of Man*, 115-16; Walsh, "Theology of Hope," 59.

69. *TKG* 109; *SW* 202 n. 17. Although Moltmann makes it appear that he is following a long train in Christian theology, he is not (see *GC* 334 n. 28; *SW* 63-64, 119).

70. *SW* 58-60; "Ernst Blochs Christologie," 9; see also Fiddes, *Creative Suffering*, 7. Moltmann follows Scholem on this "rift" of divine humiliation (*TKG* 28ff.).

71. On this matter, Fergusson fears that Moltmann's position is too close to Hegel who equated evil to finitude (Fergusson, *Cosmos and the Creator*, 27).

72. *GC* 87-88. Compare, however, *CoG* 298-99: "When the triune God restricts his omnipresence in order to permit a creation outside himself to be 'there,' he does not leave behind a vacuum, as the kabbalistic doctrine of *zimsum* suggest. He throws open a space for those he has created, a space which corresponds to his inner indwellings: he allows a world different from himself to exist before him, with him and *in him*."

73. He employs sacrificial imagery (typically related to the cross) as points of reflection for a proper understanding of God's suffering in creation, in light of industrial society and capitalistic economies. For his later elucidation of these themes, see *SW* 55-58.

> That is why God's presence in the crucified Christ gives creation eternal life, and does not annihilate it . . . By entering into the God-forsakenness of sin and death (which is Nothingness), God overcomes it and makes it part of his eternal life.[74]

For Moltmann, the annihilating Nothingness is "overcome" in the cross. His appeal to the category of kenosis for understanding creation is dependent upon his theology of the cross. While developing the Spirit's relationship to evolution and development, he consciously elaborates upon both *CG* and *TKG* by tying the Spirit's activity to suffering: "The Spirit of the universe is the Spirit who proceeds from the Father and shines forth in the Son. The evolutions and catastrophes of the universe are also the movements and experiences of the Spirit of creation. That is why Paul tells us that the divine Spirit "sighs" in all created things under the power of futility."[75] Later in *GC*, he makes a bold assertion:

> If God commits himself to his limited creation, and if he himself dwells in it as "the giver of life," this presupposes a self-limitation, a self-humiliation and a self-surrender of the Spirit. This history of suffering creation, which is subject to transience, then brings with it a history of suffering by the Spirit who dwells in creation. But the Spirit who dwells in creation turns creation's history of suffering into a history of hope.[76]

He avoids explicating why (or how) suffering becomes hope, but the basis seems generally clear. Based on his close identification of God's faithful presence in suffering, Moltmann finds hope wherever there is suffering. For the travails of creation, the kenotic Spirit engenders hope because the Spirit is present: "in the suffering history of the world of nature and human beings, we have to discern the inexpressible sighings of the indwelling Spirit, and the suffering presence of God."[77]

While this sets the frame of relating the Spirit's suffering in relation with creation (which is itself related to *Shekinah*),[78] God is not controlled by the futility of suffering; ultimately his doctrine of creation is hopeful because creation's redemption is dependent upon God's faith-

---

74. *GC* 91; see also 74.

75. Ibid., 16; he seems to be citing Rom 8:22–26; see also *SpL* 76–77.

76. *GC* 102; see also *TKG* 59: "With the creation of a world which is not God . . . *God's self-humiliation* begins."

77. *GC* 102.

78. See especially *SpL* 47–51; *ET* 314; *SW* 58–67.

fulness in redeeming it: "God's adherence to his resolve *to create* also means a resolve *to save* ... The creation of the world is itself a promise of resurrection, and the overcoming of death in the victory of eternal life."[79] While he parallels creation and the cross as kenosis for God, he insists that this is not the end of the story: "the raising of the crucified Jesus is the beginning of the End-time process of the raising of the dead, and with that the new creation of the world."[80] Indeed, the new creation is another episode in a long line of God's divine intervention, principally the Old Testament narratives of Yahweh's activity of rescue and God's active, demonstrable overcoming of death in the resurrection. By asserting that the new creation is reliant upon the God "who gives life to the dead and calls into existence the things that do not exist," Moltmann firmly identifies the God of the resurrection with the one who creates *ex nihilo*.[81] He stresses the power of the *Zukunft* to the extent that even "end of the world" apocalyptic scenarios cannot "divert" the "Creator-out-of-nothing."[82]

The New Creation: Novum *from the* Zukunft

The relationship between the new creation and the God of the future is typified in resurrection power. To be sure, these moves are inseparable from Moltmann's understanding that God needs the world. The God of the future (*Zukunft*) will ensure creation's ultimate redemption. While creation is consciously set in an eschatological frame, he explicitly rejects the eschatological new creation as a return, preferring to view it as a renewal: "the end is much more than the beginning. The outreach of hope at the end extends far further than at the beginning."[83] Indeed, in the "eschatological moment" there is both "historical similarity, in spite

---

79. *GC* 90; he cites 1 Cor 15:26, 55–57.

80. *GC* 66. Initial and continual creation, then, are identified with both cross and resurrection, because the referent for understanding the *nihil* is not the cross alone, but also the resurrection, to such an extent that Moltmann equates them: "In the light of the cross of Christ, *creatio ex nihilo* means forgiveness of sins through Christ's sufferings ... and the resurrection of the dead and eternal life through the lordship of the Lamb" (*GC* 91).

81. Rom 4:17; see *GC* 66.

82. Ibid., 93.

83. *CoG* 264; see also *EB*.

of all eschatological dissimilarity; and to this the imaginative power of hope can cling."[84]

Back in October 1967, while showing signs of turning to a theology of the cross, Moltmann parallels the action of God in the resurrection to the act of creation: "Out of chaos, darkness, and flood God created the world. In the context of nothingness he revealed his creative power ... He will raise the dead. If, for the sake of this God, Christians hope for the future, they hope for a *novum ex nihilo*."[85] The same type of language appears earlier in *TH*: "The experience of the cross of Jesus means for them [the disciples] the experience of the god-forsakenness of God's ambassador—that is, an absolute *nihil* embracing also God. The experience of the appearance of the crucified one as the living Lord therefore means for them the experience of the nearness of God in the god-forsaken one ... that is, a new totality which annihilates the total *nihil*."[86] The annihilating power of the resurrection of Christ brings a new creation: "The resurrection of Christ does not mean a possibility within the world and its history, but a new possibility altogether for the world, for existence and for history."[87] The archetype, then, of present creation's (dis)continuity with the new creation is Jesus' death and resurrection: "With the rebirth of Christ from death to eternal life we also expect the rebirth of the whole cosmos."[88]

Tensions arise in Moltmann's conception of designating the new creation as renewal. He insists, especially in later comments, that the *transformatio mundi* be rendered eschatologically, and in so doing, one must understand the new creation as not only transformation of the existing order, but rather as "new not only over against the world of sin and death, but over against the first, temporal creation too."[89] To do this, of course, is to posit a coming future as *Zukunft*. This move is

---

84. *CoG* 294; he is co-opting Bultmann's phrase and using it in a totally different way for emphasizing the future; for criticisms of Bultmann, see *CoG* 19–22, 293.

85. *RRF* 171.

86. *TH* 198; see also 85.

87. *TH* 179; see also *SoL* 122ff. "We are afraid of the future dangers of the world ... [but] we believe in God and that God will not let creation drop" ("All Things New," 30).

88. *SoL* 123; see also "The Blessing of Hope," 155; On this, see Weder, "Hope and Creation."

89. *CoG* 271.

bound up with rendering creation as the place of eschatological divine indwelling. Hope, for Moltmann, is eschatologically orientated to the future when "God will live on Earth, as in Heaven."[90] To become God's home, creation is in need of a different future than that which can come from the past (*futurum*). It needs the future from the coming God (*adventus*), when God "will dwell with them as their God; they will be his peoples, and God himself will be with them" (Rev 21:3).[91] The hope of creation is not immanent in the system itself, but is instead open to transformation, by the coming God. This conceptuality necessitates an understanding of "creation as an open system," which is important for his doctrine of creation and his eschatology.

CREATION AS AN OPEN SYSTEM

Ever since the mid-1970s Moltmann has described "creation as an open system."[92] While in *GC* he does not define this phrase with any real degree of specificity,[93] it is generally clear that open systems "exist in the direction of their future. The future is the scope of their open possibilities."[94] "Creation is not closed within itself; it is open for its his-

---

90. "Zum Gespräch," 95; see also *GC* 181–4.

91. Moltmann mistakenly cites Rev 21:4.

92. See *FC* 115–30 = *SW* 33–53 (this essay was first issued as "Creation and Redemption," 119–34). Creation is an open system, open to God (*GC* 17, 39, 63, 69, 103, 205ff, 264–65; *ET* 112; *SW* 83–84), which corresponds to his prior insistence that God is open to the world (*CG* 249; *FC* 93; *CPS* 55; *DGG* 155; *TKG* 127; *GSS* 101, 184).

Elsewhere, he stresses the importance of openness using it in numerous ways: hope is open (*TH* 335); history is an "open process" (*HP* 81; see also *TH* 276); The cross "give[s] openness to that which is fixed" (*CG* 219); christology is open (*CG* 106ff); the world is an "open process" (*TJ* 44); humanity experiences being human as "openness" (*M* 9; see also *TH* 286); "socially open companionship is the form of life which corresponds to God" (*GC* 233); the social doctrine of the Trinity describes an "open Trinity" (*GC* 242–43); and friendship in the New Testament is an open friendship (*SpL* 258f.). The open anthropology seems to be influenced by Bloch's notion of the *homo absconditus*, whose being is "not yet" (see Dabney, "Advent of the Spirit," 84–85; Wakefield, *Moltmann*, 12 n. 74).

93. In the earlier essay he delineated four necessary properties which would qualify a system as open: (1) that the system has different possibilities for alteration; (2) that its future behavior has not been totally determined by its previous behavior; (3) that it can communicate with other systems; (4) that the final condition of the system is different from its initial state (*FC* 190 n. 14 = *SW* 199 n. 15).

94. *GC* 264–65. At one point he insists: "there is no such thing as a 'closed system' . . . because they elude all observation" (*FC* 190 n. 14 = *SW* 199 n. 15); however, in 1970,

tory... If God made creation to be the kingdom of his glory, then it was he who gave it movement and set it in motion, at the same time lending it an irreversible direction... He accompanies it in this movement by opening up new possibilities... through the fellowship of his creative Spirit."[95] While some have criticized Moltmann for converting a scientific notion into theological currency,[96] the openness of creation is attractive to him because he can show creation's eschatological horizon: creation is open to the future, God, heaven, and thus available as a resource for his doctrine of hope: "Heaven and earth wait to become God's house because all creatures are created for love. The divine spirit is in all of them and opens them for God's future. God finds no rest until all of God's creatures... have returned to God's lap."[97]

Yet, for Moltmann such is God's creative power that even humanity's destruction of nature cannot prevent God's plan for creation's future.[98] This is grounded in his insistence that God requires creation for himself. Indeed, this line of thinking leads directly toward the eschatological consummation when God "will be all in all," when creation is "glorified" and "will be *the home of the Trinity*."[99] While the problems of making God in "need" of anything were elucidated above, this tenet of his thought is the most obvious way that Moltmann renders creation as a doctrine of hope: "The deliverance of the world from its contradiction is nothing other than God's deliverance of himself from the contradiction of his world."[100]

Moltmann, perhaps critically, asserts: "Between the individual man and his hope and the open possibilities in the world process, there stands society, which today is... built according to the model of the 'closed system'" (*EH* 27).

95. *GC* 207. see also *TKG* 101ff.; "Is the World Coming to an End or Has Its Future Already Begun?"

96. For example, see Walsh, "Theology of Hope," 55ff.; McPherson, "Life, the Universe and Everything," 34ff. The only scientific meaning Moltmann gives this notion is that it expresses the irreversibility of time (*ET* 112).

97. "All Things New," 31.

98. Medieval historian (and Christian) Lynn White, Jr. laid the blame of the then-current ecological crisis at the feet of the Judeo-Christian faith; see his seminal article: "The Historical Roots of Our Ecologic Crisis." It is unclear whether Moltmann agrees with White's thesis (see *GC* 324 n. 11).

99. *TKG* 105. "The creation is also 'ecological' in so far as it represents the 'house' and 'dwelling' of God" (Müller-Fahrenholz, *Kingdom and Power*, 154).

100. *TKG* 39.

To be sure, any assertions related to the (dis)continuity between creation and the new creation will be ultimately conditioned by his understanding of redemption as working or leading not from past to the future, but rather from the future to the past: "What has to be called eschatological is the movement of *redemption*, which runs counter to evolution . . . this is a movement which runs from the future to the past . . . The raising of the dead, the gathering of the victims and the seeking of the lost bring a redemption of the world which no evolution can ever achieve."[101] To this end, what about rumors of apocalyptic end-time scenarios, depicting and predicting the earth's destruction, whether via warfare (nuclear, biomedical) or natural destruction (earthquakes, tsunamis, hurricanes)? Apocalyptic fears over the "end of the world" are unfounded, in Moltmann's view.[102] Furthermore, God will not be dictated to regarding what can and cannot be done in the eschatological re-creation; indeed this is the very essence of the divine power of *Zukunft*: "How should the Creator-out-of-nothing be diverted from his intention and his love through any devastations in what he has created?"[103]

This side of God's creation is "open" to God, but while this terminology of an open system lends itself to being interpreted as open to possibilities, that is of either good or evil, destruction or consummation, Moltmann makes it explicitly clear this is not what he means, as he further delineates the separation of heaven and earth at just this point, since earth is "the determined side of this system."[104] This move to a guaranteed future is totally in line with *TH*, which also posits the notion of openness not to destruction, but only to God's fulfillment.[105]

Conclusion

At the core of Moltmann's doctrine of creation is its need of redemption. Three notions reinforce this relationship: (1) creation is integral to the being of God; (2) God's freedom to create is qualified by necessity;

101. *WJC* 303, ellipsis added, otherwise, as cited by Fiddes, *Promised End*, 190.

102. He calls on Noah narrative, concluding that even this story does not support the fear of impending doom, but rather "arouses the hope that God will remain true to his decision over creation" (*CJF* 31).

103. *GC* 93.

104. Ibid., 163.

105. Moltmann insists that this is necessary to ensure that humanity does not bring or cause the kingdom of God.

(3) creation is open to God. This train of thought in many ways ensures that the doctrine of creation is a doctrine of hope. Creation is important to God, because he requires it for the eschatological indwelling and since the new creation is a transformation of the present creation. God's need of the world becomes an eschatological goal. Even if conceived as "open," hope is only conceivable because it is grounded in the *Zukunft*, and this important view is applied to creation quite readily: in the final analysis, the world is not open to destruction, because God is not limited by the past and present. The new creation is not becoming, it is coming.[106]

The tension between God's openness to suffering and the relentless assertion that God is coming and will re-create the heavens and the earth for the new creation, when God "will be all in all" follows the same pattern as his doctrine of hope, fully reliant on the dialectic of the cross and resurrection, but as in *TH* always with an eye on the resolution fully in view.[107] Indeed, to conclude his lengthy exposition on the importance of God's self-restriction for creation, he turns to the wider frame that conditions the preceding comments: "The goal of God's *kenosis* in the creation and preservation of the world is that *future* . . . the kingdom of God and the new creation, or 'world without end.'"[108] And in the new creation God can dwell fully, so that he may "be all in all." The next chapter investigates three images that Moltmann uses to expound hope in a christological direction: cross, resurrection, and parousia.

---

106. How this relates to evolution, is not considered here; see Bauckham, *Theology of Jürgen Moltmann*, 183–98.

107. Moltmann labels his view two sides of a mirror (*TKG* 109).

108. *SW* 67.

6

Christology as Hope

Introduction

CHRISTIAN HOPE CENTERS ON JESUS CHRIST.[1] MOLTMANN HAS ADvanced this perspective since the opening of *TH*: "Christianity is eschatology, is hope" and "speaks of Jesus Christ and *his* future."[2] In *WJC*, originally planned as the centerpiece of his "contributions,"[3] Moltmann proposes a pneumatological christology,[4] because only this approach acknowledges rightly the importance of the pervasive pneumatic activity in Jesus' life.[5] Once one takes into account the Spirit's activity, the proper label for a discussion of Jesus' life is not simply the history of

---

1. For Moltmann's christology besides *WJC*, see *EH* 60–69; *CG* 86–87; *HD* 101; *HTG* 31–43; *JCTW*. For secondary comments on Moltmann's christology, see Bauckham, *Theology of Jürgen Moltmann*, 199–213; Millicent C. Feske, "Christ and Suffering in Moltmann's Thought," *ATJ* 55.1 (2000) 85–104; Donald Macleod, "The Christology of Jürgen Moltmann," 35–47; Müller-Fahrenholz, *Kingdom and Power*, 167–81; Farrow, "In the End is the Beginning," 428–30; Rasmusson, *Church as Polis*, 68–74.

2. *TH* 16, 17, respectively; see also *EB* 88.

3. The unforeseen addition of *SpL* displaces it.

4. Moltmann's label "pneumatological christology" is used instead of the more common "Spirit christology," because of the historically problematic associations of the latter (namely subordinationism), which Moltmann generally avoids (see *TKG* 132–34). Bauckham asserts correctly: "He [Moltmann] sees this [Spirit-Christology] neither as an alternative to incarnational Christology nor as leading to a degree Christology (the dangers which the tradition has seen in Spirit-Christology)" (Bauckham, *Theology of Jürgen Moltmann*, 207).

For a historical discussion of the problems associated with Spirit christology, see Kelly, *Early Christian Doctrines*, 142–45; for a modern day articulation, see Ralph Del Colle, *Christ and the Spirit*.

5. *WJC* 73ff.; see also *CPS* 37; *HTG* 34; *ET* 307. This is also in line with his rejection of the *Filioque* addition (see *TKG* 178–87).

Jesus, but rather "the Spirit-history" of Jesus.⁶ This approach is intent on avoiding any hint of "christomonism" by attending to the variety of trinitarian relationships. In other words, Moltmann's christology and his social trinitarianism are interdependent: "The doctrine of the Trinity directs all ideas of God to Jesus . . . It does not really divinize Christ, but christifies God."⁷ This move seeks to secure his christology from over-emphasizing only Jesus' birth, death and resurrection, to the exclusion of his life. Moltmann's christology is a conscious response to the lamentable fact that in the common Christian creeds (namely the Nicene and Apostles') the life of Jesus and the expectation of his parousia are skipped over as if unimportant, "reduced to a mere comma between 'born' and 'suffered.'"⁸ (Ironically, this same judgment can be lodged against his earlier work, which focused strongly on the resurrection and the cross largely to the exclusion of Jesus' teachings, miracles and preaching.⁹) Additionally, a pneumatological christology allows Moltmann to insist on christology's decidedly messianic shape and to be more in line with the "Jewish contours of the messianic promise": "according to messianic tradition, the messiah who is anointed with the Spirit of God is 'the son of God.'"¹⁰

His rejection of Chalcedonian two-natures christology continues,¹¹ and he criticizes the early church's christology for being vertical instead

---

6. *WJC* 73–94; see also *TKG* 74–75; *EJM* 81–82. To conclude the section on the pneumatic activity in Jesus' life, Moltmann also asserts its correlative: "the reverse side of the history of Jesus is the history of the Spirit" (*WJC* 94).

7. *HTG* 39. "We are searching for an emphatically *social* christology . . . we shall look at the 'social' person of Jesus" (*WJC* 71; see also 74, 145–47). The most in-depth discussion is found in *TKG* 61–96: "The History of the Son". For a lucid account detailing how Jewish monotheism was/is capacious enough for Christ's divinity, see Bauckham, *God Crucified*.

8. *JCTW* 3; quotation verbatim, but originally this is a question; see *WJC* 52ff., 74, 150, 316; *HTG* 31; see also Sobrino, *Christology at the Crossroads*, 329.

9. *WJC* 3–4. This applies to *TH* and *CG*; compare *CPS* 37: "Pneumatic christology is only realistic when it is developed into the trinitarian theology of the cross."

10. *WJC* 74; see also *TH* 141; *RRF* 214; *HTG* 33ff.; Bauckham, *Theology of Jürgen Moltmann*, 205: "A major concern of this discussion [*WJC* I] is to understand the Christian confession of Jesus as Messiah in a way that is not anti-Jewish." See also Martin Hengel, *The Son of God*, 48–51.

11. *WJC* xiii-xv, 53, 136ff; see also *CG* 227–35; *FC* 62–64. Generally, Moltmann's motivation is an attempt to avoid presenting an essentially oversimplified Apollinarian christology where Jesus' body was human and contained his (divine) mind or spirit, as

of horizontal,[12] attaching the apparently pejorative label "Jesuology" to modern anthropological christology for its narrow focus on Jesus, reliant on a methodology "from below."[13] While he previously lodged criticisms against the exclusivity of both the "from above" and "from below" methodologies,[14] now he banishes such "infelicitous phraseology" from theological discourse, because they are too weak.[15] Only a dialectical understanding can support the theological freight of a christology that seeks neither a dissolution of the divine into the human nor the human into the divine, but rather a "more complex" christology.[16]

He places hope's ground in the history of Jesus, which has been a major emphasis since *CG* at least, and he goes a step further in *WJC* by making a telling methodological decision to conclude the text by stressing the importance of the parousia for a proper understanding of messianic hope.[17] While he posits "a holistic christology,"[18] arguably, even in *WJC* he attaches greater eschatological significance to the dialectic of cross and resurrection than before. In fact, no matter how important the life of Jesus is to Moltmann's christology, the prior focus of cross and resurrection still heavily determines the importance that this life has for a proper understanding of christology: "The Christian community

---

an envelope contains a letter. For Moltmann this invalidates the truth of the incarnation from the outset. Defenders of two-natures christology, however, are right to find Moltmann's argument lacking (see especially Webster, "Jürgen Moltmann: Trinity and Suffering," 4–6).

12. *WJC* 69ff.

13. Ibid., 55ff., 69; see also *TT* 35–39.

14. *TT* 35–9; *WJC* 3. Of contemporaries, Pannenberg most famously exemplifies (and insists on) an approach "from below," while labeling Barth as typifying christology "from above" (Pannenberg, *Jesus—God and Man*, 33–7; see also Pannenberg, *Systematic Theology*, 2:288–89, 362–89).

For more on the above/below approaches, see Gunton, *Yesterday and Today*, 10–55; Lash, "Up and Down in Christology," in Sykes and Holmes, eds., *New Studies in Theology I*, 31–46; Rahner, "The Two Basic Types of Christology," *Theological Investigations*, vol. XIII: *Theology, Anthropology, Christology*, 213–23.

15. Previously Moltmann lent these approaches weight, but found them one-sided (*TT* 38; *CG* 89–91; see also *JCTW* 83).

16. *WJC* 69.

17. He avoids discussing the relationship between Christ and church by referring to *CPS*; see also *EH* 60–68. The eschatological nature of his christology comes out most explicitly in his intent to relate "the categories 'messianic', 'apocalyptic' and 'eschatological' . . . to the way of Christ" (*WJC* xv).

18. *WJC* 3; see Bauckham, *Theology of Jürgen Moltmann*, 206 n. 2.

rightly understood the cross and resurrection as the revelation of that which Jesus really is."[19] This endorsement places a heavy burden on the cross and resurrection to articulate a proper christology. In this, there is an emphasis on his first two principal works and the shadow they cast on his christology.

The present chapter seeks to show how christology is grounded in the key elements of his doctrine of hope, and in turn, builds upon this foundation by adding further dimensions to his vision of hope. After showing the advances made regarding the cross and resurrection, attention is paid to the other major pillar of Moltmann's "Christ of hope": the parousia.[20]

The Cross of Christ

In *CG*, where his strong emphasis on the cross pointed to, but intentionally did not develop, a full christology, Moltmann rightly asserted that christology can never be truly final because the "cross requires a christology . . . but it is also the mystery behind all christologies, for it calls them into question and makes them in constant need of revision."[21] Embarking on his own christology, he reinforces this perspective.[22] While no one predicted Messiah suffering and dying, Christians have maintained that this belief is a central tenet of Christian doctrine: Jesus suffered and died as Messiah.[23]

Inclusive Suffering

The present section is limited to the central advance *WJC* makes on his theology of the cross, focusing supremely on his understanding of

---

19. *WJC* 139; see also *CG* 204.

20. The phrase "Christ of Hope" was under consideration to be the title of his christology (*WJC* xiii). Elsewhere, he relates the parousia to resurrection and the new creation (see *TH* 227; *CPS* 209). For the importance of the parousia as an image of hope, see Bauckham and Hart, *Hope against Hope*, 117–22.

Moltmann's articulation of the "way of Jesus Christ" certainly moves into ethical considerations, which will not be addressed here; see "The Passion of Christ and the Suffering of God," 27.

21. *CG* 86; of course, this is a causational link to his relentless association of the cross as iconoclastic (see *CG* 108 n. 13).

22. *WJC* xiv.

23. Beyond *WJC*, see *TT* 18; *HP* 32, 43.

soteriology and its relation to hope. The thesis advanced in chapter two, that the cross is a source of hope because it acutely epitomizes God's experience of, and faithfulness in, suffering is presupposed here. Moltmann's understanding of God's relationship to suffering is repeated and developed in both *CPS* and *TKG* and related to the Spirit's experience of kenosis in *GC*;[24] these antecedent steps lead to the further step taken in *WJC*, as Moltmann presents an inclusive, seemingly all-embracing, notion of universal suffering. While previously, he developed divine passibility in the context of fellow-suffering, in *WJC* this notion is expanded. Moltmann's view that Jesus is the co-sufferer is asserted in the context of, and as a pretext to, a full-blown soteriology: Jesus' co-suffering, with both humanity and creation, has saving efficacy.[25]

While before the emphasis on the cross had decisive implications for the Trinity principally,[26] in *WJC* he views the cross from the perspective of christology. More than a rehash of *CG*, "The Apocalyptic Sufferings of Christ" (*WJC* IV),[27] uses a wider frame to investigate suffering by advocating a broader notion of the "sufferings of Christ" and to develop a theology of the cross that is more inclusive than the one propounded in 1972. At its best, this wider scope is not intended to generalize suffering, it is intended to allow him to promote a view of

24. In *GC*, the kenosis of the Spirit is a dimension of divine impassibility.

25. *WJC* 178ff. The cosmic dimension is, of course, an advance made since *CG*, leaning heavily on the major tenet of *GC*. His move in seeing God as co-sufferer is rooted in the "ancient Jewish idea" of the Old Testament (*WJC* 179).

Arguably, his theology of the sufferings of Christ is a tip of the hat to Abelard. Moltmann never mentions Abelard in *WJC*. This fact alone may rebut any linkage between them. However, the very title of the text seems to inherently point to the positive contribution of Abelard. The title promotes Jesus as a way to be followed; indeed his person is the way, his life an "example." While Peter Abelard's argument has been shown to have more texture to it than the simplistic label "exemplary" can convey (See Weingart, *The Logic of Divine Love*), Moltmann's notion of suffering as closely related to love leads him not to Anselm's notion of recompense for slighting a dignitary, but an appeal to Abelard's basic conviction of suffering and love. Moltmann writes: "we are parting company with the inadequate images of the sacrificial theories: ransom, atoning sacrifice, satisfaction, and so on . . . We ourselves have to be justified as sinners . . . That happens through the atoning love of God. In the long run, Abelard was right, not Anselm" (*HTG* 52; in his indexed works, this is the only reference to Abelard). Obversely, he ties Anselm's sacrificial view of the atonement to a functional christology of the scapegoat (*WJC* 188).

26. See especially *TKG* 83.

27. *WJC* 151–212.

suffering that places specific sufferings in "the sufferings of Christ," and vice versa. While in the earlier writings Moltmann related hope to those who suffer by insisting that God is the passible, crucified God and is not an abstract being detached from the events of history,[28] the discussion typically focused on relating other sufferings to the cross event: "There is no suffering which in this history of God is not God's suffering; no death which has not been God's death in the history on Golgotha."[29] Moltmann's mature vision espouses not only a notion of suffering in the very being of God (although this is still retained), but an openness to suffering in its universal reach. He now looks more precisely at how Christ's sufferings are not exclusively tied to one Friday two-thousand years ago on Golgotha, but actually include other sufferings manifested at present: "if we discover where God is, and sense his presence in our suffering, then we are at the fountainhead—the source out of which life is born anew."[30] By this, he identifies the cross as a source of hope for the outcasts of society, because the cross is a source of hope since it best exemplifies the suffering nature of God, who not only suffers in the event of the cross and also allows suffering to enter into the divine community, but is present in all suffering.[31] Thus, while CG relied heavily upon the cross as the site of divine suffering and its meaning for God, in WJC divine suffering is more capacious, knowing no spatial or temporal limit. It is not the mere fact that God suffers, and so knows of the pain which afflicts humanity and creation. For Moltmann, God's suffering is not limited to only the human nature of Jesus in the solitary event of the cross. The most significant development of his theology of the cross from 1972 to 1989 is that a proper understanding of divine

28. That is, not a closed circle in heaven (*CG* 249; see also *HP* 15; *CPS* 55–56; *ET* 323).

29. *CG* 246.

30. *JCTW* 46.

31. In *CG*, Moltmann proclaimed that "even Auschwitz is in God himself" (*CG* 278). What is made fully manifest in 1989 that was expressed but not expounded fully in 1972 is the reverse: God is in all suffering. Recall his approving quote of Wiesel, "He [God] is hanging here on this gallows" to answer the questioning protest: "Where is God now?" (Wiesel, *Night*, 62; *CG* 173–74). Contextually, it is unclear whether Moltmann intends this to mean that God is here hanging on this gallows and thus present, or hanging and thus impotent or dead. The difference is not minor. It may be that when he uses Wiesel's story about the boy on the gallows, he is implying or asserting such a notion (see above, 50 n. 54). Here it is not implicit, but explicit.

suffering does not confine sufferings to the cross as a singular event, but rather suffering is manifest multifariously:

> Christ's sufferings are not exclusive: they are not just his sufferings. They are inclusive—our sufferings too, and the sufferings of the time in which we are living. His cross stands between our crosses, our Brother's cross, as a sign that God himself participates in our suffering and takes our pains on himself. The suffering Son of man is so much one of us that the unnumbered and unnamed, tortured and forsaken human beings are his brothers and sisters.[32]

Suffering is taken on by God and, therefore, anyone who suffers is a member of God's family, with Christ as their brother.

Soteriological Suffering

Any doctrine of Christian hope must give an account of salvation, including both its ground and reach. Moltmann's advances in this regard show more clearly that his soteriology stems from his christology, supported strongly by his doctrine of hope, grounded in the cross and resurrection. His previous intent was to relate the cross to God, the implications of that argument are shown to be, ultimately, messianically hopeful: "Through the suffering of the Messiah, the suffering ones receive messianic hope."[33] Indeed: "Christian faith therefore has to understand the powerless suffering and the forsaken dying of Jesus, not as refutation of his messianic hope, but rather as its deepest realization under the conditions of a godless and inhuman world which stands under the coming judgment. It has therefore discovered the hope of the suffering ones in the suffering of this 'coming one.'"[34] This understanding of Messianic suffering renders soteriology viable: "the delivering up of the Son to godforsakenness is the ground for the justification of the godless and the acceptance of enmity by God."[35] Linking the cross to soteriology is something asserted in *CG*, but not developed.[36] In *WJC*

---

32. *JCTW* 39; he also includes apostolic suffering. For an emphasis on Christ as the first-born brother, see *HTG* 36–37.

33. *EH* 64.

34. Ibid.

35. *CG* 242–43.

36. Indeed, only by exaggeration can this aspect be criticized. In *CG* the focus is clearly on the cross and its meaning for God. For soteriological assertions, see *CG* 241ff.

this changes appreciably: Jesus "suffered vicariously what threatens everyone."[37] Jesus can represent "everyone" because he did not die a private death: he died as Messiah, and as the Son of man, while he suffered "and died for the new creation of all things."[38] As such, he suffered and died for Jew, Gentile, and creation in order to inaugurate the new creation. This eschatological vision with a vicarious concentration amplifies his doctrine of hope, enlarging its scope.[39] Yet, in *WJC*, drawing on Romans 4:25 (Jesus "was handed over to death for our trespasses and was raised for our justification"), Moltmann slips into language that seeks to root justification not in the death (as in the Romans passage) but in suffering: "The meaning and purpose of his suffering is our liberation from the power of sin and the burden of our guilt."[40] For a proper view of atonement, Moltmann principally locates its ground not in the death of Jesus, but in suffering, more generally.

While Moltmann opens his discussion of soteriology under the heading: "Why did Christ die?"[41] tellingly he states at the outset that his discussion seeks to show the "liberating, redeeming and creative energies" of Christ's *sufferings*.[42] The obvious advantage of framing soteriology in direct relation to suffering is the ability to identify, quite readily, non-human creation as subjected to sufferings. Furthermore, by not defining soteriology in terms of forgiveness of sin(s), this gives Moltmann the added advantage of avoiding propounding a highly anthropocentric understanding of salvation. This seeming added benefit, however, could be generated by different means. If a proper notion of atonement must give an account of sin and its relation to Christ's cross, then Moltmann should be relating soteriology to forgiveness of sin and the entrée to the non-human creation's sufferings would be a direct effect of humanity's

---

37. *WJC* 155.

38. Ibid.; see also "Child and Childhood as Metaphors of Hope," 592–614.

39. Moltmann labels suffering "fruitful" (*WJC* 153), which is problematic if taken to extreme; but Moltmann's usage of it seems to assert atonement imagery.

40. *WJC* 182; see also *CG* 242–43.

41. *WJC* 181–89. Moltmann presents most of this argument in *CG*, but it is not a central concern.

42. Ibid., 181. This may be his way of encompassing death into a larger scope of suffering, but in *CG* he maintained the (Heideggerian) notion that no one suffers death. At most one suffers dying, but not death (*CG* 243); see also Kitamori, "Buchbesprechung," 109.

sins.⁴³ This would allow him to ground his view of atonement firmly in the biblical emphasis of forgiveness of sins, and yet also strengthen an important and emerging aspect of Moltmann's program: locating the human situation in the wider frame of creation.⁴⁴ This would still enable him to focus on soteriology in a holistic way (which is one of his goals), preferring neither humanity nor creation.

The reason that he does not do this is, perhaps, an indictment on his rather underdeveloped notion of sin, specifically personal sin. In discussing the importance of "justifying faith,"⁴⁵ Moltmann is clearly reticent to discuss forgiveness of sin and thus he rarely calls the object of such forgiveness "sinners."⁴⁶ Instead he prefers to regard humanity as passively subjected to sin, so the gospel is "anticipating in believers the victory of life over death by liberating them from the power of sin."⁴⁷ This discussion is not one detailing sinners seeking forgiveness in justifying faith, but one asserting that "God is just because he makes the unjust just and creates justice for those who suffer under injustice."⁴⁸ The ramifications of such a proposal are not difficult to predict. Moltmann has grounded his soteriology in suffering, so by implication anyone or anything that suffers is inclusively placed in Christ's sufferings, and is saved. This affirms the universal scope of redemption.

Moltmann's christology is guided, to some degree, by the question: "Who is Christ for me?"⁴⁹ After reflecting on the nature of the cross, where he sees Jesus as "the brother in suffering and the liberator from guilt," Moltmann replies "The Christ for me is the crucified Jesus."⁵⁰ He does not intend, however, a one-sided focus on the cross.⁵¹ In reflecting

43. See especially *SW* 55–58.

44. Of course, his earlier work placed humanity in the wider frame of history.

45. See *WJC* 183–89.

46. Ibid., 183ff.

47. Ibid., 184.

48. Ibid.

49. *JCTW* 3. This is a revision of Bonhoeffer's question: "Who is Jesus Christ for us today?"

50. Ibid.

51. Jenson correctly names Moltmann as one who removes the cross from its previous allocated "centrality" in theology (Jenson, *Systematic Theology*, 1:179). Indeed, Moltmann claims that justification is rooted in cross and resurrection (*WJC* 184); see his criticism of the Lutheran (Jenson's own tradition) tendency to find soteriological significance in the cross (*WJC* 186).

on the cross in personal and evocative terms he cannot help but draw on the importance of the resurrection: "Jesus is the divine Brother in our distress. He brings hope to the prisoners and abandoned. He is the one who delivers us from the guilt that weighs us down and robs us of every kind of future."[52] It is not only Jesus' suffering that is important for Moltmann's christology; he also explicates his mature view of the resurrection. Showing the close relationship that the cross has with the resurrection is one of the key contributions of *WJC*.

The Resurrection of Christ

While the cross is the "ontological foundation" of cosmic christology, the resurrection is its "epistemological foundation."[53] The early church found its source of hope in the truth that the crucified Jesus had been raised from the dead.[54] The resurrection prevents one from identifying Jesus as simply a "scapegoat" or "suffering servant."[55] Such a view raises two fears for Moltmann: (1) it places christology on a functional model, instead of relational and (2) leaves no place for the resurrection, reducing the resurrection to being merely "return," unable to say anything "about the totally new thing which the resurrection has brought into the world."[56] Since *TH*, Moltmann has insisted that resurrection faith, centerd on Messiah, leads to resurrection hope.[57] In 1994 he expresses hope

---

52. *JCTW* 2–3.

53. *WJC* 281–82; both phrases are italicized originally.

54. Martin Hengel points out this connection: "The compound name Jesus Christ was above all the basic confession for the resurrected Jesus: 'Jesus is the Messiah'" (Hengel, "Jesus, the Messiah of Israel," 10).

55. *WJC* 188.

56. *WJC* 188.

57. Martin Hengel asserts that the very notion of a righteous man linked to messianic expectations due to being resurrected, "is absolutely without analogy" (Hengel, "Jesus, the Messiah of Israel," 12). Thus, in the context of messianic expectation it is surprising that Jesus' followers, at the realization that Jesus was risen, did not simply conclude " 'he lives', but that they immediately progressed to the other deduction: he is therefore (indeed) the Messiah (Acts 2.36)" (Johannes Weiss, as quoted in Hengel, "Jesus, the Messiah of Israel," 13). On this point Hengel follows Weiss and rejects Wrede, believing that Jesus' followers did not in fact falsify his intent, projecting their expectations onto his person. Similarly, I. Howard Marshall points out that "it was the resurrection of Jesus which gave the decisive stimulus to Christological thinking. The firm recognition that Jesus was Lord and Messiah stemmed from the resurrection. The expectation of his parousia received credibility from his resurrection . . . The earliest

as having two sides, both rooted in Christ's resurrection. The "personal side" is that "the raising of Christ *from the dead* means that the general raising of all the dead has begun," while the "cosmic side" of hope is that "the raising of Christ means that the destructive power of death, which is anti-God, is driven out of creation."[58] This is properly read as a critique of anthropocentric notions of salvation and eschatology. Hope impacts both human history and the created order.[59]

Based on his rejection of the "homogeneity of all historical happening," Moltmann continues to dispute the validity of analogy when discussing the historicity of the resurrection.[60] Instead of labeling the resurrection historical, he advocates "a *process* of resurrection . . . Resurrection doesn't mean a closed fact. It means a way: the transition from death to life."[61] He seems to mean that the resurrection is not a closed fact in the sense of having no further importance or effect:

> In love, resurrection is not merely expected; it is already experienced. For love makes us come alive. And love never gives anyone or anything up for lost. It sees a future [*Zukunft*] in which God will restore everything, and put everything to rights, and gather everything into his kingdom. This great hope strengthens our little hopes, and puts them straight. It is the presence of Jesus in the Spirit of life.[62]

Inveighing against Pannenberg, Moltmann addresses the relationship between cross and resurrection as they relate to hope:

> Anyone who describes Christ's resurrection as "historical", in just the same way as his death on the cross, is overlooking the new creation with which the resurrection begins, and is falling short of the eschatological hope. The cross and resurrection stand in the same relation to one another as death and eternal life. Since resurrection brings the dead into eternal life and

---

Christology stressed the way in which he fulfilled the Old Testament promises of a coming deliverer" (Marshall, *Origins of New Testament Christology*, 128).

58. *JCTW* 85; italics original.

59. The resurrection has a cosmic reach, extending even to stones (*WJC* 258; see also *EJM* 82).

60. *WJC* 244; see above, pp. 8–12. *JCTW* 77: "Can an event that has no analogy, such as Christ's resurrection, be understood in historical terms? No."

61. *JCTW* 81; contraction original.

62. Ibid., 4.

means the annihilation of death, it breaks the power of history and is itself the end of history.[63]

Central to his mature view of the resurrection is his volte-face regarding Pannenberg's view of the resurrection. In 1972 Moltmann labelled Pannenberg's understanding of the "retroactive force [*rückwirkenden Kraft*]" of the resurrection a "helpful" construct.[64] In 1989, however, calling it a "violent assumption" he jettisons it.[65] At first glance it is not clear why his view has changed, since he appears to employ a notion very similar to this.[66] First glances can be deceiving, however, and here he provides a subtle distinction, clarifying the matter. Even though he does not explain why he objects to Pannenberg's notion so vehemently, at least two reasons explain Moltmann's view.

A couple of issues intersect: as was shown in chapter one, for Moltmann the resurrection cannot be just another historical event in the life of Jesus; he now further emphasises a further dimension which complements his view by asserting that the resurrection has both a synchronic effect and a diachronic effect.[67] By this, he wants to include

63. *WJC* 214; thus the resurrection is different in kind, *contra* Pannenberg. See also Hunsinger, "The Daybreak of the New Creation," 169–75.

64. *CG* 181 [168]; see Pannenberg, *Jesus—God and Man*, 135–41. For Moltmann's rejection of Pannenberg's view of history, see *TH* 76ff.; *WJC* 76, 235–36.

Interestingly, in 1991 Pannenberg did not use the phrase "retroactive force" in the body of the discussion; instead he chooses to discuss it in a footnote, presenting the phrase as a previously held view. He implies that although he still subscribes to the concept, he now rejects the 1964 phrase "retroactive force," because it is "conceptually unclear" (Pannenberg, *Systematic Theology*, 2:303 n. 92; compare however, Pannenberg, *Systematic Theology*, 1:331).

65. *WJC* 76.

66. Ibid: "the resurrection witnesses could identify the living with the dead, the one present with the one past, the one to come with the one who had already come. It is the Easter event that prompts the confession: 'Jesus is the Christ of God.'" Compare Moltmann's 1994 comments about the disciples' record of having a christophany and Easter vision: "They were *retrospective* [*retrospektiv*] visions of remembrance: the disciples recognized Jesus from the marks of the nails and from the way he broke the bread. The One who will come is the One crucified on Golgotha" (*JCTW* 75).

67. While this issue cannot be pursued further here, it is not clear that Pannenberg understands the resurrection "as simply one more event" in the life of Jesus (*WJC* 76). Pannenberg directs this ontological notion in direct contrast to what he labels the "concept of being in the Greek philosophical tradition . . . because for Greek thought everything has always been in its essence what it is" (Pannenberg, *Jesus—God and Man*, 136). Even Moltmann can make claims that seem fit for the resurrection and apply

antecedent events in the life of Jesus that are affected by the resurrection.⁶⁸ This issue merges into another.

Against Pannenberg, Moltmann asserts: "The resurrection of Jesus from the dead by God does not speak the 'language of facts,' but only the language of faith and hope, that is, the 'language of promise.'"⁶⁹ Indeed, precisely because there can be no final the verification of the resurrection in the present, its verification is pushed to the future, because "the resurrection of a dead man falls outside the framework of history, which is dominated by death and men's dying,"⁷⁰ and furthermore in his view, "universal history" has one major "impulse": "the eschatological hope for the dead."⁷¹ While their divergence on the understanding of history is the primary cause of their disagreement at this point, more important for Moltmann's own christology, yet still levelled against Pannenberg, is the importance of the Spirit in the life of Jesus: "If Christ is present now in the eternal Spirit of God, then his history must have been determined by this Spirit from the very beginning."⁷² Indeed, this is what the nativity scenes convey: "God is bound up with Jesus of Nazareth not fortuitously but essentially. From the very beginning God is 'the Father of Jesus Christ'... the Messiah Jesus is *essentially* God's Son. He does not do so at some point in history, from a particular moment in his life. He is from the beginning the messianic Son, and his beginning is to be found in his birth from the Holy Spirit."⁷³ His stronger appreciation of the Spirit's work supplements his disagreement with Pannenberg's methodology.

---

them to the cross: the cross "give[s] future to that which is passing away, firmness to that which is unsteady, openness to that which is fixed, hope to the hopeless, and in this way to gather all that is and all that is no more into the new creation" (*CG* 219).

68. *WJC* 76.

69. *CG* 173; see also 204; *WJC* 223; for a discussion of facts and promise, see *WJC* 238–40.

70. *CG* 189. Indeed, "the resurrection of Christ is still dependent on its eschatological verification through the new creation of the world" (*WJC* 223).

71. *WJC* 240.

72. Ibid., 77.

73. Ibid., 84; Regarding Jesus' conception and birth, Moltmann writes: "talk about Christ's 'virgin birth' through Mary dangerously narrows down his humanity, if the virgin birth is taken to mean that a super-natural process takes the place of a human-natural one... We should rather view the whole process of the human begetting, conception and birth of Jesus as the work of the Holy Spirit. Christ's birth from the Spirit is a statement about Christ's relationship to God, or God's relationship to Christ. It does not have to be linked with a genealogical assertion" (ibid., 85).

The resurrection does not retroactively make Jesus Christ the son of God; he is already the son of God. Moltmann insists that both resurrection and the last judgement are to be understood diachronically:

> The symbol of the resurrection of the dead expresses a *historical hope for the future*—hence the dating "in the last days" or, as German says, *am Jüngsten Tag*—"on the Final Day," or the Last Judgment. But the resurrection symbol links this with an eschatological hope: at the end of time all the dead will be raised together and suddenly "in a moment, in the twinkling of an eye, at the last trumpet", as Paul puts it (1 Cor. 15.52)—and that means *diachronically*.[74]

It is this hope for the dead that leads Moltmann to address the parousia as a central issue. Indeed, beyond the cross and resurrection, the relative importance he gives to the parousia is a distinction of Moltmann's hope and christology: "the unity of the risen and the crucified one is grasped . . . by an eschatological Christology, a Christology 'from ahead.'"[75]

Parousia

Moltmann's inclusion of the parousia under the heading of christology, serves two functions: (1) it evidences his view that it contributes materially to christology and (2) is a methodological critique of those who place it under eschatology.[76] This inclusion can be interpreted as either a blurring of the line between christology and eschatology, or conversely one can see it as a reinforcement of it.[77] At the very least it is the hinge

---

74. Ibid., 239; as opposed to synchronically (compare ibid., 76).

75. *HD* 104; For Moltmann, christology and eschatology are closely related because "christology is no more than the beginning of eschatology and eschatology, as the Christian faith understands it, is always the consummation of christology" (*WJC* xiv; see also *HTG* 95; *EH* 65).

76. Moltmann laments the fact that the parousia is rarely treated in recent christologies, chastising works of the 1960s and 1970s (*WJC* 313, 378 n. 1). Somewhat contradictorily, only three pages after his criticism Moltmann asserts: "It is only in more recent, eschatologically oriented theology which has brought back the expectation of the parousia in christology", citing only two Käsemann articles from the early 1960s (*WJC* 316; 379 n. 3).

77. The fact that he finds it important to discuss the parousia under christology, not eschatology, seems to reinforce the notion that a distinction is both present and important; yet the parousia, christologically determined as it is in Moltmann's thought, seems to threaten to obliterate the line altogether since both christology and eschatology can claim partial ownership.

linking christology to eschatology, exemplifying the christological nature of eschatology, and vice versa.⁷⁸ Moltmann rejects totally any attempt to remove the parousia's importance via demythologization. He laments that the early church's prayer "Maranatha, come Lord Jesus, come soon" was turned into a wish for the return to be delayed by the Constantinian imperial church.⁷⁹ Seeking to retrieve the importance of the parousia as a substantive theological doctrine, he regards the parousia as integral to the person of Christ: "It is the goal of [Christ's] history," without which Christ's mission would be "incomprehensible fragments."⁸⁰ For christology, the parousia serves not as Christ's return, but as "the completion of the way of Jesus: 'the Christ on the way' arrives at his goal."⁸¹ Note well his criticisms of those unwilling to place the parousia in the category of time, regarding it as seemingly super-temporal.⁸² Yet, his regard for the parousia is similar (if not parallel) to the argument he advanced for viewing the resurrection as beyond historical investigation and yet of fundamental importance for theology (see chapter 1).

The parousia is not the "return" of Christ (as if Jesus were absent), but is rather his advent, his coming.⁸³ At his parousia, Christ will come

---

78. According to Moltmann, the New Testament speaks of the parousia in eucharistic terms; indeed, the eucharist is the "practical testimony" to the parousia (*WJC* 338). A few lines later he equates the eucharist to the "Lord's supper", the latter being his favored label in seeking to unite the Orthodox Eucharist, the Catholic Mass, and the Protestant communion (see *CPS* 242–60; *WJC* 207–9).

79. *WJC* 313, citing 1 Cor 16:22; Rev 22:20. For a brief discussion of *maranatha*, see Marshall, *The Origins of New Testament Christology*, 101ff. It can mean "our Lord, come" or "our Lord has come" (1 Cor 16:22); it can be imperative "Come, Lord Jesus" (Rev 22:20) or indicative "The Lord is at hand" (Phil 4:5).

80. *WJC* 316; he calls the parousia the "keystone" of christology (ibid.).

81. *WJC* 314, also 316. Additionally, in 1989 the notion of a "second coming" is perhaps even more problematic for Moltmann due to his stronger understanding of the Spirit (compared with 1964), since the term second coming "presupposes his absence and suppresses his presence in the Spirit" (*WJC* 379 n. 10).

82. Ibid., 317–18; he names Bultmann, Barth, and Althaus.

83. See Oepke, "*parousia, pereimi*," 865; see also Rowland, "Parousia." As early as 1964 (following Oepke), Moltmann rejected the terms "return" and "second coming" for the parousia (*TH* 227; see also *CPS* 130, 138; *GL* 105–12; *WJC* 319, 379 n. 10; *CoG* 25; "Foreword," in Althouse, *Spirit of the Last Days*, viii; *EB* 89; "The Blessing of Hope," 158–59).

Moltmann would dispute Placher's main contention, that in the present Christ is absent (see Placher, "Present Absence of Christ," 169ff.).

(*adventus*)⁸⁴ from heaven.⁸⁵ His intent is not to outline or map the events of the eschaton,⁸⁶ but to show the christological basis of the parousia. The meaning of the parousia should not be taken in the (all too often) contemporary American sense of the church awaiting its rapture, meeting Christ in the clouds: an "eschatology of Christ 'coming' can be of help in overcoming a chronological dispensationalism through an eschatology of advent."⁸⁷

From beginning to end, *WJC* is concerned with messianic christology.⁸⁸ He explicitly frames the text with messianic concerns, opening *WJC* with the messianic shape of christology and closing with a discussion on the parousia. The first chapter deals explicitly with Jewish-Christian relations and the concluding chapter deals with the parousia, specifically its expectation and delay.⁸⁹ The parousia acutely manifests the division of Jews and Christians: the former still awaiting Messiah's arrival, the latter believing Messiah has come already and awaiting his second advent. The parousia is the quintessential problem when dealing with messianic christology.⁹⁰ Moltmann, following Paul, sees the parousia as hope for both Jew and Gentile.⁹¹ This discussion, however, necessarily pulls in both directions. For it is the delay of the parousia

84. *FC* 29; for a concurring opinion on this point, see Ben Witherington III, *Jesus, Paul and the End of the World*, 150.

85. For more on his view of heaven, see *WJC* 332; *GC* 158ff. Moltmann rejects a tripartite view of the universe. Moltmann rejects the cloud imagery as literal and instead relates it to the veiling of God's presence.

86. He speaks against the very notion of an eschatological calendar (see *CoG* 13); for options of relating the parousia to the millennium, see the various contributions in Darrell L. Bock, ed., *Three Views on the Millennium and Beyond*.

87. "Foreword," in Althouse, *Spirit of the Last Days*, ix; he is endorsing Christoph Blumhardt's eschatology.

88. Compare, however, *WJC* 136–50.

89. Moltmann does not solve the "delay" aspect that perpetually lingers in the background of the imminence of the parousia. For an extensive and lucid discussion on the delay of the parousia, see Witherington, *Jesus, Paul and the End of the World*.

90. In *WJC* the parousia relates to both creation and humanity, although the accent falls on the latter. It is true that he discusses the eschatological conclusion of the Lurian notion of *zimsum*, whereby God ends his initial self-restriction (*WJC* 328–31), however, this discussion would be better placed in *CoG* since it relates not materially to Christ's parousia but more generally to eschatology.

91. The omission may be due to a desire to focus on the Gentile/Jewish angle of hope, saving the cosmic dimension of eschatology for *CoG*. Indeed, Paul is absolutely convinced that in the end "all Israel will be saved" (Rom 11:26).

Christology as Hope 169

that makes christology problematic, placing a question mark on claims that Jesus is Messiah: "if Jesus is the redeemer, why is the world still so unredeemed?"[92] While this pertinent question seems to be limited to theodicy, it penetrates christology only as deep as a doctrine of the parousia allows. This is especially true the more one includes Jewish concerns: "The humanly irreconcilable difference between Jews and Christians will not be settled until God redeems the entire world as promised in Scripture."[93] Until then christology can appear to be a doctrine of misplaced trust in a failed Messiah.[94]

Moltmann understands the parousia adjectively as "the parousia hope,"[95] and seeks to clarify two issues. The first is the correct understanding of judgment in theological discourse. He unequivocally renders the traditional scheme of separating the sheep from the goats obsolete.[96] He pronounces a wholly positive expectation of the parousia. Instead of the fantastic images conceived throughout church history and depicted in art, whereby divine and human revenge is exacted in excruciating detail,[97] Moltmann insists that the parousia should be centrally linked to its "criterion," the crucified Christ:[98] "The crucified One will be the judge, and he will judge according to his gospel.[99] His

92. So aptly put by Moberly, "The Christ of the Old and New Testaments," 186. This viewpoint shows that while Christians are prone to wonder why Israel responds with a "no" (to the question: "are you the one who is to come?"), the question boomerangs: why, in light of suffering, do Christians say "yes"?

93. "A Jewish Statement on Christians and Christianity," xvii, italics original.

94. Over against a "false" messiah; see Greenberg, "Judaism and Christianity: Covenants of Redemption," 156–57.

95. *WJC* 314.

96. See Matt 25:31–46.

97. Beyond *WJC*, see *PPL* 19–27.

98. *WJC* 314.

99. He rightly asserts that the criterion is the crucified Christ. However, Moltmann asserts Christ's role as judge by quoting a passage that identifies not Christ, but God as the judge (see *WJC* 336, referencing Acts 17:31). Based on Moltmann's own customary usage of God as referring to the Father specifically, this is problematic. While Christ will certainly have some role in the last judgement, identifying Christ as the judge at the last judgement is not a unanimous view in the New Testament: Jesus (or the Son of Man) is portrayed as the Judge in the Gospels, Acts, and Paul (Matt 10:32–33; Mark 14:62; perhaps also Luke 13:25–27; Acts 10.42; 1 Cor 4:5; 2 Cor 5:10). Alternatively, the expectation that God is the Judge is broadly asserted (4 Ezra 7:33ff.; Matt 6:4, 15, 18; Acts 17:31), even by Paul (Rom 2:3ff.; 3:6; 14:10; 1 Cor 5:13; 1 Pet 4:5; see also Rev 20:11). Paul also names the saints as judges of the world (1 Cor 6:2; see Matt 19:28).

saving righteousness will renew the world. Only when the apocalyptic expectation of judgment is completely Christianized does it lose its terror and become a liberating hope, in which we go to meet the future with heads held high ... Then the fear of judgment will no longer hinder and paralyse the expectation of the parousia."[100] Moltmann draws on language that portrays Jesus as the presiding judge who comes "to judge both the quick and the dead,"[101] yet, asserts that "Jesus does not come to judge. He comes to raise up."[102] "He will come as the familiar brother. We may hope for his judgment. We do not have to be afraid of it."[103] This is not contradictory for Moltmann, but biblical.[104] He strips away any vestige of an apocalyptic expectation of the last judgment where the judge simply enacts retaliation, reacting to the facts of the case, resulting in "good being requited with good, evil with evil."[105] Indeed, Jesus does not condemn, for the love that Jesus "embodied" is "unconditional love," which will be evidenced at the last judgment and "prevail" among all.[106] At this point, Moltmann seems to be advancing an argument for universal salvation. While earlier in *WJC* he affirmed "the reconciliation of all things,"[107] when discussing the last judgment, in the final chapter, precisely where his position seems to call for it, he draws back: "this [universal reconciliation] does not have to be affirmed in order to spread confidence about the judgment."[108] And while speaking of a

---

100. *WJC* 315.

101. See the entire section ibid., 334–38.

102. He is following Blumhardt's "confessions of hope"; see the approving quotation (ibid., 382 n. 36; *CoG* 238–39, 254).

103. *TKG* 91; see also *JCTW* 142; "The Blessing of Hope," 160–61; *CoG* 314. It is, perhaps, a weakness that Moltmann does not deal with the role of Christ as the advocate of the believers at the Father's judgment (1 Thess 1:10). This might have been the way for him to promote universalism in a more satisfactory way. As it stands Christ is both the judge of all and the believers' advocate.

104. This view seems to cohere with Johannine assertions (see John 3:17; 12:47), yet Moltmann does not present the other side of this perspective: "are condemned already" (John 3:17).

105. *WJC* 336; see also *EB* 48; in *CoG* he criticizes such a view by equating it with atheistic anthropocentrism, whereby God validates the human decision for heaven or hell.

106. *WJC* 337.

107. Ibid., 304; see also 182, 186.

108. Ibid., 338.

purifying fire, he maintains a hopeful outcome for all, while refusing to unequivocally affirm universalism.[109] Yet still, the parousia will not be a time of judgment, but rather a time of hope. Accordingly, the parousia is not a doctrinal basis for evangelistic scare tactics of impending doom or existential self-examinations regarding salvation.[110] Understood this way, judgment is redefined and in Moltmann's view, corrected, indeed "Christianized" when it is divested of fear and replaced with hope.[111] This is in line with his program of turning every doctrine into hope. It is not "horrible visions of hell" that are appropriate to the last judgment, but rather salvation: the crucified one will judge "so as to make the saving righteousness of God prevail among them all."[112] The parousia "brings something new" and therefore "it works upon the present by awaking hopes and establishing resistance."[113]

Besides correcting the historic notion of judgment (which separates the sheep from the goats) taking place at the parousia, another issue raises Moltmann's ire. He is concerned that the parousia be correctly identified with the future, effectively replacing the "modern stress on the presentative experience of salvation" which renders the very notion of future salvation "meaningless,"[114] since it relegates the parousia to serving a mere disclosive function: "It has all taken place; the only thing wanting is that the covering be removed and all may see it."[115] Moltmann rejects this view totally. While insisting that the parousia is a future event, he also asserts that it is not sudden: it is not "an

---

109. In 1995 he sees the full effect of his confident expectation at the last judgment and affirms universalism unequivocally, even the salvation of the devil (*CoG* 235–55); for more, see below, pp. 205–10.

110. *JCTW* 142. This would seem to apply to either corporate or individual self-examination.

111. *WJC* 320, 326; 315: "The judgment of the living and the dead is one more reason to hope for Christ's coming; it is not a subject for fear."

112. Ibid., 315. The next chapter will discuss more closely Moltmann's universalism; here the discussion is confined to the relationship between the parousia and hope.

113. *TH* 227.

114. *WJC* 318; he references Barth as typifying this view.

115. Barth, *Church Dogmatics in Outline*, 133; as quoted in *WJC* 318. This criticism repeats Moltmann's 1964 argument, although it appears 25 years later that his conviction has hardened, since earlier he was less adamant in rejecting "unveiling" as appropriate, instead seeking to balance it out with the notion of fulfillment (see *TH* 228–29; compare, however, *ET* 37).

unforeseeable day" it is a "day which is already dawning."¹¹⁶ The parousia commences "the kingdom that shall have no end," Israel's redemption and the new creation.¹¹⁷ For Moltmann the future is still outstanding, events must still take place.

Moltmann uses both angles to recast the parousia as a hopeful doctrine. While he is certainly correct in attempting to articulate a wider understanding of the importance of the parousia, there is a problem. A strength of his eschatology is its goal of overcoming notions of the eschaton as simply disclosing matters as they are. Because he does not promote universalism in the section on the parousia, his bold statements modifying the parousia seem misplaced. The fact that he wants to convey the parousia as still outstanding seems to lead him to withdraw predictions of universal salvation; since it is not merely disclosive, its outcome cannot be presumed. Yet, because he is confident that the *Zukunft* will bring the *novum*, Moltmann is absolutely confident in the future, which leads him to unequivocally assert that the parousia is a time of hope, not fear. Yet, since he does not assert universalism, it seems implausible that he interprets the parousia in *purely* hopeful terms. One cannot presume the results of the parousia precisely because the eschaton, as Moltmann insists in reaction to others, is made up of events that must take place, not merely a disclosure of reality.

Conclusion

Moltmann's christology develops and extends his doctrine of hope, precisely because it is an elaboration of hope's ground. The resurrection ensures that redemption extends from the future to the past, while the cross renders Christ's sufferings soteriological. To these he adds the parousia, which is an event to be hoped for, not feared. These three overriding images are the essence of hope in christological terms.

Moltmann's conclusion to *WJC* transitions from christology to eschatology.¹¹⁸ And toward the beginning of *CoG* he discusses "The Rebirth of Messianic Thinking in Judaism,"¹¹⁹ which seems to lend itself

---

116. *WJC* 326.

117. Ibid., 319.

118. Of course the demarcation (if that is the right term) between the two is very slim in Moltmann's theology.

119. See *CoG* 29ff.

to a text on christology, rather than eschatology. Both sections show the close relationship between christology and eschatology.[120] These complementary transitional sections are interrupted, however: between christology and eschatology Moltmann publishes an unforeseen pneumatological text, *SpL*.[121] While his concluding chapter on the delay of the parousia transitions to eschatology, in some ways it is more appropriate to discuss the role of the Spirit before eschatology proper, since it is the person and work of the Spirit that is centrally active after Christ's ascension and before his parousia.[122] So, unbeknownst to him at the time,[123] *WJC*'s concluding chapter on the parousia is actually put into better service since it transitions to pneumatology, instead of directly to eschatology. His pneumatology will be considered, with special reference to the developments made over the years, and, of course, most centrally how the Spirit impacts his understanding of hope.

---

120. *HTG* 96: There is "no messianism without eschatology" and christology thus leads to eschatology; they are mutually informing.

121. Del Colle sees *WJC* and *SpL* as a two-part contribution to Spirit-Christology (*Christ and the Spirit*, 216 n. 68).

122. See especially John 14:15ff; 16:9ff.

123. It is clear in the conclusion of *WJC*, that the next "contribution" on his agenda is eschatology, not pneumatology (*WJC* 321, 382 n. 33; see also *HTG* 182).

7

Pneumatology as Hope

Introduction

A volume devoted to pneumatology was unforeseen in Moltmann's original plan of "contributions".[1] Even in the final pages of *WJC*, a mere two years before *SpL* was published, he advertised that the next "contribution" would cover eschatology.[2] First, however, he publishes his pneumatology, centrally relating the work of the Spirit to life in all its manifestations. Though a text devoted to pneumatology was unforeseen by Moltmann it is an entirely intelligible development in his thought.[3]

The Transition

While the importance of the Spirit for hope in *TH* was comparatively scarce, even in 1964 he linked resurrection hope to the Spirit: "as the urge of hope is towards the life that is promised and finally attained, so the urge of the raising of Christ is towards life in the Spirit and

---

1. His contributions were originally designed as a five-volume offering (*GC* xvii).
2. See *WJC* 382 n. 33.
3. *SpL*; for his other pneumatological discussions, see principally: *CPS*; *TKG* 122–28, 168–70, 178–90; *HTG* 59–67; *GC* 9–13, 98–103, 262–70; *WJC* 73–94, 174, 247–50, 288–90; *SpL* 289–306; *SoL*; *JCTW* 86–87; "The Trinitarian Personhood of the Holy Spirit," 302–14 (this article is remarkably similar to *SpL* 289–306); *ET* 145ff.

For secondary comments on Moltmann's pneumatology, see principally: Bauckham, *Theology of Jürgen Moltmann*, 151–70, 213–47; Bauckham, "Jürgen Moltmann," 221–22; Dabney, "The Advent of the Spirit," 81–107; Jaeger, "Pneumatological Developments in the Theology of Jürgen Moltmann"; Müller-Fahrenholz, *Kingdom and the Power*, 182–99; Wood, "From Barth's Trinitarian Christology to Moltmann's Trinitarian Pneumatology," 51–69.

towards the eternal life that is the consummation of all things."[4] In *SpL* Moltmann repeats the link: pneumatology has "a justification of its own between the christology which is its premise and the eschatology towards which it is aligned," based on the resurrection of Jesus Christ.[5] To the question, "Why did Christ come, die and rise again?" Moltmann answers: "in order *to send the Spirit* who sanctifies life and opens up the future".[6] Indeed, he shows that a theology desiring to be thoroughly eschatological must have a robust pneumatology. And while he concluded *WJC* with a discussion of the delay of the parousia, the concern with the delay is enigmatically both warded off and exacerbated because of the Spirit, the other paraclete.[7] Indeed, on one hand, the Spirit "brackets together our present with this divine future. That is why we wait in the Spirit for God's coming".[8] On the other, "The experience of Spirit is the reason for the eschatological longing for the completion of salvation."[9] Calling on Revelation 22:17 ("The Spirit and the bride say, 'Come'"), Moltmann asserts that "It is not that we call on the God who is coming, but rather the Spirit of God, who is already in us, presses for the parousia of Christ, because the Spirit is the parousia's 'prepayment.'"[10] Unbeknownst to him at the time, then, Moltmann's concluding chapter aptly transitioned from christology to pneumatology before proceeding to eschatology.

The Affirmation of Life

Moltmann insists that the affirmation of life is counter-intuitive, and although *SpL* was published only six years after *GC* (which of course was written in light of the ecological crisis), Chernobyl (1986) and the

---

4. *TH* 213.

5. *SpL* 152.

6. *ET* 145.

7. *SpL* 123; para/klhtoj is the masculine Greek term for advocate. Since Jesus is named advocate, the Holy Spirit is "another" advocate (see 1 John 2:1; 14:16–17).

8. Ibid., 34.

9. Ibid., 73.

10. "A Response to my Pentecostal Dialogue Partners," 66; he also quotes Rev 20:20. The beginning of Moltmann's quote is a rather odd and unnecessary division between the Spirit and the individuals who await the parousia, because the exhortation to say "Come" is directed to "everyone who hears" (Rev 20:17).

Gulf war (1991)[11] have arguably made the affirmation of life even more difficult, but more crucial. To open *SpL* he asserts: "We have got used to death, at least to the death of other creatures and other people. And to get used to death is the beginning of the freezing into lifelessness oneself."[12]

Because Moltmann intends his "contributions" to be messianic in nature (which is, perhaps, the reason for the omission of pneumatology at the outset), his volume on pneumatology might have logically followed Paul with the title *Spirit of Christ* or, perhaps more generally, *Spirit of God*.[13] Yet, *SpL*, does in fact echo Paul and goes a long way in giving the reader a clue as to Moltmann's focus.[14] The title avoids any appearance of subordination of the Spirit to either the Father or the Son and so Moltmann can easily take up other "titles" while going beyond them,[15] especially in the context of not displacing the importance of Yahweh's *ruach* or Shekinah in the Old Testament.[16] He discusses the importance of life and the Spirit's role in all of life's multifarious forms, and as such

11. Moltmann signed the preface to *SpL* on April 2, 1991, just after Iraq accepted the cease-fire in line with U.N. Security Council resolution 686 (March 3, 1991). For reference online, see: http://usinfo.state.gov/products/pubs/iraq/timeline.htm

12. *SpL* xii; see also *GSS* 54. Although, for Moltmann, it is Auschwitz that most stamps German life: "it is a vital part of collective self-experience for Germans to see themselves and their own world through the eyes of Auschwitz victims" (*SpL* 26) it is peculiar that he does not have more to say about the central geo-political event since *WJC*, the fall of the Berlin wall (1989); on this, see "Political Reconciliation," 17–31.

13. See *TKG* 125. For Paul, these two phrases are equivalent (Rom 8:9; Gal 4:6). Moltmann refuses the limitation implied by both titles, believing they affirm the *Filioque* addition (*ET* 320).

14. Rom 8:2: "For the law of the Spirit of life in Christ Jesus has set you free from the law of sin and of death." In English *SpL* repeats the English New Testament, but the German title "Der Geist des Lebens" does not follow the German New Testament: "Denn das Gesetz des Geistes, der lebendig macht in Christus Jesus" (Rom 8:2, Luth). The fact that he avoids crediting Paul for his choice of title is justified, since the German would have most likely precluded the appreciation.

15. He uses a variety of labels: beyond the "Spirit of God" and "Spirit of Christ," the Spirit is "the redeeming Spirit"; "the divine Spirit"; "the Spirit of redemption"; "of creation"; "of the resurrection and the new creation of all things"; "of the passion"; "of the crucified one"; "of holiness"; "of the resurrection of the dead"; "the cosmic Spirit"; "of community" (*SpL* 8–9, 62, 94, 227, 229, respectively; see also *HG* 81); he also uses "Spirit of the church, and the Spirit of faith" but disagrees with the implied restriction (*SpL* 8–9). More specifically, he asserts that the Spirit is concerned with the church "not as such" but in relation to the kingdom of God (*SpL* 230).

16. *SpL* 9; see also 47–51, 279; *Is There Life After Death?* 14.

the designation "Spirit of Christ" or "Spirit of God" might impose a limit on the person and work of the Spirit:[17] "The operations of God's life-giving and life-affirming Spirit are universal and can be recognized in everything which ministers to life and resists its destruction."[18] This application of the Spirit's work is intended to reinforce lessons which he learned from scripture: the Old Testament attests to the working of the Spirit before and after Christ.[19]

From the opening page of *SpL*, he presupposes and pursues the understanding that permeates *CPS* and *GC*, namely that the work of the Spirit is universal,[20] not confined to the institutional church.[21] Because Moltmann's pneumatology is generally concerned with countering "the apathetic, meaningless life of people in the Western world,"[22] he believes that what people need is not a defense of reality's status quo (what Pope John Paul II properly labeled the "culture of death"), but rather life.[23] First, however, his view of the personhood of the Spirit is assessed briefly.

The task of the present chapter is to show the various ways in which Moltmann's pneumatology provides hope for everything living, by focusing on two areas:[24] (1) the Spirit's involvement in the cross and

17. See *ET* 320.

18. *SpL* xi. Regarding the criteria for reading scripture, Moltmann asserts: "We shall work out what in the texts *furthers life*, and we shall subject to criticism whatever is *hostile to life*" (*ET* 149). Realizing that this is by no means self-evident, he attempts to illuminate what "furthers life" by affirming that which promotes "integration," "spreads reverence," "liberates life," and "whatever makes *Christ* present"; for the full list, see *ET* 149–50. Moltmann's view of scripture is highly informed by his pneumatology.

19. *SpL* xi.

20. The English subtitle "A Universal Affirmation" is an attempt to follow the original: "Eine ganzheitliche Pneumatologie." The German *ganzheitliche* is not clear: it may mean comprehensive, integrated, or holistic, but in each case there is an obvious German word for each: *umfassend, integrieren, holistisch*, respectively.

21. Moltmann avoids discussing Pentecost again, but he closes *SpL* quoting Rabanus Maurus'"Veni Creator Spritus," a hymn for the feast of Pentecost (*SpL* 310–11). He states that the experience of life in the Spirit is more likely to be found "in self-encounter . . . Many people express this personal experience of the Spirit in simple words: 'God loves me'" (*SpL* 3).

22. *SoL* 18–19.

23. See John Paul II, *Evangelium vitae*, ch. 1, 12 (March 25, 1995). For reference online, see: http://www.vatican.va/holy_father/john_paul_ii/encyclicals/index.htm

24. Kuzmic labels *SpL* Moltmann's "pneumatology of hope" ("A Croatian War-Time Reading [of *SpL*]," 17).

resurrection; and (2) his altered understanding of experience in light of his mature pneumatology.

Personhood of the Spirit

Based on the orientation of *CPS* around Pentecost and ecclesiology, the social trinitarianism of *TKG*, the suffering of the Spirit in *GC*, and the Spirit christology in *WJC*, Moltmann has already argued for, while also developing, the personality of the Spirit. And regardless of the valid criticisms of the lacks in his early pneumatology,[25] even in *TH* he has a personal understanding of the Spirit, citing the "historical and eschatological character of the Holy Spirit".[26] And in 1965, Moltmann asserted that "the Holy Spirit is first the Spirit of the raising of the dead and then as such the third person of the Trinity."[27] While in the pre-*CG* era there is a pneumatology of life already, it is only a general concept:

> the spirit which moves out of the resurrection of Christ like a strong, irresistible wind through the life of the believing and the hoping ... [T]his spirit of resurrection confers to life an indestructible direction and openness to the future that reaches out over death into a life which overcomes death.
>
> This spirit is not a substance in us, but a direction of our whole spiritual and corporal life. Wherever we give ourselves wholly to this direction ... we overcome death ...[28]

The "spirit" is not explicitly a person or even bond, but rather is a "direction". Yet, even here this understanding of the spirit has one central affirmation, which has two sides: (1) the spirit affirms life and (2) overcomes death. While he is strongly impressed by the metaphorical language of

---

25. See *DGG* 184–87; *HTG* 174; Claybrook, rather hastily, asserts that in *TH* and *CG* "one could not so much as 'glean' a doctrine of the Holy Spirit! It was simply nonexistent" (Claybrook, "The Emerging Doctrine of the Holy Spirit in the Writings of Jürgen Moltmann," 185); see also Dabney, "Advent of the Spirit," 96–100. See, however, *TH* 23, 57, 215; Bauckham, *Theology of Jürgen Moltmann*, 151; Jaeger, "Pneumatological Developments," 71; Deane-Drummond, *Ecology in Jürgen Moltmann's Theology*, 123.

26. *TH* 57. He indicates the possibility of sinning against the Holy Spirit (*TH* 23). Although he admits to not having a well-developed pneumatology up until the late 1970s, already in 1964 he had a clear understanding of "the Spirit of the resurrection" (*TH* 215).

27. See "Letter to Barth," 348. This assertion, of course, stems from his preference of the economic over the immanent Trinity.

28. *GL* 135–36.

the Spirit,[29] only after which does he promote the "personhood of the Spirit,"[30] he avoids both subordinationism and modalism. Building on his social trinitarianism, Moltmann issues a direct attack on deficient perspectives of pneumatology: the Spirit is no "external bond" through which humanity relates to the divine, but rather the fellowship of the Holy Spirit "issues from the essential inward community of the triune God . . . gather[ing] into itself these men and women and all other created things, so that they find eternal life."[31] This is not merely a "unitarian sense of *community of essence*" but can only be comprehended through a robust trinitarianism, which for Moltmann can only be "a *community of persons*."[32] It is important to recall that ever since *CPS* Moltmann has refused the limitation of the traditional *taxis* of trinitarian relations.[33] He affirms not solely Father—Son—Spirit, but calling on the biblical narrative he finds multiple expressions of the perichoretic relations. Thus, the identifiable relations found in the economy are not merely apparent (while the *taxis* of the immanent Trinity remains unchanged), but rather are constitutive for the Trinity. Thus, God is not only seemingly involved in history, he is influenced by it, and in Moltmann's terms, passible and open to suffering. The importance of pneumatology is found, specifically, in the weight he confers it for one's knowledge of God generally: "in the operation of the Spirit we experience the operation of God himself . . . An understanding of the unique personhood of the Spirit is therefore decisive of the understanding of God in general."[34]

29. Here Farrow's question of Moltmann's pneumatology promoting a "sub-personal" definition of the Spirit has some justification (Farrow, "In the End is the Beginning," 431). However, Moltmann is to be commended for not leaving the Old Testament notions out of his pneumatology (*SpL* 269–85). And the major thrust of his doctrine of the Trinity speaks against Farrow's assertion.

30. This is the title of chapter XII, but he devotes considerable space to the impersonal notions.

31. *SpL* 219; The Spirit "enter[s] into fellowship with believing men and women—if he indeed becomes their fellowship—then 'fellowship' cannot merely be a gift of the Spirit. It must be the eternal, essential nature of the Spirit himself" (*SpL* 218, see also 225, 309; *ET* 150). Bauckham disputes whether this understanding of the Holy Spirit translates as easily as Moltmann desires (Bauckham, *Theology of Jürgen Moltmann*, 161–70).

32. *SpL* 219; see *TKG* 168ff.

33. See above, pp. 75–78; compare, however, *SpL* 285–86.

34. *SpL* 286.

Earlier, he asserted: God is not "in us or over us but always only before us, who encounters us in his promises for the future".[35] Indeed, his view had a strong future orientation: "God is not 'beyond us' or 'in us,' but ahead of us".[36] As pneumatology became more important, however, Moltmann changed his mind: "God acts *in* and *through* the activity of his creatures; God acts *with* and *out of* the activity of his creatures".[37] Even though he insists on the personhood of the Spirit, some of Moltmann's best language for the Spirit is impersonal, revealing the switch in perspective: "Our true hope in life is wakened and sustained and finally fulfilled by the great divine mystery which is above us and in us and round about us, nearer to us than we can be to ourselves."[38] And this is the effect of a more substantial pneumatology: the accent clearly lies on the immanence of God and the presence of the Spirit. Recall that some of the initial reactions to *TH* criticized Moltmann's almost exclusionary relationship between God and the world. In *SpL* Moltmann is easily able to take up Macquarrie's prior assertion: "We need presence as well as promise."[39] Those critiques shall not be repeated, except only to say that whatever faults *TH* has, regarding God's presence or immanence, they are set in sharp relief in *SpL*.[40] Indeed, Moltmann's stress on the Spirit's "immanent transcendence" has invited criticism.[41] For example, calling on Jeremiah 23.23: "Am I a God near by, says the Lord, and not a God far off?" Mark Stibbe asks, "Where is the far-away God in Moltmann's pneumatology?"[42] Ironically, this critique appears at the very time and place that Moltmann most clearly overcomes his previous view. While Moltmann replies by pointing to the Old Testament generally,[43] he could have specifically pointed Stibbe to the next verse in Jeremiah: "Who can hide in secret places so that I cannot see them? Says the Lord.

---

35. *TH* 16.
36. "Theology as Eschatology," 10.
37. *GC* 211.
38. *SoL* 39.
39. Macquarrie, "Eschatology and Time," 123.
40. Meeks asserts that Moltmann has "steadily moved to an eschatology of immanence and presence" ("Systematic Contributions," 96); see also Farrow, "In the End is the Beginning," 428–39.
41. *SpL* ch. 1 §3.
42. Stibbe, "A British Appraisal [of *SpL*]," 12.
43. "A Response to my Pentecostal Dialogue Partners," 64–66.

Do I not fill heaven and earth?"[44] Indeed, here one finds the both/and affirmation that Moltmann intends for pneumatology. For Moltmann, it is only appropriate to discuss the Spirit in ways and forms of both/and: "as power and as person, as energy and as space, as wellspring and as light."[45] Moltmann makes it clear that the Spirit is both immanent and transcendent, although he claims that the Spirit is transcendent eschatologically in "otherness and newness," not ontologically.[46] In *SpL*, despite the clear affirmation of the non-human aspects of the Spirit in life, Moltmann's pneumatology develops a strongly personal notion of the Spirit: while the essential nature of God was the future in the 1960s,[47] now Moltmann asserts that God's essential nature is "the community of divine Persons."[48]

When asserting the personhood of the Spirit, one is confronted with a difficulty, which is two-fold: first, the Bible does not use this way of describing the Spirit; and second, humans do not experience the Holy Spirit as a person.[49] These two reasons, at least, lead Moltmann (and anyone else for that matter) into problems when relating the Spirit to humanity as a person.[50] The Spirit is a person who acts upon the Father and Son as a subject, and in this sense Moltmann is right to insist on this line of thought.[51] The real test, however, of the personhood of

---

44. Jer 23:24.

45. *SpL* 288.

46. "A Response to my Pentecostal Dialogue Partners," 65.

47. See the discussion on "God's Essential Nature" above (pp. 25–27).

48. *SpL* 309; see also 219, 225; *ET* 150. He also mentions the Old Testament understanding of God's essential nature as a "devouring fire" (*SpL* 279, quoting Deut 4:24).

49. John Taylor captures well this thought: "We can never be directly aware of the Spirit, since in every experience of meeting and recognition he is always the go-between who creates awareness . . . You cannot commune with the Holy Spirit, for he *is* communion itself" (John V. Taylor, *The Go-Between God*, 43). While his comments are related to another matter, Bauckham rightly rejects Moltmann's attempt to portray the Spirit as related to humanity as humans relate to each other (Bauckham, *Theology of Jürgen Moltmann*, 169–70).

50. For impersonal language of the Spirit in Paul, see 1 Cor 2:4–5; for more operative language, that denotes some level of personal agency by a subject, see Rom 8:2, 10–11, 14, 16, 26–27; 15:16; 1 Cor 2:10, 13; 12:1ff; 2 Cor 3:6, 17; 6:4–6; Gal 4:5–7; 1 Thess 1:5.

51. "Response to my Pentecostal Dialogue Partners," 65–66. But his move into gender language and deity is open to mislead, because he is conflicted, evidenced by his changing positions. For his various contributions to gender language and God, see "I

the Spirit for Moltmann's project at least is how he articulates the Spirit's role in the cross and resurrection. If, as Moltmann has been claiming since *CG*, the cross is a trinitarian event, and if the Spirit is a subject, indeed a person and not merely a "bond" in the trinitarian event of the cross, then he must be able to account for the Spirit's role. The section following details this development in his theology, and shows its implication for his doctrine of hope.

Cross and Resurrection in Pneumatological Perspective

Pneumatology of the Cross

For Moltmann the cross is a trinitarian event: "the cleavage [*der Riß*] of death on the cross goes right through God himself."[52] This is the result of rejecting two natures christology, which he equates with relegating God to being an apathetic deity uninvolved in history, unaffected by the world and so untouched by suffering.[53] If indeed "the Trinity is no self-contained group [*Kreis*] in heaven"[54] and the cross does indeed affect not only Jesus Christ but also the triune God,[55] then what affect does the cross have on the Spirit and vice versa? Moltmann fully answers this question in *SpL*.[56]

Developments from *CG* to *SpL*

In its earliest expression Moltmann's theology of the cross one-sidedly concentrated on the implications of the cross via christology, with an insufficient focus on pneumatology.[57] In *CG* the Spirit's role is not am-

---

believe in God the Father" (*HTG* 1–18); see also "The Motherly Father and the Power of His Mercy" (*HTG* 19–25); "God as Mother" (*GHH* 33–8); *HG* 92–3, 100–4; *SoL* 35–7, 114.

52. *FC* 65 [73].
53. See especially *CG* 227–35.
54. *CG* 249; see also *CPS* 55–56.
55. *FC* 65.
56. By developing a pneumatology of the cross Moltmann moves further away from Luther; for an explanation as to why Luther may not have followed through with a discussion on the cross and the Spirit, see Ngien, *Suffering of God*, 158, 165.
57. For criticisms of the pneumatological neglect in *CG*, see Dabney, "Advent of the Spirit," 98; Hill, *Three-Personed God*, 174; Miskotte, "Das Leiden ist in Gott," 86–88; Kühn, "Rezension," 55–56; Sölle, "Gott und das Leiden," 113; Zimany, "Moltmann's Crucified God," 54; for Moltmann's response, see *DGG* 184–87; *HTG* 174. However,

plified.⁵⁸ Later, Moltmann himself concedes the point, admitting that in *CG* he "did not get further than seeing a binity of God the Father and Jesus the Son of God. Where was the Holy Spirit . . . ?"⁵⁹ Accordingly, in *CG* he maintains: "The Son suffers in his love being forsaken by the Father as he dies. The Father suffers in his love the grief of the death of the Son. In that case, whatever proceeds from the event between the Father and the Son must be understood as the spirit of the surrender of the Father and the Son, as the spirit which creates love for forsaken men, as the spirit which brings the dead alive."⁶⁰ Because of the pneumatological neglect in *CG*, the most remarkable element in this passage is that he mentions the Spirit at all. The Spirit not only "creates love" and brings to life the dead, the Spirit is identified as this very love.⁶¹ Dabney asserts that in *CG* Moltmann "is held captive to the pneumatological tradition of continental Reformation theology."⁶² However, Moltmann is more precise by being more general and assigning the problem not only to "Reformation theology" specifically, but to the entire West.⁶³ In

---

others disagree; see Meeks, "Foreword," xi; O'Donnell, "Doctrine of the Trinity," 163; Bauckham maintains that "Moltmann's theology became strongly trinitarian" in *CG* (Bauckham, *Theology of Jürgen Moltmann*, 5; see also Bauckham, *Moltmann*, 91). Compare, however, his assertion that only after *CG* "Moltmann's theology becomes fully trinitarian" (p. 157). It is not apparent which statement is more recent.

58. In the section "Trinity and Eschatology" (*CG* 256–66), the focus is squarely on the Father and Son relationship, whereas he mentions the Spirit once (265; see also *UZ* 143–47; "Der Gekreuzigte Gott," 407ff.).

59. *HTG* 174; see also see also *UZ* 142–47; *JM* 52–56; Miskotte, "Das Leiden ist in Gott," 79; compare, however, Moltmann's 1964 reference to sinning against the Holy Spirit (*TH* 23). Yet, in places, he lapses into non-trinitarian language (see *CG* 203; *WJC* 137–45; *JCTW* 36–38). In *CG*, he mentions the need to relate the death of the Son to the Father and Spirit, yet his theology of the cross is generally binitarian (*CG* 206).

60. *CG* 245; "*der Geist*" is used both times for "spirit" here. The translators are unhelpfully unpredictable at this point: "*der Geist*" is rendered "Spirit" (*CG* 244, 246, 247, 248 [231–35]) and "spirit" (*CG* 245, 246, 248 [231–35]; see also "The 'Crucified God,'" 294–95.

61. "It [the spirit] is the unconditioned and therefore boundless love . . ." (*CG* 245).

62. Dabney, "Advent of the Spirit," 97; while Dabney identifies the problems with Moltmann's pneumatology related to the cross, he (like the rest of secondary scholarship consulted) does not discuss the major advances made in this regard in *SpL*, or the implications of such a move.

63. Replying to the charge of a "gap [*Lücke*]" at the point of the personality of the Spirit in *CG* he points readers to *CPS* and asserts that it is not his problem alone but rather a "material problem" with the West's doctrine of the Trinity (*DGG* 184–85). He

SpL, Moltmann shows his discontentment with his previous descriptions. Here the discussion maps Moltmann's perceivable attempt to overcome the deficit in his theology of the cross prior to *SpL*.

Because of his attachment to a social Trinity, Moltmann explores the Spirit's relationship to the cross, further than he did in his previous work. The cross and the Trinity belong together, each defining and conditioning the other. If this is not so, for Moltmann at least, the real meaning of the cross is emptied and the doctrine of the trinitarian God is unintelligible as he simply evades the suffering of Christ, and so suffering generally. He has been claiming since *CG* that it is the cross that makes the Trinity necessary, yet interestingly here the situation is reversed: his doctrine of the social Trinity, with the personhood of the Spirit now fully explored, ultimately requires that his theology of the cross be seen pneumatologically, instead of principally in Father-Son terms. While in *CPS*,[64] *TKG*,[65] and *WJC*[66] he added to his prior proposal in *CG*, and only in *SpL* does he develop a pneumatology of the cross.[67] Moltmann builds on the importance of the *Shekinah*, his theology of the cross and his concomitant attachment to God's passibility to argue for a pneumatology of the cross. These prior moves are taken up in his argument for a pneumatology of the cross: "On Golgotha the Spirit suffers the suffering and death of the Son, without dying with him."[68] Although the history of the Son is also the history of the Spirit,[69] this differentiation at the point of death opens up an interesting pneumatological advance in both his theology of the cross and his pneumatology, forming an explicit pneumatology of the cross. In his social trinitarianism the Spirit is a subject, able to act on the Father and the Son: "The Spirit

---

points to Augustine and Richard of St. Victor for reducing the Spirit to a relation, a "bond of love" between Father and Son, instead of a person (ibid.).

64. See *CPS* 53–65.

65. See *TKG* 80–83; for his views on the subjectivity of the Spirit, see *TKG* 125–26.

66. Revealing the newness of this understanding, even in his "Spirit christology," Moltmann does not mention the Spirit at the most opportune time; see "*The Death of God's Child*" (*WJC* 165–67; compare, however, *WJC* 174). Of course, Moltmann's Spirit christology led him to assert the kenosis of the Spirit had a specifically christological dimension: the Spirit emptied himself in Jesus Christ (*WJC* 93).

67. *SpL* 60–65. Of course Moltmann does develop the kenosis of the Spirit in *GC*, but this does not concern the cross *per se*.

68. Ibid., 64.

69. Ibid.; *SoL* 15.

is *the unifying God*. In this respect the Spirit is not an energy [*Kraft*] proceeding from the Father or from the Son; it is a subject from whose activity the Son and the Father receive their glory and their union . . ."[70] Also in *TKG*, Moltmann described the Spirit's activity in the cross of Christ, thusly: "the source or 'well of life' [i.e., Holy Spirit] rather flows into death and hell."[71] Still, however, these advances do not approach the relationship of Spirit and cross that he details in *SpL*.[72] While the central question of *CG*: "what does the cross mean for God?" was only answered in a discussion of Father and Son, even in *TKG*, he still maintained that Jesus' passion "takes place between the Father and the Son."[73] In *SpL*, however, Moltmann seeks a specific answer in pneumatological terms.[74]

In *SpL* he is exercised by the "seldom asked" question: how does the Spirit relate to the cross?[75] And in so doing, he moves well beyond the language of the Spirit as the "bond" or the link "of separation,"[76] relating the cross more directly to the Spirit as a person.[77] This should

---

70. *TKG* 126 [141]; see also *CPS* 60: "As the force that glorifies, the Holy Spirit is also the power of unification."

Note: The translation includes "it" unnecessarily. The relevant section reads: "ist der Geist nicht . . . sondern ein Subjekt" and is probably better rendered: "the Spirit is not . . . but rather [is] a subject" which would leave to one side the question of personal or impersonal agency, much less of relating gender to deity, or personhood to spirit.

71. *TKG* 234 n. 34; here he is disagreeing with Adrienne von Speyr's view that on the cross the Holy Spirit was "sealed up and closed" on the cross.

72. The cross is still primarily related to christology, whereas pneumatology is related to creation (see *TKG* 161).

73. *TKG* 76. Dabney locates the late 1970s as the "turning point in Moltmann's approach to pneumatology" (Dabney, "Advent of the Spirit," 99). However, at least regarding Christ's passion, the turn must take place after *TKG*.

74. *SpL* 60–65.

75. Ibid., 62; with the development of a pneumatology of the cross, it might now be asked: if this had been taken up in *CG* and *TKG* could Moltmann so easily have included Jewish sources in his claim? Ironically, he is now espousing what *only* a Christian trinitarian doctrine can support, not Heschel's dipolar *pathos* theology. This new development pushes him even more into espousing a trinitarian understanding while also making it more problematic to call on Jewish sources. The way round this seems to be his espousal of *Shekinah* theology (developed in *GC*; see above, pp. 135, 147–8), making it parallel while not replacing his pneumatology of the cross; see *SpL* 47–51; also "Ernst Blochs Christologie," 9.

76. *TKG* 82; *WJC* 174; he refers to Heb 9:14. He explicitly rejects "bond" language in 2000 (*ET* 317).

77. Bauckham rightly sees Moltmann's declaration of the Spirit as "proceeding" from the cross as an explicit move beyond both Augustine and Barth (Bauckham, *Theology*

not be seen as a recantation, but rather an extension of his earlier pronouncements.

Pneumatological Kenosis in the Cross

Rejecting the view of the atonement as sacrifice,[78] Moltmann refuses to relegate the Spirit to being a non-participant in the suffering of the cross.[79] The Spirit did not forsake the Son prior to the passion, thus being able to exert a "merely external influence," for this would disallow the Spirit's experience of suffering, an experience which reaches each person of the Trinity. Previously he held: the Son suffers as he is forsaken by his Father, while the Father suffers as he abandons his Son to death, and the Spirit is what proceeds from this event as the "spirit of surrender."[80] During the passion of the Christ[81] each is suffering in this trinitarian event. Although Moltmann does not explicitly recant his earlier paradigm of "God against God" it must be reframed by a pneumatology of the cross.[82]

The cross, especially the more one promotes social trinitarianism, has to be approached not through one angle, but three: the Father, Son and Spirit. While he reflected on Rublev's icon of the Trinity when writing *TKG*, it is even more useful here in depicting the cross, which now takes full measure of its meaning for the Spirit as a *subject* experiencing

---

of Jürgen Moltmann, 154); elsewhere in the chapter, Bauckham refers to *SpL*, but makes no comment about Moltmann's pneumatology of the cross, instead confining himself to pre-*SpL* writings.

78. He states that there are two angles from which to view the Spirit's role in cross of Christ: suffering and power; he explicitly rejects the option of power (*SpL* 67; see *SpL* 60–71). He previously merged the two angles, viewing the Spirit as a "suffering power" (*WJC* 174).

79. See *SpL* 67–70, explicitly pointing to the sacrificial language found in mediaeval theology. For support, he calls on 2 Cor 5.19: "God was in Christ reconciling the world to himself," a passage which he found problematic in *TKG* because of its monotheistic tone (see *SpL* 70).

80. *CG* 245.

81. Jesus' passion begins "in Gethsemane with the experience of God's hiddenness, and ends with the experience of God-forsakenness on the cross" (*SpL* 63–4; see also *TKG* 76; *WJC* 166; "The Passion of Christ and the Suffering of God," 20–3).

82. For this paradigm without referencing the Spirit, see *UZ* 142–7, *TKG* 80; and also *HG* 75–8, where the Spirit is the "binding force" and the "medium" of the sacrifice.

the cross.[83] Indeed, his assertions regarding the cross draw strongly on his social understanding of God's triunity, stressing the three subjects rather than their unity. And now that his theology of the cross is fully developed in trinitarian form, the dimensions are clear:

1. The Father, from Gethsemane to Golgotha, is the "rejecting Father."[84] First, the Father does not hear[85] the prayer of the Son in Gethsemane, and then on the cross is continually silent as he abandons the Son to death. So, the Father suffers as the one abandoning his Son.
2. The Son, from Gethsemane to Golgotha, is the abandoned Son. The first part of his plea to the Father (Abba[86]): "remove this cup from me"[87] goes unanswered, while the second half "yet, not what I want [θέλω], but what you want" is answered according to the Father's will.[88] So, the Son suffers actively[89] as the one who both "through the eternal Spirit offers himself without blemish to God"[90] and passively as the one abandoned by his Father.
3. The Spirit, from Gethsemane to Golgotha, is the Spirit of Christ.[91] The Spirit suffers, but does not die and is "Jesus' strength in suffering."[92] Thus, the Spirit is the "real determining subject of

---

83. Rublev's icon vividly depicts the Trinity as three persons; see *HTG* 19–25; *ET* 305–6.

84. *SpL* 65; see also *WJC* 173ff.

85. *SpL* 64; this is an odd interpretation, and "unanswered" would seem to convey the same meaning; see also *WJC* 173; "The Passion of Christ and the Suffering of God," 20–23.

86. *Contra* Moltmann, who asserts that "Jesus always addressed God only as 'Abba'" (*HTG* 10; compare, however, *SpL* 62). Mark 14:36 is the only instance of Abba in the Gospels; compare the parallels: Matt 26:39; Luke 22:42.

87. Mark 14:36; he cites Mark's account as "original," while Matthew and Luke sound "more modest" (*TKG* 76).

88. Mark 14:36; θέλω occurs once (UBS⁴). In seeming contrast to this assertion, Moltmann finds no problem with stating: there is "an inward conformity between the will of the surrendered Son and the surrendering will of the Father" (*WJC* 174).

89. *CG* 243. For a discussion of the criticisms of this theology of surrender as child abuse, see *WJC* 172–81; *GHH* 75; *JCTW* 38; see also p. 63 n. 121, above.

90. Heb 9:14; Moltmann takes liberty with this passage and states that "Jesus *offered himself up* to suffer-God-forsakenness," instead of "to God" (*SpL* 65).

91. Or perhaps Moltmann would say "becomes the Spirit of Christ" (*SpL* 68; see 59–71).

92. *SpL* 64; *WJC* 174.

this special relationship of Jesus' to God, and of God's to Jesus."[93] Accordingly, the Spirit "frames the Son's response: 'Not my will, but thine be done.'"[94] The Spirit also "reveals to Jesus the 'will' of God [the Father]."[95]

So each experiences the passion differently according to their different roles. This entails understanding the cross in pneumatological perspective:

1. Regarding the "unheard prayer": the Spirit neither prays nor answers.
2. Regarding the suffering abandonment: the Spirit suffers neither like the Father nor the Son; the Spirit neither abandons like the Father, nor is abandoned like the Son, yet suffers as Jesus' strength.
3. Regarding the death: the Spirit, like the Father, experiences the death of the Son, but does not die.

Here the "God against God" paradigm is mitigated slightly because, beyond the Spirit's role as "bond," Jesus experiences the Spirit's presence in the midst of the Father's absence.[96] Yet, his understanding of the divine suffering becomes clearer and more complex: "the Father suffered *with* and *in* the Son; and he did so by virtue of his indwelling in the Son through the Holy Spirit."[97] Showing the different angles of divine passibility seems to render his notion of perichoresis stronger compared with *CG* or *TKG*.

This vital development in his theology of the cross does not prevent Moltmann from asserting: the Spirit is "very much more the one who

93. *SpL* 61; see also *WJC* 174: "The Spirit is the divine subject of Jesus' life-history; and ... passion history"; this statement does not capture the dialectic involved in the Son's relationship to the Spirit. Compare *SpL* 61, 63, 68. *SpL* 63 captures well the difficulties at this point: "It is Christ himself who is the truly active one, through the operation of the divine Spirit who acts in him."

94. *SpL* 64.

95. Ibid.; here again the need to be more specific in naming the Father, instead of God, especially regarding the "will" which in Moltmann's reading places the Son and the Father at odds here.

96. *SpL* 65. It is not entirely clear whether the "God against God" paradigm is still helpful since he still stresses divine abandonment, yet now insists on divine presence in the its very midst.

97. Ibid., 68.

brings Jesus up out of death."[98] Indeed, the explication of the Spirit's role in the cross transitions quickly to resurrection: "Looked at pneumatologically, Christ's death and rebirth belong within a single movement. They are one event."[99]

Pneumatology of the Resurrection

While in *SpL* Moltmann makes an advance over his prior theology of the cross, he also directly identifies the Spirit's role in the resurrection of Christ.[100] Christology leads to pneumatology because of the resurrection: being "in" Christ is equated with being indwelt by the Holy Spirit.[101] The Spirit of life will "give life to our mortal bodies" as he raised Christ Jesus from the dead.[102] And it is when discussing the "Spirit of the resurrection" that Moltmann too easily slips into positive experiences of the Spirit. Moltmann cites joy and peace, quickly and rightly warning that the many other experiences "seem to be purely positive and somewhat illusory," adding the corrective that it is easy, yet incorrect, to lose sight of reality when reading of these experiences.[103] Unfortunately, he does not heed his own advice, as he instead moves to discuss "Easter joy" and proclaims that during experiences of the Holy Spirit there are "unlimited potentialities."[104] (This is precisely the opposite conclusion he reached during the "breakdown" of hope: "At that time we came to understand the future as by no means open, or an antechamber of unlimited possibilities, but as occupied by counter-forces and counter-utopias."[105]) He

---

98. Ibid., 65; see also *TH* 215; "A Response to my Pentecostal Dialogue Partners," 64; *ET* 147–48.

99. *SpL* 65; see also *WJC* 214; *SoL* 15.

100. Beyond *SpL*, see *GHH* 56; "The Blessing of Hope," 151.

101. Rom 8:1, 9.

102. Rom 8:11; see also *JCTW* 86; *SpL* 87.

103. *SpL* 154; he cites Gal 5:22 which lists the fruit of the Spirit.

104. Ibid., 155. Kuzmic makes some of these charges as well, but unfairly represents Moltmann's position as unaware of war, pain, suffering and death (Kuzmic, "A Croatian War-Time Reading [of *SpL*]," 19–21; see also "A Response to my Pentecostal Dialogue Partners," 68–9); conversely, the point made here is that Moltmann is aware of these but still does not bring out the implications of a *pneumatologia crucis* for his theology generally or his hope specifically. The difference is crucial. Unfortunately, Kuzmic makes it appear that there are not resources in Moltmann's theology to overcome such onesidedness.

105. *EJM* 118–19.

insists on relating the Spirit to both the cross and resurrection, but notice the altered perspective: "Christ was 'crucified in (the) weakness (of God) but lives in the power of God' (2 Cor. 13.4)."[106] This is true, but this statement does not require the conclusion Moltmann reaches, which pits resurrection power over against the Spirit's presence in suffering. He avoids balancing the discussion of the present experience of suffering, which would seem to require him to relate experience to "limited," rather than "unlimited potentialities."

For example, while briefly discussing the importance of the disabled and handicapped for a proper understanding of the church[107] he cannot avoid pitting the Spirit of resurrection against the Spirit of suffering: "The astonishing energies [*Kräften*] of the Spirit reveal God's marvellous power to rise [*sic*]. The weaknesses and disabilities and the sufferings of the Spirit reveal the even more marvellous suffering power of God."[108] But recall, that for Moltmann, the Spirit is "very much more" the Spirit of resurrection, a view that runs through all of *SpL*.[109] A theology of healing is important for Moltmann because "according to the Gospels, people in the nearness of Jesus are not revealed as 'sinners' [as with Paul] but rather as *sick*; while 'demons' are 'personal images for powers of disorder and of destruction.'"[110]

According to Paul, "we groan inwardly" awaiting redemption,[111] because the Christian life is, by definition, a struggle, an acknowledgement of the lack until the future. The tension in the Christian life is that, on one hand, when identifying with the cross, one experiences some measure of suffering in relation to Christ's. Yet, on other, one also can

---

106. *SpL* 67; Moltmann's parenthesis. Unfortunately, Moltmann does not develop the second sentence in a pneumatological contour.

107. See *SpL* 192–3; see also p. 89 n. 125 above.

108. *SoL* 68 [71]; this quote needs clarification: 1. the first statement ends with a typo: "rise" should be "raise" (*Auferstehungsmacht*) [71]; 2. *wundebare* might be better rendered (in theological parlance) as "miraculous" instead of the more aesthetic "marvellous"; 3. the second statement could be read as the Spirit having disabilities, but contextually it appears that Moltmann is distinguishing "weaknesses and disabilities [of the disabled]" from "the sufferings of the Spirit."

109. *SpL* 65; see also "A Response to my Pentecostal Dialogue Partners," 64; *ET* 147–48.

110. "Jesus and the Kingdom of God," 8. This interpretation serves Moltmann well, seemingly providing a precondition for his lack of a personal doctrine of sin.

111. Rom 8:22–24.

experience some measure of resurrection joy in relation to Christ's. Both of these are only conceivable by way of the Spirit. Moltmann affirms just this notion: "the experience of the Spirit . . . makes Christians in every society restless and homeless."[112] Yet, the dialectic of Christian living (as he explicated in *CPS*) is that both cross and resurrection determine the experiences of life. And it is therefore rather odd that despite the desire to relate the Spirit to the cross and resurrection, Moltmann has quite intentionally placed supreme weight on the Spirit of resurrection. This methodology, while not inherently flawed, opens Moltmann's understanding of the Spirit, perhaps especially here, to being too one-sided, dogmatically favoring the Spirit's presence in power over presence in suffering. This is most appreciable in his understanding of experience, which helps him to underscore the importance of "the Spirit of life."

A Theology of Experience

It would be unfair to assert that in his pneumatology, Moltmann avoids mentioning the nature of suffering in the present. He knows full well that Christian discipleship is invariably open to suffering: "life in the Spirit is always discipleship of Jesus, and discipleship leads to conflict with the powers and the powerful of 'this world,' and to the bearing of the cross."[113] He introduces this understanding, however, not to develop a theology of experience tied to suffering, whereby the Son and the Spirit help humanity and all creation endure the conflicts, but rather to recast it: "In *faith* we experience the peace of God, in *hope* we look ahead to a peaceful world."[114] This recasting moves too quickly to define experience of God in light of the resurrection: "We call these experiences of peace with God and Easter joy in the rebirth to life, *experiences of the Holy Spirit* . . . If this Spirit of God is 'the Spirit of resurrection,' then we are possessed by a hope which sees unlimited possibilities ahead, because it looks to God's future."[115]

The move from the cross to resurrection is not problematic, the urgency with which he makes the transition points to an underdeveloped (or underappreciated) understanding of the Spirit's role in pres-

112. *SpL* 73.
113. Ibid., 154; see also 74–77.
114. Ibid., 154.
115. Ibid., 155.

ent suffering. Admittedly, this seems impossible: inspect any one of Moltmann's major works post-*CG* and suffering is clearly a vital component. The Spirit will "be poured out on all flesh," but for Moltmann this is too easily transferred to the present, without reserve. He is to be commended for his desire to inform the culture of death with an affirmation of life. But his discussion is one-sided.[116] The clearest example of the problems associated with his view is related to his positive understanding of experience and reality.

Experience and Reality

On one hand he opts for a highly positive understanding of life. This is certainly due to his understanding of life sourced in the Spirit. On the other, he is too dismissive of keeping this in proper perspective of the variety of experiences: the overall presentation of *SpL* is the promotion of life in seemingly utter positivity.[117] This is surprising and problematic. Moltmann explicates his mature trinitarian theology of the cross in *SpL* devoted to showing the Spirit's role. It should follow, but unfortunately does not, that in the same text is the appropriation of the Spirit's work in suffering. Indeed, the fact that he explores the Spirit's role in the cross exacerbates the lack of sustained discussion of exploring the Spirit's role for creation's suffering. Enigmatically, Moltmann stresses life to the detriment of his pneumatology. While Moltmann affirms the "fathomless complexity"[118] of the Holy Spirit, this seldom renders his discussions equally complex. Calling to mind *TH*'s insistence on the surplus of hope, Moltmann points to the "eschatological immeasurability in the experience of the Spirit."[119] The dialectical ground of his doctrine of hope should have prevented him from falling into this trap; it does not.

---

116. And while he asserts that his pneumatology is "drawn less on the *Zeitgeist*" (*SpL* xiii), it appears that the result of this historical self-awareness leads him too quickly to confront the *Zeitgeist* with a much-needed dose of life affirmation, instead of an insistence on the Spirit's presence as co-sufferer.

117. Perhaps typified by his penultimate quotation:

"Let's get together and be alright,
one love, one heart.
Give thanks and praise to the Lord
and be alright" (*SpL* 309, quoting Bob Marley, "All in One").

118. *ET* 338.

119. *SpL* 152.

And because it fails to keep him from this, his pneumatology of experience appears one-sided and unbalanced.

Experiences of Life, Experiences of God

Experiences can be positive, of course, but just as easily (more, perhaps?) they can be negative.[120] Moltmann knows this; he is fond of asserting: "When freedom is close, the chains begin to hurt."[121] And while experiences can be spoken of as active, they are more likely to be connoted in passive terms: "experience is something that 'happens to us,' something that overpowers us without our intending it, unexpectedly and suddenly."[122] And by asserting, "There is no experience without jeopardy" he captures well the inherent ambivalence of experience, or rather the potentiality and possibility of every experience. Because Moltmann is always concerned with bringing hope to the present, his pneumatology is a significant contribution to this orientation. For, pneumatology is the way to bring the history of Christ to bear on human living: it is through the Spirit that one experiences God.

Before exploring what Moltmann means by "experiences of God" in pneumatological perspective, first a brief glance at his view of this relationship earlier.[123] Indeed, his emphasis in TH on the radical discontinuity between the future and the present is not easily forgotten: "Hope's statements of promise, however, must stand in contradiction to the reality which can at present be experienced."[124] Thus, Moltmann was concerned with relating hope to experience as contradiction: "Present and future, experience and hope, stand in contradiction to each other ... [humanity] is drawn into the conflict between hope and experience."[125] Drawing on the New Testament, he asserted that "Christian hope is ...

---

120. See ibid., 18–28, for Moltmann's view of experience related to consciousness, reason, perception, and the like.

121. Ibid., 75; italics original. For a discussion of the importance, and limitation, of the negation of the negative, see ibid., 75–77; *EB* 91.

122. *SpL* 22.

123. While Bauckham assert that the differences between the early and late Moltmann on the notion of experience is a "striking contrast" (Bauckham, *Theology of Jürgen Moltmann*, 214), he finds a strong measure of continuity between *TH* and *SpL* on this point (216).

124. *TH* 18; see also 103ff.

125. Ibid., 18.

a 'hoping against hope' and thereby brands the visible realm of present experience as a god-forsaken, transient reality that is to be left behind."[126] From the same time period, he writes: "that which is Christian does not correspond to reality that can be known or experienced."[127] In *SpL* Moltmann turns this understanding of experience on its head: "Experience and hope mutually reinforce each other."[128] Clearly, much has changed between *TH* and *SpL*.

In light of the cross his early orientation was altered: "God and suffering are no longer contradictions . . . but God's being is in suffering and the suffering is in God's being itself, because he is love."[129] The more Moltmann identifies present reality as a time and place that God himself experiences, the easier he can locate divine activity in the present, not as God with "future as his essential nature,"[130] but as experiencing human history in a relationship of reciprocity. The key to this development in Moltmann's thought is the emergence of pneumatology between *TH* (1964) and *SpL* (1991). From *CG* forward, he insists that God is involved in human history. It appears that Moltmann wants to affirm the contradiction between reality and the promised future, while also affirming God's experience of precisely this reality.[131]

In explicating pneumatology Moltmann is keen to dispense with the unfortunate division between divine revelation and human experience, which he finds prevalent in pneumatological discussions.[132]

---

126. Ibid.; hope contradicts "our present experience of suffering, evil and death" (19).

127. *HP* 15–16.

128. "Jesus and the Kingdom of God," 12.

129. *CG* 227.

130. *TH* 16, 141; *RRF* 216.

131. See *EB* 90–93. In *SpL* Moltmann devotes space to the mystical tradition and this surely influences his own view of experience (see Bauckham, *Theology of Jürgen Moltmann*, 213–47).

One might wish to defend Moltmann at this point by asserting that he is focused on religious experience, which is positive. This argument is highly questionable based on even a cursory reading of his work, but it reaches the realm of improbability when this argument is compared to recent events. Indeed, even Moltmann points to some tragic incidents of death due to their involvement in religion (see *EJM* 119–20). One might also cite the radical elements in Islam, Judaism and Christianity.

132. *SpL* 5–8. This view he finds typified in Barth, who draws a sharp distinction between the Spirit of God and the spirit of human beings; the relationship is one Moltmann describes of "utter contradiction" (ibid., 6). Furthermore, Moltmann faults

Moltmann refuses any such limitation: "By experience of the Spirit I mean an awareness of God in, with and beneath the experience of life, which gives us assurance of God's fellowship, friendship and love."[133] "The presence of [the] Kingdom is *experience of the Spirit*. The future of our experience of the Spirit is the *Kingdom of God*. So we also experience the coming Kingdom in the present Spirit of God which makes us alive."[134] Thus, for Moltmann, the source of life can also be designated as the kingdom of God, which "is the *open vast space* in which we can develop because there are no more limitations in it."[135] This is highly illuminating and his impulse is correct in so far as the work of the Spirit is aligned to the future kingdom; however, such a stress also mitigates his calls elsewhere for the place of suffering. Relating the kingdom to the future, Moltmann stresses the following: "Exactly because the Kingdom of God is experienced in the present . . . its completion is hoped for in the future. Experience and hope mutually reinforce one another."[136] And it is this statement that Moltmann could use to reflect on how this is not always the case, pointing out that in fact hope(s) are not always fulfilled in experience, and there are times that experiences call hopes into question, causing a re-evaluation of hope, to ensure they it is sufficiently grounded.[137] (Moltmann's own turn to the cross should be a resource to avoid asserting without qualification that "Experience and hope mutually reinforce one another.") Indeed, there is a tension to be had, and Moltmann is finding it hard to maintain. This is the case because he too often interprets experience in highly positive ways; there is too little discussion of the ambiguity of life, experience and

---

Barth's eschatology for reducing pneumatology to revelation: "the Holy Spirit is holy because 'it is *eschatologically* present to the human spirit in God's revelation, and in no other way'" (ibid.; quoting Karl Barth).

133. Ibid., 17.

134. "Jesus and the Kingdom of God," 9; Bauckham finds Moltmann's view of experience "one of his more emphatic rejections of Barth's theology" (Bauckham, "Jürgen Moltmann," 221).

135. "Jesus and the Kingdom of God," 8.

136. Ibid., 12.

137. As Adams rightly points out (referencing Aquinas): "Experience cannot be said straightforwardly to cause hope: it will depend on what kind of experience it is upon which one draws, and experience can be a cause of despair as well as of hope" (Adams, "Hope," 310). Hope and experience only reinforce one another if one believes that "suffering tend[s] to call forth hope" (Tinder, *The Fabric of Hope*, 135).

potential failures. His basic impulse of talking in pneumatological terms is in phrases related to life, divine field of force, source of energy, power, fellowship, renewal, new life, spirituality, fellowship, vitality and experience.[138] These locutions however are restrictive in Moltmann's hands, and allowed only a positive meaning.

It is puzzling why Moltmann's pneumatology moves so quickly to positive dimensions. To be sure, he validly asserts: "'The Spirit of the resurrection' is there at the places where we experience the shadow of the cross."[139] Yet, this statement has the possibility of being either helpful or detrimental in expressing the Spirit's role. As quickly as he places the accent on the suffering power of God in the Spirit, his understanding of the Spirit of resurrection too often carries the freight of his material argument.[140] In a striking statement, yet emblematic of *SpL*, he asserts: "The experience of the Spirit makes Christ—the *risen* Christ—present, and with him makes the eschatological future present too."[141] While this is a statement seeking to offer hope, it needs to be informed by the knowledge of the crucified one, too.

While his approach to pneumatology is completely understandable on one level, on another it detracts from the very important notion of the suffering Spirit. His pneumatology can only begin to point in the right direction and he fails to follow through with his own intentions of developing a pneumatology of the cross. The result is a pneumatology that at once affirms the kenosis of the Spirit while passing it over in favor of the Spirit of the resurrection. The basis for this move is not hard to predict; it should not be surprising that the roots go all the way back to *TH*:

> His experience of reality as history in all its possibilities of change is not . . . conditioned by whether history can be made at the whim of the human subject. For him, the world can be changed by the God of his hope. . . The subject of the transfor-

---

138. This list leaves out the various aspects of soteriology (like liberation, justification, regeneration, sanctification; see *SpL* 83–213).

139. Ibid., 192; he is quoting Käsemann. Oddly this statement is removed from the later and virtually identical discussion (*SoL* 66).

140. *SpL* 192.

141 Ibid., 147; the context is a discussion on rebirth and justification, but the assertion, while correct, is emblematic of the entire volume's tendency to focus on the resurrection, instead of taking up the importance of the Spirit's role for suffering.

mation of the world is for him therefore the Spirit of the divine hope.¹⁴²

His understanding of the resurrection impels him to prefer resurrection power over suffering power, because the Spirit is not limited by possibilities within history, but brings about "a new possibility altogether for the world, for existence and for history."¹⁴³

The most problematic aspect of Moltmann's view of the universal Spirit is not that he contends that the Spirit is active in all people, regardless of religious affiliation (or none),¹⁴⁴ but that this concern to see the Spirit in all experience is too easily undermined by what Moltmann really intends. If he intends to say that every experience is an experience of God,¹⁴⁵ then he should, by definition, seek to relate this to both positive aspects of the Spirit and also the negative dimensions of life: suffering, disappointment, death, etc. His pneumatology is too one-sided in favor of fulfilled experiences, not disappointed failures.¹⁴⁶

Conclusion

A Critique and the Offering of an Alternative

The conclusions of Moltmann's doctrine of hope in pneumatological perspective have been building throughout the chapter. The disconnect in Moltmann's appropriation of the Spirit is that, unlike the Spirit who has experienced the raising of Jesus and thus can be rightly called the Spirit of life, people living in the present do not have that "experience" to call upon; instead people hope for the resurrection. Moltmann

---

142. *TH* 289-90.

143. Ibid., 179; these comments originally refer to the resurrection, but it seems clear that, in 1991 especially, what can be said about the resurrection must apply to the Spirit.

144. Clark Pinnock explores these dimensions as well (*Flame of Love*, 200-208).

145. This phrase intentionally echoes *EG*.

146. For a notable exception, see the early discussion of the openness of experience: open to fulfillment or disappointment, acceptance or rejection. The roots of Moltmann's move to the positive realm of experience might be explained in a comment early on: "Every severe disappointment in life diminishes the basic trust with which life is affirmed, and restricts a persons interest in life as such. Every despair constricts expectations about living, and diminishes the openness for new experiences" (*SpL* 27). To be sure, Moltmann is not entirely positive in *SpL*, but it appears to be the basic impulse throughout.

however does not develop this thinking, but instead writes in highly positive terms about life lived in the Spirit.

Jesus' ministry was one of divine healing, but recall that along with the healing command to "stand up, take your mat and go to your home" is his instruction to his followers to "take up [your] cross and follow me."[147] Because the Spirit of life is the dominating motif of his pneumatology, the Spirit of suffering is too easily passed by without further elaboration. Indeed, if there is a place for extended ethical reflection on the meaning of the cross for humanity it is in pneumatological assertions about the place of suffering in God, through the Spirit. Yet, the very book that develops a pneumatology of the cross fails at precisely this point.

Because he develops fully the pneumatological contour of his theology of the cross, the 1991 version (not the original 1972 version) should be better suited to articulate a doctrine of hope. In *SpL*, especially, Moltmann could have brought out the solidarity in suffering that his theology of the cross entails, with the pneumatology that now supplements it. While he follows the dialectical pattern formally, almost without exception the Spirit is not the source of suffering presence but of resurrection power. For Moltmann, the Spirit does not merely begin working after the cross. What is needed in his pneumatology of life is a coherent vision of the Spirit as fellow sufferer, rooted in the fact that the Spirit has already been involved in the abandonment of the Son by the Father. It may be that the relative newness of this development prevented him from seeing its benefits for an application of his doctrine of hope. It is this understanding that Moltmann can bring to bear on present suffering. The following section is an attempt to show what he might have done to explicate the results of his pneumatology of the cross in the context of hope.

The underlying premise of Moltmann's mature pneumatology is his insistence that "We have got used to death . . . And to get used to death is the beginning of the freezing into lifelessness oneself."[148] "So the essential thing" he writes, "is to affirm life—the life of other creatures— the life of other people—our own lives."[149] The affirmation of life is,

147. See Mark 2:11; 8:34, respectively.
148. *SpL* xii.
149. Ibid.

arguably, most crucial in the context of suffering and death. On this point, Moltmann's pneumatology has a decided advantage over those that do not make the Spirit a real subject participating in the cross. God is on the side of the outcasts, the godless, and the suffering: "the 'crucified' God is the human God of all godless men and those who have been abandoned by God."[150] Moltmann is no defender of the status quo, of human progress, but knows that hope must be found in the crucified one: "God has not begun the future of man at the extremities of human progress, but with this humiliated man. Hope, which is born of the memory of the crucified Lord, therefore leads to hope where there is nothing to hope for. It sees the future of man not in progress, but in his sacrifices."[151] His pneumatology has the resources to supplement such a concept of hope and thereby make it more applicable to the present. It is unfortunate that he does not develop this line of thought. This critique is not the same as Stibbe's, who asks: "do we not need some discussion concerning unholy and destructive energies in the cosmos? Do we not need a chapter on 'the spirit of death'?"[152] No; Moltmann does not need to develop the spirit of death, what he needs is a full application of the implications of his mature, pneumatological theology of the cross.

It is not only in success that the Spirit of life is active, but in suffering too. "The Son of God" writes Moltmann, "is not first at work in his exaltation and glory, but in his humiliation and lowliness."[153] Indeed, "the true God is therefore not recognized by his power and glory . . . but through his helplessness and his death on the scandal of the cross of Jesus."[154] This understanding of finding God in suffering, however, can now be supplemented with an understanding of the Spirit as the "*companion* in [Jesus'] suffering,"[155] building on the relevant gains made in his mature christology. Just as *WJC* showed the wider frame of Jesus' suffering, *SpL* can explicate how the Spirit, as Jesus' companion in suffering, is creation's companion is suffering too.[156] While this was done

150. *CG* 195.

151. *M* 117.

152. Stibbe, "A British Appraisal," 13.

153. *CG* 192.

154. Ibid., 195.

155. *SpL* 62.

156. Moltmann comes close to this notion by drawing on the theology of the *Shekinah*, but unfortunately avoids doing so in relation to the cross (ibid., 47–51).

in *GC* related to creation, in *SpL* he needs to relate this role of the Spirit in relation to humanity. In light of his explicitly trinitarian theology of the cross, he can now bring out the point that the Spirit provides no insulation from pain, but rather, just as with Jesus on the cross, sustains the sufferer in the very midst of suffering. God is not aloof, distant in heaven, but rather the Spirit is present in suffering. Furthermore, the "suffering Spirit" is the same Spirit of Christ's resurrection. Moltmann, especially, can go even further. The Spirit suffers, not as one enjoined in creation's plight and thus unable to ultimately overcome, but as the one who raises the dead: "If you are reviled for the name of Christ, you are blessed, because the spirit of glory, which is the Spirit of God, is resting on you."[157] In relation to creation the Spirit is both resurrection power and suffering presence.[158] There is no need to attempt to show how one role is more important than another: the Spirit suffered through the "God against God" abandonment on the cross, and on the third day raised the Son.[159] Christian hope takes full measure of the deadliness of death, and despite the present suffering of creation and humanity, awaits the work of the Spirit who will again overcome death and affirm life now and in the eschaton.

The chapter following is devoted to Moltmann's eschatology. The transition from pneumatology to eschatology is entirely natural in Moltmann's program, because pneumatology "prepares the way for eschatology."[160] His penultimate "contribution" brings together his previous theological assertions, relating them to Christian eschatology. The angle taken surveys how his doctrine of hope influences and is influenced by "the coming of God."

---

157. 1 Pet 4:14–15

158. The analogy, of course, breaks down at some point, and here it may well be the problem of relating the Spirit to personhood and suffering. To press Moltmann's conceptuality: does the Spirit work to overcome suffering now, or must creation wait for the future resurrection? This is probably a false dichotomy; yet unless the Spirit is placed on the side of the abandoning Father, Moltmann, surely, must say that the Spirit is on the side of the abandoned Son, and endures but still does not yet overcome the suffering. For Moltmann, in relation to the cross specifically, this conceptuality is true because in the midst of the abandonment the conformity of will is present for the Father, Son and the Spirit.

159. *TH* 162; *SpL* 66; see also Rom 8:11.

160. *SpL* 18.

8

Eschatology as Hope

Introduction

UNTIL NOW CONCENTRATION HAS BEEN DEVOTED PRINCIPALLY TO THE ground and implications for hope in Moltmann's theology. This chapter seeks to show more definitively the conclusions of the development of his doctrine of hope.

Moltmann's program, from 1964–2004, relentlessly shows how one overcomes eschatology's confinement to a discussion of merely "the last things" (traditionally: death, judgment, heaven and hell) but rather interpenetrates all others.[1] That said, however, theologians still tend to treat eschatological topics after dealing with virtually all others.[2] To a degree, Moltmann takes exception with this notion, untrammeled by the example set by others in his field: "Eschatology should not be its [theology's] end but its beginning."[3] Ultimately, however, his approach is unexceptional compared with other theologians because he issues his Christian eschatology toward the end of his contributions. (His final "contribution" is methodological and largely retrospective,[4]

---

1. See *CoG* x–xvii; *PG* 87; *EB*; see also Sauter, *What Dare we Hope?* 210. Moltmann would certainly agree that eschatology is not "the final piece in the jigsaw of Christian belief" (Fergusson, "Eschatology," 226).

2. Compared with other theologians, trying to draw limits around Moltmann's eschatology, distinct from other topics, poses an insoluble problem. Nevertheless, "eschatology" is employed to describe the topics of *CoG*, while admitting that all of them could have (or have already) appeared in his previous works, and perhaps in a prior chapter in the present study.

3. *TH* 16.

4. Placing methodology at the end is natural to him. In 1979 (regarding his early trilogy) he writes: "Actually one can judge the meaning [*Bedeutung*] of the individual steps on a theological way only from the goal or from the end" (*DGG* 168).

containing no major developments in his doctrine of hope.) For Moltmann, "*Christian* eschatology has nothing to do with apocalyptic 'final solutions'... its subject is not 'the end' at all ... Christian eschatology is the remembered hope of the raising of the crucified Christ, so it talks about beginning afresh in the deadly end."[5] Moltmann's point now, as then, is central: "The presence of salvation therefore only has a future if God's universal future is present in it in particular terms."[6] This language about the future in the present is intelligible in Moltmann's thought, with qualification. And the qualification lies not in identifying the radical divergence between eschatology and apocalyptic (Rahner), but rather in their convergence.[7] Rahner asserts: "To extrapolate [*Aussage*] from the present into the future is eschatology, to interpolate [*Ein-sage*] from the future into the present is apocalyptic."[8] The German reveals what the English does not, as Moltmann turns Rahner's phrase in on itself: "Our statements spoken *out* [*Aus-sagen*] of our present *into* the divine future are possible on the basis of the divine word spoken *into* [*Ein-sage*] our present *out* of God's future."[9] Indeed, "distinctively Christian hope brings eschatology into apocalyptic: in the end—new beginning."[10]

The discussion below follows Moltmann's order (personal eschatology, cosmic eschatology and divine eschatology),[11] whereby he reverses the ontic order of cause to effect, by advancing his eschatology in ever-widening concentric circles, noetically: from effect to cause.[12]

---

5. *CoG* xi; see also *EB* 48–52; *FC* 20 [28].

6. *FC* 22; future = *Zukunft* [30].

7. Moltmann does not seek an absolute conflation of the two; see especially, his 1974 article: "Methods in Eschatology" (*FC* 41–48).

8. Rahner, "Eschatological Assertions," 336 (as quoted in *Zukunft der Schöpfung*, 54).

9. *FC* 45 [54]; see also "God's Kenosis," 138.

10. "From the Beginning of Time in God's Presence," 62.

11. *CoG* xii; four questions outline the focus of *CoG*: (1) What is hope for eternal life? (2) What is hope for the kingdom of God? (3) What is hope for the new heaven and the new earth? (4) What is the hope of glory for God himself?

12. "Love, Death, Eternal Life," 5–6; *CoG* xvi.

Anthropological Eschatology[13]

For the doctrine of hope, one's position on universalism can be symptomatic, revealing the relative dogmatism that accompanies eschatology generally. Moltmann clearly envisions an eschatological soteriology that is universal in scope.[14] He does not invoke an agnostic claim of uncertainty regarding future salvation. Even if he did not explicitly address this issue, his eschatology surely demands it. While some commentators, even in the face of his explicit denials, have not been deterred from finding universalism in Barth's doctrine the situation is entirely different regarding Moltmann.[15] There is no getting round his affirmations on this point, which become more pronounced over the years (save his enigmatic and short-lived ambivalence in WJC). Both the structure of his theology and his affirmations lead to universalism, stemming from the theocentricity of his eschatology.[16] Without question his understanding of God's inner-trinitarian relations and God's relationship to the world essentially demands that in the future all will be saved. With this in mind, the question that leads Moltmann to universalism should not be surprising: "what does God lose in losing anyone?"[17] Noticeably, the question is not anthropologically driven: "what does universalism mean for humanity?" but rather theocentrically driven: "what does

---

13. Moltmann develops his doctrine of eschatological soteriology under the heading "Historical Eschatology," but here personal salvation is discussed under the more fitting label "Anthropological Eschatology" because Moltmann's discussion of the millennium (*CoG* II: "Personal Eschatology") is not addressed at length.

14. See *CG* 101–2, 176–80, 194–95, 242–4; *CoG* 235–55; *EJM* 43–47; "The End of Everything is God: Has Belief in Hell Had Its Day?" 263–64. However, he mitigates the force of his argument at times (see *WJC* 334–8; *EB* 118; "The Blessing of Hope," 161).

15. Secondary readers of Moltmann are not (or rather should not be) confused about Moltmann's intent on the matter (as is sometimes the case when reading Barth). Indeed, regardless of one's interpretation of Barth on this point, he explicitly denies dogmatic universalism, because salvation history is not complete (Barth, *Church Dogmatics*, II/2:306ff.). The irony is that while Moltmann rejects Barth's view of eschatology because of its primarily disclosive function (see *CoG* 239, 249), Moltmann's own espousal of dogmatic universalism seems to tend in this direction, too.

16. Among the faults of my earlier study, devoted to the theological underpinnings of the modern-day proliferation of universalism, is its failure to bring out enough the theocentricity of Moltmann's universalism (see Neal, "The Doctrine of Universalism, with Special Reference to Jürgen Moltmann," 51–68).

17. See *CoG* 324.

universalism mean for God?" His doctrine of God supplies the answer to this question.

Back in 1974, Moltmann's formal argument for universal salvation was rooted in his theology of the cross: "Therefore the theology of the cross is the true Christian universalism. There is no distinction here, and there cannot be any more distinctions. All are sinners without distinction, and all will be made righteous without any merit on their part by his grace which has come to pass in Christ Jesus (Rom. 3.24)."[18] Moltmann adjudicates the issue of the resurrection of the body or immortality of the soul by turning the question on its head,[19] as he defends eschatological resurrection and immortality, not by hiding behind the question and issuing tautologies, but rather by having the former lead to the latter:[20] "the Spirit of life is stronger than death and must therefore be called immortal ... In this Spirit, it is not just one part of life ... that is already immortal here and now; it is the whole of this mortal life."[21] In *CoG*, he writes:

> The great turning point from disaster to salvation took place on Golgotha; it does not just happen for the first time at the hour when we decide for faith [*Glaubensentscheidung*], or are converted ... If salvation and damnation were the results of human faith or unfaith, God would be dispensable ... It is only if a qualitative difference is made between God and human beings that God's decision and human decision can be valued and respected. God's decision "for us," and our decisions for faith or disbelief no more belong on the same level than do eternity and time.[22]

---

18. *CG* 194–95; see also *TH* 196–97; *TKG* 40; *WJC* 336–38; "Talk-Back Session with Dr. Jürgen Moltmann," 39–47. Back in 1964, Moltmann seems to identify hope as specifically for Christians (*TH* 17); yet, he includes all people, even those outside the church, in the invitation to the Lord's supper (*CPS* 246, 273). Balthasar discusses universalism as a possibility based on the cross (Balthasar, *Dare We Hope "That All Men Be Saved?"* 225–54).

19. He makes it clear that the immortality of the soul, as traditionally conceived, is erroneous (*CoG* 58–65; *EB* 103ff.; "The Blessing of Hope," 156).

20. "Love, Death, Eternal Life," 6–10; Is There Life after Death?; *CoG* 58–77.

21. *CoG* 71ff; see also *EB* 103–8.

22. *CoG* 245 [273]; see also *WJC* 213–15; *SpL* 147–49; *EJM* 44–47; *EB* 54ff., 140–43.

The decision, then, is God's. The stated motivation is a desire not to "overstress man's activity" which thereby "makes God passive."[23] While in *WJC* Moltmann recanted the dogmatism of his previous universalistic view of salvation,[24] his pneumatology leads him back to support universalism fully: "all those he has created will participate in his eternal vitality and will live eternally."[25] In this, he explicitly follows Johann Christian Blumhardt's "confession of hope": "The confession of hope has completely slipped through the church's fingers . . . The end has to be: Behold, everything is God's! Jesus comes as the one who has borne the sins of the world. Jesus can judge but not condemn."[26] This endorsement typifies a doctrine of soteriology that is heavily deterministic, which reaches to his entire eschatological program.[27] In *CoG* soteriology is not a possibility, but an eschatological certainty.

Eschatological Determinism

In *TH* Moltmann criticized Pannenberg's preference for viewing history as a whole over against his own view of history's open future.[28] The problem with Pannenberg's view, according to Moltmann, is that it closes history giving the future essentially a disclosive function, resulting in "the disappearance of the real movements, differences and prospects in

---

23. "God's Kingdom," 100.
24. See *WJC* 334–38.
25. *SoL* 65; see also *SpL* 189–90.
26. Shortened, but otherwise, as quoted in *CoG* 254–55; see also *WJC* 382 n. 36; "The Blessing of Hope," 161. Moltmann labels Christoph Blumhardt (Johann Christian's son) "a master of hope" ("Foreword," in Althouse, *Spirit of the Last Days*, vii). Moltmann is further indebted to the Blumhardts because beyond anthropological soteriology, they also expected "the restoration of all the things of nature in the new creation" (viii-ix; see also *CoG* 239).
27. Indeed, despite his thoroughgoing rejection of God's immutability, Moltmann cannot be counted as a supporter of "open theism." Growth in this literature continues seemingly unabated; see the seminal collection: Clark Pinnock, *et al.*, *The Openness of God*; see also the *JETS* volume devoted to this issue: *JETS* 45.2, 193–341. While this issue seems to exercise only evangelicals in North America (thus far), Fiddes discusses (and rejects), with more philosophical erudition than the "open theists" typically do, the notion of a programmed future based on a traditional theistic metaphysic (see Fiddes, *Creative Suffering of God* 97–106; idem, *Promised End*, 175–80).
28. *TH* 78–79, 275–79; see also *ET* 35.

history."²⁹ In *CoG* Moltmann maintains an open future that reaches the past.³⁰ In so doing, he places a question mark squarely on Pannenberg's approach of historical investigation via analogy and comparison, fearing that this results in a formal acceptance of the contingent, while at the same time disallowing a place for it: "For the raising of Christ involves not the accidentally new, but the expectational category of the eschatologically new."³¹ Compared with Pannenberg, then, Moltmann does not support eschatological determinism. In an entirely different way, yet with arguably similar results, Moltmann posits his own version of determinism based not in seeking historical unity (Pannenberg), but by having the eschatologically new determine the meaning of the present, which is precisely where a strong notion of the ontological priority of the future leads. Here Moltmann's view of universal salvation is assessed and a question mark is placed on his view of the open future.

Moltmann hopes to link separationism with the modern concentration on human subjectivity, thereby showing its cultural bias and basis, in order to discredit it. This move leads him to a dubious conclusion: "The doctrine of the double outcome of Judgment is a relatively modern doctrine compared with the doctrine of universal salvation."³² His view, then, returns to the past to find the proper answer. In doing so, however, he only goes back as far as Barth's "open universalism"³³ and the Blumhardts³⁴ for support as he pushes to one side the "terrible"

---

29. *TH* 276; while Moltmann's overall critique of Pannenberg implicitly stems from Bloch's influence, he concludes his assessment by quoting Benjamin: "That is why there is sense in asking about the future of past people . . . in order to 'kindle in the past the spark of hope.'" (*TH* 279; see also 268). Bloch's influence on Moltmann certainly brings into focus one of the central differences between Moltmann and Pannenberg: the openness of the future.

30. See *CoG* 44ff.; *ET* 56. In *CoG* he calls on the same figures as in *TH* (see references in the preceding note).

31. *TH* 179.

32. *CoG* 245; see also *EJM* 45; he provides no references to back up this claim. An abundance of literature would argue precisely the opposite. The reasons, starting point, and extent of the growth of universalism are disputed. For introductions to the literature, see Bauckham, "Universalism: A Historical Survey," 48–54; *The Nature of Hell*, 24–34; Cameron, *Universalism and the Doctrine of Hell*.

33. *CoG* 248-9; he avoids subscribing to Barth's view, but neither does he critique it.

34. He finds the Blumhardts a helpful resource (whom Barth also relies on; see *CoG* 239), citing them with approval numerous times (*WJC* 382n.36; *CoG* 254-55; *EJM* 47; *ET* 26).

Calvinist particularism of double predestination, whose major strength, he asserts, was its "aesthetic of juxtaposition" which was appealing due to its artistic symmetry of antithesis.[35] Predestination and soteriology, Moltmann posits, are not conceived in terms of symmetry with the yes and no on equal planes but rather in terms of asymmetry:[36] "In the divine Judgment all sinners, the wicked and the violent, the murderers and the children of Satan, the Devil and the fallen angels will be liberated and saved from their deadly perdition through transformation into their true, created being, because God remains true to himself, and does not give up what he has once created and affirmed, or allow it to be lost."[37] Besides the fact that he goes beyond even Origen in asserting the devil's ultimate redemption,[38] it seems difficult to demand precise details, especially regarding human beings, perhaps the most sophisticated of "open systems." To assert universalism dogmatically, however, Moltmann must refuse his own assertion: "The human person and human societies are the most complex systems which we know. They exhibit the highest level of indeterminate behaviour as well as the broadest degree of openness to time and the future."[39] Indeed, "Hope is the opposite of fatalism and decionism."[40] Moltmann, however,

---

35. *CoG* 247; he attributes this to Augustine's introduction of Aristotelian "juxtaposition."

36. Ibid., 246–49.

37. Ibid., 255.

38. Despite his reputation, Origen is difficult to interpret on this point; see Daley, *The Hope of the Early Church*, 56–60. Moltmann's inclusion of the devil and fallen angels in final salvation is "something of a *non sequitur*, since Moltmann has not suggested (and seems never to suggest) that Christ suffered and died in solidarity with (fallen) heavenly beings" (Bauckham, "Eschatology in *The Coming of God*," 13 n. 9). Perhaps however Moltmann's soteriological version of suffering gets him beyond the requirement of death.

39. "Creation and Redemption," 131. He goes on: "Because any actualization of a possibility by open systems itself creates a new openness for possibilities and does not merely actualize a given possibility and, thereby, transfer the future into the past, we cannot conceive of the kingdom of glory . . . as a system that is finally brought to its conclusion and, as such, closed but, on the contrary, as the openness of all finite life systems for the infinity of God" (131). Creation, then, remains open even in glory. He clearly wants to argue against eternity being a state of fixed, rigidity *contra*, perhaps, Kant (see Kant, "The End of all Things," 217–31).

40. *HP* 182; for decionism he uses "Dezisionismus" rather than "Determinismus" [254]. Fiddes opposes this view: "When we are concerned with persons, the route to the

insists that openness is only to God: "all open systems . . . will participate unhindered in God's indwelling fullness of possibility without being destroyed by it, and become that for which God has destined them."[41]

Moltmann's position is not based on "multiple salvations" (Heim),[42] a vision of God as "divine therapist" (Hick),[43] or "anonymous Christians" (Rahner),[44] resulting in the salvation of all. His methodology requires universalism because it stems from his doctrine of hope. Indeed, his adoption of universalism is understandable, since it is virtually unavoidable. As has been argued throughout, his fundamental theological impulse is to conceive of doctrine, every doctrine, as hopeful. Universal salvation has been implicit throughout his writings. If Moltmann had avoided reaching this conclusion it would be tantamount to disrupting his entire program. And while in both 1964 and 2003 he proffers a vision of hope that explicitly avoids both despair and presumption,[45] ultimately his doctrine of hope asserts universalism, not as possibility,[46] but as fact. Because he conceives hope as certainty based on the promises of God regarding the future (*Zukunft*) and the atoning work of Christ's death and suffering, Moltmann is able to avail himself of pronouncing universalism as dogma. This lack of resistance toward dogmatic universalism is a self-assured confidence that disallows mystery; there are no dark corners of theology, everything is clearly in view. Thus, the still-to-be-determined open future is actually closed. To his credit, he does not argue for eschatology as divine disclosure of how things are,

---

end shapes the content of the end; . . . There is room then for tragedy as well as triumph in God's victory over evil and suffering" (Fiddes, *Promised End*, 178).

41. "God's Kenosis," 151; ironically, these comments appear in a tribute for W. H. Vanstone, who refuses to assert universalism dogmatically; see also *EB* 17.

42. S. Mark Heim's thesis critiques Christian pluralism's insistence on a common end instead of evaluating each religion's conception of a desired ultimate state (Heim, "Salvations: A More Pluralistic Hypothesis").

43. For John Hick, God is "a divine therapist, working . . . in unlimited time, with perfect knowledge . . . [so] there is no final opposition between God's saving will and our human nature acting in freedom" (Hick, *Death and Eternal Life*, 254).

44. Moltmann is sympathetic to Rahner's notion, but does not subscribe to it (*CPS* 153; *HTG* 110–22); see Rahner, "Christianity and the Non-Christian Religions," Rahner, "Anonymous Christians."

45. *TH* 22ff.; *EB* 87–95. These are, of course, Pieper's terms.

46. For a more ambiguous appraisal of universalism, see Balthasar, *Dare We Hope "That all Men be Saved"?*

but rather eschatology is understood to be a future that is coming, and events still must take place. This argument seems to call for one to hope for universalism, but avoid guaranteeing it.

Jesus' discussion of the coming judgment[47] in terms of sheep and goats is one entrée into understanding the lack of certainty with which one should perhaps approach details of the future, especially regarding the destiny of human beings. Jesus places one group on his left and another on his right. Neither group thinks the depiction is accurate. The "sheep" on his right unwittingly ask: "When was it that we saw you hungry and gave you food, or thirsty and gave you something to drink?" And the "goats" on his left ask the same question albeit in the negative. Notice the lack of confidence in each group's questioning answer to Jesus.[48] Both groups are uncertain as to their placement in the judgment, and are surprised by Jesus' response. Indeed, God works in unpredictable ways. Moltmann's conception, however, contains no surprises.[49]

Moltmann's doctrine of universalism is ultimately a symptom of the fundamental problem of his doctrine of hope: certainty. The result is predictable: universalism is not a question of hope, but is certain. This, Moltmann believes, turns salvation into a hopeful doctrine: everyone will be saved. Yet, ultimately this is contrary to the nature of hope *qua* hope: dogmatic universalism cannot be hopeful, because it does not hope for salvation, it presumes it. And it is his stress on the coming of God that should have kept him from making such a presumptuous eschatological assertion. That the cross is a victory, because of the resurrection, is true, but it is not yet a total victory. Admittedly, the eschatology espoused here has a higher threshold for ambiguity in eschatology, which is an option Moltmann explicitly disallows,[50] but which resources in his project could ground. Regardless of the rejection of the scope of his soteriology, it is fully grounded in his doctrine of hope. Moltmann

---

47. Its more well-known title is "the parable of the sheep and goats" (Matt 15:31–46). Moltmann briefly addresses this passage (*CoG* 241).

48. Matt 25:37–38, 44.

49. This is due to his exegetical decision to regard all scriptural depictions of coming judgment as apocalyptic, and as having no place in Christian eschatology. He uses Matt 25 as showing that salvation and judgment are "a-symmetrical" (*CoG* 242). The remainder of his discussion is a theological development of universalism based on interpreting "separationist" passages in accordance with universalism (*CoG* 243–55).

50. "Creation and Redemption," 129.

makes it clear that the full reality of human salvation will only take place when creation is "consummated through the indwelling of God, then the unlimited possibilities open to God will indwell the new creation and glorified man will be free to participate in the unlimited freedom of God."[51] To be sure, Moltmann's vision of eschatological soteriology is not anthropocentric; it is cosmic in scope.

Cosmic Eschatology

In 1975 Moltmann asserted that the nature of "Christian eschatology is not merely eschatology for Christians; if it is to be the eschatology of the all-embracing kingdom, it must also be unfolded as the eschatology . . . of nature."[52] The life-giving Spirit will be poured out "on all flesh": "mean[ing] not just human life but all earthly living things."[53] A vision of eschatological salvation that encompasses humanity to the exclusion of creation is inconceivable for Moltmann.[54] Just as he refuses the view that the soul needs to flee the body, so also he refuses the view that humanity needs to flee creation: "Love for Christ and hope for him embrace love and hope for the earth."[55] Modern anthropocentricity is not a proper angle to discover the authentically Christian doctrine of humanity or creation.[56]

A key focus of *GC* is how God both suffers along with creation and will overcome creation's afflictions in the new creation. Most appreciably from *SpL* forward, Moltmann tends to focus on God's re-creating activity.[57] While he admits that at first sight the biblical apocalypses can appear to be visions of catastrophe on a global scale, his major discussion of creation from *CoG* through *EB* is not the catastrophic end-times, but the new beginning at the cosmic end, through which he seeks to

---

51. Ibid., 130.

52. *CPS* 135; see also *EB* 150–51. Already in *TH* he had a fairly broad view of future salvation (*TH* 216, 223).

53. *EJM* 82; see also *CoG* xiii; *WJC* 258.

54. Besides *GC* and *CoG*, see *CPS* 283; *SoL* 20.

55. *CoG* 279; while he relates this to christology, it seems that pneumatology is the driving premise of his argument.

56. *GSS* 130ff.

57. Namely, *CoG, ET, EB, PG*.

recover the original impetus of the biblical apocalypses as "messages of hope in despair."[58]

The New Creation

Inveighing against the traditional understanding of the creation-eschatology relationship, which sees eschatology as consummation of the creation as return, he writes: creation in the end "is more than the beginning: in the beginning creation—at the end the kingdom; in the beginning God in himself—at the end God all in all."[59]

In *TH* Moltmann referred to the resurrection as a *"nova creatio"* and *"novum ultimum"* that "shows [God] to be the *creator ex nihilo*."[60] While he calls on biblical support for this understanding,[61] the main intent of his assertion seems to be his insistence that eschatology is neither extrapolation (Rahner) nor *Futurum* (Bloch); it is concerned with the activity of God, who is not tied to the inevitable march of history, but is free as the power of the future to bring about the *novum*. Here it is crucial to qualify this activity lest Christian eschatology posits a new *creatio ex nihilo*, as Moltmann did previously: "in the context of nothingness he revealed his creative power . . . He will raise the dead. If, for the sake of this God, Christians hope for the future, they hope for a *novum ex nihilo*."[62] In *CoG* he recants the implication that he intended such a sharp discontinuity: "Raising is not a new creation; it is a new creating of this same mortal life for the life that is eternal,"[63] apparently meaning that there is continuity to be found in the *novum*, yet not constrained by the past. That God has defeated death and suffered vicariously is a

---

58. *EB* 51.

59. *CoG* 335; compare with Bloch: "*The real genesis is not at the beginning, but at the end*" (as quoted in *RRF* 160).

60. *TH* 179–80, 200, 221, respectively. "The resurrection of Christ does not mean a possibility within the world and its history, but a new possibility altogether for the world, for existence and for history" (*TH* 179).

61. See *RRF* 4, where he cites Rev 21:5: "Behold, I make all things new"; and *CoG* 27, where he cites Isa 43:18–19: "Remember not the former things, nor consider the things of old. For behold, *I* purpose to do a new thing." This latter quote picks up on von Rad's depiction of Israel's self-identity, linked to the prophets (see Meeks, *Origins*, 73–6).

62. *RRF* 171.

63. *CoG* 75; 350 n. 50; compare, however, *CoG* 271. The continuity of this new creating extends even to "personal sexual characteristics" (*CoG* 75). He compares this to the relationship between a caterpillar and a butterfly (*PG* 90).

reason for hope. In *CoG* he stresses that God is not subject to the limitations of this world in recreating it, while also asserting that the transient creation does not have the capacity for eternity, of its own accord. This emphasis continues on from *GC* and *SpL*, seemingly resulting from the emergence of pneumatology, as Moltmann more easily finds the Spirit immanently working in all of life's manifestations.

The Consummation of the World

God's creation has been spoilt by sin and evil; signs of imperfection, transience, tears, death, and suffering are only present in the temporal creation, not in the new.[64] For Moltmann this necessitates a view that waits hopefully for the new creation of the whole cosmos.[65] For the sabbath of creation goes back, presupposing the old creation, to gather up the beginning, not as a circle would return to the beginning,[66] but it "brings back everything that had ever been before."[67] Hope in the new creation, then "is not a one-way street on which one leaves the present behind in order to flee into the future."[68] "When all things are subjected to him," writes Paul, "then the Son himself will also be subjected to the one who put all things in subjection under him, so that God may be all in all."[69] In scripture, the Christian hope for the new heaven and the new

---

64. "Resurrection as Hope," 146; see also *CoG* 90–91; Bauckham, "Eschatology in *The Coming of God*," 17–19.

65. *CPS* 28–33; *FC* 115–30; *GC* 276–96; *WJC* 189–92, 260–70; *CoG* 68–71, 112, 131–3, 277–79. He details the interconnectedness of humanity, community and nature. This eschatological hope is for all life, and the "fulness of the times" will be expressed when the "unfurled times of history will be rolled up like a scroll" (*CoG* 294–95).

66. This is a specific rejection of the mythical view, held by Bultmann, that time is circular and the end returns to the beginning (*CoG* 263); see also *FC* 115–30; *GC* 1–19, 104–39, 276–96; "Liberation of the Future," 283–84.

67. *CoG* 265; God is involved in saving his entire creation, not as a restoration of the beginning, but specifically a renewal of all things (259–65).

68. "Resurrection as Hope," 138; Christian hope "draws the future into the sufferings of the present" (138). The new creation must avoid becoming "a gnostic doctrine of redemption" that only teaches an escapist rejection of the world and the body (*CoG* 259). Human beings are bestowed a responsibility as caretakers of the world.

69. 1 Cor 15:28; 1 Cor 15:22–28 is the underlying passage for Moltmann's entire eschatology. This undergirds his panentheistic vision of creation. Additionally, Moltmann regards "Isaiah's vision: 'The whole earth is full of his glory' (6.3)" as "[t]he key promise" for his eschatological vision ("World in God," 39; see also *TKG* 90–6).

earth[70] is "the redemption of human history and the consummation of creation."[71] The new creation is "a finitude that embraces infinity"[72] where "the indwelling of God and the indwelling of believers" is the basis of "the new creation of all things."[73] Using the abiding theme of love found in 1 John 4:16, Moltmann conceives of a glorification of perichoretic love when "the world will find space in God" and "God indwells the world."[74] God's indwelling is accorded universal significance where his omnipresence is unmediated to the extent that "we shall be able to look upon his face without perishing"[75] enabling humanity to "know him 'face to face.'"[76]

For Moltmann the restoration of all things does not focus solely on human beings, it must be a total consummation, because only then does Rev 21:5 become true: "Behold I make *all things* new."[77] The most appropriate image Moltmann employs to express this relationship is the sabbath.

The Eschatological Sabbath[78]

Moltmann transposes the days of creation (Genesis 1) to eschatology: "the day of Christ's resurrection is the first day of the new creation," it is the eschatological sabbath which Christians "early on" labeled "the eighth day."[79] For Moltmann, it is not the individual "restless heart" (Augustine)[80] but the whole creation "search[ing] for the rest in which it

---

70. *CoG* 305–6: For Moltmann, the new heaven, new earth theme of Rev 21 is both the Jewish and Christian hope found in the promises of Ezek 37.27 as well as a New Testament theme: John 1:14; 1 Cor 6:19; 2 Cor 5:17–9; Col 2:9.

71. "World in God," 39; see also "Resurrection as Hope," 145–47.

72. "World in God," 40; see also *GC* 277–79; *CoG* 44–46, 265–67, 280–84, 302–8.

73. *CoG* 306; see also "Resurrection as Hope," 146.

74. "World in God," 41.

75. *CoG* 317.

76. *CoG* 295; see also "Resurrection as Hope," 146–47; *CG* 264–66; *TKG* 91–93; *CoG* 335. Following 1 Corinthians, this will be the final stage of God's trinitarian process of "giving life to mortal creation" (Bauckham, "Eschatology in *The Coming of God*," 23).

77. As quoted in *EB* 150.

78. His clearest exposition of the sabbath is in *GC*; see also *CoG* IV.

79. *SoL* 122.

80. Augustine: "The thought of you stirs him so deeply that he cannot be content unless he praises you, because you made us for yourself and our hearts find no peace

can abide"; a rest which is not God, but the sabbath.[81] Disagreeing with Barth, Moltmann opts for an eschatological reading of the christological relationship between covenant and creation,[82] by essentially expanding the covenant to include not only humanity, but also non-human creation as well.[83] Relying on the New Testament[84] he explicates this dimension: "Without a new earth there is no hope of resurrection. So it is an incomplete description of Christian hope to say that only human beings will be 'eternalized and glorified' in God."[85] His eschatological hope of the new creation is the operative lens that places creation in the covenant.

Dismissing the notion of creation as only a past event Moltmann states: "The messianic doctrine of creation therefore sees creation together with its future—the future for which it was made and in which it will be perfected."[86] Reflecting on John's record from Patmos, Moltmann states: "God comes in order to live with God's temporal creatures on this earth and to come to rest in God's creation just like in the beginning on the Sabbath day. God does not want to find a dwelling place in particular temples or cathedrals but rather in God's entire creation."[87] Following Rosenzweig, Moltmann labels the sabbath "the feast of

---

until they rest in you." (Augustine *Confessions* I.i.1). Discussing the relationship between space and time and God, Moltmann labels God a "restless God" (*ET* 313).

81. *GC* 282; see also *GC* 181; *TH* 276.

82. Regardless of any specific objections to the details, this inclusion is a commendable tenet of his doctrine of creation. For a full appraisal, see especially *HTG* 125–42; see also *FC* 119 = *SW* 38; *WJC* 188; Torrance, "*Creatio ex Nihilo*," 85ff.

83. *HTG* 129, citing Ephesians 1 and Colossians 2. Arguably, his eschatology directs his doctrine of creation: "the creation itself is already God's covenant, and not just the enabling of such a covenant with just one creature" (*HTG* 129).

84. One Old Testament passage shows God's covenant with creation: A covenant with "Noah and his sons . . . and every living creature" (Gen 8:9–17; and perhaps also Jer 33:25).

85. *HTG* 139; see also *JCTW* 83. He also disagrees with the dualism of body-soul because he believes that it leads to a further separation of humanity from nature (*HC* 130; see also *TH* 329ff.; *GC* 236–43).

86. *GC* 5.

87. "All Things New," 31; see also "Zum Gespräch," 95. Alternatively, Kathryn Tanner proposes a future in God, yet does not require a spatially conceived world, where God dwells (Tanner, "Eschatology Without a Future?" 230). For expert exegesis of Revelation in relation with Moltmann's eschatology, see Michael Gilbertson, *God and History in the Book of Revelation*, VI.

creation"[88] which is the "prefiguration of the world to come" [because] "Every sabbath is a sacred anticipation of the world's redemption."[89] The sabbath has the dual role of casting one's gaze both to the past and the future: it recalls the divine rest, while also serving as "anticipation" to the future. This, indeed, is where Moltmann breaks his reliance on the Jewish sabbath and undergirds his doctrine of creation with a future perspective in distinctly Christian terms.[90] His stress on the importance of the sabbath is transposed for Christian theology by relating it to the importance of the resurrection. Because Christians "celebrate the first day of the week as the feast of the resurrection: it is the first day of the new creation."[91] Moreover, to achieve the intended result, he must transfer the importance of the Jewish sabbath to Sunday in light of the resurrection: "The light of Christ's resurrection is the light of the Christian sabbath."[92] Feasting, then, is rooted in the sabbath and the resurrection.[93] Moltmann makes it clear that the sabbath is "the crown of creation"[94] not humanity.[95] Once this is stressed, cosmic eschatology becomes a matter of course, enabling Christian theology to refuse the one-sided doctrine

---

88. *GC* 5, see also 277; *GSS* 114.

89. *GC* 6.

90. *GC* 295: "Israel's sabbath turns our gaze back to God's works in creation ... the Christian feast of the resurrection looks forward into the future of a new creation. ...Israel's sabbath is pre-eminently a day of a remembrance and thanksgiving, so the Christian feast of the resurrection is pre-eminently a day of a new beginning, and of hope."

91. *GC* 6–7; see also 277; *TH* 179–80; *GSS* 114.

92. *GC* 7.

93. Nicholas Adams picks up on one alteration between the early trilogy and *CoG*. He writes: "In later work, Moltmann modifies this picture and arguably abandons it: his account of feasting in *The Coming of God* concentrates on the risen, rather than the crucified, Christ and the dominant theme is not solidarity but laughter. Moltmann does not explain why" (see Adams, "Jürgen Moltmann," 236–38).

94. He credits Barth for the phrase "crown of creation" (*HTG* 129). Moltmann simultaneously praises Barth for his high view of the sabbath, while condemning his anthropocentric covenantal view of creation (*HTG* 128–29).

95. *GC* 197; see also *TJ* 42; *M* 108–11; *GC* xvi, 6, 18, 36; "Verschränkte Zeiten der Geschichte," 227; "The Ecological Crisis," 5–18; *GSS* 114–16. Otto labels Moltmann's theology anthropocentric (*God of Hope*, 99); Stephen Platten labels Moltmann's view of creation theocentric, yet unrealistic, because humanity's motive in caring for, and thus inherent attitude toward, creation necessarily focuses on fulfilling its own needs (Platten, "Authority and Order in Creation," *Theology* 94, 27).

of human redemption from the world.⁹⁶ As such, Christian theology can only discuss salvation in the wider frame of creation's salvation.⁹⁷ The way he relates creation and eschatology goes far in surmounting the thrust of escapist eschatologies that present the future as a time or place of humanity fleeing from God's creation. This "hostile" vision of eschatology undermines human stewardship of creation.⁹⁸

In the end God comes to his creation and indwells everything living. As such, the future is not a return to the beginning but instead is a new beginning. While creation in the beginning was very good, the new creation in the future will be much more than very good. This vision cannot be the certain outcome of the past and present, as if it could be plotted into the future (extrapolation). To overcome this, Moltmann must rely on his understanding of the future as the coming future which God brings: "In God's creative future [*Zukunft*], the end will become the beginning, and the true creation is still to come."⁹⁹ It is new in so far as the future brings not consummation and return, but instead "transforms not man alone, but all things."¹⁰⁰ Eschatological justification does not return creation and humanity to the beginning as it was, but brings about what was never there, a freedom for the divine, instead of oppressing nothingness.¹⁰¹ The hope of creation, in eschatological terms, is the future indwelling of creation by God, when "the finite is able to contain the infinite."¹⁰²

Moltmann views creation as necessary for God.¹⁰³ This orientation is important to remember: Moltmann sets the doctrine of creation in an eschatological perspective, and his doctrine of creation, with its adoption of *zimsum* and the necessity of creation, is complemented by his eschatology which necessitates creation's renewal and God's derestriction.¹⁰⁴ Eschatology and creation are closely linked in Moltmann's

---

96. *CoG* 259–67.

97. He seems to imply that humanity only truly has a "special dignity" as caretakers of creation, which can be lost if exploitation occurs (*GSS* 132).

98. *EB* 149ff.

99. *CoG* xi [12].

100. *FC* 170.

101. *FC* 168–70.

102. *EJM* 37.

103. See chapter 5, above.

104. Moltmann mediates between the one-sided Orthodox insistence on deification and the mutually one-sided Lutheran annihilation of the world by following Calvin's

program. Previously opposed members of the created order will be reconciled in the eschaton,[105] but even more importantly, creation must be renewed because the new creation is God's eschatological dwelling place, when "the glorification of the triune God *in* the new heaven and new earth" takes place.[106] This is not a return to the original state or paradise regained. Moltmann vehemently objects to this understanding, equating it with mythical notions of the circularity of time.[107] The time of eternity is "aeonic": "Aeonic time can be thought of as a time corresponding to the eternity of God: a time without beginning and end, without before and after."[108] This is an important concept in his eschatology: every time must be open to the future, open to redemption and open to hope. As such, the new creation is the time and space,[109] and the goal of God's relationship to creation: "The city of God is the centre of the new creation."[110] Cosmic eschatology "is the transition from temporal creation to the new creation of an eternal 'deified' world."[111]

Divine Eschatology

"The great eschatological question is this: What is the ultimate goal? Is it the world in God, or God in the world?"[112] In *TKG* Moltmann focused on the world in God,[113] but even there, his eschatology was directed toward God's future indwelling: "If God is love . . . he also expects and needs love: his world is intended to be his home. He desires to dwell in it."[114] In *CoG* he adds more detail: "the mutual relationships of the

---

notion of transformation, because only the latter takes into account both the cross and resurrection (*CoG* 272–75).

105. See Isa 11:6–9.

106. *EJM* 39.

107. *HP* 146; *CoG* 262ff.

108. *CoG* 282. Eternal time, then, is pictured as a cycle. Fiddes laments the fact that this seemingly deems eternal time static (Fiddes, *Promised End*, 132–34).

109. Or more specifically, the end of both time and space in the eternity of God (*CoG* 279–308); for a helpful introduction to these notions, see Bauckham, "Eschatology in *The Coming of God*," 10–16; idem, "Time and Eternity," 155ff.

110. *CoG* 308; see also *ET* 31.

111. *CoG* 265–66.

112. *EJM* 37; both questions are originally italicized.

113. *TKG* 90–96.

114. Ibid., 99.

Trinity are so wide open that in them the whole world can find a space, and redemption, and its own glorification."[115] In *WJC*, but not in *CoG*, this cosmic aspect resulted from Christ's resurrection: "The transition of Christ [into the new creation] has more than merely historical significance. It has cosmic meaning too. Through this transition resurrection has become the universal 'law' of creation, not merely for human beings, but for animals, plants, stones and all cosmic life systems as well."[116] *CoG* focuses specifically on God in the world: "In this divine eschatology God acquires through history his eternal kingdom, in which he arrives at his rest in all things, and in which all things will live eternally in him."[117] Consequently, "all created beings are drawn into the mutual relationships of the divine life, and into the wide space of the God who is sociality."[118]

Although only the final sixteen pages of *CoG* deal centrally with "divine eschatology,"[119] the book (like his theological program) is thoroughly theocentric: "*The God of hope* is himself *the coming God* (Is. 35.4; 40.5). When God comes in his glory, he will fill the universe with his radiance, everyone will see him, and he will swallow up death for ever. The future [*Zukunft*] is God's mode of being [*Seinsweise*] in history. The power of the future is his power in time."[120] While this quote brings to the fore the fact that the future is God's mode of being (although to be sure it is *Zukunft*, not *Futurum*), he finishes the assertion with the vital addition "in history" (words not included in the same description in *TH*). Moltmann's eschatology continues his strong insistence that the future is "above" the past and present: "By virtue of hope for the coming God, the expected future [*Zukunft*] acquires an inexhaustible 'added

---

115. *CoG* 335.

116. *WJC* 258.

117. *CoG* 335; see also *EJM* 39. Notice the unmistakeable reference to the importance of the economic Trinity and its effect on the immanent.

118. *CoG* 336; notice the restriction to living things, thus no mention of stones.

119. See *CoG* 323–39; *EJM* 35–41.

120. *CoG* 24 [41]. Notice the usage of *Seinsweise* and how he uses it entirely different than Barth (see *DGG* 183 nn. 34–35). This is an eschatology that appreciates more the aesthetic than the ontological (this is not to assert that these are mutually exclusive): "the fulness of God is the rapturous fulness of the divine life; a life that communicates itself with inexhaustible creativity; . . . a life from which everything living receives its vital energies and its zest for living" (*CoG* 336).

Eschatology as Hope 219

value' over against present and past in the experience of time."¹²¹ With this, Moltmann does not seek to adjudicate the time/eternity dilemma, but rather move beyond it insisting that it has no capacity to properly depict Christian eschatology. Instead he stresses, following von Rad and in opposition to Bultmann,¹²² the importance of understanding properly the future by deploying the importance of the category *novum* that rests firmly on the *Adventus/Futurum* distinction. The category *novum* "does not *emerge* from the old; it makes the old obsolete. It is not simply the old in new form. It is also a new creation."¹²³ As such, Moltmann posits the coming God in contradistinction from the Greek notion of "timeless and simultaneous eternity: Zeus was, Zeus is, and Zeus will be: Zeus is eternal."¹²⁴ Rather, "Grace to you and peace from him who is and who was and who is to come," is the proper description of the coming God.¹²⁵ The final turn of phrase provides the correction; somewhat unexpectedly, the future tense "who will be" is not asserted but instead the "ontological concept of eternity is broken through by the expression 'who is to come.'"¹²⁶ This emphasis goes back to the opening pages of *TH*, and he puts forward its importance again in *CoG*: "His [God's] name is declared in the mysterious 'I am who I am' or 'I will be who I will be' (Ex. 3.14). Whereas the first rendering stresses the reliability of the God who remains true to himself, the second emphasizes his futurity [*Zukünftigkeit*]. Ernst Bloch therefore talked about a God 'who has future [*Futurum*] as the essence of his Being.'"¹²⁷

Moltmann does not correct Bloch's conception, but instead rather confusingly adds it to support his own view. (In light of the strong

121. *CoG* 24 [41].

122. Bultmann asserts: "Newness is not a category which is determinative for the divine. That category is eternity" (as quoted in *CoG* 27).

123. *CoG* 27; see also Gilbertson, *God and History*, 173–74; and see pp. 27–32 above.

124. *CoG* 23; see also *UZ* 156; *FC* 25–27. Bauckham points out (not specifically related to Moltmann) that this phrase would have been understood by "Later Jewish interpretation . . . as statements of divine eternity" (Bauckham, *The Theology of the Book of Revelation*, 28).

125. Rev 1:4; compare Rev 1:8; 4:8; 11:17; 16:5. For expert analysis, see Bauckham, *The Theology of the Book of Revelation*, 23–30; see also Gilbertson, *God and History*, 116.

126. *FC* 26.

127. *CoG* 23 [41].

distinction he makes between *Futur* and *Advent* for concepts of *Zukunft* both prior to and in *CoG* itself, this attempt is incorrect and careless.)

The operative questions guiding divine eschatology are not the traditionally asked ones, such as Reformed theology's emphasis on the glorification of God as the meaning and purpose of human existence.[128] Rather, Moltmann develops divine eschatology by looking at these matters the other way round: "'What does God get from the world?' Is the world a matter of indifference for him, because he suffices for himself? Does he need it, in order to complete himself? Does it perhaps give him pleasure, because he rejoices in the echo of those he has created?"[129] Moltmann's divine eschatology is highly theocentric, instead of christocentric, because eschatology is not primarily concerned with the coming of Christ, but the coming of God.[130] Indeed, "the different horizons of eternal life, the eternal kingdom and the eternal creation draw together to a single focus: *the cosmic Shekinah of God.*"[131] At the eschaton, God will be present in all things. Moltmann describes this vision thusly: "[God] interpenetrates their finitude with his infinity. For this Paul takes the image: 'God will be all in all' (1 Cor. 15.28).[132] That is the vision of God's kingdom in his glory. The divine and the earthly are not intermingled, the divine is not pantheistically absorbed into all things, but the divine and the earthly interpenetrate each other mutually: unmingled and undivided."[133] This vision calls for "nothing less than the cosmic incarnation of God."[134] Divine eschatology is the direction to which all of his theology, as a doctrine of hope, points: "hope for the whole community of creation, is ultimately hope that its Creator and Redeemer will arrive at his goal, and may find in creation his home."[135]

---

128. See *CoG* 323ff., where Moltmann proceeds in typical fashion of summarizing a view only to alter or reject it.

129. *CoG* 324; the first question is Balthasar's, which he refers to as "too stringently economic" (*CoG* 381n.5).

130. Thus the apt title: *CoG*. He assigns this view to the early church (*ET* 52).

131. *CoG* xii-xiii; see also *CoG* 261–67.

132. See Lewis, *So That God May Be All in All*, 14–15. Lewis refers to *TH*, but does not pronounce judgment on Moltmann's use of the passage.

133. *EB* 158.

134. Ibid.; incarnational language fits Moltmann's point.

135. *CoG* xiii.

The awaited goal of Christian hope is the triune God's indwelling "on earth as it is in heaven."[136]

Interestingly, the tone calls to mind neither *TKG* nor *WJC*, but rather *GC* and *SpL*. In light of the strongly trinitarian orientation of Moltmann's theology, it is rather surprising (and unacceptable, perhaps) that the final chapter of *CoG* is scarce in explicit trinitarian language.[137] This, however, is not the most central concern. Perhaps more surprising, and certainly more unacceptable, is the lack of an *eschatologia crucis*. The trinitarian language problem might be defended on the basis of style, rather than substance, but the lack regarding the cross is more substantial, indeed an aporia based on Moltmann's own claims.

In *CG* and *TKG*, he made it clear that the impress of the cross is not confined to the human nature of Jesus, one Friday, but affects God from "eternity to eternity": "The meaning of the cross of the Son on Golgotha reaches right into the heart [*Mitte*] of the immanent Trinity. From the very beginning, no immanent Trinity and no divine glory is conceivable without 'the Lamb who was slain' . . . God is from eternity to eternity 'the crucified God'. Only 'the Lamb that was slain is worthy to receive power, and riches, and wisdom, and strength, and honour, and glory and blessing' (Rev. 5.12)."[138] The impress of the cross on the economic Trinity culminates at the eschaton: "When everything is 'in

---

136. See *CoG* 323–39; *EB* 158.

137. *CoG* is not devoid of christological considerations; but tellingly even the usually sympathetic Bauckham admits that "There is hence a danger that the eschatology of *The Coming of God* looks christological in the sense of being grounded in the history of Jesus, but not in the sense of being focused on his own eschatological role, as redeemer and judge, at his parousia" ("Eschatology in *The Coming of God*," 4). Bauckham, in defending Moltmann, points to *WJC* for a more detailed look at, for example, the importance of Christ's parousia for eschatology ("Eschatology in *The Coming of God*," 4–5.)

However, it is odd for a theologian, who is as avowedly committed to promoting and explicating both eschatology and Messianic doctrine as essential to Christian theology, to provide not more detail of their relation, but less in a comprehensive vision of Christian eschatology. In fact, the emerging pattern previously displayed is not repeated. For example, *TKG* develops a more detailed vision of the Trinity in relation to the cross and suffering compared to *CG*. A similar comment can be made in relation to *SpL*, which takes up reflections from both *CPS* and *GC*. Unfortunately, however, this helpful technique is not repeated in *CoG* in relation to *WJC*. If *WJC* is presupposed in the discussion then Moltmann has missed out on an opportunity to relate messianic christology to eschatology. See here: *HTG* 95; *WJC* xiv.

138. *TKG* 159.

God' and 'God is all in all,' then the economic Trinity is raised into and transcended [*ist aufgehoben*] in the immanent Trinity. What remains is the eternal praise of the triune God in his glory."[139] In *CoG* this emphasis is almost entirely missing.

Conclusion

Properly Relating TH *and* CoG

Before issuing this study's final, overall conclusion, some brief remarks on *CoG* and its relationship to *TH* conclude chapter 8. Moltmann opens *CoG*, his penultimate "contribution" devoted to Christian eschatology, with the programmatic assertion: "*In the end is the beginning.*"[140] This dictum, at once, grasps his view of eschatology's role in dogmatics, while also pointing to his own theological journey's beginning: "This eschatology . . . is entirely in line with that doctrine of hope [in *TH*]."[141] Indeed, more than any other, *CoG* (which Bauckham correctly identifies as the "concluding synthesis"[142] of Moltmann's program) calls to mind *TH*. Moltmann's first programmatic work does not deal with the "last things," but instead clearly asserts eschatology's importance for every doctrine, moving it from the periphery to the center of the theological enterprise. While typically eschatology deals with "the end," Moltmann propounds eschatology not as expectation of the end only, but an end that is a new beginning.[143] Although he only recently began using the phrase "In the end is the beginning" (echoing T. S. Eliot's *East Coker*), this emphasis reaches back to *TH*, wherein Moltmann relentlessly proffers the events of the Exodus and resurrection as decisively showing

139. Ibid., 161 [178].

140. *CoG* x, xi; see especially *EB* ix–xii, 46; see also *SW* 75; "From the Beginning of Time in God's Presence," 62. As the primary locus of Moltmann's eschatology, *CoG* is the focus of this chapter; see also his post-*CoG* writings, especially *EJM*, *ET* and *EB*. For secondary material on *CoG*, see principally the contributions in *EJM*; see also Müller-Fahrenholz, *Kingdom and Power*, 200–218.

141. Certainly the former is the main intention of the assertion, but his agreement to it manifests itself in his own theological movement.

142. Bauckham, "Eschatology in *The Coming of God*," 1.

143. *CoG* x–xi; "Lived Theology," 13; *EB* ix–xii; *PG* 87ff; *BP* 105. Pannenberg's view of universal history stresses not the beginning, but the end: "revelation is not comprehended completely in the beginning, but at the end of the revealing history" (Pannenberg, "Dogmatic Theses on the Doctrine of Revelation," 131 [thesis 2]).

that where there is an end, there is a new beginning. Moltmann's doctrine of hope was grounded in the resurrection in *TH*, and this focus returns with renewed vigor in *CoG*.[144]

Whereas *TH* was "only prolegomena to eschatology,"[145] *CoG* is concerned with eschatological content. Moltmann makes the dual-claim that *TH* is prolegomena to eschatology and also an *eschatologia crucis*.[146] That he intends *CoG* to develop the eschatological direction of *TH* is unquestioned; it does so, quite well. The justification for this conclusion is ironic, however: *CoG* is most closely related to *TH* because neither in method nor conclusion is it an eschatology of the cross. Indeed, Moltmann's dual-claim is untenable: in light of *CoG* only one claim can be correct. And here the irony becomes even stronger: the very text meant to fulfill what was started in *TH*, is the same text that undermines the very claim that *TH* is an eschatology of the cross. Thus, the very fact that *CoG* fulfils *TH* is the source of its own undoing, because it contains the same one-sided ground of hope, lacking a material development of an eschatology of the cross. This serves as a double-indictment against both *TH* and *CoG*.

For Moltmann, it is not the cross that is the true mark of Christian eschatology, but rather the glory of the resurrection.[147] The most consequential flaw in the development of Moltmann's doctrine of hope can be found most easily in the beginning and end of his career. Where *TH* erroneously, and too easily, based hope on the resurrection alone, *CoG* suffers from the same imbalance. While Moltmann is correct, in the Pauline sense, that the resurrection keeps Christian faith from being "in vain" he is incorrect insofar as he intends to displace the ground of hope (the cross and resurrection) with a singular basis, relying only on the resurrection.

Indeed, Moltmann's dialectic is, in principle, designed to hold a tension. His intended purpose of keeping the cross and resurrection in dialectical relation, however, is undermined from the very beginning with an inevitable result. *CoG* is not an eschatology of the cross precisely because it relies on the root impulses so central to *TH*. What

---

144. For example, compare *TH* 34ff. with *CoG* 22ff.
145. "Letter to Barth," 348.
146. *TH* 83, 160.
147. See especially *CoG* 323–39; *PG* 90.

was sown in *TH*, then, is reaped in *CoG*: an eschatology of the resurrection. Admittedly, this is not necessarily a damning conclusion. For a theologian who so strenuously demands that the ground of hope be the cross and resurrection, however, his eschatological conclusions are problematic since they tend toward presumption.

For Moltmann, the cross is iconoclastic and reveals a God who suffers while being involved in human history. His divine eschatology, while presenting the eschaton as a time and place where creation and God interact, shows no hint of this iconoclasm. The critique lodged here is based in Moltmann's own work: the "cross requires a christology . . . but it is also the mystery behind all christologies, for it calls them into question and makes them in constant need of revision."[148] Applied to eschatology the result is similar: the cross makes all eschatologies in need of revision, lest they presume too much. The lesson that Moltmann brings out in his theology of the cross is that God does the unexpected. God does not forgo suffering; God enters it. In Jesus Christ, God experiences abandonment. Additionally, God's Spirit is involved in suffering in, and with, creation. These emphases are essentially missing from the material discussion in *CoG*. While it would have been odd, perhaps, for Moltmann to argue for eschatological passibility, it seems equally odd that his theology of the cross is non-effectual for his eschatology; it is passed over. This seems doubly odd when his earlier comments are taken into account regarding the centrality of the cross for all of Christian theology.

Fulfillment of God's promises, however, occurs in surprising ways. Indeed the very term fulfillment is capacious. God is faithful, but no one (least of all his closest followers) foresaw a suffering, dying messiah. The cross reveals God to be faithful. Yet, the partial fulfillment of the promise shows the surplus of the promise: opening up a new future, unexpected from present experience. All of this is designed to show that Moltmann's theological program has the resources to overcome its own deficiencies, if appropriated. God will fulfill his promises, but the details of this fulfillment are not fully known. Regarding the future, Moltmann might have been better guided by a passage connoting, perhaps, a notion of the surplus of promise: "What no eye has seen, nor ear heard,

---

148. *CG* 86; of course, this is a causational link to his relentless association of the cross as iconoclastic (see *CG* 108 n. 13).

nor the human heart conceived, what God has prepared for those who love him."[149]

---

149. 1 Cor 2:9; admittedly Paul goes on to express that these things have been revealed to him.

Conclusion

THE CONCLUSIONS OF THIS STUDY HAVE BEEN EMERGING THROUGHOUT, and some have already appeared in chapter 8. Some brief comments sufficiently draw the threads together. Moltmann's doctrine of hope is both the wider framework and also the intricate thread that holds all other doctrines together.

More than three decades after first subscribing to the dialectic pattern at the root of his theology, in his final contribution he affirms the fundamental dialectic that grounds his doctrine of hope, which is the core of his entire theology: "In the light of the eschatological future to be disclosed [zu erschließende], one-sided theologies of the cross and one-sided Easter theologies are both inadmissible."[1] Indeed, it is remarkable that the initial dialectic, while waxing and waning throughout, has remained resilient from *TH*, his first programmatic work, to *ET*, the final contribution. As stated at the outset of this study, one could nominate several doctrines in Moltmann's program as the determining center. Each, however, is determined and conditioned by his doctrine of hope.

The veritable and ostensible strength of Moltmann's doctrine of hope is its ability to maintain the tension of the cross and resurrection. The composition of this ground, however, is precisely the problem that pervades the implications. At times he stresses divine passibility to such a degree that one might be led to think that this is the core of his thought. Yet, in each instance his concentration on suffering, both divine and human, is always conditioned by his resolute confidence in the coming God whose intent is to "be all in all." This is funded by his earliest impulse in the power of the resurrection, which receives renewed force and vigor as he develops his pneumatology. While he continually grounds Christian hope in the dialectic, the primary (in the dual-sense of first and of first importance) referent for hope is the resurrection.

---

1. *ET* 37 [45]; one might press Moltmann's usage of "disclosed" here; for Moltmann, eschatology is more about fulfilment than disclosure (see *WJC* 318).

Unfortunately, his hopeful vision is insufficiently capacious to hold the tension of both cross and resurrection. While he emphatically insists on the theological importance, even centrality, of the cross, his vision is ultimately framed by the triumph of the resurrection. Indeed, his doctrine of hope both changes and remains remarkably the same from beginning to end.

Moltmann's development of the ground of hope is best characterized as reactionary: to Bloch in *TH*, and to protest atheism in *CG*. These dual-moves are only problematic in so far as reactionary claims can overstate matters, since they seek to overcome an opposing view. As he establishes the ground of hope, it is clear now, that his first impulse of finding hope in the resurrection was supplemented by his claims in *CG*. The result is a hope that finds hope (as was seen in *SpL*) in all experiences: suffering and success, presence and power. Indeed, it is his pneumatology that supplements his initial findings.

As pneumatology gained importance in his theology, it helped to buttress resurrection and fulfillment and this had two implications: it (1) seemed to pass over the importance of a theology of the cross, and (2) enigmatically sought to deepen the critical error of his theology of the cross which was to make certain claims about God, with little, if any, room for mystery. This was due to the fact that the central understanding of his doctrine of the Spirit is the Spirit of resurrection and life. Broadly speaking, *SpL* is the culmination of the trend his theology has taken since *CPS* (or perhaps closely thereafter). The viability of this picture has enhanced viability in light of *CoG*, especially the divine eschatology therein.[2] It seems highly probable that his pneumatological developments have slowly turned the major emphasis of his theology away from the cross which he so strenuously argued for as the center of all theology in *CG* and *TKG*, and have lead him to focus more upon the resurrection as the vital key to understanding God and eschatology. The Spirit of resurrection (one of his favorite labels) is the Spirit of life, immanently bringing forth creation and life. This designation seemed to lose sight of the notion of the Spirit suffering with and for creation. These moves, coupled with the fact that already in *TH*, Moltmann chose (in reaction to Bloch) to assert hope as certainty led, invariably it seems, to a doctrine of future certainty, rather than maintaining the dialec-

---

2. *CoG* V.

tic that he presents in *CPS*, whereby the community draws from both events as constitutive for life before "the coming of God". Indeed, form seemed to determine function, as his doctrine of hope as formed in *TH*, was never altered sufficiently, never subjected to severe questioning.

Admittedly, this claim has a tinge of irony to it, lingering below the surface. An element of this study questions the continuity between *TH* and *CG*. To a degree, however, the broader conclusions reached in this study actually call this into question. Arguing against virtually unanimous opinion that a major turn occurred in Moltmann's early theology in the 1960s, this study concludes by seeking to show that in reality the change was not as fundamental as it first appeared. Even this however can be explained by another major thrust of this paper. This doubt about the turn actually reinforces its veracity. The turn was real, but it was not as deep as it first appeared. Retrospectively, his theology of the cross does not ask questions of his theology of the resurrection, so much as it provides him with further resources for comprehending God's relationship with the world. This had implications throughout his theology, because his turn to the cross provided him the opportunity to make theological assertions while also calling them into question. Yet, this is indeed the "crux" of the matter: the cross, Moltmann explicitly asserts, when understood rightly is iconoclasm of the highest order for the Christian faith. Not, though, for his resurrection-based doctrine of hope. His turn to the cross rescued his theology from funding a utopian oriented understanding of reality. Thus, the cross could have been used to place a question mark on his resurrection-focused doctrine of hope in the 1960s. Instead he kept much of his previous thought structure, and added the cross to it, rather than integrating them. The cross neither questioned his earlier theology enough nor provided a necessary antithesis. His early hope theology knew too much, and initially it appeared that *CG* would temper that clear vision by a call to iconoclasm which would bestow a measure of modesty on his program, including its central doctrine. Instead, however, his findings in *CG* actually propelled his initial vision, because over the decades he becomes more certain of God's nature and actions, which evidently makes his hope more certain. Both *TH* and *CG*, in a relationship of complementarity, ground and inform his doctrine of hope.

For all his efforts to properly reorient theology to take seriously the future and its impact on the present, there is a lingering suspicion that in his desire to show how the future impacts the present, he moves out of the realm of hope and into the realm of presumed fulfillment. His vision of hope slips too easily into certainty, an option he clearly wishes to avoid (see the conclusion to chapter 1, above). This he does because a more hesitant, restrained vision does not allow full assurance of what the future holds, which in turn, he believes presumably, gives it less applicability for the present. To be sure, Moltmann does not prescribe a future that simply discloses a reality, but rather God's future enacts reality. He envisions a future of events, not merely a future revelation. On the other hand, while the future is still open and undecided since it has not occurred, Moltmann closes the future by declaring too precisely what the future holds. This actually detracts from the very point of his doctrine of hope: one can hope in the future because it is not already decided; it is open. Salvation is not yet complete; creation needs redemption; judgment has not been exacted; the Spirit is active. This is a major emphasis of, and contribution from, Moltmann's program. In the end, however, the temptation is too strong: his open future is not as open as he maintains.

Moltmann has made hope the theme of this entire project, both implicit and explicit. If all theology must be eschatological, and all eschatology is hope, then for Moltmann all theology is hope. Hope is his method. His programme is rightly understood in a three-word dictum: theology as hope. Supremely, Moltmann should not be identified with his theology of the cross but rather with his doctrine of hope. While the cross helps determine the identity of God, the resurrection most fully determines his vision of Christian theology.[3] While the cross supplements his doctrine of hope, unfortunately, at times, it threatens to be rendered merely supplemental instead of constitutive to his theology. Perhaps the more general reason for this is his view that the 20th century is best deemed "the age of anxiety" or a time of abyss.[4] In part, because he deems angst the setting of his career, Moltmann speaks a message of hope. This valiant attempt is undermined however by the very nature of hope that he expounds.

---

3. Perhaps Hunsinger confirms this view: "Moltmann thus sketched out that 'complete theology of the resurrection' which Barth had planned but never developed" ("The Daybreak of the New Creation," 181).

4. See especially "Progress and Abyss," 15–19 (which he contrasts with the age of progress: 1789–1914).

Ultimately his theology has the resources to ground and articulate a proper doctrine of hope. Christian hope must be crucified: it must, precisely because of the cross, speak; but it must always be aware of (and thus forgo) the temptation to speak when it should be silent, or to assert rather than question. Moltmann clearly asserts that the cross is iconoclastic, but he needs to take this into consideration for the hope he pronounces. The cross renders assertions as to God's future activity, uncertain. God fulfills his promises, but as the cross shows, he acts in surprising ways. Presumption of God's future activity has no place in theology. As such, resurrection hope must always avoid passing over the cross and insist on passing through it, so that it can be fully (in)formed. For, such a passing renders Christian hope a hope against hope.

The preceding interpretation of his program finds a triumphant tone, which too easily lapses into an articulation of Christian hope that borders on presumption. In the end is the beginning: a doctrine of hope planted firmly in the soil of resurrection power, connoting presumptive fulfillment, instead of an equal commitment to crucifixion presence, connoting the unknowable future. And so as he began, he finishes. From first to last, the true orientation of his theology is hope: it is the beginning, the main plotline and the end. He never escapes its grasp.

Bibliography

Jürgen Moltmann's Works

Books, Articles, and Essays

"The Adventure of Theological Ideas." *RelSRev* 22 (1996) 102-5.
"The Alienation and Liberation of Nature." In *On Nature*, edited by Leroy S. Rouner, 133-44. Boston University Studies in Philosophy and Religion 6. Notre Dame: University of Notre Dame Press, 1984.
"All Things New: Invited to God's Future." *ATJ* 48 (1993) 29-38.
"Antwort auf die Kritik an 'Der gekreuzigte Gott.'" In *Diskussion*, edited by Michael Welker, 165-90.
"Antwort auf die Kritik der Theologie der Hoffnung." In *Diskussion*, edited by Wolf-Dieter Marsch, 201-38.
"Befreit Euch—Nehmt einander an." In *Diakonie im Horizont des Reiches Gottes: Schritte zum Diakonentum aller Gläubigen*, 52-73. Neukirchen-Vluyn: Neukirchen, 1984.
"The Bible, the Theologian and the Exegete." Translated by Margaret Kohl. In *God Will Be All in All*, edited by Richard Bauckham, 227-32.
"The Blessing of Hope: The Theology of Hope and the Full Gospel of Life." Translated by Margaret Kohl. *JPT* 13 (2005) 147-61.
A Broad Place: An Autobiography. Translated by Margaret Kohl. Minneapolis: Fortress, 2008.
"The Challenge of Religion in the '80s: How My Mind Has Changed." *Christian Century* 97.15 (1980) 465-68.
"Child and Childhood as Metaphors of Hope." *ThTo* 56 (2000) 592-614.
"Christ in Cosmic Context." In *Christ and Context: The Confrontation between Gospel and Culture*, edited by H. D. Regan and Alan J. Torrance, 180-91, 205-9. Edinburgh: T. & T. Clark, 1993.
"Christianity in the Third Millennium." *ThTo* 51 (1994) 75-89.
The Church in the Power of the Spirit: A Contribution to Messianic Ecclesiology. Translated by Margaret Kohl. London: SCM, 1977. First Fortress Press edition, with a new Preface, Minneapolis: Fortress, 1993. German edition consulted: *Kirche in der Kraft des Geistes: Ein Beitrag zur messianischen Ekklesiologie*. Munich: Kaiser, 1975.
The Coming of God: Christian Eschatology. Translated by Margaret Kohl. Minneapolis: Fortress, 1996. German edition cited: *Das Kommen Gottes: Christliche Eschatologie*. Gütersloh: Kaiser, 1995.

Creating a Just Future: The Politics of Peace and the Ethics of Creation in a Threatened World. Translated by John Bowden. London: SCM, 1989.

"Creation and Redemption." Translated by R. W. A. McKinney. In *Creation, Christ and Culture: Studies in Honour of T. F. Torrance,* edited by Richard W. A. McKinney, 119–34. Edinburgh: T. & T. Clark, 1976.

"The Cross and Civil Religion." Translated by T. Hughson and P. Rigby. In *Religion and Political Society,* edited and translated by The Institute of Christian Thought, 14–47. New York: Harper & Row, 1974.

The Crucified God: The Cross of Christ as the Foundation and Criticism of Christian Theology. Translated by R. A. Wilson and John Bowden. London: SCM, 1974. First Fortress Press edition, with a new Preface, Translated by Margaret Kohl. Minneapolis: Fortress, 1993. German edition cited: *Der gekreuzigte Gott: Das Kreuz Christi als Grund und Kritik christlicher Theologie.* Munich: Kaiser, 1972.

"The 'Crucified God': A Trinitarian Theology of the Cross." *Int* 26 (1972) 294–95.

"The Crucified God." *ThTo* 31 (1974) 6–18.

"Descent into Hell." *Duke Divinity School Review* 33 (1968) 115–19.

"The Diaconal Church in the Context of the Kingdom of God." Translated by T. Runyon. In *Hope for the Church,* edited by Theodore Runyon, 21–36.

"'Dialektik, die umschlägt in Identität'—was ist das? Zu Befürchtungen Walter Kaspers." In *Diskussion,* edited by Michael Welker, 149–56.

"The Disarming Child." In *Watch for the Light: Readings for Advent and Christmas,* 311–22. Maryknoll, NY: Orbis, 2004.

"The Ecological Crisis: Peace with Nature?" *Colloquium* 20 (1988) 8–11

"The End of Everything Is God: Has Belief in Hell Had Its Day?" Translated by J. Bowden. *ExpTim* 108 (1997) 263–64.

"Ernst Blochs Christologie." *EvTh* 64 (2004) 5–19.

Experiences in Theology: Ways and Forms of Christian Theology. Translated by Margaret Kohl. Minneapolis: Fortress, 2000. German edition consulted: *Erfahrungen theologischen Denkens: Wege und Formen christlicher Theologie.* Gütersloh: Kaiser, 1999.

Experiences of God. Translated by Margaret Kohl. London: SCM, 1980. German edition consulted: *Gotteserfahrungen: Hoffnung, Angst, Mystik.* Kaiser Traktate 47. Munich: Kaiser, 1979.

The Experiment Hope. Edited and translated by M. Douglas Meeks. London: SCM, 1975. German edition consulted: *Das Experiment Hoffnung: Einführungen.* Munich: Kaiser, 1974.

"The Fellowship of the Holy Spirit—Trinitarian Pneumatology." *SJT* 37 (1984) 287–300.

"Foreword." In *Spirit of the Last Days,* edited by Peter Althouse, vii–ix.

"Foreword." In Richard Bauckham, *Moltmann,* vii–x.

"Foreword." In A. J. Conyers, *God, Hope, and History,* vii–ix.

"Foreword." In M. Douglas Meeks, *Origins,* ix–xii.

"Foreword." In Dennis Ngien, *The Suffering of God,* xi–xii.

"From the Beginning of Time in God's Presence." In *The End of Time? The Provocation of Talking about God,* edited and translated by J. Matthew Ashley, 54–64. Proceedings of a Meeting of Joseph Cardinal Ratzinger, Johann Baptist Metz,

Jürgen Moltmann, and Eveline Goodman-Thau in Ahaus. Mahwah, NJ: Paulist, 2004.
The Future of Creation. Translated by Margaret Kohl. London: SCM, 1979. German edition consulted: *Zukunft der Schöpfung: Gesammelte Aufsätze.* Munich: Kaiser, 1977.
"Der Gekreuzigte Gott, Neuzeitliche Gottesfrage und trinitarische Gottesgeschichte." *Concilium* 8 (1972) 407–13.
"Die Gemeinschaft des heiligen Geistes: Zur trinitarischen Pneumatologie." *TLZ* 107 (1982) 705–15.
God for a Secular Society: The Public Relevance of Theology. Translated by Margaret Kohl. Minneapolis: Fortress, 1999.
God in Creation: A New Theology of Creation and the Spirit of God. Translated by Margaret Kohl. The Gifford Lectures 1984–85. London: SCM, 1985. First Fortress Press edition, Minneapolis: Fortress, 1993. German edition consulted: *Gott in der Schöpfung: Ökologische Schöpfungslehre.* Munich: Kaiser, 1985.
"God is Unselfish Love." In *The Emptying God: A Buddhist-Jewish-Christian Conversation*, edited by John B. Cobb and Christopher Ives, 116–24. Faith Meets Faith. Maryknoll, NY: Orbis, 1990.
"God's Kenosis in the Creation and Consummation of the World." In *The Work of Love: Creation as Kenosis*, edited by John Polkinghorne, 137–51. Grand Rapids: Eerdmans, 2001. Subsequently published as "God's Self-Restriction and the History of the Universe," in Moltmann, *Science and Wisdom*, 54–67.
"God's Kingdom as the Meaning of Life and of the World." Translated by T. Weston. In *Why Did God Make Me?* edited by Hans Küng and Jürgen Moltmann, 97–103. New York: Seabury, 1978.
"Der Gott der Hoffnung." In *Gott heute: Fünfzehn Beiträge zur Gottesfrage*, edited by Norbert Kutschki, 116–26. Mainz: Matthias-Grünewald, 1967.
Gotteserfahrungen: Hoffnung, Angst, Mystik. Munich: Kaiser, 1979.
History and the Triune God: Contributions to Trinitarian Theology. Translated by John Bowden. London: SCM, 1991.
"Hope and Confidence: A Conversation with Ernst Bloch." Translated by M. Douglas Meeks. In Moltmann, *Religion, Revolution, and the Future*, 148–76. German text consulted: "Anhang: 'Das Prinzip Hoffnung' und 'Theologie der Hoffnung': Ein Gespräch mit Ernst Bloch." In Moltmann, *Theologie der Hoffnung*, 61966: 313–34. Originally published in *EvTh* 23 (1963) 537–57.
Hope and Planning. Translated by M. Clarkson. London: SCM, 1971. German text consulted: *Perspektiven der Theologie: Gesammelte Aufsätze.* Munich: Kaiser, 1968.
"Hope and Reality: Contradiction and Correspondence: Response to Trevor Hart." Translated by Margaret Kohl. In *God Will Be All in All*, edited by Richard Bauckham, 77–85.
"Hope and the Biomedical Future of Man." In *Hope and the Future of Man*, edited by Ewart H. Cousins, 89–105.
"Hope Beyond Time." *Duke Divinity School Review* 33 (1968) 109–14.
"The Hope for Israel and the Anabaptist Alternative." In *God Will Be All in All*, edited by Richard Bauckham, 149–54.

"Hope without Faith: An Eschatological Humanism without God." Translated by J. Cummings. In *Is God Dead?* edited by Johann Baptist Metz, 25–40. Concilium 16. New York: Paulist, 1966.

"Ich glaube an Gott den Vater: Patriarchalische oder nichtpatriarchalische Rede von Gott?" *EvTh* 43 (1983) 397–415.

Im Gespräch mit Ernst Bloch: Eine theologische Wegbegleitung. Kaiser Traktate 18. Munich: Kaiser, 1976.

In the End—the Beginning: The Life of Hope. Translated by Margaret Kohl. Minneapolis: Fortress, 2004. German text consulted: *Im Ende—der Anfange: Eine kleine Hoffnungslehre.* Gütersloh: Kaiser, 2003.

"Israel's No: Jews and Jesus in an Unredeemed World." *Christian Century* 107.5 (1990) 1021–4.

"Is Protestantism the 'Religion of Freedom'?" In *On Freedom*, edited by Leroy S. Rouner, 30–45. Boston University Studies on Religion and Philosophy. Notre Dame, IN: University of Notre Dame Press, 1989.

"Is the World Coming to an End or Has Its Future Already Begun? Christian Eschatology, Modern Utopianism and Exterminism." Translated by Margaret Kohl. In Fergusson and Sarot, *The Future as God's Gift*, 129–38.

Is There Life after Death? Edited and translated by D. Lyle Dabney. The Père Marquette Lecture in Theology 1998. Milwaukee: Marquette University Press, 1998.

Jesus Christ for Today's World. Translated by Margaret Kohl. London: SCM, 1994. German text consulted: *Wer ist Christus für uns heute?* Kaiser Taschenbücher 129. Gütersloh: Kaiser, 1994.

"Kein Monotheismus gleicht dem anderen: Destruktion eines untauglichen Begriffs." *EvTh* 62 (2002) 112–22.

"Kind und Kindheit als Metaphern der Hoffnung." *EvTh* 60 (2000) 92–102.

"Letter to Karl Barth." In Karl Barth. *Letters: 1961–1968.* Edited by J. Fangmeier and H. Stoevesandt. Edited and translated by Geoffrey W. Bromiley, 348–49. Edinburgh: T. & T. Clark, 21981.

"Liberating and Anticipating the Future." Translated by Margaret Kohl. In *Liberating Eschatology: Essays in Honor of Letty M. Russell*, edited by Margaret A. Farley and Serene Jones, 189–208. Louisville: Westminster John Knox, 1999.

"Liberation in the Light of Hope." *Ecumenical Review* 26 (1974) 413–29.

"The Liberation of the Future and its Anticipations in History." Translated by Margaret Kohl. In *God Will Be All in All*, edited by Richard Bauckham, 265–89.

"The Life Signs of the Spirit in the Fellowship of the Community." In Runyon, *Hope for the Church*, 37–56.

"Lived Theology: An Intellectual Biography." *ATJ* 55 (2000) 9–13.

"The Logic of Hell." Translated by Margaret Kohl. In *God Will Be All in All*, edited by Richard Bauckham, 43–47.

"The Lordship of Christ and Human Society." Translated by Reginald H. Fuller and Ilse Fuller. In Moltmann and Weissbach, *Two Studies in the Theology of Bonhoeffer*, 19–94.

"Love, Death, Eternal Life: Theology of Hope—the Personal Side." In *Love: The Foundation of Hope*, edited by Frederic B. Burnham et al., 3–22.

"The Motherly Father and the Power of His Mercy." In Moltmann, *History and the Triune God*, 19–25.

"The Motherly Father: Is Trinitarian Patripassianism Replacing Theological Patriarchalism?" Translated by G. W. S. Knowles. In *God as Father?* edited by Edward Schillebeeckx, Johann Baptist Metz, and Marcus Lefebure, 51–56. Edinburgh: T. & T. Clark, 1981.

"Nachwort." In Peter F. Momose, *Kreuzestheologie: Eine Auseinandersetzung mit Jürgen Moltmann*, 174–83. Freiburg: Herder, 1978.

On Human Dignity: Political Theology and Ethics. Translated by M. Douglas Meeks. London: SCM, 1984.

The Open Church: Invitation to a Messianic Life-style. London: SCM, 1978. = *Passion for Life: A Messianic Lifestyle*. Translated with an Introduction by M. Douglas Meeks. Philadelphia: Fortress, 1978.

"An Open Letter to José Miguez Bonino." *Christianity and Crisis* 36 (1976) 57–63.

"The Passion of Christ and the Suffering of God." *ATJ* 48 (1993) 19–28.

Perspektiven der Theologie: Gesammelte Aufsätze. Munich: Kaiser, 1968.

"Political Reconciliation." In *Religion, Politics, and Peace*, edited by Leroy S. Rouner, 17–31. Boston University Studies in Philosophy and Religion 20. Notre Dame, IN: University of Notre Dame Press, 1999.

"Political Theology." *ThTo* 28 (1971) 6–23.

"Politics and the Practice of Hope." *Christian Century* 87 (1970) 288–91.

The Power of the Powerless. Translated by Margaret Kohl. San Francisco: Harper & Row, 1983.

"Progress and Abyss: Remembrances of the Future of the Modern World." In *The Future of Hope: Christian Tradition amid Modernity and Postmodernity*, edited by Miroslav Volf and William Katerberg, 3–26. Grand Rapids: Eerdmans, 2004.

"Die Rehabilition Behinderter in einer Segregationsgesellschaft." In *Diakonie im Horizont des Reiches Gottes: Schritte zum Diakonentum aller Gläubigen*, 42–51. Neukirchen-Vluyn: Neukirchener, 1984.

Religion, Revolution, and the Future. Translated by M. Douglas Meeks. New York: Scribners, 1969.

"Response." In *Hope for the Church*, edited by Theodore Runyon, 128–36.

"A Response to My Pentecostal Dialogue Partners." *JPT* 4 (1994) 59–70.

"Response to the Essays." Translated by R. T. Cornelison. *ATJ* 55 (2000) 129–34.

"Response to the Opening Presentations." In *Hope and the Future of Man*, edited by Ewart H. Cousins, 55–59.

"Resurrection as Hope." *HTR* 61 (1968) 129–47.

"Resurrection: The Ground, Power and Goal of Our Hope." Translated by John Bowden. In *2000: Reality and Hope*, edited by Virgil Elizondo and Jon Sobrino, 81–89. Concilium 1999/5. London: SCM, 1999.

"Schöpfung aus nichts." In *Wenn nicht jetzt, wann dann? Aufsätze für Hans-Joachim Kraus zum 65 Geburtstag*, edited by Hans-Georg Geyer, Johann M. Schmidt, and Werner Schneider, 259–67. Neukirchen-Vluyn: Neukirchener, 1983.

Science and Wisdom. Translated by Margaret Kohl. Minneapolis: Fortress, 2003.

The Source of Life: The Holy Spirit and the Theology of Life. Translated by Margaret Kohl. London: SCM, 1997. German edition consulted: *Die Quelle des Lebens: Der Heilige Geist und die Theologie des Lebens*. Kaiser Taschenbücher 150. Gütersloh: Kaiser, 1997.

The Spirit of Life: A Universal Affirmation. Translated by Margaret Kohl. Minneapolis: Fortress, 1992.

"Talk-Back Session with Dr. Jürgen Moltmann." *ATJ* 48 (1993) 39–47.

"Theological Proposals Towards the Resolution of the Filioque Controversy." In *Spirit of God, Spirit of Christ: Ecumenical Reflections on the Filioque Controversy*, edited by Lukas Vischer, 164–73. Faith and Order Paper 103. London: SPCK, 1981.

"Theologie der Hoffnung. Eine kleine Autobiographie." In *Entwürfe der Theologie*, edited by Johannes B. Bauer, 235–57. Graz: Styria, 1985.

Theology and Joy. Translated by Reinhard Ulrich. Introduction by David E. Jenkins. London: SCM, 1973.

"Theology as Eschatology." In *The Future of Hope*, edited by Frederick Herzog, 1–50.

"Theology in Germany Today." Translated and introduction by A. Buchwalter. In *Observations on "The Spiritual Situation of the Age": Contemporary German Perspectives*, edited by Jürgen Habermas, 181–205. Cambridge, MA: MIT Press, 1984.

Theology of Hope: On the Ground and the Implications of a Christian Eschatology. Translated by J. W. Leitch. London: SCM, 1967. First Fortress Press edition, with a new Preface, translated by Margaret Kohl. Minneapolis: Fortress, 1993. German edition cited: *Theologie der Hoffnung: Untersuchungen zur Begründung und zuden Konsequenzen einer christlichen Eschatologie.* Beiträge zur evangelischen Theologie, Band 38. Munich: Kaiser, 61966.

"The Trinitarian Personhood of the Holy Spirit." Translated by D. L. Dabney. In *Advents of the Spirit: An Introduction to the Current Study of Pneumatology*, edited by Bradford E. Hinze and D. Lyle Dabney, 302–14. Marquette Studies in Theology 30. Milwaukee: Marquette University Press, 2001.

"Trinitarier und Antitrinitarier." *EvTh* 46 (1986) 293–4.

The Trinity and the Kingdom: The Doctrine of God. Translated by Margaret Kohl. London: SCM, 1981. First Fortress Press edition, with a new Preface. Minneapolis: Fortress, 1993. German edition cited: *Trinität und Reich Gottes: Zur Gotteslehre.* Munich: Kaiser, 1980.

Umkehr zur Zukunft. Gütersloher Taschenbücher Siebenstern 154. 2nd edition. Munich: Kaiser, 1970; Gütersloh: Mohn, 1977.

"The Unity of the Triune God: Remarks on the Comprehensibility of the Doctrine of the Trinity and its Foundation in the History of Salvation." Translated by O. C. Dean. *SVTQ* 28 (1984) 157–71.

"Verschränkte Zeiten der Geschichte: Notwendige Differenzierungen und Begrenzungen des Geschichtsbegriffs." *EvTh* 44 (1984) 213–226.

The Way of Jesus Christ: Christology in Messianic Dimensions. Translated by Margaret Kohl. London: SCM, 1990. First Fortress Press edition. Minneapolis: Fortress, 1993. German text consulted: *Der Weg Jesu Cristi: Christologie in messianischen Dimensionen.* Munich: Kaiser, 1989.

Wer ist Christus für uns heute? Kaiser Taschenbücher 129. Gütersloh: Kaiser, 1994.

"What Has Happened to Our Utopias? 1968 and 1989. A Response to Timothy Gorringe." Translated by Margaret Kohl. In *God Will Be All in All*, edited by Richard Bauckham, 115–21.

"What is a Theologian?" Translated by Margaret Kohl. *ITQ* 64 (1999) 189–98.

"The World in God or God in the World? Response to Richard Bauckham." Translated by Margaret Kohl. In *God Will Be All in All*, edited by Richard Bauckham, 35–41.
"Zum Gespräch mit Christian Link." *EvTh* 47 (1987) 93–5.

Edited Works

Moltmann, Jürgen, editor. *How I Have Changed: Reflections on Thirty Years of Theology*. Translated by John Bowden. London: SCM, 1997.

Collaborative Works

Lapide, Pinchas, and Jürgen Moltmann. *Jewish Monotheism and Christian Trinitarian Doctrine: A Dialogue*. Translated by Leonard Swidler. Philadelphia: Fortress, 1981.
Moltmann, Jürgen, and Jürgen Weissbach. *Two Studies in the Theology of Bonhoeffer*. Translated by Reginald H. Fuller and Ilse Fuller. Introduction by Reginald H. Fuller. Scribner Studies in Contemporary Theology. New York: Scribner, 1967.
Moltmann, Jürgen, with M. Douglas Meeks. "The Liberation of Oppressors." *Christianity and Crisis* 38 (1978) 310–17.
Moltmann-Wendel, Elisabeth, and Jürgen Moltmann. *God: His and Hers*. Translated by John Bowden. New York: Crossroad, 1991.
———. *Humanity in God*. New York: Pilgrim, 1983.
———. *Passion for God: Theology in Two Voices*. Introduction by M. Douglas Meeks. Louisville: Westminster John Knox, 2004.

Secondary Works Cited

Adams, Nicholas. "Eschatology Sacred and Profane: The Effects of Philosophy on Theology in Pannenberg, Rahner and Moltmann." *IJST* 2 (2000) 283–306.
———. "Jürgen Moltmann." In *The Blackwell Companion to Political Theology*, edited by William T. Cavanaugh and Peter Scott, 227–40. Blackwell Companions to Religion. Oxford: Blackwell, 2003.
———. "Hope." In *The Oxford Companion to Christian Thought*, edited by Adrian Hastings, Alistair Mason, and Hugh Pyper, 309–11. Oxford: Oxford University Press, 2000.
Althouse, Peter. *Spirit of the Last Days: Pentecostal Eschatology in Conversation with Jürgen Moltmann*. Foreword by Jürgen Moltmann. Journal of Pentecostal Theology Supplement Series 25. London: Sheffield Academic, 2003.
Alves, Rubem A. *A Theology of Human Hope*. Washington, DC: Corpus, 1969.
Augustine. *Confessions*. Translated by R. S. Pine-Coffin. Reprinted, Harmondsworth, UK: Penguin, 1961.
Balthasar, Hans Urs von. *Dare We Hope "That All Men Be Saved?" With a Short Discourse on Hell*. Translated by David Kipp and Lothar Krauth. San Francisco: Ignatius, 1988.
———. "Zu einer christlichen Theologie der Hoffnung." *MTZ* 32 (1981) 81–102.

Bibliography

Barth, Karl. *Church Dogmatics*, I/1. Edited and and translated by Geoffrey Bromiley and Thomas F. Torrance. Edinburgh: T. & T. Clark, 21975.

———. *Church Dogmatics*, II/2. Edited and and translated by Geoffrey Bromiley and Thomas F. Torrance. Edinburgh: T. & T. Clark, 1957.

———. *Church Dogmatics*, IV/1. Edited and and translated by Geoffrey Bromiley and Thomas F. Torrance. Edinburgh: T. & T. Clark, 1956.

———. *Letters: 1961–1968*. Edited by Jürgen Fangmeier and Hinrich Stoevesandt. Edited and translated by Geoffrey W. Bromiley. Edinburgh: T. & T. Clark, 21981.

Bauckham, Richard. "Eschatology." In *The Oxford Companion to Christian Thought*, edited by Adrian Hastings, Alistair Mason, and Hugh Pyper, 206–9. Oxford: Oxford University Press, 2000.

———. "Eschatology in *The Coming of God*." In *God Will Be All in All*, edited by Richard Bauckham, 1–34.

———. "The Future of Jesus Christ." In *The Cambridge Companion to Jesus*, edited by Markus Bockmuehl, 265–80. Cambridge Companions to Religion. Cambridge: Cambridge University Press, 2001.

———. *God Crucified: Monotheism and Christology in the New Testament*. Didsbury Lectures, 1996. Carlisle, UK: Paternoster, 1998.

———. "Jürgen Moltmann." In *The Modern Theologians: An Introduction to Christian Theology of the Twentieth Century*, edited by David F. Ford. Rev. ed. Oxford: Blackwell, 1996.

———. "Jürgen Moltmann." In *One God in Trinity*, edited by Peter Toon and James D. Spiceland, 111–32. London: Bagster, 1980.

———. "The Millennium." In *God Will Be All in All*, edited by Richard Bauckham, 123–47.

———. *Moltmann: Messianic Theology in the Making*. Foreword by Jürgen Moltmann. Contemporary Christian Studies. Basingstoke, UK: Pickering, 1987.

———. "Moltmann's Eschatology of the Cross." *SJT* 30 (1977) 301–11.

———. *The Theology of the Book of Revelation*. New Testament Theology. Cambridge: Cambridge University Press, 1993.

———. *The Theology of Jürgen Moltmann*. Edinburgh: T. & T. Clark, 1995.

———. "Time and Eternity." In *God Will Be All in All*, edited by Richard Bauckham, 155–226.

Bauckham, Richard, editor. *God Will Be All in All: The Eschatology of Jürgen Moltmann*. Edinburgh: T. & T. Clark, 1999.

Bauckham, Richard, and Trevor Hart. *Hope against Hope: Christian Eschatology in Contemporary Context*. Trinity & Truth. London: Darton, Longman & Todd, 1999.

Berkhof, Hendrikus. "Über die Methode der Eschatologie." In *Diskussion*, edited by Wolf-Dieter Marsch, 168–80.

Billings, David. "Natality or Advent: Hannah Arendt and Jürgen Moltmann on Hope and Politics." In *The Future of Hope: Christian Tradition amid Modernity and Postmodernity*, edited by Miroslav Volf and William Katerberg, 125–45. Grand Rapids: Eerdmans, 2004.

Bloch, Ernst. "Kann Hoffnung enttäuscht werden?" In *Verfremdungen*, vol. 1. Frankfurt: Suhrkamp, 1962.

———. "Man as Possibility." Translated by Walter H. Capps. In *The Future of Hope*, edited by Walter H. Capps, 50–67. Philadelphia: Fortress, 1970.

———. *The Principle of Hope*. 3 vols. Translated by N. Plaice, S. Plaice, and P. Knight. Oxford: Blackwell, 1986.

———. *The Spirit of Utopia*. Translated by Anthony Nassar. Meridian. Stanford: Stanford University Press, 2000.

Bloesch, Donald. *The Holy Spirit: Works and Gifts*. Christian Foundations. Downers Grove, IL: InterVarsity, 2000.

Bock, Darrell L., editor. *Three Views on the Millennium and Beyond*. Grand Rapids: Zondervan, 1999.

Bockmuehl, Markus, editor. *The Cambridge Companion to Jesus*. Cambridge Companions to Religion. Cambridge: Cambridge University Press, 2001.

Boff, Leonardo. *Trinity and Society*. Translated by Paul Burns. Theology and Liberation Series. Maryknoll, NY: Orbis, 1988.

Bonhoeffer, Dietrich. *Letter and Papers from Prison*. Edited by Eberhard Bethge. Translated by Reginald H. Fuller. 3rd ed. London: Fontana, 1959.

Bonino, José Míguez. "Love and Social Transformation in Liberation Theology." In *Love: The Foundation of Hope*, edited by Frederic B. Burnham et al., 60–76.

———. "Reading Jürgen Moltmann from Latin America." *ATJ* 55 (2000) 105–14.

Bowie, Andrew. *Introduction to German Philosophy: From Kant to Habermas*. Cambridge: Polity, 2003.

Braaten, Carl E. "Toward A Theology of Hope." In *New Theology No. 5*, edited by Martin E. Marty and Dean G. Peerman, 90–111. New York: Macmillan, 1968.

———. "A Trinitarian Theology of the Cross." *JR* 56 (1976) 113–21.

Breshears, Gerry. "Creation Imaginatively Reconsidered: Review of *God in Creation*." *Journal of Psychology and Theology* 14 (1986) 337–51.

Brueggemann, Walter. *An Introduction to the Old Testament: The Canon and Christian Imagination*. Louisville: Westminster John Knox, 2003.

Brunner, Emil. *Eternal Hope*. Translated by Harold Knight. London: Lutterworth, 1954.

Buckley, Michael. *At the Origins of Modern Atheism*. New Haven: Yale University Press, 1987.

Burnham, Frederic B., Charles S. McCoy, and M. Douglas Meeks, editors. *Love: The Foundation of Hope: The Theology of Jürgen Moltmann and Elisabeth Moltmann-Wendel*. San Francisco: Harper & Row, 1988.

Cabestrero, Teófilo. *Faith: Conversations with Contemporary Theologians*. Translated by Donald D. Walsh. Maryknoll, NY: Orbis, 1980.

Cameron, Nigel M. de S., editor. *Universalism and the Doctrine of Hell: Papers Presented at the Fourth Edinburgh Conference in Christian Dogmatics, 1991*. Scottish Bulletin of Evangelical Theology Special Study 5. Grand Rapids: Baker, 1992.

Capps, Walter H. *Hope against Hope: Moltmann to Merton in One Theological Decade*. Philadelphia: Fortress, 1976.

———. "Mapping the Hope Movement." In *The Future of Hope*, edited by Walter H. Capps, 50–67.

———. *Time Invades the Cathedral: Tensions in the School of Hope*. Philadelphia: Fortress, 1972.

Capps, Walter H., editor. *The Future of Hope*. Philadelphia: Fortress, 1970:

Carson, D. A., editor. *From Sabbath to Lord's Day: A Biblical, Historical, and Theological Investigation*. Grand Rapids: Zondervan, 1982.

Carter, Dee. "Foregrounding the Environment: The Redemption of Nature and Jürgen Moltmann's Theology." *Ecotheology* 10 (2001) 70–84.

Chapman, G. Clarke. "On Being Human: Moltmann's Anthropology of Hope." *AJT* 55 (2000) 69–84.

Charlesworth, James H., editor. *Jesus' Jewishness: Exploring the Place of Jesus within Early Judaism*. Shared Ground among Jews and Christians 2. New York: Crossroad, 1991.

Chopp, Rebecca S. 1986. *The Praxis of Suffering: An Interpretation of Liberation and Political Theologies*. Maryknoll, NY: Orbis.

Claybrook, Donald A. "The Emerging Doctrine of the Holy Spirit in the Writings of Jürgen Moltmann." Ph.D. dissertation, Southern Baptist Theological Seminary, 1983.

Clutterbuck, Richard. "Jürgen Moltmann as a Doctrinal Theologian: The Nature of Doctrine and the Possibilities for its Development." *SJT* 48 (1995) 489–505.

Cobb, John B., Jr. "Jürgen Moltmann's Ecological Theology in Process Perspective." *ATJ* 55 (2000) 115–28.

———. "Reply to Jürgen Moltmann's 'The Unity of the Triune God.'" *SVTQ* 28 (1984) 173–77.

Collins, John J. *Introduction to the Hebrew Bible*. Minneapolis: Fortress, 2004.

Cone, James H. "Martin, Malcolm, and Black Theology." In *The Future of Theology*, edited by Miroslav Volf, Carmen Krieg, and Thomas Kucharz, 185–95. Grand Rapids: Eerdmans, 1996.

Congar, Yves. *I Believe in the Holy Spirit, Vol. 3: The River of Life Flows in the East and in the West*. London: Chapman, 1983.

Conyers, A. J. *God, Hope, and History: Jürgen Moltmann and the Christian Concept of History*. Foreword by Jürgen Moltmann. Mercer, GA: Mercer University Press, 1988.

———. "History as Problem and Hope." *ATJ* 55 (2000) 29–39.

Cousar, Charles B. *A Theology of the Cross: The Death of Jesus in the Pauline Letters*. Overtures to Biblical Theology. Philadelphia: Fortress, 1990.

Cousins, Ewart H., editor. *Hope and the Future of Man*. The Teilhard Study Library. London: Garnstone, 1973.

Cox, Harvey. "Ernst Bloch and 'The Pull of the Future.'" In *New Theology No. 5*, edited by Martin E. Marty and Dean G. Peerman, 191–203.

———. "Gedanken über Jürgen Moltmanns Buch: Der gekreuzigte Gott." In *Diskussion*, edited by Michael Welker, 126–39.

Dabney, D. Lyle. "The Advent of the Spirit: The Turn to Pneumatology in the Theology of Jürgen Moltmann." *ATJ* 48 (1993) 81–108.

Deane-Drummond, Celia E. *Ecology in Jürgen Moltmann's Theology*. Texts and Studies in Religion 75. Lewiston, NY: Mellen, 1997.

Del Colle, Ralph. *Christ and the Spirit: Spirit-Christology in Trinitarian Perspective*. New York: Oxford University Press, 1994.

———. "Review of *God in Creation: A New Theology of Creation and the Spirit of God*." *USQR* 41 (1987) 69–74.

Dillistone, F. W. "The Theology of Jürgen Moltmann." *Modern Churchman* 18 (1974–75) 145–50.
Eckardt, Burnell F. "Luther and Moltmann: The Theology of the Cross." *Concordia Theological Quarterly* 49 (1985) 19–28.
Fairhurst, Alan M. "'Dare We Hope . . .' From C. F. D. Moule (1953) to Jürgen Moltmann (1996)." *ExpTim* 111 (2000) 373.
Falcke, Heino. "Phantasie für das Reich Gottes: Der theologische Weg Jürgen Moltmanns." *EvTh* 61 (2001) 155–6.
Farrow, Douglas. "In the End is the Beginning." *ModTh* 14 (1998) 425–47.
Fergusson, David A. S. *The Cosmos and the Creator: An Introduction to the Theology of Creation*. London: SPCK, 1998.
———. "Eschatology." In *The Cambridge Companion to Christian Doctrine*, edited by Colin E. Gunton, 226–44. Cambridge: Cambridge University Press, 1992.
———. "Interpreting the Resurrection." *SJT* 38 (1985) 287–305.
Fergusson, David, and Marcel Sarot, editors. *The Future as God's Gift: Explorations in Christian Eschatology*. Explorations in Contemporary Theology. Edinburgh: T. & T. Clark, 2000.
Feske, Millicent C. "Christ and Suffering in Moltmann's Thought." *ATJ* 55.1 (2000) 85–104.
Fiddes, Paul S. "Creation out of Love." In *The Work of Love: Creation as Kenosis*, edited by John Polkinghorne, 167–91. Grand Rapids: Eerdmans, 2001.
———. *The Creative Suffering of God*. Oxford: Clarendon, 1988.
———. *The Promised End: Eschatology in Theology and Literature*. Challenges in Contemporary Theology. Oxford: Blackwell, 2000.
———. "Review of *God in Creation*." *JTS* 38 (1987) 263–5.
Fiorenza, Francis P. "Dialectical Theology and Hope 1." *HeyJ* 9 (1968) 143–63.
———. "Dialectical Theology and Hope 2." *HeyJ* 9 (1968) 384–99.
———. "Dialectical Theology and Hope 3." *HeyJ* 10 (1969) 26–42.
Frei, Hans W. "Review of Moltmann's *Theology of Hope*." *USQR* 23 (1968) 267–72.
French, William C. "Returning to Creation: Moltmann's Eschatology Naturalized." *JR* 68 (1988) 78–86.
Frymer-Kensky, Tikva et al., editors. *Christianity in Jewish Terms*. Boulder, CO: Westview, 2000.
Genovesi, Vincent J. *Expectant Creativity: The Action of Hope in Christian Ethics*. Washington, DC: University Press of America, 1982.
Gilbertson, Michael. *God and History in the Book of Revelation: New Testament Studies in Dialogue with Pannenberg and Moltmann*. Society for New Testament Studies Monograph Series 124. Cambridge: Cambridge University Press, 2003.
Gilkey, Langdon. *Reaping the Whirlwind: A Christian Interpretation of History*. New York: Seabury, 1979.
———. "The Universal and Immediate Presence of God." In *The Future of Hope*, edited by Frederick Herzog, 81–109. New York: Herder & Herder, 1970.
Goetz, Ronald. "The Suffering God: The Rise of a New Orthodoxy." *Christian Century* 103 (April 13, 1986) 385–9.
Gorringe, Timothy. "Eschatology and Political Radicalism: The Example of Karl Barth and Jürgen Moltmann." In *God Will Be All in All*, edited by Richard Bauckham, 87–114. Edinburgh: T. & T. Clark, 1999.

Greenberg, Irving. "Judaism and Christianity: Covenants of Redemption." In *Christianity in Jewish Terms*, edited by Tikva Frymer-Kensky et al., 141–58. Boulder, CO: Westview, 2000.

Gregerson, Niels Henrik. "The Final Crucible: Last Judgment and the Dead-End of Sin." Translated by S. Drew. In *The Future as God's Gift*, edited by Fergusson and Sarot, 169–80.

Grellert, Manfred. "The Eschatological Theology of Jürgen Moltmann." Th.D. dissertation, Southern Baptist Theological Seminary, 1970.

Grenz, Stanley J., and Roger E. Olson. *20th Century Theology: God & the World in a Transitional Age*. Downers Grove, IL: InterVarsity, 1992.

Gunton, Colin E. *Act and Being: Towards a Theology of the Divine Attributes*. London: SCM, 2002.

———. "Dogmatic Theses on Eschatology: Conference Response." In *The Future as God's Gift*, edited by David Fergusson and Marcel Sarot, 139–43. Edinburgh: T. & T. Clark, 2000.

———. *Yesterday and Today: A Study of Continuities in Christology*. 2nd ed. London: SPCK, 1997.

Gunton, Colin, editor. *The Cambridge Companion to Christian Doctrine*. Cambridge Companions to Religion. Cambridge: Cambridge University Press, 1997.

Hall, Christopher A. "Stubborn Hope." *Christianity Today* 37 (Jan 11, 1993) 30–33.

Hardy, Daniel W. "Creation and Eschatology." In *The Doctrine of Creation: Essays in Dogmatics, History and Philosophy*, edited by Colin E. Gunton, 105–33. Edinburgh: T. & T. Clark, 1997.

———. "Eschatology as a Challenge for Theology." In *The Future as God's Gift*, edited by David Fergusson and Marcel Sarot, 151–58. Edinburgh: T. & T. Clark, 2000.

Hart, Trevor. "Imagination for the Kingdom of God? Hope, Promise, and the Transformative Power of an Imagined Future." In *God Will Be All in All*, edited by Richard Bauckham, 49–76. Edinburgh: T. & T. Clark, 1997.

———. "Person and Prerogative in Perichoretic Perspective: The Triunity of God." In *Regarding Karl Barth: Essays Toward a Reading of His Theology*, 100–116. Downers Grove, IL: InterVarsity, 1999.

Hays, Richard B. *The Moral Vision of the New Testament: A Contemporary Introduction to New Testament Ethics*. San Francisco: HarperCollins, 1996.

Hefner, Philip. "Theological Reflections (4). Questions for Moltmann and Pannenberg." *Una Sancta* 25.3 (1968) 32–51.

Heim, S. Mark. "Salvations: A More Pluralistic Hypothesis." *ModTh* 10 (1994) 341–60.

Heinitz, Kenneth. "The Theology of Hope According to Ernst Bloch." *Dialog* 7 (1968) 34–41.

Hegel, Georg Wilhelm Friedrich. *Lectures on the Philosophy of Religion*. 3 vols. Edited by Peter C. Hodgson. Translated by R. F. Brown, Peter C. Hodgson, and J. M. Stewart. Berkeley: University of California Press, 1984–87.

Hengel, Martin. "Christological Titles in Early Christianity." Translated by P. Cathey. In *Studies in Early Christology*, 359–89. Edinburgh: T. & T. Clark, 1995.

———. "Jesus, the Messiah of Israel." Translated by P. Cathey. In *Studies in Early Christology*, 1–72. Edinburgh: T. & T. Clark, 1995.

———. *The Son of God: The Origin of Christology and the History of Jewish-Hellenistic Religion*. London: SCM, 1976.

Herzog, Frederick, editor. *The Future of Hope: Theology as Eschatology*. New York: Herder & Herder, 1970.

———. "Towards the Waiting God." In *The Future of Hope*, edited by Frederick Herzog, 51–71.

Heschel, Abraham. *The Prophets*. New York: Harper & Row, 1962.

Hill, William J. *The Three-Personed God: The Trinity as a Mystery of Salvation*. Washington, DC: Catholic University Press of America, 1982.

Holten, Wilko van. "Eschatology with a Vengeance: Hell as the Greatest Conceivable Evil." In *The Future as God's Gift*, edited by David Fergusson and Marcel Sarot, 181–88. Edinburgh: T. & T. Clark, 2000.

Hudson, Wayne. *The Marxist Philosophy of Ernst Bloch*. London: Macmillan, 1982.

Hunsinger, George. "The Crucified God and the Political Theology of Violence: A Critical Survey of Jürgen Moltmann's Thought: 1." *HeyJ* 14 (1973) 266–79.

———. "The Crucified God and the Political Theology of Violence: A Critical Survey of Jürgen Moltmann's Thought: 2." *HeyJ* 14 (1973) 379–95.

———. "The Daybreak of the New Creation: Christ's Resurrection in Recent Theology." *SJT* 57 (2004) 163–81.

———. Review of Jürgen Moltmann, *The Trinity and the Kingdom*. *The Thomist* 47 (1983) 129–39.

Irish, Jerry A. "Moltmann's Theology of Contradiction." *ThTo* 32 (1975–6) 21–31.

Jacobsen, Hans-Adolf. "The Role of the Federal German Republic of Germany in the World, 1949–1982." In *Contemporary Germany: Politics and Culture*, edited by Charles Burdick et al. Boulder, CO: Westview, 1984.

Jaeger, John D. "Pneumatological Developments in the Theology of Jürgen Moltmann." Ph.D. dissertation, Baylor University, 2003.

Jantzen, Grace M. "Christian Hope and Jesus' Despair." *King's Theological Review* 5 (1982) 1–7.

Jenson, Robert W. "The Bible and the Trinity." *Pro Ecclesia* XI (2002) 329–39.

———. "Second Thoughts about Theologies of Hope." *EvQ* 72 (2000) 335–46.

———. *Systematic Theology*, 2 vols. New York: Oxford University Press, 1997–99.

"A Jewish Statement on Christians and Christianity." In *Christianity in Jewish Terms*, edited by Tikva Frymer-Kensky et al., xv–xviii. Boulder, CO: Westview, 2000.

John Paul II. *Evangelium vitae*. Published 25 March 1995. Online: http://www.vatican.va/holy_father/john_paul_ii/encyclicals/index.htm

Jones, Gareth. *Bultmann: Towards a Critical Theology*. Cambridge: Blackwell, 1991.

Jowers, Dennis. "The Reproach of Modalism: A Difficulty for Karl Barth's Doctrine of the Trinity." *SJT* 56 (2003) 231–46.

———. *The Trinitarian Axiom of Karl Rahner: The Economic Trinity Is the Immanent Trinity and Vice Versa*. Lewiston, NY: Mellen, 2006.

———. "The Theology of the Cross as Theology of the Trinity: A Critique of Jürgen Moltmann's Staurocentric Trinitarianism." *TynBul* 52 (2001) 245–66.

Juel, Donald. *Messianic Exegesis: Christological Interpretation of the Old Testament in Early Christianity*. Philadelphia: Fortress, 1988.

Jüngel, Eberhard. *God as the Mystery of the World: On the Foundation of the Theology of the Crucified One in the Dispute between Theism and Atheism.* Translated by Darrell L. Gruder. 3rd ed. Edinburgh: T. & T. Clark, 1983.

Kaiser, Walter C. Jr. *The Messiah in the Old Testament.* Studies in Old Testament Biblical Theology. Grand Rapids: Zondervan, 1995.

Kant, Immanuel. *The Conflict of the Faculties* (1798). Translated by M. J. Gregor and R. Anchor. In *Religion and Rational Theology*, edited by Allen W. Wood et al., 233–328. Cambridge: Cambridge University Press, 1996.

———. *Critique of Pure Reason.* Translated by N. K. Smith. 2nd edition. London: MacMillan, 1933.

———. "The End of All Things." Translated by A. W. Wood. In *Religion and Rational Theology*, edited by Allen W. Wood et al., 217–32. Cambridge: Cambridge University Press, 1996.

Kasper, Walter. *The God of Jesus Christ.* Translated by Matthew J. O'Connell. London: SCM, 1983.

———. "Revolution im Gottesverständnis? Zur Situation des ökumenischen Dialogs nach Jürgen Moltmanns 'Der gekreuzigte Gott.'" In *Diskussion*, edited by Michael Welker, 140–48.

Kelly, J. N. D. *Early Christian Doctrines.* Rev. ed. San Francisco: Harper Collins, 51978.

Kenny, Anthony. *A Brief History of Western Philosophy.* Oxford: Blackwell, 1998.

Keuss, Jeff. Letter to the author. 10 June, 2003.

Kitamori, Kazoh. "Buchbesprechung." In *Diskussion*, edited by Michael Welker, 108–10.

———. *Theology of the Pain of God.* Translated by M. E. Bratcher. 1966. Reprinted, Eugene, OR: Wipf & Stock, 2005.

Kolakowski, Leszek. *Main Currents of Marxism: Its Origins, Growth, and Dissolution*, vol. 3: *The Breakdown.* Translated by P. S. Falla. Oxford: Oxford University Press, 1978.

Krötke, Wolf. "Hope in the Last Judgement and Human Dignity." Translated by P. G. Ziegler. *IJST* 2 (2000) 270–83.

Kühn, Ulrich. "Rezension." In *Diskussion*, edited by Michael Welker, 54–56. Munich: Kaiser, 1979.

Lash, Nicholas. "Considering the Trinity." *ModTh* 2 (1986) 183–96.

———. "Up and Down in Christology." In *New Studies in Theology I*, edited by Stephen Sykes and Derek Holmes, 31–46. London: Duckworth, 1980.

Law, Jeremy Thomson. "The Future of Jesus Christ: A Constructive Analysis of the Development of the Eschatological Structure of Jürgen Moltmann's Theology: 1964–1996." D.Phil. thesis, Oxford University, 1998.

Leighton, Christopher M. "Christian Theology After the Shoah." In *Christianity in Jewish Terms*, edited by Tikva Frymer-Kensky et al., 36–48.

Lessing, G. E. "Über den Beweis des Geistes und der Kraft." In *Gotthold Ephraim Lessings sämtlichen Schriften*, vol. 13, edited by Karl Lachmann. Berlin: Göshen.

Lewis, Scott M. *So that God May be All in All: The Apocalyptic Message of 1 Corinthians 15.12–34.* Tesi Gregoriana Serie Teologia 42. Rome: Editrice Pontificia Università Gregoriana, 1998.

Link, Christian. "Schöpfung im messianischen Licht." *EvTh* 47 (1987) 83–92.

Lochman, Jan Milič, and Hermann Dembowski. "Gottes Sein ist im Leiden. Zur trinitarischen Kreuzestheologie Jürgen Moltmanns." In *Diskussion*, edited by Michael Welker, 26–38. Munich: Kaiser, 1979.

Lodahl, Michael E. *Shekhinah/Spirit: Divine Presence in Jewish and Christian Religion*. Studies in Judaism and Christianity. New York: Paulist, 1992.

Lunn, Andrew J. "The Doctrine of Atonement: (3) The Significance of the Cross for Moltmann and Dillistone." *Epworth Review* 19.1 (1992) 26–34.

Luther, Martin. *Die Bibel, mit Apokryphen*. Stuttgart: Deutsche Bibelgesellschaft, 1985.

MacLeod, Donald. "The Christology of Jürgen Moltmann." *Themelios* 24.2 (1999) 35–47.

Macquarrie, John. "Eschatology and Time." In *The Future of Hope*, edited by Frederick Herzog, 110–25. New York: Herder & Herder, 1970.

———. "Theologies of Hope: A Critical Examination." In *Thinking about God*, 221–32. London: SCM, 1975.

Maitland-Cullen, Pratick S. "The Theodicy Problem in the Theology of Jürgen Moltmann." Ph.D. dissertation, University of Edinburgh, 1990.

Marsch, Wolf-Dieter, editor. *Diskussion über die "Theologie der Hoffnung" von Jürgen Moltmann*. Munich: Kaiser, 1967.

———. "Die Hoffnung des Glaubens." In *Diskussion*, edited by Wolf-Dieter Marsch, 122–24.

———. "Zur Einleitung: Wohin—jenseits der Alternativen." In *Diskussion*, edited by Wolf-Dieter Marsch, 7–18.

Marshall, I. Howard. *Origins of New Testament Christology*. Rev. ed. Downers Grove, IL: InterVarsity, 1990.

Marty, Martin E., and Dean G. Peerman, editors. *New Theology No. 5*. New York: Macmillan, 1968.

Marx, Karl. *Early Writings*. Translated by R. Livingstone and G. Benton. New York: Penguin, 1975.

McCosker, Philip. "Joined-Up Thomism and the Second Quest for Trinitarian Renewal." *RRT* 12 (2005) 331–7.

McDade, John. "The Trinity and the Paschal Mystery." *HeyJ* 29 (1988) 175–91

McGrath, Alister E. *Luther's Theology of the Cross*. Oxford: Blackwell, 1985.

———. *The Making of Modern German Christology: 1750–1990*. Leicester, UK: Apollos, 21994.

McIntyre, John. "Review of Moltmann's *God in Creation*." *SJT* 41 (1988) 267–73.

McPherson, Jim. "Life, the Universe and Everything: Jürgen Moltmann's *God in Creation*." *St. Mark's Review* 128 (1986) 34–46.

McWilliams, Warren. "Trinitarian Doxology: Jürgen Moltmann on the Relation of the Economic and Immanent Trinity." *PRS* 23 (1996) 25–38.

Meeks, M. Douglas. "Foreword." In Moltmann, *The Experiment Hope*, ix–xvii.

———. "Jürgen Moltmann's *Systematic Contributions to Theology*." *RelSRev* 22 (1996) 95–102.

———. "Moltmann's Contribution to Practical Theology." In *Hope for the Church*, edited by Theodore Runyon, 57–74. Nashville: Abingdon, 1979.

———. *Origins of the Theology of Hope*. Philadelphia: Fortress, 1974.

Meesmann, Hartmut. "An Account of the Symposium." Translated by John Bowden. In Moltmann, *How I Have Changed*, 112–30.

Metz, Johann Baptist. "The Last Universalists." Translated by D. Stott. In *The Future of Theology*, edited by Miroslav Volf, Carmen Krieg, and Thomas Kucharz, 47–51. Grand Rapids: Eerdmans, 1996.

———. "Theological Interruptions." In Ekkehard Schuster and Reinhold Boschert-Kimmig, *Hope against Hope: Johann Baptist Metz and Elie Wiesel Speak Out on the Holocaust*, 12–18. Translated by J. Matthew Ashley. New York, NY: Paulist, 1999.

Milbank, John. "The Second Difference: For a Trinitarianism without Reserve." *ModTh* 2 (1986) 213–34.

Miles, Margaret R. *The Word Made Flesh: A History of Christian Thought*. Oxford: Blackwell, 2005.

Miskotte, Hermannus Heiko. "Das Leiden ist in Gott. Über Jürgen Moltmanns trinitarische Kreuzestheologie." In *Diskussion*, edited by Michael Welker, 74–93. Munich: Kaiser, 1979.

Moberly, R. W. L. "The Christ of the Old and New Testaments." In *Cambridge Companion to Jesus*, edited by Markus Bockuehl, 184–99. Cambridge Companions to Religion. Cambridge: Cambridge University Press, 1999.

Molnar, Paul D. "The Function of the Trinity in Jürgen Moltmann's Ecological Doctrine of Creation." In *Divine Freedom and the Doctrine of the Immanent Trinity: In Dialogue with Karl Barth and Contemporary Theology*, 197–233. Edinburgh: T. & T. Clark, 2002.

———. "Toward a Contemporary Doctrine of the Immanent Trinity: Karl Barth and Current Discussion." *SJT* 49 (1996) 311–57.

Moltmann-Wendel, Elisabeth. *Autobiography*. Translated by John Bowden. London: SCM, 1997.

Mommsen, Wolfgang J. "The Germans and Their Past: History and Political Consciousness in the Federal Republic of Germany." In *Coping with the Past: Germany and Austria after 1945*, edited by Kathy Harms, Lutz R. Reuter, and Volker Dürr, 252–69. *Monatshefte* Occasional Volumes, No. 10. Madison: University of Wisconsin Press, 1990.

Momose, Peter Fumiaki. *Kreuzestheologie: Eine Auseinandersetzung mit Jürgen Moltmann*. Ökumenische Forschungen, Soteriologische Abteilung 7. Freiburg: Herder, 1978.

Mondin, Battista. "Der gekreuzigte Gott." In *Diskussion*, edited by Michael Welker, 94–107. Munich: Kaiser, 1979.

Morse, Christopher. "God's Promise as Presence." In *Love: The Foundation of Hope*, edited by Frederic B. Burnham et al., 143–57.

———. *The Logic of Promise in Moltmann's Theology*. Philadelphia: Fortress, 1979.

Müller-Fahrenholz, Geiko. *The Kingdom and the Power: The Theology of Jürgen Moltmann*. Translated by John Bowden. London: SCM, 2000.

The Nature of Hell. A Report by the Evangelical Alliance Commission on Unity and Truth among Evangelicals. Carlisle, UK: Paternoster, 2000.

Neal, Ryan A. "The Doctrine of Universalism, with Special Reference to Jürgen Moltmann." M.Th. thesis, University of Edinburgh, 2001.

———. "Good Friday." In *Encyclopedia of Christian Civilization*, edited by George Kurian. 3 vols. Oxford: Blackwell, forthcoming.
———. "J. Moltmann." In *Encyclopedia of Theologians*, edited by Ian Markham. Oxford: Blackwell, 2008.
———. "Minority Report: Reconsidering Jürgen Moltmann's Turn to a Theology of the Cross." *IJST* (forthcoming).
Neuhaus, John. "Moltmann vs. Monotheism." *Dialog* 20 (1981) 239–43.
Ngien, Dennis. *The Suffering of God according to Martin Luther's "Theologia Crucis."* 1995. Reprinted, Eugene: Wipf & Stock, 2001.
O'Collins, Gerald. "The Principle and Theology of Hope." *SJT* 21 (1968) 129–44.
———. *The Tripersonal God: Understanding and Interpreting the Trinity*. London: Chapman, 1999.
Oberdorfer, Bernd. *Filioque: Geschichte und Theologie eines ökumenischen Problems*. Forschungen zur systematischen und ökumenischen Theologie 96. Göttingen: Vandehoeck & Ruprecht, 2001.
O'Donnell, John J. "The Doctrine of the Trinity in Recent German Theology." *HeyJ* 23 (1982) 153–67.
———. "Exploring the Human: Theology in Dialogue." *Gregorianum* 67 (1986) 125–32.
———. *Trinity and Temporality: The Christian Doctrine of God in the Light of Process Theology and the Theology of Hope*. Oxford Theological Monographs. Oxford: Oxford University Press, 1983.
Oepke, Albrecht. "παρουσία, πάρειμι." In *TDNT* 5:865.
Ogden, Schubert. "Response Jürgen Moltmann." In *Hope and the Future of Man*, edited by Ewart H. Cousins, 109–16. London: Garnstone, 1973.
Olson, Roger. "Trinity and Eschatology: The Historical Being of God in Jürgen Moltmann and Wolfhart Pannenberg." *SJT* 36 (1983) 213–27.
O'Regan, Cyril. *The Heterodox Hegel*. SUNY Series in Hegelian Studies. Albany: State University of New York Press, 1994.
Otto, Randall E. *The God of Hope: The Trinitarian Vision of Jürgen Moltmann*. Lanham, MD: University Press of America, 1991.
———. "Moltmann and the Anti-Monotheism Movement." *IJST* 3 (2001) 293–308.
———. "The Use and Abuse of Perichoresis in Recent Theology." *SJT* 54 (2001) 366–84.
Pannenberg, Wolfhart. "Can Christianity Do Without an Eschatology?" In G. B. Caird, Wolfhart Pannenberg, I. T. Ramsey, James Klugmann, Ninian Smart, and W. A. Whitehouse, *The Christian Hope*, 25–34. Theological Collections 13. London: SPCK, 1970.
———. "Dogmatic Theses on the Doctrine of Revelation." In *Revelation as History*, edited by Wolfhart Pannenberg, 123–58.
———. "The God of Hope." In *Basic Questions in Theology: Collected Essays*, vol. 2, 234–49. Translated by George H. Kehm. Philadelphia: Fortress, 1977.
———. *Jesus—God and Man*. Translated by Lewis L. Wilkens and Duane A. Priebe. Philadelphia: Westminster, 1968.
———. "Probleme einer trinitarischen Gotteslehre." In Baier, Walter, ed. *Weisheit Gottes—Weisheit der Welt: Festschrift für Joseph Kardinal Ratzinger*, vol. 1, 329–34. St. Ottlien, Germany: EOS, 1987.

———. editor. *Revelation as History*. Translated by David Granskou and Edward Quinn. 2nd ed. London: Sheed & Ward, 1979.

———. *Systematic Theology*. 3 vols. Translated by Geoffrey W. Bromiley. Grand Rapids: Eerdmans, 1991–98.

———. *Theology and the Kingdom of God*. Edited by Richard John Neuhaus. Philadelphia: Westminster, 1969.

Peters, Ted. *God as Trinity: Relationality and Temporality in the Divine Life*. Louisville: Westminster John Knox, 1993.

———. "Trinity Talk: Part One." *Dialog* 26 (1987) 44–8.

Phillips, Benjamin Blair. "The Crisis of Creation: A Critical Analysis of Jürgen Moltmann's Panentheism." Ph.D. dissertation, Southwestern Baptist Theological Seminary, 2003.

Pieper, Josef. *Faith, Hope, Love*. San Francisco: Ignatius, 1997.

Pinnock, Clark H. *Flame of Love: A Theology of the Holy Spirit*. Downers Grove, IL: InterVarsity, 1996.

Placher, William. "The Present Absence of Christ: Some Thoughts on Pannenberg and Moltmann." *Encounter* 40 (1979) 169–79.

Platten, Stephen. "Authority and Order in Creation." *Theology* 94 (1991) 22–30.

Polkinghorne, John C., and Michael Welker, editors. *The End of the World and the Ends of God: Science and Theology on Eschatology*. Theology for the Twenty-First Century. Harrisburg, PA: Trinity, 2000.

Powell, Samuel M. *The Trinity in German Thought*. Cambridge: Cambridge University Press, 2001.

Pulzer, Peter. *German Politics: 1945–1995*. Oxford: Oxford University Press, 1995.

Rahner, Karl. "Anonymous Christians." In *Theological Investigations, Vol. VI: Concerning Vatican Council II*, 390–98. Translated by K.-H. Krüger and B. Krüger. London: Darton Longman and Todd, 1969.

———. "Christianity and the Non-Christian Religions." In *Theological Investigations, Vol. V: Later Writings*, 115–34. Translated by K.-H. Krüger. Baltimore: Helicon, 1966.

———. "The Hermeneutics of Eschatological Assertions." In *Theological Investigations, Vol. IV: More Recent Writings*, 323–46. Translated by K. Smyth. London: Darton, Longman & Todd, 1966.

———. "On the Theology of Hope." In *Theological Investigations, Vol. X: Writings of 1965–67, 2*, 242–59. Translated by D. Bourke. London: Darton, Longman & Todd, 1973.

———. "On the Theology of the Incarnation." In *Theological Investigations, Vol. IV: More Recent Writings*, 105–20. Translated by K. Smyth. London: Darton, Longman & Todd, 1966.

———. "*Theos* in the New Testament." In *Theological Investigations, Vol. I: God, Christ, Mary, and Grace*, 138–48. Translated by C. Ernst. London: Darton, Longman & Todd, 21965.

———. *The Trinity*. Translated by J. Donceel. New York, NY: Herder & Herder, 1970.

———. "The Two Basic Types of Christology." *Theological Investigations, vol. XIII: Theology, Anthropology, Christology*, 213–23. Translated by D. Bourke. London: Darton, Longman & Todd, 1975.

Rasmusson, Arne. *The Church as Polis: From Political Theology to Theological Politics as Exemplified by Jürgen Moltmann and Stanley Hauerwas*. Rev. ed. Notre Dame, IN: University of Notre Dame Press, 1995.

Rauser, Randal. "Rahner's Rule: An Emperor without Clothes?" *IJST* 7 (2005) 81–94.

Rhodes, J. Stephen. "The Church as the Community of Open Friendship." *ATJ* 55 (2000) 41–9.

Ricœur, Paul. "Der gekreuzigte Gott von Jürgen Moltmann." In *Diskussion*, Michael Welker, 17–25. Munich: Kaiser, 1979.

Ritschl, Dietrich. "Historical Developments and Implications of the Filioque Controversy." In *Spirit of God, Spirit of Christ: Ecumenical Reflections on the Filioque Controversy*, edited by Lukas Vischer, 46–65. Faith and Order Paper 103. London: SPCK, 1981.

Roberts, Richard H. *Hope and its Hieroglyph: A Critical Decipherment of Ernst Bloch's Principle of Hope*. American Academy of Religion Studies in Religion 57. Atlanta: Scholars, 1990.

Rosenfeld, Alvin H., and Irving Greenberg, editors. *Confronting the Holocaust: The Impact of Elie Wiesel*. Bloomington: Indiana University Press, 1978.

Rowland, Christopher. "Parousia." In *ABD* 5:166–70.

Rubenstein, Richard L., and John K. Roth. *Approaches to Auschwitz: The Holocaust and Its Legacy*. Atlanta: John Knox, 1987.

Rublev, Andrei. *Trinity*. <http://members.valley.net/~transnat/trinlg.html>

Runyon, Theodore, editor. *Hope for the Church: Moltmann in Dialogue with Practical Theology*. Translated by Theodore Runyon. Nashville: Abingdon, 1979.

———. "Introduction." In *Hope for the Church*, edited by Theodore Runyon, 57–74.

Sarot, Marcel. "Auschwitz, Morality and the Suffering of God." *ModTh* 7 (1991) 135–52.

———. *God, Possibility and Corporeality*. Studies in Philosophical Theology. Kampen: Kok Pharos, 1992.

Sauter, Gerhard. *What Dare We Hope? Reconsidering Eschatology*. Theology for the Twenty-First Century. Harrisburg, PA: Trinity, 1999.

Scaer, David. "Review of *Hope and Planning*." *ThTo* 28 (1971) 363–4.

Scholem, Gershom G. "Seventh Lecture: Isaac Luria and His School." In *Major Trends in Jewish Mysticism*. Based on the Hilda Strook Lectures Delivered at the Jewish Institute of Religion, New York. Rev. ed. New York: Schocken, 1946: 244–86.

Schwarz, Hans. *Christology*. Grand Rapids: Eerdmans, 1998.

———. *Eschatology*. Grand Rapids: Eerdmans, 2000.

Schweitzer, Donald. "The Consistency of Jürgen Moltmann's Theology." *SR* 22 (1993) 197–208.

Schwöbel, Christoph. "Last Things First?" In *The Future as God's Gift*, edited by David Fergusson and Marcel Sarot, 217–41. Edinburgh: T. & T. Clark, 2000.

Seitz, Christopher R. "Old Testament or Hebrew Bible?" In *Word without End: The Old Testament as Abiding Theological Witness*, 61–74. Grand Rapids: Eerdmans, 1998.

Sobrino, Jon. *Christology at the Crossroads: A Latin American Approach*. Translated by John Drury. Maryknoll, NY: Orbis, 1978.

Sölle, Dorothee. "Gott und das Leiden." In *Diskussion*, edited by Michael Welker, 111–17. Munich: Kaiser, 1979.

———. *Suffering*. Translated by Everett R. Kalin. London: Darton, Longman & Todd, 1975.
Spence, Brian John. "Von Balthasar and Moltmann: Two Responses to Hegel on the Subject of the Incarnation and 'the death of God.'" Ph.D. dissertation, St. Michael's College, University of Toronto, 1996.
———. "The Hegelian Element in Von Balthasar's and Moltmann's Understanding of the Suffering of God." *Toronto Journal of Theology* 14 (1998) 45–60.
Stibbe, Mark W. G. "A British Appraisal [of *SpL*]." *JPT* 4 (1994) 5–16.
Swartley, Willard M. *Slavery, Sabbath, War and Women: Case Issues in Biblical Interpretation*. The Conrad Grebel Lectures, 1982. Scottdale, PA: Herald, 1983.
Sykes, Stephen W. "The Dialectic of Community and Structure." In *Love: The Foundation of Hope*, edited by Frederic B. Burnham et al., 113–28. San Francisco: Harper & Row, 1988.
Tang, Siu-Kwang. "God's History in the Theology of Jürgen Moltmann." Ph.D. thesis, University of St Andrews, 1994.
Tanner, Kathryn. "Eschatology Without a Future?" In *The End of the World and the Ends of God*, edited by John Polkinghorne and Michael Welker, 222–37. Harrisburg, PA: Trinity, 2000.
Taylor, Iain. "In Defence of Karl Barth's Doctrine of the Trinity." *IJST* 5 (2003) 33–46.
Taylor, John V. *The Go-Between God: The Holy Spirit and the Christian Mission*. London: SCM, 1972.
Thistlethwaite, Susan Brooks. "Comments on Jürgen Moltmann's 'The Unity of the Triune God.'" *SVTQ* 28 (1984) 179–82.
Thompson, John. *Modern Trinitarian Perspectives*. Oxford: Oxford University Press, 1994.
Tinder, Glenn. *The Fabric of Hope: An Essay*. Emory University Studies in Law and Religion. Atlanta: Scholars, 1999.
Torrance, Alan J. "*Creatio ex Nihilo* and the Spatio-Temporal Dimensions, with special reference to Jürgen Moltmann and D.C. Williams." In *The Doctrine of Creation: Essays in Dogmatics, History and Philosophy*, edited by Colin E. Gunton, 83–103. Edinburgh: T. & T. Clark, 1997.
Torrance, Thomas F. *The Christian Doctrine of God, One Being Three Persons*. Edinburgh: T. & T. Clark, 1996.
Tracy, David. "God as Trinitarian: A Christian Response to Peter Ochs." In *Christianity in Jewish Terms*, edited by Tikva Frymer-Kensky et al., 77–84. Boulder, CO: Westview, 2000.
Tripole, Martin R. "Ecclesiological developments in Moltmann's Theology of Hope." *TS* 34 (1973) 19–35.
———. "A Church for the Poor and the World: At Issue with Moltmann's Ecclesiology." *TS* 42 (1981) 645–59.
Tuggy, Dale. "Divine Deception, Identity, and Social Trinitarianism." *Religious Studies* 40 (2004) 269–87.
Volf, Miroslav. "After Moltmann: Reflections on the Future of Eschatology." In *God Will Be All in All*, edited by Richard Bauckham, 223–57. Edinburgh: T. & T. Clark, 2000.
———. "The Lamb of God and the Sin of the World." In *Christianity in Jewish Terms*, edited by Tikva Frymer-Kensky et al., 313–19. Boulder, CO: Westview, 2000.

Volf, Miroslav, Carmen Krieg, and Thomas Kucharz, editors. *The Future of Theology: Essays in Honor of Jürgen Moltmann.* Grand Rapids: Eerdmans, 1996.

Volf, Miroslav, and Maurice Lee. "The Spirit and the Church." In *Advents of the Spirit: An Introduction to the Current Study of Pneumatology,* edited by Bradford E. Hinze et al., 382–409. Milwaukee: Marquette University Press, 2001: 382–409.

Wakefield, James. L. *Jürgen Moltmann: A Research Bibliography.* ATLA Bibliography Series. Lanham, MD: Scarecrow, 2002.

Walker, Graham B. *Elie Wiesel: A Challenge to Theology.* Jefferson, NC: McFarland, 1988.

Walsh, Brian J. "Theology of Hope and the Doctrine of Creation." *EvQ* 59 (1987) 53–76.

Webster, John B. "Jürgen Moltmann: Trinity and Suffering." *Evangel* 3.2 (1985) 4–6.

Weder, Hans. "Hope and Creation." In *The End of the World and the Ends of God,* edited by John Polkinghorne and Michael Welker, 184–202. Harrisburg, PA: Trinity, 2000.

Weinandy, Thomas G. *Does God Suffer?* Edinburgh: T. & T. Clark, 2000.

———. *In the Likeness of Sinful Flesh: An Essay on the Humanity of Christ.* Edinburgh: T. & T. Clark, 1993.

Weingart, Richard. *The Logic of Divine Love.* Oxford: Oxford University Press, 1970.

Welker, Michael, editor. *Diskussion über Jürgen Moltmanns Buch "Der gekreuzigte Gott."* Munich: Kaiser, 1979.

White, Lynn, Jr. "The Historical Roots of Our Ecological Crisis." *Science* 155 (March 10, 1967) 1203–7.

Wiesel, Elie. "Hope, Despair and Memory." In Abrams, Irwin ed. *Nobel Lectures in Peace (1981–1990),* edited by Irwin Abrams, 174–79. Singapore: World Scientific, 1997.

———. *Night.* Translated by Stella Rodway. 1960. Reprinted, Harmondsworth, UK: Penguin, 1981.

———. "Why I Write." Translated by R. C. Lamont. In *Confronting the Holocaust: The Impact of Elie Wiesel,* edited by Alvin H. Rosenfeld and Irving Greenberg, 200–206. Bloomington: Indiana University Press, 1978.

Williams, Rowan. *On Christian Theology.* Challenges in Contemporary Theology. Oxford: Blackwell, 2000.

Willis, W. Waite, Jr. *Theism, Atheism and the Doctrine of the Trinity: The Trinitarian Theologies of Karl Barth and Jürgen Moltmann in Response to Protest Atheism.* American Academy of Religion Academy Series 53. Atlanta: Scholars, 1987.

Witherington, Ben III. *Jesus, Paul and the End of the World: A Comparative Study in New Testament Eschatology.* Downers Grove, IL: InterVarsity, 1992.

Wood, Laurence W. "Editorial Note." *ATJ* 55 (2000) 5–6.

———. "From Barth's Trinitarian Christology to Moltmann's Trinitarian Pneumatology." *ATJ* 55 (2000) 51–69. Note: all citations refer to the 2000 paper, which is a revision of the earlier version: "From Barth's Trinitarian Christology to Moltmann's Trinitarian Pneumatology: A Methodist Perspective." *ATJ* 48.1 (1993) 49–80.

Wright, Nigel Goring. *Disavowing Constantine: Mission, Church and the Social Order in the Theologies of John Howard Yoder and Jürgen Moltmann.* Paternoster Biblical and Theological Monographs. Carlisle, UK: Paternoster, 2000.

Zimany, Roland D. "Moltmann's Crucified God." *Dialog* 16 (1977) 49–57.
Zizioulas, John D. *Being as Communion: Studies in Personhood and the Church.* Crestwood, NY: St. Vladimir's Seminary Press, 1985.

www.ingramcontent.com/pod-product-compliance
Lightning Source LLC
Chambersburg PA
CBHW071246230426
43668CB00011B/1605